The Music of
Carly Simon

Songs from the Vineyard

Michael Francis Taylor

NEW HAVEN PUBLISHING LTD

Published 2020
First Edition
NEW HAVEN PUBLISHING LTD
www.newhavenpublishingltd.com
newhavenpublishing@gmail.com

Front Cover image © Clive Limkin, *Daily Mail* 1988
Rear cover picture © Kathy Hutchins, Oceana's Partners Awards
Gala, Beverly Hills CA September 30th 2013

Cover design © Pete Cunliffe
pcunliffe@blueyonder.co.uk

Contents

Foreword by Jimmy Ryan

Jimmy Ryan is a longtime friend of Carly's, having worked alongside her as guitarist, bassist, singer, arranger, and collaborator for 52 years, and has performed with her on songs such as 'That's the Way I've Always Heard It Should Be', 'Anticipation', 'You're So Vain', and 'Let the River Run', as well as many of her major albums, tours and television specials.

© Maggie Ryan

It was the summer of 1968, a year of protests and love-fests, and I was a 22-year-old musician. Curious and excited about life, and enjoying a career as a recording and touring musician, I was always on the lookout for the next cool thing. I left college to make music a full-time job, and so far, no regrets. Who would have thought that one night in a basement New York club, an unfamiliar singer in an unknown band would one day change my life? Here's how it all began....

On a warm Saturday night in June, bored in New Jersey, I decided to hop in my '66 Austin Healy and take a ride into New York City. I pulled up and parked on West 46th Street, meeting my friends and looking forward

5

to a relaxing evening at a club called Steve Paul's Scene. We were met at the club entrance by Teddy, the evening's host, and were led down the stairs into the noisy, smoky, underground cavern that was the Scene, a haunt for many a rock star. The room was filled with music fans and showbiz people, and the Chambers Brothers 'Time' was playing through the club sound system. At around 10:30pm, while my friends and I were sitting at our table talking about the usual - music, politics, whatever, the canned music faded and the owner, Steve Paul, stepped up onto the small stage and tapped the center mic. Steve always sported a wide-eyed, deer-in-the-headlights expression on his face as he looked at the ceiling awkwardly announcing each show. He, Skipper the karate chopping bouncer, and Tiny Tim were some of the quirky attractions that helped make the Scene popular and the go-to New York dive for John Lennon, Jimi Hendrix, Keith Emerson, Johnny Winter, Joe Cocker, The Rascals, Traffic, Pink Floyd, The Doors and many other rock stars of the day. Steve leaned into the mic. "Good evening everybody. Thanks for coming out and joining us at the Scene. Please give a warm welcome to Elephant's Memory."

Hmmm - not familiar with that name. Hope they're not too loud. After a few snare drum hits, the usual buzzes from plugging in live guitar jacks and the obligatory "testing, one-two, one-two," they kicked off their set with… a song no one knew. They were okay. I didn't pay much attention to them, but when I looked up from my third lime and lager, I saw a tall, beautiful woman singing lead. It was an odd match because her voice was far more interesting than their music. No one in the band mentioned her name, but in a vote of who gets to stay on the island, I'd say with that voice, she was the keeper. I didn't give it much further thought, and continued my conversation with my friends about Lyndon Johnson's resignation and how long it would be before the terrible war in Vietnam would end.

That year I had been recording a third album with my band, The Critters. We were high school heroes who made it to the big time with a couple of hits, 'Younger Girl', and 'Mr. Dieingly Sad'. On one of the last mixing sessions, our producer, Dan Armstrong, showed up with his girlfriend who was a musician/singer. He wanted her to meet us but mostly wanted to impress her with his production skills! I immediately recognized her as the Elephant's Memory lead singer I had seen earlier that year. Dan simply introduced her by her first name, "Carly," as they took off their winter coats and scarves and settled into the control room sofa. When I told her how much I enjoyed hearing her that night at the Scene, she seemed to appreciate the compliment but confessed she hadn't done much in music since then. I was utterly baffled, but had a strong feeling her current musical silence wouldn't last. I was also starting to lose interest in the Critters and fantasized: wouldn't it be cool to be in a band with someone who was

6

THAT good? Anyway, I thoroughly enjoyed chatting with her while Dan made comments and suggestions to our engineer about the mixes. The evening ended on a happy, "hope to see you again soon" note. That hope would soon be fulfilled.

The album we played for Carly that night barely made it into the top 200 and did not produce any hits. With the Critters 'subsequent decline, and no new songs shooting up the charts, our final year was spent playing high school senior proms and sock hops. After a depressing gig at a Lido Beach country club on Long Island, I ended the band. For me, unemployment and financial frustration would surely be better than a slow, painful descent into irrelevance. Within a month or two my savings evaporated, and the pressure was on to look for a day job, anything to sustain me until I could find another interesting and hopefully lucrative musical project. I recalled that Dan Armstrong had a popular music store in Greenwich Village and decided to inquire there. He needed a store manager, and I got the gig. Things started looking up. His girlfriend Carly would often show up at the store to meet him for dates, and occasionally I'd grab a guitar off the wall and we'd sing a song or two together while waiting for Dan. We all became good friends and enjoyed double dating, Carly, Dan, my girlfriend, KC, and me.

I worked at the store for about a year, while developing a studio musician career during the evenings and days off. Eventually I gathered enough recording session and Broadway orchestra work to quit the store, and ironically, Carly and Dan split up around the same time. She and I stayed in touch over the next year, both enrolling in the same music copying course at the Juilliard School. We used to joke about why we were even taking the course, as neither of us had any ambition to be copyists (the people who create sheet music when needed for recording sessions or live performances). Also, the jingle business was thriving in those days. Carly and I often found ourselves standing side by side in studios, singing about dish soap, diapers and occasionally when we got a lucky break, national cigarette commercials. They were legal then, and I was a smoker, so no foul. Eventually I quit, and both lungs are still functioning well.

One day in mid-1970, Carly called me to say she had been signed as a singer/songwriter to Elektra Records. I grinned ear to ear and cheered in my mind, "YES, finally!!" She asked if I'd like to play guitar on her upcoming album. This time I said YES out loud. Before my first recording with her, she played me a song she had just finished at Jimi Hendrix's studio, Electric Ladyland. The band was Carly on piano, accompanied by an A-list group of studio musicians. From the first verse of the song, my jaw was on the floor - it was spectacular. She never shared any of her original songs with me in all the time I had known her, so I wasn't even aware she could write.

I liked her recordings with her sister Lucy, but this song was in a category all of its own. The song was 'That's The Way I've Always Heard It Should Be', and I immediately knew it was going to be a huge hit.

I didn't play on the entire album, but I heard enough of what she was doing to know her music was going to be very important in her life and the lives of people all over the world. Her unique perspective on life, her unusual and mesmerizing songwriting style, and her beautiful voice, would soon be charming the masses.

Fast forward: 'That's The Way I've Always Heard It Should Be', her first release, started climbing up the charts, and she was getting pressure from Elektra to perform live. In early March 1971, she called me and asked if I'd like to be her guitarist for a series of concerts at the famous Troubadour in LA - we'd be opening for Cat Stevens. It was scheduled for April 6th. A dream had just come true. Not only would I meet and open for one of my favorite artists, but I'd be doing it with one of my favorite people, my old Juilliard and jingles, guitar store boss's girlfriend, Carly… and she was about to begin a journey that would make history, rocketing her into international stardom.

She asked if I would help her put a band together. Two musician buddies came to mind. I had recently returned from a festival tour as bassist with The Crazy World of Arthur Brown, and I suggested Arthur's keyboard player, Paul Glanz. I had known Paul for several years as he had also been keyboardist for the Critters. Paul and I had recently been jamming with an excellent drummer named Andy Newmark, so I invited him to her apartment to try out the combination. They both passed the audition with flying colors. Unfortunately, as good as Andy was, budget concerns would prevent him from joining us on this first gig. Instead, we would be using Russ Kunkel, a legendary LA drummer who just happened to be available. His current tour with James Taylor had come to a temporary halt due to James being involved in a motorcycle accident. Russ was available and eager to work with us. With this wonderful dream unfolding, Carly and I put together a set list, and she, Paul and I went through it song by song, coming up with our instrumental parts, working out harmonies, having meals together, laughing and jamming, and creating what was to become her live band and the core musicians for the recording of *Anticipation*.

The days passed quickly, we became tighter and tighter, and were super-excited about opening for Cat Stevens and playing at this famous LA venue that had showcased so many iconic stars over the years. April 4th was our departure date, and we gathered that morning at Carly's apartment on East 35th St. A limo picked us up, whisked its way through the twisted, intertwined Long Island highways, and, with all the comfort and luxury of the rock stars we hoped we would become, gently deposited us in front of

United Airlines at LaGuardia Airport. In my mind, we were on our way to the big time, and after the Critters debacle, I was ready!

An odd little aside - Elektra put us up at the famous Continental Hyatt House on Sunset Blvd for that week. The room they picked for Carly had a curious bed raised up on a platform and surrounded by four stanchions, connected by thick red velvet ropes. I'll stop there. The hotel had stories that could fill several chapters all by itself.

When we arrived at the Troubadour the next afternoon, the owner, Doug Weston, met us with a huge bouquet of flowers and an expensive bottle of champagne. We truly felt more than welcome. Russ Kunkel was set up and ready for us, every bit the consummate professional we had hoped he would be. He had already learnt our songs the week before, and the sound check and run-through went without a hitch. Well, one hitch. They didn't have enough mics to go around, so on songs that I sang backgrounds (most), I had to sit on the stage floor and sing into my guitar mic. Yes, stiff neck and a very silly look, but hey, it was Carly's show, not mine. Opening night was magical, the venue was packed, and our half-hour show was met with deafening cheers and a standing ovation. For a new artist and support act, this was an incredible accomplishment. If Carly was experiencing any of her well-known stage fright, there was no sign of it that night. She was absolutely riveting and received uniform rave reviews from the music press and the many Hollywood stars who came out to see this new music sensation. Warren Beatty was one of them. Whatever you're thinking... Yep.

That was the beginning of my all-time favorite collaboration. Year after year, Carly and I recorded together, performed live at venues like New York's Schaefer Festival in Central Park, Chicago's Quiet Night, Carnegie Hall, Boston Symphony Hall, filmed two HBO television specials, commiserated about our neurotic lovers, held hands on nerve-wracking, turbulent plane rides, and over the many miles that often came between us, remained good friends.

Though the Critters got me going in the music business, it was Carly who brought me into the top tier of that world, introducing me to Cat Stevens, Elton John, James Taylor, Paul McCartney, Mick Jagger and so many others who shaped and influenced my music. Of all the amazing guitarists, bassists and arrangers she chose to work with over her thirty albums, she always found a place for me on at least one song, and often many per album.

There are few hearts as big as Carly Simon's, few writers of either music or prose who are her equal, and few who can claim active, productive careers like hers in the forefront of international, multi-generational audiences over a span of fifty-six years and counting. I am eternally grateful for her including me in this incredible journey, and look forward to the next time we meet, to either make music or just sip a glass of wine and reminisce.

Final Note: We had planned to meet again in person on March, 17th, 2020. An all-star, Carnegie Hall tribute to Carly's music had been planned, and we were completing the final details of the production. Then the sad news came from Carnegie that they were closing down due to the pandemic, and the concert was cancelled. As of this writing, this disease has put on hold the plans and careers of almost every live-performing artist, Broadway actors, stage crews, lighting and sound crews, film crews, recording studios, theaters, clubs, bars and venues, sports arenas, many hotel and restaurant workers, agents, managers and support people the world over. I hope that this wonderful tribute to her will be rescheduled someday when we eradicate this terrible disease. Until then, all my love to this incredibly talented woman who lit up my life in so many ways, for so many years.

Jimmy Ryan
August 22nd 2020

Introduction

"I find answers to questions I have about myself in the lyric and melody. My writing is quite introspective, like a journal in musical verse."

It's no wonder that Richard Simon's three girls grew up to be bright, gifted artists. Born into a privileged and highly cultured family environment, it was not unusual for them to see the cream of New York's artistic luminaries dropping by for lunch at their family homes in New York and Connecticut. But the story of Carly Simon, the youngest of the daughters, is a journey from childhood to immeasurable success that was fraught with physical and emotional obstacles that would have to be overcome if she was going to succeed in life.

Beginning her solo career in 1970, Carly became one of her generation's most successful female artists, accumulating in a short space of time three gold singles and five gold albums without even undertaking expansive record-promoting tours. Always more interested in her music than becoming a huge star, Carly likened herself to contemporaries such as Judy Collins and Odetta, but not to others who at the start of their careers were creating personas they would then have to strive to live up to. As a performer she wanted to be different, and even as a young girl, her mother had put pressure on her to "stand out" in her own way. And stand out she did, but inevitably it came at a cost. As years went by, performing in front of large crowds would often bring on anxiety attacks, a legendary stage fright, and a fear of flying that would eventually impact on her touring. To the chagrin of her record labels, it would also affect both her public awareness and ultimate record sales.

But Carly's reluctance to sing before large audiences takes nothing away from her amazing voice. Always note-perfect, singing comes as easy to her as to a trained opera star, her incredible range so finely tuned that, by projecting a sudden change of emotion, it's sometimes hard to believe we are listening to the same singer. When emotions run high, her voice can heave with anxious tremors, and in an instant return to her trademark warm and soothing tone. This is the paradox of Carly the reluctant performer, and the perfection of Carly the singer. Before even stepping into a recording studio, she saw her future in only writing songs for others artists to perform. But it is as singer-songwriter that Carly truly excels, and in a career spanning over fifty years she has written and co-written some of the most honest, autobiographical songs of her generation. Compositions such as

'Orpheus', 'We're So Close', 'Libby', and 'Scar' are not just lyrically strong, they are nothing less than works of art.

Carly readily admits that melodies can come into her head like water dripping from a faucet, and over the years her amazing lyrics have covered a diversity of themes - fervently romantic, candidly confessional, cynically realistic, and even sarcastically scathing - all like carefully woven stitches in a tapestry of the human condition. At the start of her career her sophisticated writing led to some criticism for her having a soulless rich-girl persona, one lacking the empathy of the more authentic, rags to riches female artists of her time. But the fact is that she was writing from the gut and wearing her heart on her sleeve. There are signs of fragility and vulnerability in many of her songs; a gritted assertiveness in others; and even anger and depression in some: "I write when I feel frustrated, and I get frustrated most over issues of the heart. I can't talk to other people about my feelings so I write about them."

The wonderful artist Ellen Questel perhaps best sums up Carly: "You have two eyes - one says yes to the world, the other says no. You need to see with both of them. Carly sees more with the eye that says yes and that makes her so vulnerable. She belongs in another century, the era of grand feelings and penned love letters."

Carly has never shied away from her original concepts, despite the temptation to do so. Some of her earlier confessional lyrics struck a chord with the women's lib movement and unconsciously made her a feminist pioneer, without her really having a clear picture of the female angst and the shifting social landscape of the early 70s. But she was always willing to take risks and put her career on the line so as not to be left behind in the ever-changing music trends.

Carly never wrote more candidly than she did during her eleven-year marriage to fellow singer-songwriter James Taylor, a period when they were dubbed the golden couple of pop, "the two lanky aristocrats," and seldom out of the public gaze. The unfolding drama of their marriage would be a defining time and foster some of Carly's most introspective work about love in all its guises. Almost every turn of the page in her well-worn diary found a story that could be turned into a song, and, in what would ultimately amount to an outstanding canon of over thirty albums, she was, maybe unknowingly, compiling an audio journal of her life.

During her long career, Carly would be much sought after for both collaborations and for composing music for stage, television and movies. Greatly raising her profile in the entertainment business, it led to a number of prestigious awards and nominations along the way. To enhance her already impressive catalog of achievements, she was even commissioned to write a modern opera, as well as authoring a fine collection of well-received children's books. Her lifelong love for the popular standards of another era brought another dimension to her already diverse repertoire. Seldom has there been an artist who has contributed so much to so many facets of the music industry.

Carly's achievements owe a great deal to her having had the opportunity to work alongside some of the finest producers, engineers and musicians in the business, and it would be an injustice not to mention their valuable contributions as being an integral part of her continuing success. But behind that success there would be darker times - a frustrating period of writer's block, having no record label, and, above all, a harrowing and painful battle with cancer. But all of this would spur her on to make what many consider to be her masterpiece, *The Bedroom Tapes*, and one of the most inspiring albums of her career.

2021 will see the fiftieth anniversary of Carly's debut album, and the perfect time to celebrate and focus on the outstanding body of work that followed. In the intervening years since the day she hailed a cab to take her to the studio to record that first album, Carly has become one of the most glamorous, photographed, interviewed and successful female singers of the era, and that famous Simon smile with that wild feather-like hair still depicts a strong independent woman with a huge heart and a great love for life.

With Carly Simon there will always be a glowing aura around her that seems she is forever being touched by the sun.

About this book

Carly Simon has always been the darling of the chat shows, never holding back on revealing intimate stories about her personal life. Everyone still wants to hear about what it was like to be married to James Taylor, or the true identity (or identities) of the much celebrated "vain" man. No doubt they will continue to do so for many years to come.

However, the stories and recollections of her life do form a foundation for this work, as do the countless television, newspaper, and magazine interviews conducted over the years during which she relates those same stories almost word for word. All extracts and soundbites in this book have been judiciously chosen for their succinctness and to give a clearer understanding of Carly's thought processes during her career. My deep appreciation goes out to all those reviewers, interviewers and commentators, who, like me, have shared Carly's journey over the years. The sources of their wonderful and valuable contributions have been listed at the end of the book. Bouquets for everyone.

Long before Carly had released her memoirs, her life story had already been laid bare in the very songs she had written, and it's that music, that gorgeous music, which is where the main focus of this book lies. In the following pages I will present a summary of Carly's rise to fame, and give my appraisal of her amazing body of work and the impact it has had on various stages of her personal and professional life. Sadly, I am no musician, nor do I even profess to be a music critic. I will however exhaust all adjectives in describing those songs that are nailed to my heart, but equally point out disappointment for certain others, which of course are very few. Music has always been subjective, as it should be, but sometimes lyrics can also be hard to define. What you experience in life can influence how you may interpret lyrics, and therefore each of us should take from the words in Carly's songs what is meaningful to us. These are just my humble opinions, so please, no brickbats.

By any definition this book you now hold in your hands is a labor of love, and the one person I really need to thank is Carly herself, for her amazing words and music, remarkable voice, incredible stage presence, and, of course, that dazzling smile, all of which conspired to hook and captivate a young college student all those wonderful years ago.

Michael Francis Taylor
October 2020

14

Acknowledgments

To Jimmy Ryan, Carly's longtime friend and guitarist for graciously writing the foreword.

To Teddie Dahlin at New Haven Publishing for not losing faith in me.

To Sarah Healey for her painstaking work on editing the draft.

To Peter Cunliffe for his amazing work on the cover.

To Ronni Simon for permission to use Peter Simon's iconic picture of his sister.

To James Court, friend and fellow author, who said if I didn't do this book, he would.

To my wife Angela for her encouragement and guidance in good grammar.

To all the members of Carly's online fan groups around the world.

And especially to Carly, for just remaining a large part of my life.

Michael is also the author of
Harry Chapin - The Music Behind the Man
New Haven Publishing 2019

Song ratings

1 star - disappointing
2 stars - average
3 stars - good
4 stars - very good
5 stars – outstanding

Note from the author
This body of work takes the form of a critical review and promotion of the artist's musical career. All short extracts of comments, reviews and interviews are done under Fair Use guidelines.

New York City 1970
Carly Simon hailing a cab to take her to Electric Lady Studios to
record her first album©Peter Simon

A Girl Born with Feathers

*"I don't want people to concentrate on my looks, because I don't think
they'll like what they see"*

The Simons, the Heinemanns and the King of Spain

Carly's father was Richard Leo Simon, born in New York City on March
6th 1899 to Leo Simon and Anna Meier. Leo had been born in Hartford,
Connecticut on October 14th 1866, the son of German-Jewish immigrants
Leopold Simon and Sophie Friedenburg. They had sailed to America in the
mid-19th century to start a new life in the Constitution State and there had
three sons, Leo, Alfred and Bernard.

In 1896, Leo married German immigrant Anna Meier, who had been
born in Frankfurt, Germany, on January 18th 1869 to William Meier and
Rosine Mendel. Leo made his small fortune in New York by importing
exotic bird feathers and silk ribbon from around the world, and selling them
on to the thriving millinery trade for the manufacture of the wide-brimmed
hats that were essential dress for ladies in this most fashionable Edwardian
era.

Marriage to Anna produced five children, all named after British
monarchs - Richard, Henry, Alfred, George and Elizabeth. The family's
New York home was on West 86th Street, and the children all enjoyed
private education at the Ethical Culture School on Central Park West. Apart
from eldest child Richard, the boys would all go on to have successful
careers in music, while their sister would marry noted New York physician
Arthur Seligmann. Although not making music his profession, Richard
shared his brothers' love for classical music and in time became an
accomplished pianist himself, with friends claiming he was even better than
some professionals. But for Richard, it would remain just an enjoyable
pastime.

Carly's mother, Andrea Louise Heinemann, was born in Philadelphia
on March 24th 1909. Andrea's father was Frederick Adolph Heinemann,
born in Pittsburgh on August 10th 1870, the son of German immigrants
August Heinemann and his wife Dora. Her mother was (Ofelia Maria) Elma
Oliete/Ollright, born in the Spanish colony of Cuba on June 3rd 1888, and
later affectionately known as "Chibie" (pronounced Shee-bee). Frederick
married Chibie in New York on July 15th 1907, and their first child
Frederick Adolph (Dutch) was born there that same year. Shortly after, the

family relocated to Germantown, a suburb of Philadelphia, where Andrea was born, followed by her brother Peter Dean in 1911.

Chibie's story is as mysterious as it is intriguing. Over the years there were several stories relating to her background, but the most popular one had her being the illegitimate child of Spain's King Alphonse XIII (1886-1941) and a Moorish servant. Banished from the country, the mother gave her baby to a woman who had managed to get passage to America, where the child was eventually raised by a family in New Orleans. In another version of the story, Chibie had been sent to England to be educated in a convent, before eventually going to America. But the truth was out there, and Carly herself would see the mystery unravelled many years later.

Chibie's marriage to Frederick was short lived, as both his alcoholism and often violent temper led him to abandon the family, leaving Chibie to raise her three children in near-poverty (Frederick would die in 1933, aged 62). Undaunted, Chibie put her education to good use (she could speak eight languages) to ensure that they had the kind of cultured upbringing that would stand them in good stead. In 1922, after leaving school at the age of fourteen, Andrea started work at Wanamaker's luxury department store in Philadelphia, bringing home much-needed money for her struggling mother.

Birth of a publishing empire

After graduating from Columbia University and serving his country in Europe in the dying months of the Great War, Richard became involved, like his father before him, in the import trade, but this time dealing in sugar. He then settled into a job as a salesman for the Aeolian Piano Company on West 42nd Street, where, with his charismatic charm and being able to demonstrating his playing skills to prospective buyers, he quickly became a leading salesman. One of the customers he had dealings with was an old college friend called Max Schuster, who would later become his business partner.

When Richard's mother Anna died at the age of 57, on October 26th 1926, the family's former childminder Jeanette (Jo) Hutmacher, a Swiss-born professional nurse, moved into the home to look after Richard's younger siblings. In time, Richard would develop a deep fondness for Jo, eighteen years his senior, and despite one time having his marriage proposal turned down, he would never lose his affection for her.

Richard's next job was as a salesman for Boni & Liveright, a publisher of trade books, and a company which had gained notoriety for its dubious marketing strategies and for opposing the censorship laws of the day, leading it to be called "the most magnificent but messy publishing firm this century has seen." Despite this, Richard's hard work and dedication soon earned him promotion to sales manager. In the cut-throat world of publishing, he had developed a keen eye and acute understanding of the mechanisms involved.

In 1924, while Andrea and her brothers were doing their best to support their mother in Germantown, 25-year-old Richard, thanks to an aunt, was now looking at a golden opportunity. An avid lover of daily newspaper crossword puzzles, particularly those in the *New York World*, she had complained to him how she had to wait a whole day for the next one to come out, and wondered why there wasn't a book of word puzzles that could satisfy both her passion and impatience. Richard could see for himself that, despite its growing national popularity, there indeed appeared to be a gap in the market for this kind of book.

Richard talked about the idea of setting up their own publishing company with his friend Max, who was already involved in publishing motor trade magazines. Max liked the idea, and between them they pooled together $8,000 to start Simon & Schuster. Working out of their small one-room office on West 57th Street in mid-town Manhattan, they began their operation by commissioning some fifty puzzles for a series of cheap crossword books. Richard, with his innovative marketing brain, suggested that each book came with a little yellow pencil attached. A small gimmick maybe, but before the year was out the company had a best-seller on its hands, with some 370,000 copies sold.

The two entrepreneurs now went into overdrive, and to get the edge on their Publishers Row rivals, approached the business with aggressive marketing strategies, spending vast amounts on advertising and promotion to become the first publisher to apply mass market production and distributing techniques to books. They also launched the low-price paperback revolution by co-founding Pocket Books, and one of their first successes was Charles Coran's *Contract Bridge for Beginners*, which sold a million copies in the first year alone. But there were also some missed opportunities, and Carly recalled in a later interview that the company had turned down the chance to publish a new novel called *Gone with the Wind* in 1936.

By the end of the decade, Richard was at the very top of his game - wealthy, well-renowned, and highly respected in New York's high society. At six feet five inches, he had enormous presence, and remained both charismatic and utterly charming, a culture vulture with a keen interest and love for both people and the arts, with people loving him in return. But one lady in particular was yet to steal his heart.

Around the same time as Richard's publishing empire was growing, Chibie and her family had relocated to New York, and Andrea was now working as a sales clerk at B Altman's opulent department store on the corner of Fifth Avenue and 34th Street. But with the Great Depression now casting a somber shadow over the nation, Andrea suddenly found herself on short time, and through some friends was lucky enough to find work at the nearby H Ditson's popular music store, whose regular customers included the young George Gershwin, already one of Richard's many musical acquaintances. Andrea found the work highly enjoyable but taxing on her feet, and regrettably had to find something less strenuous. Another friend, a young editor at Simon & Schuster, managed to pull strings and get her a job as a switchboard operator, albeit a low-paid position. In the summer of 1933, although not having the necessary experience, Andrea began working for Richard's company, but with an affinity for communicating with people, she soon had the task mastered and became a popular asset to the company.

With Max Schuster being ever present in the day-to-day running of the business, Richard was often out of the office having lunch appointments with clients. Andrea had heard great things about the mysterious man she had yet to meet, although there were times when she had put calls through to his office.

Hello little woman

There were many things about Andrea that would turn a man's head. Not only was she petite like her mother; her natural high cheekbones, sculptured nose, and hair swept up in the French style gave her a striking similarity to the current matinee idol Katherine Hepburn. With a similar fireball personality, she was the life and soul of any party, incredibly funny, very athletic, and highly intelligent, often wearing eye-catching but unusual outfits and applying very little makeup other than red lipstick. Not only that, she could sing like a nightingale, and had a pure soprano.

Chibie Heinemann must have felt so proud of her only daughter, seeing in her a little of the glamorous princess that, maybe in a dream, had pictured herself sitting in the court of the King of Spain.

All this, of course, was indicative of having her mother's influence and working in some of the most glamorous fashion stores in the country. With all these attributes, she was fast becoming a popular face among the city's glitzy nightlife society, and could easily hold her own in the company of some of her high-profile would-be admirers. They included a young (Neil) Cornelius Vanderbilt, who at the time was working as a staff writer for the company. There was also circus magnate, John North Ringling, showing more than a passing interest. If things didn't happen soon, this woman was going to be swept away and this story would be coming to an end right here.

But, of course, it did happen. Richard came into the building one morning, passed by the switchboard room, and saw Andrea. As she turned to look at him, he noticed how her smile lit up the room. Leaning toward her, he tipped his hat and smiled back at her, saying, "Hello little woman," and, perhaps without even thinking, she shot back with the flirtatious, "Hello, big man." In that fleeting, life-changing moment, there was mutual admiration, a certain chemistry that would lead to a fairytale romance of matinees, carriage rides and cocktail parties, and the announcement of their engagement in July 1934.

The following year, 36-year-old Richard Simon married Andrea, ten years his junior. Their first home was a six-story doorman town house at 133 West Eleventh Street, between Sixth Avenue and Seventh Avenue South, in the leafy area of Greenwich Village. The Simons occupied the two top apartments, while the remaining floors were shared by relatives, close friends and even some business associates. As well as Chibie and Jo Hutmacher sharing an apartment, Richard's sister Elizabeth also lived there with her husband Arthur and their children Mary and Jeanie, along with Andrea's brothers, Peter and Dutch.

On October 20th 1940 the Simons had their first child. Joanna (Joey) was reputedly named after both Richard's mother Anna and Jo Hutmacher, and she would soon take after her mother in both glamor and refinement. Even from an early age, it was to be expected that her singing voice would one day place her firmly in the spotlight, a diva in waiting. Around this time the Simons began spending vacations in rented houses on the island of Martha's Vineyard off Cape Cod, Massachusetts, thus beginning the family's long association with that idyllic location.

A second child, Lucy, was born on May 5th 1943. While not quite sharing her sister's elegance, she did however have an adorable, sweet-as-apple-pie cuteness. Carly would later refer to her two older sisters as "Daddy's darlings."

In 1944 Richard and Max decided to sell their publishing business to 51-year-old Marshall Field III, heir to his grandfather's mercantile fortune and owner of the *Chicago Sun-Times*, for an estimated sum of $3 million. This was only on the proviso that the two founders stayed on to run the company and on the added condition that, if Field died, they were given first option to buy it back. The sale of the company made Richard a fortune, and with it he bought a 64-acre Georgian mansion in Stamford, Connecticut, where his growing family could escape the city and spend their summer months.

The left-over sister

Carly Elizabeth Simon was born in New York City on June 25th 1945. As the story goes, she was either named after her parents' close friend, Caroline "Carly" Wharton, or, as they were hoping for a boy had already chosen the name Carl, and now decided to simply add a "y," thus giving her what at the time was quite an unusual name for a girl. Almost waif-like in appearance, Carly differed from her more feminine sisters, being more of a rough and tumble tomboy, gawky and gangly, with a pronounced overbite, and blonde, wild hair, feather-like in texture, sprouting every which way and so difficult to brush that she went to bed with it in braids.

Carly later confessed her feelings at the time: "The story about our family was that my father adored Joey for the first four years, and then when Lucy came along, he adored her, and then when I came along, it was too much to have another girl. I didn't look the way he wanted and I wasn't a boy. It was like he'd had *enough*."

The fact that Carly was a little dissimilar in looks to her siblings may have come as a disappointment to her father, and his subsequent remoteness and uneasiness around her made her feel like "the leftover sister," an outsider within the bosom of her own family. Carly would never forget those days of low-esteem and it would have a lasting effect. In a later interview she confessed: "Even now, I don't want people to concentrate on my looks, because I don't think they'll like what they see." Heartbreaking words from someone who was destined to become one of the most glamorous and photographed artists of her generation.

Carly later recalled the difficulties of growing up: "I'm a third child and there are lots of problems a third child has to go through in trying to find her own identity. My older sisters were extremely talented and very attractive and they got all the attention. I had to find some niche of my own where I could feel proud of myself or make my parents notice me."

As with most young girls, in Carly's young innocent eyes her father was everything, and she dearly craved the love that she felt was being denied to her. Just the thought of this, and not believing those who told her otherwise, was enough to have a deep impact on her childhood. While she felt that her father was seeing Joey as his graceful young queen, and Lucy his glamorous princess, Carly saw herself as "the ugly girl down the block." She had to find a way to compensate for not being the pretty one, and the answer was to stand out and be noticed in her own unique way. Even her mother had said that it might be the best way of attracting her father's attention.

Carly recognized that her sisters had adopted individual personas, and realized that she probably had the strongest ego of them all. Where Joey was allowed to be sophisticated, poised and overtly theatrical, and Lucy was just becoming sweeter and more adorable, Carly had to assume an identity. But what would it be?

In later interviews Carly explained: "The ingenue had been filled. The sophisticate had been filled. So, I chose my role. The comedian hadn't been filled yet." It was a role she readily embraced: "I knew I couldn't be prettier than my sisters, or more lovable to him, but I had certain faces or gestures or little moves that would make him laugh."

On January 26th 1947, Andrea gave birth to her fourth child, Richard Peter (but always known as Peter, after his maternal uncle.) With Richard seemingly now having the son he wanted, Carly must have felt like her father's attention would now be diverted away from her even more.

By the spring of 1950 the Simon family had moved from Greenwich Village to a large, six-bedroom brick house at 4701 Grosvenor Avenue in Fieldston, a part of the Riverdale section of The Bronx. Richard had the house extended, with a library wing and even a dark room for his photography, a passionate hobby that almost rivaled his love for the piano, and one that he would eventually pass on to his son Peter. These two houses - Riverdale in the winter, and the Stamford mansion in the summer - became the two rich environments in which the four children would spend their formative years.

The new decade was one spent nurturing the children's growing appetite for culture. What Carly lacked in her father's affection was compensated for in the education that he gave all his children in the arts. Evenings were often spent in the library with readings from classical literature or listening to their father playing Chopin or Brahms, or even the latest music by his friends George Gershwin, Richard Rodgers and Oscar Hammerstein.

Carly was also given piano lessons, but there was always the fear that she would upset her hypercritical father, and eventually she gave them up. Yet, there were rare tender moments between the two of them, and she later recalled a time when he was reading her a poem and it brought tears to his eyes, a fleeting show of emotion in front of the very daughter he was otherwise emotionally detached from. But, by allowing Carly to become engrossed and seduced by the work of great poets, writers and musicians, the seeds were slowly being sown for what would be her destiny as a musician, songwriter and author. Richard must have reveled in watching how keenly his children were embracing their "baptism of emotions and language." Although failing to show her real affection, his influence on Carly could never be dismissed.

Andrea, in turn, did her very best to educate her girls in the social graces, just as her mother had taught her years before. Joey and Lucy proved keen students, and Carly, too, if only people would notice her. With Andrea

23

also having a wonderful voice, she encouraged them all in turn to sing along when it came to bedtime lullabies.

There was another way for Carly to gain her father's attention. Richard loved his baseball, especially the Brooklyn Dodgers, and was a regular visitor to Ebbett's Field to watch them play their home games. Andrea suggested to Carly that if she learned all about the game - players 'names, batting averages, etc - she could engage with him in sporting conversations. For a time, it worked, and the two of them spent quality time sharing hotdogs and statistics.

The Simons also became great friends of Dodgers' hero Jackie Robinson, who had broken the color barrier back in 1947, ending racial segregation in the sport. Through the tenacious campaigning of Richard and Andrea, the Robinson family were able to overturn what was outright racism and finally be allowed to buy a house in Stamford.

Music was the one thing guaranteed to bring the family together, and it became the heartbeat of the Simon home. Theater, too, was something that the girls readily embraced, thanks to Helen Gaspard, who looked after young Peter and shared their home. She taught them and their cousins Mary and Jeanie how to rehearse and perform plays for the whole family. Joey, of course, always got the lead part, but in doing so, made sure that young Carly and Jeanie felt their minor roles were just as important. One story reveals what Joey's mindset was like at the age of twelve. When asked by a dinner guest what she wanted to become - a dancer, an actress, or an opera singer - not surprisingly, she replied: "Which one has more maids?"

Pass the butter

By the age of six, Carly was already suffering with anxieties, but now a new complication emerged. While rehearsing her part in *Little Women* for a family guest, writer James Thurber, she was about to read a line when her throat went into spasm, the words seemingly being strangled. It was the first signs of a stammer that would grow steadily worse and affect both her schooling and confidence.

But it was Andrea who came up with a solution, and one that would change Carly's life forever. At the dinner table one day Carly attempted to say "pass the butter" without stammering, and after a number of failed attempts, her mother suggested she tried singing the words instead. With repeated practice using different melodies, and tapping along with her foot with increasing tempo, it soon began to work, no doubt helped along by her siblings singing and tapping along in joyous harmony. It became a meal time ritual and the butter dish and other items must have been passed around many times.

This seemingly insignificant episode proved to be a turning point. From that moment on, Carly realized that with this handicap under some sort of control, maybe in time it could be eradicated altogether. Here was a girl who had found she had a voice to match a burning desire to perform, even if it was just to impress her father and win him over. But there was also a new-found confidence, a self-belief that maybe now she could have ambition too. She had a voice, and now she could sing.

Carly could turn to two of her favorite uncles for their undivided attention. A lot of support came from Harry Simon, Richard's brother, who was now making a name for himself as a classical conductor. He had been organizing weekly choral sessions with the adults ever since the Village days, and now was doing it for the whole family, singing mainly hymns. Joey, of course, was only too willing, but Carly and Lucy soon got bored with this kind of somber music and goofed around enough to get them "expelled." But then there was maternal Uncle "Snake Hips" Peter, who was always guaranteed for a laugh. Peter had musical pedigree and had been one of Sam Cooke's early managers. Carly adored him with a passion. She not only inherited her clowning and silliness from Peter (especially his ability to wiggle his hips), but also had him to thank for teaching her to play the ukulele and to write little songs together. His girlfriend, singer Betty Ann Grove, also encouraged the girls to sing some of the popular songs of the day.

Stranger in the house

By 1953 it became increasingly evident that Richard was growing more depressed, less active, and increasingly preoccupied, an underlying indication that there were problems outside of the family. His gradual estrangement, even from Andrea and Peter, was now becoming a deep concern. Andrea feared that six-year-old Peter's mental and physical well-being would suffer without a male companion in a house full of girls. In answer to the problem she placed an ad in Columbia University's newspaper for a part-time student to act as both coach and counsellor for her son.

Ronnie Klinzing, a 20-year-old scholarship student from Pittsburgh, was given the job, commuting from his dorm during the week but having his own room at Riverdale at weekends. Andrea was attracted to the handsome, athletic student, and, as it turned out, he neglected his duties in favor of spending more time with her. Their clandestine affair would last a number of years, and apart from Carly, everyone knew what was taking place, including Richard.

In her final school year at Fieldston, Lucy was given an assignment in which she had to learn a famous poem and then recite it in class. She chose Eugene Field's 'Wynken, Blynken and Nod', but, apparently suffering from what may have been an early form of dyslexia, found it very difficult to read. Repeating the episode with Carly and the butter dish, her mother suggested she sang it in class, and with a few simple chords on her guitar, Lucy came up with a melody, turning the poem into a song, and then played it to the delight of both teacher and classmates. The Simons now had another musician in the family.

In 1955 Ronnie was drafted into the army and posted to Europe, and during the summer Andrea went out to France to be with him. While Andrea was abroad Richard suffered a massive heart attack that nearly killed him, and Jo Hutmacher was brought in to look after the family and nurse him back to health until Andrea eventually returned.

The following summer, with Richard still recuperating, Andrea and the family vacationed on Martha's Vineyard, and while they were there Carly and Lucy met up with a young friend called Davy Gude, who was playing his guitar outside the local store with his friend, eight-year-old Jamie. Although Carly never got to talk to young Jamie that day, it would be another fifteen years before she finally did get the chance. By then he would be better known as James Taylor.

At the age of eleven Carly began her first year at the private Riverdale Country Day Girls School, and was put on a course of speech therapy to help control her stammer. She also began to notice subtle changes in her father, which she later described as being like a "slow-motion fall." Although she couldn't understand what was happening to him, she also began to notice changes in herself. Having always been anxious and insecure, she now suffered from a fear of the dark, just one of the many neuroses that would plague her for years. Her father's lack of empathy toward her may have had something to do with what was going on in both his business empire and his personal life, but they were things that Carly would have to wait to discover.

In November 1956 it was announced that Marshall Field III had died from brain cancer at the aged of 38. The Field estate, eager to get out of publishing, arranged to sell Simon & Schuster back to its original owners. The attorney in charge asserted that Richard chose not to buy back in, and the sale proceeded without him. But the Simon family were convinced that Max Schuster, along with other colleagues, some of whom Richard considered great friends, had, due to his continuing poor health, put pressure on him to cash in and sell his shares.

Finding love but losing her father

Over the next couple of years Carly became more and more popular with the other students at Riverdale school, thereby boosting her confidence enormously, even to the extent that she and her best friend Jessie Hoffman became energetic cheerleaders. Despite the anxieties brought on by her continuous stammer and worries over her father's health, Carly now threw herself into the one thing she loved to do - performing, and she participated in various school plays, as long as they were all singing parts, and indulged herself in the kind of music her father had played to her by now watching them being performed live in Broadway shows. Around this time Carly had her first steady boyfriend in Tim Ratner, a student at Riverdale's boys' school, and they spent many hours together singing folk songs and listening to the popular radio show on WBAI hosted by Jonathan Schwartz.

By 1958 Carly had followed in Joey's footsteps to become a freshman at the prestigious Sarah Lawrence College for girls in Yonkers, with Joey now moving on to study opera at New York's Julliard School of Music. Lucy, meanwhile, had just started her first term at Bennington College in Vermont, and, by embracing the growing beatnik culture, was now finding that folk music, not jazz, was the new "cool." Carly was also getting more interested in the folk scene and had started taking guitar lessons with Jessie at the Manhattan School of Music.

In the fall of 1959 Richard suffered another heart attack and was sent off to rest at Stamford, again to be nursed by Jo. Each time Carly believed he was going to die, she convinced herself that by knocking on wood she could save him, and for a time it seemed to work. But this great powerhouse of a man, loved and admired by many, was now just a frail shadow of his former self. Carly had never been given the chance to see him drop his guard and allow her to peek behind the dark veil which concealed a man hiding his physical and emotional turmoil in silence. Not being allowed to do so would be the greatest tragedy of Carly's young life.

In the spring of the following year, Carly was introduced by a friend to Nick Delbanco, a Harvard freshman, and began what was to be her first serious relationship. London-born Nick was a gifted writer, handsome and highly intellectual. Not only would his love of culture inspire Carly, but he was there to provide her an emotional crutch in the dark days that followed.

One day in June, Carly chose to accompany her father to his office and noticed for the first time how his former colleagues and employees were now doing their best to avoid him. It broke her heart to see this, and she swore to herself that she would always stand by the father she loved so much, and now, as she took his arm and he gave her a smile, she had to finally believe that he loved her too.

In the early hours of the morning of July 29th, Richard suffered a third heart attack and died. He was 61. His death had an enormous and lasting effect on everyone, especially 15-year-old Carly, who saw it as unfinished business, the chance of a deep and meaningful father-daughter relationship now cruelly snatched from her just when she was beginning to see cracks in his emotional armor: "I wanted him to live longer so that I could see him and my mother really love each other. I couldn't bear the thought that they didn't have the perfect marriage, with the perfect house, and the perfect car, and the perfect apple pie cooling on the window ledge."

In a later candid interview Carly would look back on the effect her father had had: "I also have such enormous compassion for him. I feel so much like him in a lot of ways. It's like a concentric circle. That's the way I felt when my father died. I swallowed him so that I could *become* him."

All the personal struggles Carly would encounter in the years to come would in some way hark back to those tragic days of the summer of 1960.

"You Two Should Form a Group"

"I didn't want to sing, even when I was singing with my sister. I just wanted to be a little college girl"

Two little sisters

Soon after Richard's death, Andrea sold the Stamford mansion, and along with it the cherished memories of endless summer cocktail parties, celebrity luncheons, and those magical nights of music and laughter. For Carly, those memories would remain with her for the rest of her life, but now as she approached adulthood, it was time for her to focus on the future and whatever new challenges lay ahead.

That September, with Nick back at Harvard, Carly was beginning her junior year at Sarah Lawrence, while Lucy had embarked on a new career by enrolling at Cornell's New York School of Nursing. As for Joanna, her career in opera was about to explode. After studying in both Zurich and Italy, she would soon be going on to make her professional theater debut in 1962 with the New York City Opera's performance of *The Marriage of Figaro*, in which she played Cherubino opposite Norman Treigle in the title role. With excellent reviews she would then go on to win the Metropolitan Opera auditions and the Marion Anderson Prize. All the hard work and dedication had paid off, and Joanna now looked forward to even greater success. Meanwhile, 13-year-old Peter was also doing well and finding his calling in photography, an interest inherited from his late father, and one that would eventually see him becoming a well-respected professional.

Carly was now studying harder than ever, excelling in both Russian literature and painting. But in her dorm room she spent much of her free time with a new guitar, chosen for her by Lucy, singing and writing songs with her best friend Jessie. She also teamed up with fellow-folkie Helen Rheinhold to perform little concerts on campus. Most weekends, however, were spent back home with Lucy, practicing guitar techniques and perfecting their vocal harmonizing. Whilst watching the two girls sing one evening, Uncle Peter, who had already recognized Carly's potential from an early age, said to them, "You two should form a group." The off-the-cuff remark must have come as no surprise to Lucy, but, for Carly, with her self-deprecation being in constant conflict with her yearning to perform, it would be looked on as one more obstacle to overcome.

Lucy was already quite an accomplished guitarist, and she certainly looked the part of a budding folk singer, which, of course, Carly had to try and imitate: "I studied every detail. I copied her style. I wore tight suits and tight sweaters. When she wore her hair with a dip over her eyes like Veronica Lake, I did too. I was Lucy for a number of years."

During their time together, Lucy taught Carly new chords, vocal techniques, and even how to control her breathing whilst singing. Lucy's high soprano and strong vibrato was comparable to that of newcomer Joan Baez, whose debut album was making giant waves on the folk scene. In contrast to Lucy, Carly admired singers like Carolyn Hester and Judy Henske, but her greatest idol was Odetta (Holmes), the black opera singer-now turned folk singer and activist, who had a powerful and deep voice that resonated with Carly's own contralto. Credited for being one of Dylan's inspirations, Odetta would soon be dubbed "The Voice of the Civil Rights Movement." Carly had already had the chance to see her perform at Carnegie Hall in support of Harry Belafonte, another singer whose voice she greatly admired. Another inspiration came in the form of another new folkie on the scene called Judy Collins, who had lately switched instruments from piano to guitar, and whose debut album *A Maid of Constant Sorrow* had been widely acclaimed. While Lucy favored Baez's voice, Carly found she could best imitate Judy's, while at the same time still dream of having one like Odetta's.

Apart from some traditional folk songs and one or two other standards, Lucy was now perfecting the melody of the old children's poem, 'Wynken, Blynken and Nod', the one she had nervously played in class, and giving it a new folk-like arrangement. Although the sisters found it easy to sing in close harmony, it soon became apparent that there was something quite unique in Carly's voice that set it in sharp contrast to Lucy's. And no one knew that more than Carly herself, having spent years singing before her bedroom mirror, trying different ways to perfect certain words and phrasing due to the ongoing frustration of her speech impediment.

For want of a better name, the girls decided that if they were going to perform in public, they would simply call themselves the Simon Sisters. For Carly in particular, the weekends now meant juggling time between rehearsing with Lucy, spending time with Nick up in Cambridge, and making pilgrimages to Greenwich Village's bohemian boutiques shopping for the mandatory folk-ware of pleated skirts, turtle-necks, slave sandals, cheap beads and bangles, or anything else that would match what her sister was already wearing. At least it would make her look hip among her own college friends.

By the summer of 1962, the girls had given fresh arrangements to a number of traditional folk songs using the three or four essential chords, and they felt they now had the confidence (at least as far as Lucy was concerned) to try their luck out in the wider world. Despite the fact that they were being told by family and friends that they sounded really good, and that Lucy was willing to give up further education for a chance to become a professional singer, Carly was still unsure that she wanted to make a career of it, and saw this as being just a bit of fun.

The little girl who had shown no ambition, other than to make her father notice her more, had now grown into a young lady, but one still shackled by that dreaded fear of being placed in the spotlight in front of people she didn't know. Carly would now be putting her complete faith in her sister, realizing that whatever difficulties lay ahead, Lucy would always be there to support her and never let her down.

There were lots of new songs out there that they could now put their own stamp on. Later that year a young, gruff-voiced Bob Dylan had just released his debut album, full of arrangements of traditional folk songs, and although sales were moderate, it had ignited great interest in folk circles. His second album *The Freewheelin' Bob Dylan*, consisting mainly of self-penned songs, hit the folk world like a storm, with the anthemic track 'Blowin in the Wind' becoming a staple part of every singer's repertoire, including the Simon Sisters.

P-Town

By the summer of 1963, the Simon Sisters were ready to test the water, but instead of staying local, and despite their mother's reservations, decided to travel to Provincetown, the small coastal community on the tip of Cape Cod. If nothing else came of it, at least they were guaranteed to have a good time by just hanging together and honing their guitar skills. But this was P-Town, now a favorite holiday destination for both artists and the gay community and noted for its exhilarating club scene. If the girls played their cards right (and guitars), they might get the chance to perform to a live audience. Lucy had the determination to do all she could to assure her kid sister that, whatever they did next, they were in it together. They had always been Simon sisters, but now they were *the* Simon Sisters.

Arriving in P-Town that July, the girls rented a room and next day managed to get work at a bar called the Moors on the outskirts of town, where the owner had just lost his resident act to the draft. With an audience of mainly leather-clad bikers, the girls emerged from the tiny bathroom dressed in matching white-pleated Mexican blouses, knee-length skirts and slave sandals before being introduced by the owner. Nervously they opened their short set with 'East Virginia', a song from Baez's debut album, and, after several other numbers, ended the short set with Lucy's arrangement of 'Wynken, Blynken and Nod', which may have either raised eyebrows or induced sleep in some members of the audience. Still, their mixture of ballads and lullabies received quite a warm reception. The girls knew they had sung well, and even Carly sounded more assertive than before. Over the coming nights, their confidence grew and their stage presence became more fluid and relaxed.

One night, Charlie Close, a friend of Lucy's, came to see them perform at the Moors and realized straight away that they had real potential. Close was a New York talent scout and business partner of Harold Leventhal, the one-time manager of Pete Seeger's folk group, the Weavers. He had resurrected their stalled career in the mid-50s after Seeger had been blacklisted for reputed communist sympathies.

Over the next few days, and in between stints at the Moors, Close shadowed and prepared the girls in readiness for an audition which he said could be arranged once back in New York. He not only gave them hope, but also tips on everything from improving their guitar techniques, songwriting, performing, and their all-important image. For the Simon Sisters, the chance for the big time was now just a nerve-jangling month away.

Sisters on the brink

Returning to New York in mid-July, Carly spent some time with her boyfriend Nick in a rented shack near Menemsha on the Vineyard. Andrea was also renting a property on the island at the same time, and one day in August had to break the news to Carly that her grandmother Chibie had died of a heart attack at the age of 75.

Whilst on the Vineyard that summer, Lucy joined her sister to perform at the Mooncusser coffee house, a popular venue for folk musicians that had just been converted from an old grocery store in Oak Bluffs. Mondays were always reserved for Hootenanny nights and the girls were always well received. Charlie Close would soon become one of the business partners in the venture, and would bring rising stars like Alan Arkin, Tom Rush and Don McLean to the island. There were even times when the girls got to see the young Davy Gude and Jamie Taylor perform.

Around this time Nick was planning to go off to the south of France in the fall to write his long-cherished novel, and he had asked Carly to go with him, but the double pressure of continuing her education at college and not letting Lucy down on the chance of a future musical career persuaded her to stay. Before summer's end the girls travelled to Lenox, Massachusetts, where they made two appearances at the popular Potting Shed (July 30th and August 11th) before returning to New York for their audition at Leventhal's office. Impressed by what he heard, particularly with Lucy's arrangements, he offered the girls his management. Good news for sure, but in Carly's mind, it seemed that it would be Lucy, not her, that was destined for success.

Once they were signed up, word got passed around the Village clubs that there were two bright new faces on the scene, and a rare sister act at that. One of the first club owners to audition them was Fred Weintraub, who was impressed enough to sign them up for two three-week stints at his prestigious Bitter End nightclub and coffeehouse on Bleecker Street, one of the best folk music venues in town. The girls also secured a few gigs at the Gaslight Café on nearby MacDougal Street.

With the Simon Sisters hoping to continue performing in the fall, they had to consider their further education. For Lucy, it would mean continuing her nursing education, and Carly returning for her final semester at college. Until then, Carly found herself back on Martha's Vineyard, spending the remaining weeks of August with Nick in a one-room rented house in Menemsha. Whilst there, Carly discovered he had been seeing another girl. Nick denied it all, and not wanting to lose him, Carly forced herself to believe he was telling the truth.

When the time came to perform at the clubs, Carly had to travel down from her college to meet Lucy at Cornell and then get a cab to Greenwich Village. Most nights they performed their usual five-song set in support of artists on the very cusp of stardom - comedians like Joan Rivers, Woody Allen, Dick Cavett, and Johnny Carson, and singers such as Judy Collins, Judy Henske and Randy Newman. The sisters' reputation grew with each performance, and the applause they received was some consolation for the times they would get into trouble returning to their dorms post-curfew.

Carly was still unsure of whether she wanted a singing career. In an interview in the early 70s she admitted: "I didn't want to sing, even when I was singing with my sister. I just wanted to be a little college girl. I mean, I really loved college and I loved dormitory life and I felt a kind of resentment at not being able to have more of it."

The following month they would secure their first record deal and step into a recording studio for the first time. All that friendly sibling rivalry, those hours spent refining and rehearsing vocal styles and guitar playing, the tentative first experiences of performing live, and all the various attempts to control Carly's anxieties, had come down to this one moment - the Simon Sisters' first shot at the big time.

Sister Act

"Even when we were unsophisticated and unsure of who we would be eventually, as musicians and as people, we knew we wanted to reassure and comfort and hold the babies of the world in our voices"

Winkin, Blinkin and Nod

With folk music now becoming the voice of the country's conscience, 44-year-old Harold Leventhal was the man responsible for making that voice heard, and he had become folk music's most successful promotor. Now he was keen to get the Simon girls a recording contract. Whilst they were singing at The Bitter End, Charlie Close managed to get one or two representatives of local record companies to come down and see them perform. Within days they were snapped up by Kapp Records, an independent label owned by David Kapp, whose brother Jack had established US Decca Records back in 1934. Following stints working for Decca and RCA Victor, David had set up his own label in 1954, licensing its recordings for release in Britain on London Records. In 1960, the label had released one of the first cover versions of songs from the Broadway musical, *The Sound of Music*, and soon would be releasing Louis Armstrong's 'Hello Dolly', which would top the US charts in 1964, ending the Beatles 'run of three consecutive number ones.

On October 18th 1963, Lucy and Carly met up with Close at the Kapp studios in New York to begin recording the thirteen songs they had shortlisted for their debut album. It was to be promoted as *Meet the Simon Sisters*, but subsequently changed to *The Simon Sisters (Lucy and Carly)*, although a later release would have it re-titled *Winkin 'Blinkin 'and Nod*, to coincide with the song's release as a single. With a budget of less than $5,000, it took a matter of days to complete. Produced by Close, and with the music arrangement handled by guitarist Stuart Scharf, the only other accompaniment to the girls' guitars came from jazz bassist Bernie "Will" Lee (father of future film director Spike Lee), and session cellist Seymour Barav. Photographer Norman Snyder provided the cover image of the girls in their matching knee-length red dresses, with Lucy standing and Carly seated on a wire-framed chair.

Besides the now polished and re-spelt 'Winkin, Blinkin and Nod', seven of the remaining songs were credited as being "arranged and

34

adapted" by Lucy and Carly, with one written by the girls, and four composed by others.

THE SIMON SISTERS (LUCY AND CARLY)
Kapp KL-1359
Recorded - Kapp Studios, New York, October 18-21 1963.
Released - April 1964
Producer - Charles Close
Arranger - Stuart Scharf
Did not chart
Lucy Simon - guitar; Carly Simon - guitar; Stuart Scharf - guitar; Bernie "Will" Lee - bass; Seymour Barav - cello

Side 1

So Glad I'm Here *(Barnie Krause - Clarence Cooper - Dan Smith - Stuart Scharf)* ***
Recording date unknown.
A relatively recent spiritual song co-written by Scharf, gospel and folk singer Clarence Cooper, songwriter Dan Smith and Barnie Krause, who had recently replaced Pete Seeger in the Weavers. The song would be chosen as the flip-side to the 'Winkin' single.

Breton Lullaby *(Arranged and adapted by Carly Simon & Lucy Simon)* **
Recorded October 21 1963.
A fishermen's lullaby of Canadian origin.

Delia *(Arranged and adapted by Carly Simon & Lucy Simon)* **
Recorded October 18 1963.
A much-recorded Appalachian folk song based on the murder of 14-year-old African-American Delia Green in 1900. Also known as 'Delia's Gone', it has Carly and Lucy singing alternate verses.

Will You Go, Laddie, Go *(Arranged and adapted by Carly Simon & Lucy Simon)* **
Recorded October 18 1963.
Short a capella version of a traditional song of Irish/Scottish origin, which, according to many scholars, is derived from a song written by Scottish poet Robert Tannahill and composer Robbie Smith in the late 18th century. It was later adapted by an Irish musician into the more familiar 'Wild Mountain Thyme'.

Chicken Road *(Joe Greene)* ***
Recorded October 21 1963.

Written in 1954, this was a departure from their usual material and gave Carly the chance at lead vocal, adding her own touch to what is an otherwise somber tale. Composer Joe Greene was also remembered for writing 'Don't Let the Sun Catch You Crying', a hit for Gerry and the Pacemakers.

Once I Had a True Love *(Arranged and adapted by Carly Simon & Lucy Simon)* ***
Recorded October 21 1963.
An old English folk song that has its origins in 19th century Australia and sung here to perfection by Lucy. The longest track on the album.

Wind Spiritual *(Billy Edd Wheeler)* ***
Recorded October 18 1963.
A gentle song with some wonderful guitar playing by the girls. Singer-songwriter Wheeler was better known as co-writer of the smash hit 'Jackson' for Johnny Cash and June Carter, and later 'Coward of the County' for Kenny Rogers.

Side 2

Winkin, Blinkin and Nod *(Eugene Field - Lucy Simon)* ****
Single Kapp K-586 b/w So Glad I'm Here
Recorded - October 1963
Released - April 1964 (UK - London Records HLR 9893, May 22 1964)
US Billboard Pop Singles #73
Adapted by Lucy and based on Eugene Field's children poem, first published in 1899, it tells the story of three children who go sailing and fishing among the stars in a wooden shoe that serves as a boat. The name suggests a sleepy child's blinking eyes and nodding head. Sung in perfect harmony, it will become their signature tune in the years that follow.

A La Claire Fontaine (by a clear fountain) *(Arranged and adapted by Carly Simon & Lucy Simon)* ***
Recorded October 21 1963.
This centuries old children's song with its adult theme of lost love is a showcase for the girls' knack of sounding even better singing in French, a nod perhaps to singer Francois Hardy, an early inspiration.

Rise Up *(Carly & Lucy Simon)* **
Recorded October 18 1963.
Although the sisters must have written other material that was considered for the album, this interesting track is one of their rare attempts at a protest song.

Lorca Lullaby *(Eric Regner - Frederico Garcia Lorca)* ***
Recorded October 21 1963.
A moving song adapted by Eric Regner, and based on the apparent murder by fascists of poet Frederico Garcia Lorca at the start of the Spanish Civil War. Notable for some fine Spanish guitar playing by Scharf.

Waley, Waley (The Water Is Wide) *(Arranged and adapted by Carly Simon & Lucy Simon)* ***
Recorded October 21 1963.
One of the highlights of the album, with Lucy given the chance to shine with her amazing clear soprano on what is a traditional Scottish song, the lyrics of which date back to the 17th century.

San Duso *(Arranged and adapted by Carly Simon & Lucy Simon)* **
Recorded October 18 1963.
A flamenco-flavored Serbian folk song, with lyrics transcribed by Lyuben Dossev.

Lee Hays of the Weavers wrote the liner notes to the album: "Spontaneous, immediate as they seem on stage…. Lucy's voice, a subtle, clear soprano would seem to have no kinship, no possible relation to Carly's rich and driving alto sound….but time after time, and always surprisingly, they merge. Singing in unison they are indistinguishable, one from the other. It is perhaps the fruit of their long musical association, or possibly ingrained, but the sisters complement each other vocally. Haunting, rhythmic, fragile, happy, full whether duet or solo, they maintain a new timbre and style."

Whilst taking an incredible six months for the album and single to be released, Lucy and Carly continued with their college studies, playing the folk circuit in the winter evenings and usually closing their short sets with the ever-popular 'Winkin'. Meanwhile, Weintraub managed to get them a slot on the popular folk music television show *Hootenanny*, for which he acted as a sort of talent scout. Filmed at the University of Tennessee in Knoxville, and introduced by the Smothers Brothers, they performed 'Turn! Turn! Turn!' and 'Winkin'. When aired on ABC on March 7th 1964, their television debut did much to raise their profile, especially with their fellow college students.

Toward the end of 1963, it was time to make a decision on their future. Lucy wanted to continue performing and even to make another album, although college studies were getting in the way. Carly was happy to go along with her, knowing that her days at Sarah Lawrence were soon coming to an end. But Carly was also missing Nick, who had since graduated and gone off to Europe. Just after Christmas, Carly had made her mind up. Taking formal leave from college, putting her performing on hold, and leaving a frustrated Lucy to finish off her nursing education, she sailed to Europe to stay with Nick for the next couple of months.

Staying in a rented house near Cannes, Carly and Nick toured both Italy and Spain, having an idyllic time savoring all that Mediterranean culture had to offer, and even writing songs together. After a time, Carly became both physically unwell and homesick. Suffering bouts of boredom, confusion, and depression, it was made even worse when she discovered that Nick indeed had another lover, although once again she went along with his denials. When Andrea got to hear of her symptoms, she urged her daughter to come home and seek help. Her manager was also anxious to have her return to promote their debut album with Lucy. When she did come back to New York a month or two later, she left Nick in Europe to complete his book.

After a few sessions with a psychoanalyst to establish the causes of her problems, Carly now needed to patch things up with Lucy and get the Simon Sisters back to writing songs and performing. In April, David Kapp informed them that their long-delayed album had finally been released. Although not a commercial success, the single 'Winkin' had manage to strike a chord with radio listeners, especially in San Francisco, and it received just enough airplay to have it peak at a credible #73 on the *Billboard* Pop Singles chart on April 25th, remaining on the chart for six weeks. It was their inaugural flush of success. In April 1971 *Rolling Stone* magazine looked back on the album as being a "minor masterpiece."

The Happiness Blanket

On June 24th 1964, the girls were back in the studio to cut their second album, *Cuddlebug (The Happiness Blanket)*, produced by Close and arranged by Gary McFarland. Among the session musicians were several members of Count Basie's famous jazz orchestra, as well as guitarist Stuart Scharf and a young keyboard player by the name of Al Kooper, later to become famous as Dylan's organist. Although the twelve songs chosen had less traditional arrangements than before, they had an almost melodious fairytale feel to them. It would also see the debut of Carly as a solo songwriter.

CUDDLEBUG
Kapp KL-1397
Recorded - Kapp Studios, New York, June 24-29 1964
Released - 1966
Producer - Charles Close
Arranger - Gary McFarland

Side 1

Cuddlebug (The Happiness Blanket) *(Alan Arkin - Josef Berger)* ***

Single Kapp K-586 b/w No One To Talk My Troubles To
Recorded - June 29 1964
Released - October 1964 (UK - London Records HLR 9984, August 20 1965)
A song about a child's comfort blanket, co-written by Alan Arkin, the former
singer and guitarist of the folk group the Tarriers (and later Oscar-winning actor).
Jonathan Schwartz praised the song as a "fine example of their refreshing
harmonies and their unique treatment…altogether irresistible."

If You Go Down to the Water *(Carly Simon- Nick Delbanco)* **
Recorded June 25 1964.
One of the songs that Carly had written with her boyfriend in France. Sung in
harmony with Lucy.

Dinks Blues *(Arranged and adapted by Carly Simon & Stuart Scharf)* ****
Recorded June 24 1964.
A traditional blues number, dating back to 1904 and first published in 1934.
Originally known as 'Dink's Song', it relates the story of a black woman who
works on the levee and sings while drowning her sorrows with a bottle of gin.
Carly's passionate lead vocal is stunning, and she later includes it on her 1995
box set *Clouds in My Coffee*.

Turn! Turn! Turn! *(Adapted by Pete Seeger)* ****
Recorded June 25 1964.
Seeger's adaptation of verses from the Bible's Book of Ecclesiastes, already
covered by Judy Collins, and soon to be made famous by the Byrds.

Hold Back the Branches *(Carly Simon - Lope De Vega)* ***
Recorded June 24 1964.
Adapted by Carly from a poem by 17th Century Spanish novelist and playwright
Lope de Vega. Once more she takes lead vocal, augmented with a distinctive
oboe solo.

Ecoute Dans Le Vent (Blowing in the Wind) *(Bob Dylan)* ****
Single Kapp KJB-43 b/w Feuilles Oh
Recorded June 29 1964
Released -1965
Did not chart
A surprisingly good adaptation of the Dylan standard, with French translation by
Pierre Dorsey. Schwartz wrote that the "slight rock and roll feeling in no way
detracts from the simplicity and strength of the song itself."

Side 2

Motherless Child *(Adapted by Frank Hamilton & Ronnie Gilbert)* ***
Recorded June 29 1964.
A traditional Negro spiritual, also known as 'Sometimes I Feel Like a Motherless
Child'. Adapted from the Gilbert-Hamilton version, it relates the pain and

suffering of a child torn from her parents. Odetta had included it on her recent album, *Odetta at Carnegie Hall*, and it was also covered a capella by Ronnie Gilbert of the Weavers, as is this version. Schwartz commented that it has an "infectious beat that ripples through it in a commanding but subtle rhythm."

No One To Tell My Troubles To *(Dick Weissman)* ***
US Promo Kapp K 624 b/w Cuddlebug
Recorded June 29 1964.
Released August 20 1965
Written by a member of The Journeymen and covered by the Kingston Trio on their recent album, *No Time to Think*. Here Lucy and Carly give moving lead vocals on the verses. Also chosen as the flip-side to the single 'Cuddlebug'.

My Fisherman, My Laddie Oh *(Earl Robinson - Waldo Salt)* ***
Recorded June 29 1964.
Adapted from an old Scottish ballad by blacklisted screenwriter Salt and songwriter Robinson, Schwartz noted how the girls had produced a "melancholy texture of a popular ballad of unrequited love."

Feuilles-Oh (Leaves) *(Harold Bernz - Lee Hays - Ruth Bernz)* ***
Recorded June 29 1964.
Co-written by Hays, a member of the Weavers, and sung in French by Lucy. Chosen as the flip-side to the single 'Ecoute Dans Le Vent'.

If I Had A Ribbon Bow *(Hughie Prince - Louis Singer)* ***
Recorded June 24 1964.
A dance song originally recorded by Maxine Sullivan in 1936, and sung here by Lucy. According to Schwartz, a "soaring interpretation of the song."

Pale Horse and Rider *(Carly Simon)* ***
Recorded June 29 1964.
A new song written by Carly in country and western style and sung in harmony with Lucy, and making her debut on record as a solo songwriter.

The sisters' radio station friend Jonathan Schwartz gladly contributed the liner notes and summed up the album: "Lucy and Carly Simon are most assuredly folk singers, and this, their second album for Kapp Records, shows what can be done with instinctive phrasing, an individual sound, and, most important, a point of view."

Alex Greco supplied the cover photograph of the girls wearing matching pink sweaters, perhaps not the image they would have chosen themselves. For reasons not clear, Kapp did not release the album until 1966, but the single 'Cuddlebug', coupled with 'No One To Tell My Troubles To', was released in October 1964 and received a fair bit of airplay, but not enough to have it charted. A follow-up single, 'Ecoute Dans Le Vent (Blowing in the Wind)' backed with 'Feuilles Oh (Leaves)' was released in Canada to attract French-speaking music lovers, but met with similar results.

With the recording completed, a touring schedule of eastern seaboard clubs began, but with Carly's fear of flying, every venue had to be within a nine-hour train ride from New York. Dates were arranged exclusively at weekends to fit around Lucy's schooling, and although mostly in support of other acts, there were times when they actually topped the bill. Unsure of how their album would be received, Carly and Lucy must now have wondered what their futures held and which direction they would take. But the truth was that Carly was still undecided if this was what she really wanted to do, as she still had no great ambition to make it her career. But that was soon to change.

Touring and a trip to London

The summer of 1964 was a pivotal time for popular music. The folk scene was still catching its breath after the release of Dylan's second album, while radio stations across the country were now filling the airwaves with the feel-good, dance-to music of Motown. What's more, there was a whole generation of teenagers being swept along by the tidal wave of the so-called British Invasion, with girls in absolute adolescent ecstasy and boys begging parents to buy them guitars or drum kits. Lucy and Carly would be taking all this in, but perhaps this resonated more with Carly, especially in October, when she tuned in to watch the Rolling Stones make their television debut on the *Ed Sullivan Show*, with Mick Jagger at his swashbuckling, primal best, performing 'Little Red Rooster'.

This was as far removed from folk music as it could possibly get, and in her mind, Carly could see there was another side to performing. She dreamt of what it must be like to be where it was all happening. She needed to be in London.

In the meantime, the girls continued to raise public awareness by performing and appearing both on radio and television. Returning to Lenox, they performed at the Potting Shed the same night that singer Odetta had her own concert at the nearby Berkshire Music Barn. Before taking to the stage themselves, they managed to see Odetta's performance, which must have been a thrill for Carly, but afterward they found to their delight that she had also come to watch them and was now in the audience, front and center, to see their eight-song set. Carly suddenly realized she was going to be singing in front of her great idol, and she fainted, only to be brought around backstage with Odetta fanning her. They eventually managed to complete their set, but it was a night that Carly would never forget.

At a concert at The Second Fret in Philadelphia that fall, Carly's cousin Jeanie Seligmann was in the audience and was enthralled by Carly's performance, predicting that she would be a future star. On October 6th the girls were invited to appear on the New York radio show *The World of Folk Music*, hosted by Canadian-born folk singer Oscar Brand, and they performed two songs, one from each album. 'Winkin' was introduced by Carly, who gave credit to her "modest" sister Lucy, a sure sign that she was becoming more assertive and brimming with new-found confidence (albeit not in front of a live audience). This was followed by the hauntingly beautiful 'Ecoute Dans La Vent', sung in perfect French harmony. On November 9th they made the first of two guest appearances on television's popular *Mike Douglas Show*, along with fellow guest, singer Roberta Sherwood.

By now, Carly's relationship with Nick was gradually coming to an end, both of them feeling that they were too young to get married, despite the fact that some of Carly's close friends were married by now. But while she was disengaging with her boyfriend, Lucy was about to get engaged to her psychiatrist boyfriend David Levine. It seemed like the Simon Sisters' days were now numbered.

Around this time, Carly got a chance to contribute to an album issued by Chevrolet's merchandising department to promote better and safer driving. Titled *Chevrolet Sings of Safe Driving and You* and credited to the First Team, it had to be one of Carly's strangest assignments, as she had to sing the recommendations for what the company billed as an "innovation in driver education."

On May 18th 1965, the Simon Sisters made one of their last television appearances when they travelled up to Canada to guest on Oscar Brand's *Let's Sing Out*, a popular music show inspired by *Hootenanny*, and featuring contemporary folk music filmed at various universities. During the show the girls shared the stage with Brand for a humorous rendition of the old English folk song, 'Oh, no John'.

Despite fears of the act breaking up, the summer brought the possibility that a booking agent in England could get their careers launched over there. With that in mind, the girls planned a trip, but, at the last minute, Lucy went down with flu, leaving Carly to travel on her own with the hope that Lucy could follow on. Sailing over on the *Queen Mary*, Carly met up with 30-year-old Willie Donaldson, well known in the London theater and music business. He was the epitome of an English gent - charming, sharp-witted, and well-educated. But he also had a reputation for being what was referred to as a rake and a serial womanizer. Still, Carly fell head over heels for his charming ways and embarked on a relationship.

With the promise of getting the two sisters auditions and an opportunity to make money performing at club venues around Soho, he managed to get Carly to persuade Lucy to join them. Once she arrived, they had several auditions with nine-song sets, but despite being well received, it all came to nothing. Kapp's British label insisted they would not release their two albums there unless they intended to stay and promote them in a series of concerts. The label had already released the single of 'Winkin' back May 1964, and 'Cuddlebug' would shortly follow, but neither would gain much notice. With touring out of the question, the girls realized they needed to get back home. All that resulted from the trip was that Carly had fallen deeply in love.

Carly would continue to fall in love quite easily, and in a later interview admitted that it was due to her being unable to win her father's love as a child: "I was left with this unresolved dilemma. As a result, I've tried ever since to win the love of those who were unobtainable. It's a mental trap I had to learn to release myself from."

Following their six-week stay in London, the girls headed home. On the voyage back to New York, they got acquainted with fellow passenger, actor Sean Connery - James Bond himself, and they spent the rest of the voyage wining and dining with him, with most of his attention paid to Lucy. As for Carly, she came away with the unlikely dream of one day singing a theme song to a Bond movie.

Once back in New York, Carly decided to move away from their Riverdale home and live with Joey at her midtown apartment at 400, East 55th Street, where she saw for herself the trappings of her sister's success. Carly insisted she paid her way, while in turn she was told to abide by Joey's strict house rules. Although Carly still got together with Lucy to work on some new material, their lives now seemed to be moving in different directions. Lucy had moved in with her boyfriend, with marriage already being planned for the following spring. Without a job, hardly any money, and no longer hearing from her British boyfriend, Carly suddenly felt quite alone in the world, and, without Lucy, now found herself in the one place she didn't want to be - center stage.

20-year-old Carly was still under the impression that for girls her age to have an ambition was not seen as important as getting married and having a family, as Lucy was about to do. At the time, the average age for marriage for American women was just 21. The perception remained that ambition was just not the right thing for a woman to have, and not looked upon as a feminine attribute. For a woman to achieve it, it usually came about through other people noticing their potential and spurring them on. For Carly it

43

would happen just that way. Whether performing for family and friends, or at parties, or even when singing with her sister, she was told so many times just how good she was.

"I'm not that green"

Before joining her sister in England, Lucy had managed to obtain a new manager in John Court, who, along with his senior partner Albert Grossman, had founded the management company Grosscourt, and now had big names like Dylan, Odetta, and Peter, Paul and Mary on their books. Court, like Donaldson, had already hinted that with Lucy on the verge of marriage, Carly had what it took to make a success as a solo artist. But to do so, she needed to shake off the rich-girl image she had, break away from her folk music roots, and develop what they saw was a hidden personality that was trying to surface.

40-year-old Grossman had enormous presence, and had already helped steer the careers of a number of artists, but his aggressive commitment to commercial success for his clients had also generated some hostility in the music business. Like Court, his junior partner, he listened to Carly's demo tapes and recognized that there was indeed potential, but it just needed the right platform for her to make an impact. One of his first ideas was to have her as part of a double-act with a black male singer to be dubbed "Carly and the Deacon." One of the artists he had in mind was folk singer Richie Havens, another of his signings, but with to take part, Havens' unwillingness the plan was eventually shelved. Instead, Grossman now thought of launching Carly as a female Dylan. He envisaged a single, maybe even an album, with Carly imitating Dylan's voice and possibly using his own musicians. It may have sounded like a long shot, but Grossman had a reputation for giving his clients the best possible chance of success. All that was needed was a song, and, with that in mind, he suggested that Dylan himself could write or re-write a suitable one for her to record.

This was the chance for Carly to break away from Lucy's influence and become independent. There were female artists out there like Janis Joplin and Grace Slick who would soon make giant waves in an ocean of psychedelia, and the once glowing flame of folk music would be reduced to just a flicker. This was Carly's chance to make her mark, and she would now have to put her trust in Grossman to make it happen.

In June 1966 Carly met up with a disheveled, almost incoherent, Bob Dylan at the Grosscourt office in New York, and it resulted in him offering to give her the song 'Baby, Let Me Follow You Down', an old blues number he had recorded on his first album. Since then, it had become quite popular in folk circles. Dylan said he could re-write it to suit her vocal range, and although the style of the song was unlike anything she had performed or tried to imitate before, she put her complete faith in both Court and Dylan and went along with it.

Just a few days later Dylan was involved in a motorbike accident that would prevent him from touring for another eight years. Grossman had lost his prime recording artist, but at least he now had the Hawks, Dylan's excellent band of musicians, free for Carly to work with. Without Lucy there to lean on, Carly's jangled nerves were on edge. To give her confidence a boost, Court introduced her to Robbie Robertson, the Hawks' gifted and modest Canadian guitarist. Traveling up to Woodstock, Carly spent some time with him, and he did his best to reassure her by writing a new arrangement of the song.

A few days later Carly met up with Grossman at Columbia's office on West 57th Street, where he listened to her voice and, although recognizing her evident talent, disparaged her rich-girl background. Carly later recalled that he told her that as a woman on a one-to-ten scale, she was a nine, and, although flattered, when asked where she had missed out, he said that she hadn't "suffered enough," and had had an easy life, never knowing what it was like to have to work hard for a living. Carly once said that "all backgrounds are inescapable," and she was now finding out that she was in danger of being a victim of her very own upbringing and frowned upon by the music business, whose perception of her seemed to be that of a "poor little rich girl" with no soul.

But that was not all. Carly now experienced first-hand the unsavory side of the business when Grossman told her straight: "If you're nice to me…I'll make you a nice record." Without having had any experience of sexual harassment, Carly shot him down by saying, "I'm not that green." With no further arguments, and despite what had been said, the recording session went ahead the following day.

The musicians assembled were among the most talented in the business. Besides Robertson and his band, there were also Paul Butterfield, Paul Griffin, and Mike Bloomfield, all masters of their craft. Carly was determined to do her best and make the record Grossman wanted, and once the music track was laid down, with Grossman and producer Bob Johnston in the control room, Carly stepped into the booth to record her vocals. It was only then that she found the music was completely in the wrong key and much too low for her range. If Grossman really did want her to sound like Dylan, it wasn't going to happen by doing it this way. They also recorded a Bob Johnston-Wes Farrell song called 'Goodbye Lovin' Man' for the intended flip-side to the single. Although in the end Grossman appeared to be satisfied with the result, Carly always believed this was his deliberate attempt at retaliation.

But Carly's difficult experience didn't end there. When it came to the mixing, Johnston had the same expectation as Grossman. With a brave Carly standing up to him, Johnston refused to do the mixing, even telling Grossman, falsely, that she had been disparaging them both. In the end, it was all too obvious to her that there would be no further recordings, and that the idea of a single record or even an album was now dead.

These unsavory episodes were a sobering wake-up call for Carly. She would go on record as calling Grossman's studio "Meat City," and the whole experience was one she would never forget: "Whatever Bob said to Albert, I was shelved. This was the end for me for a very long time. I was frozen."

The Big Break

"I find it very difficult sometimes, when I'm feeling something, or even thinking something - a rational thought - to make it come out through my mouth into exactly what I mean. Jake does it beautifully...he has the ability to get inside of other people."

Meeting Jake

Around the time of Carly's failed recording, there was also a suggestion made that the Simon Sisters team up with fellow New Yorkers, the Chapin Brothers, to create a Mamas and the Papas-style group to be called Brothers and Sisters. Harry Chapin, with his siblings Tom and Steve, had had some minor success that year with their debut album *Chapin Music!* and, like Carly, Harry would eventually kick off a successful career with Elektra Records. Harry and Carly would eventually meet up, but by then they would both be successful solo acts.

By the fall of 1966, Carly was deeply depressed, having been made to feel almost worthless by the whole recording experience. Still without work, she was finding it harder to pay Joey rent for sharing her apartment. The Simon Sisters were making no money, and Lucy was now giving indications that their singing days together were coming to an end. What little of her father's inheritance Carly had received had been spent on years of therapy in an attempt to alleviate her anxieties. Now she had to find some kind of work, and, through a friend, got a job working as a secretary for the producer of the short-lived television music show *From the Bitter End*, where she got to meet and greet many of the current folk singers, including Peter, Paul and Mary and a young Janis Ian.

In March 1967 Lucy married David Levine, more or less rubber-stamping the end for the Simon Sisters. If Carly still had a future in music, she now saw it as a songwriter, not as a recording artist with all the trauma and dangers she now associated with it. Taking stock of the last few months, she reflected on a series of unfortunate episodes - losing her boyfriend, the sexual harassment, the failure to get a solo recording contract, and a boring office job. Carly was in need of a new environment, and that summer she would find it.

It was the Summer of Love, and on June 25th, her twenty-second birthday, Carly took a job as a counsellor at the Indian Hill Summer Camp in the beautiful pine forests of the Berkshires near Stockbridge, Massachusetts. The camp offered arts programs for mainly upper-middle class kids, and it was as if Carly had been born to do it, teaching guitar and literature to the keen campers. Within days, she had formed a little band called Lust 4 Five, and as guitarist and lead singer, was joined by campers on bass and drums, and a young pianist called Billy Mernit. One of the songs she had written for them was called 'Secret Saucy Thoughts (of Suzy)'.

A few weeks went by before the head counsellor arrived after having suffered a bout of illness. This was the man who everyone had told her she just had to meet. Jacob "Jake" Brackman was a couple of years older than Carly and a Harvard graduate. He was not only intelligent, tall, and handsome, but also an ambitious and gifted writer, having started out as a journalist for *Newsweek* before replacing Wilfred Sheed as film critic for *Esquire* and contributing articles for *The New Yorker*'s Talk of the Town section. At their very first meeting at a campfire party, something clicked. The other counsellors knew it would happen, as if there had been a divine intervention that made this union happen. There was chemistry for sure, even a kind of celestial intimacy, but it remained a mutually platonic attraction between a music-girl and a word-man, and the beginning of a lifelong friendship. In her memoir Carly recalls how they were somehow "destined to merge." Whatever the reason, it was another defining moment in her life.

Carly later described what it was like working with Jake: "I find it very difficult sometimes, when I'm feeling something, or even thinking something - a rational thought - to make it come out through my mouth into exactly what I mean. Jake does it beautifully. He has the ability to get inside of other people."

Carly had found her musical soulmate at a time when her confidence and social esteem had been at an all-time low. For the remainder of her time at Indian Hill, the two of them became the most popular team in the camp, organizing concerts, dances, plays and readings. When September finally came, they parted ways, with Carly back to Joey's apartment and Jake up to his borrowed house in Vermont. But they exchanged addresses and continued to correspond. Their future together, after all, had seemingly been written in the stars.

Elephant memories

During the fall, Carly's cousin Jeanie managed to get her a job as an editorial assistant at *Newsweek*, working in their readers' letters department: "I would write the same letter over and over again to someone who hadn't renewed their subscription." It didn't last long. She also signed up with an agency to write commercial jingles for all manner of businesses and products. Continuing to write songs in her spare time, she tried to get established artists interested in them, even some of the songs she had written at the summer camp.

1968 brought mixed fortunes. One of her songs, 'Summer Is a Wishing Well', adapted from one of her jingles, was accepted by the New York Symphony Association for a project in which rock bands collaborated on classical music. The chosen seven-piece band called Elephant's Memory asked Carly to become their lead singer and perform the song, along with others she had contributed, at the upcoming concert at Carnegie Hall. It turned out to be a big mistake. She accompanied the band for a run of local gigs, but during that time, whatever rapport they may have had soon evaporated when they began to resent her privileged background, despite liking the songs and her performance. The short-lived but acrimonious relationship ultimately led to the band trying, but failing, to sue Carly for the rights to the songs she had given them, but only after she had become famous.

Another of Carly's songs called 'Play with Me' so impressed some people that she had a demo cut by a family friend, classical music producer John McClure, who then handed it over to Jerry Ragovoy, a producer and songwriter working for the Warner subsidiary, Loma Records. Ragovoy had already penned the classic songs 'Time is on My Side' and 'Piece of My Heart'. But when Carly met up with him, he told her he couldn't quite decide in which music category to place her, and, sadly, it all came to nothing.

The remainder of the year saw Carly taking a notating course at the Julliard School of Music with the hope of being able to write down the melodies that she was creating in her head, although she never did get to master the art. There was also love in the air when one day she took her guitar to be repaired and met Danny Armstrong, owner of a prestigious guitar shop on West 48th Street and a focal point for many of the great guitarists of the day. 33-year-old Danny, a father of five, with a marriage on the rocks, became Carly's romantic interest for nearly two years. During that time, she helped him out with secretarial work and was introduced to some of his musician friends, including guitarist Jimmy Ryan, whose band, the Critters, had just broken up and who was now manager of Danny's guitar store. Jimmy struck up an instant friendship with Carly and he would later write one or two jingles with her before becoming a member of her first touring band. Danny suggested that she used whatever notating skills she had learnt to send off music sheets of her songs for other artists to consider, while encouraging her to give up on her own career as a singer.

Swansong for the sisters

It was now early 1969, and the Simon Sisters were resurrected to cut a new album. Lucy, now expecting her first child, had been busy setting well-known poems to music, and through contacts had been offered a record contract with the Columbia Children's Library of Recorded Books. Carly was more than happy to be back singing with her sister, and they recorded eleven of Lucy's musical adaptations. The producer was Arthur Shimkin, well known to Lucy and Carly since childhood. Dubbed the premier children's music producer of the baby-boom era, Brooklyn-born Shimkin had had a long association with Simon and Schuster.

Joining the company in 1948, he had been tasked with developing new marketing concepts, and after reading scores of letters sent in by parents tired of reading the same stories to their children, he pitched the idea of introducing an audio companion to their existing Little Golden Books series with Little Golden Records, tailored for playing colorful little plastic discs on tiny record players. It became the first US label exclusively devoted to children's music, and was later expanded to traditional vinyl releases, attracting many famous artists such as Danny Kaye, Bing Crosby, Burl Ives, and Jimmy Durante to recite stories backed by top session musicians. Shimkin went on to be executive producer of thousands of recordings, and in 1961 won a Grammy for *Peter and the Wolf*, recorded by Leonard Bernstein and the New York Philharmonic.

In the capable hands of Shimkin, the album was arranged and conducted by Sam Brown and engineered by Fred Plaut and Roy Segal. With Lucy credited with writing the music, there was the usual blend of duets and a sprinkling of solo performances, showcasing Lucy's tender soprano and Carly's husky contralto.

THE SIMON SISTERS SING THE LOBSTER QUADRILLE AND OTHER SONGS FOR CHILDREN
Columbia CR-21525
Recorded - Early 1969
Released - 1969
Producer - Arthur Shimkin
Arranger - Sam Brown
Engineers - Fred Plaut & Roy Segal.

Side 1

Wynken, Blynken and Nod ***
A new arrangement of the Eugene Field poem with a folk-like banjo and flute.

Calico Pie ***
Lucy's beautiful solo rendition of the Edward Lear poem with guitar and flute.

The Lamplighter ***
A poem by Robert Louis Stevenson, published in 1885 in *Penny Whistles* (aka *A Child's Garden of Verses*). Short but compelling, with banjo, flute and a drumbeat.

The Owl and the Pussycat ***
The famous poem by Edward Lear, first published in 1871 as part of his book, *Nonsense Songs, Stories, Botany and Alphabets*. Wonderful adaptation, again heavy with banjo and flute.

Sleep, Baby, Sleep **
A lullaby adapted from Mother Goose, the name synonymous with children's stories, and originating in the 17th century. A compilation *Mother Goose's Melody, or, Sonnets for the cradle* was first published in around 1780. With just a piano accompaniment, this is guaranteed to send little ones to sleep.

Side 2

The Lamb ***
A poem by William Blake published in *Songs of Innocence* in 1789 as a counterpart to 'The Tyger'. Sung here with just a flute and percussion accompaniment.

The Lobster Quadrille ***
A song recited by the Mock Turtle in Lewis Carroll's *Alice in Wonderland* (1865). The most upbeat track on the album.

Who Has Seen the Wind? ***
A poem by English pre-Raphaelite Christina Rossetti, hauntingly sung by Lucy with prominent flute, guitar and a subtle cello.

I Heard the Bells on Christmas Day **
A carol written by Henry Wadsworth Longfellow, based on his poem 'Christmas Bells' and written during the American Civil War.

A Red, Red Rose ****
A song by Robert Burns written in 1794, and also known as 'My Love is Like a Red, Red Rose'. Perhaps Carly's finest solo performance with the Simon Sisters, with just Lucy's guitar accompaniment. On hearing this at the session, even

51

Danny Armstrong finally admitted what a good singer she was. The track will later be included on Carly's 1995 box set *Clouds in My Coffee*.

A Pavane For the Nursery ***
A poem by William Jay Smith, the first African-American to be made Poet Laureate. A pavane is a slow processional dance that was common in Renaissance Europe. A final example of perfect harmony, once again with just a subtle guitar and flute.

With the accompanying hardcover book containing the poems and illustrated by Wisconsin-born Susan Bennet (who also designed the cover), the album was released later that year, with a blue label. That same year it would also be issued without the book and now with a red label.

Four years later, with Carly now an established star, Columbia re-issued the album, again without the book, under the title *Lucy & Carly - The Simon Sisters Sing for Children*, now with additional instrumentation arranged by Tim Geelan and Jim Timmens to give it a more pop-oriented sound, and a new cover image of the girls taken by Barry Brown.

On July 13th Lucy gave birth to a daughter, Julie Levine, and Carly would later pay tribute to her niece in the wonderful song 'Julie Through the Glass'. After two more television appearances that year, it finally brought the story of the Simon Sisters to an end. On December 26th they made their final appearance on the *Mike Douglas Show*, again with a splendid performance of 'Winkin'.

The Simon Sisters' legacy was that it determined each girl's destiny, defined by their individual personalities and ambitions. With marriage and motherhood now a priority for Lucy, for her younger sister it would herald a moment in her life when she had to decide for herself just what road to take next. That road was now lying just around the corner.

Songwriter, not singer

In the meantime, Carly had borrowed some money off her mother to rent her first apartment on East 35th Street, between Lexington and Third Avenue, in New York's Murray Hill. As luck would have it, this was just a block away from where Jake Brackman was now living after moving down from Vermont. With her focus now on working more with Jake, her relationship with Danny would soon be coming to an end. At the same time, she began another lengthy process of therapy to get answers to her ongoing anxiety issues.

With Carly and Jake now re-igniting their working relationship, he encouraged her to write more new songs, and, in return, she began to open up to him more and more by divulging episodes about her childhood, her parents and siblings, her relationships, and even her phobias, all of which Jake absorbed, and within days he knew more about how her mind worked than Carly did herself. He was becoming almost telepathic. Carly would just have to play a la-la-la melody to him and give him an idea of what she wanted to say, and in no time at all he could turn her thoughts into meaningful lyrics.

One of the first songs they worked on had its origins in the award-winning NBC television documentary *Who Killed Lake Erie?* which premiered on September 12th 1969 and raised public awareness of the grave national pollution crisis. Whilst doing freelance work, Carly had been asked by the film's producer, an old college classmate, to contribute the theme song and background music. Although not inspired enough to write lyrics, fragments of her original music remained in the film, while the theme song finally chosen was Malvina Reynolds ''From Way Up Here'.

Carly's melody, the first she had ever written on piano, remained a dormant fixture in her head for months. But when she played it to Jake one evening, they began working closely together to create what would become a magical song, and ultimately one of her finest compositions. Without even deciding on a theme, Jake drew inspiration from what he had learned of Carly's early life - the dynamics of her parents 'marriage; how her friends were married and now leading unhappy lives; how her boyfriend's enthusiasm for marriage came with a controlling nature; and how a woman's initial resistance to marriage ultimately ended with capitulation. The result was a song with the slightly ungainly title of 'That's the Way I've Always Heard It Should Be'.

The beginning of the new decade heralded the start of Carly's solo career. One evening that spring, Jake and his live-in girlfriend, Erica (Ricky) Johnston, introduced an unsuspecting Carly to dinner-guest Jerry Brandt. Brandt was an aggressive music impresario and owner of several nightclubs, including the Electric Circus, and had also been credited with discovering Chubby Checker. Jake asked a rather embarrassed Carly to sing a few songs to him, including 'Alone', 'Please Take Me Home (to Bed) With You', and, of course, their most recent collaboration. Brandt was impressed with what he heard, and although nothing was agreed that evening, in a matter of days he had offered to manage her, assuring her he could get a record deal.

Once Carly was signed up to his management company, Brandt took her to a studio to record five songs for a demo tape, and enlisted several top musicians, including David Bromberg, a multi-instrumentalist who was soon to launch his own solo career. The songs included 'That's the Way I've Always Heard It Should Be', 'Alone', and 'I'm All It Takes to Make You Happy', as well as two cover versions.

At this stage, Carly still saw herself as solely a songwriter, writing material for others artists. She was well aware that others considered her to be a good songwriter, but following her recent studio experiences, she could no longer visualize herself as a recording artist. Fortunately, that was all about to change, although it didn't get off to a positive start.

Brandt first took the cassette of the demo to Clive Davis at Columbia, who after hearing a little about her background and listening to just two tracks, allegedly told him, "What do I want with a Jewish girl from the Bronx?" and threw the tape across the room. Undeterred, Brandt next offered it to Jac Holzman, president of Elektra Records, who had an eclectic list of artists on his books, including Judy Collins and Phil Ochs. On hearing the name Carly Simon, Holzman asked if she was one of the Simon Sisters, as he loved their single 'Winkin, Blinkin and Nod'. With an imminent trip to Tokyo planned, Holzman agreed to take the tape with him, and while there he listened to it in his hotel room. He loved what he heard and called Brandt to tell him that he wanted to sign her.

On his return to New York, Holzman played the demo tape to his A&R (Artists & Repertoire) staff at their weekly lunch meeting, but none of them liked it, judging some of the songs to be too wordy and completely out of fashion to be a success. But Holzman disagreed, and he had the final say.

Elektra Carly

In the spring of 1970 Carly Simon was signed to Elektra. The label had been around for twenty years, founded by Holzman and Paul Rickolt in a college room for a joint investment of $300 each. 39-year-old Holzman was a visionary and while at first concentrating on folk music, by the mid-60s he had embraced the new wave of folk-rock and psychedelic rock with signings that included the bands Love and the Doors.

But what of Carly? At first no one could figure out how to market her. Holzman saw her main strength was her voice, and he had a vision of her singing covers of songs by established stars such as Jeff Buckley, Cat Stevens, Donovan, and Tim Hardin. Looking around at some of the current more gritty and soulful female artists, he saw there was a niche for a well-bred, sophisticated female singer. Carly may have agreed with him over the latter observation, but she remained insistent that she wanted to record her own material. Over the next few days, she had to convince him her songs were good enough.

After listening to a succession of demos, there was no doubt that Holzman was impressed. The next thing to do was to find a producer, and the first person who sprang to mind was South African-born Eddie Kramer, who was not only one of the top producers in the business, but also one of the toughest. Having already worked with stellar artists like Jimi Hendrix, the Doors, and Joe Cocker, he was presently engaged in designing Electric Lady Studios, a state-of-the-art underground recording venue at 52, West Eighth Street in Greenwich Village, which was due to open that June.

In a meeting with Kramer arranged by Holzman, Carly sang several songs to him, some which were still work in progress, but the only one that stood out to him was 'That's the Way…' Despite some initial reservations, Kramer agreed to produce the album, and it would be one of the first to be recorded at the new studio.

With Kramer now at the helm and recording dates arranged, all that was needed now were the songs, many of them still only melodies in Carly's head, and some just half-finished. In the following weeks Jake would work with Carly night and day to get them into shape. What wasn't completed would have to be finished off in the studio. Several demos later, Kramer had the list of songs to be recorded.

Seven years after first stepping into a recording studio with Lucy, and four years after her bad experiences with Grossman, 25-year-old Carly, for so long in the shadows, had now stepped into the light and found her independence. She was about to make her first solo album with one of the best producers and record labels in the business. That long path to success was now getting shorter every day.

No Remarks and Apricot Scarves

"I don't consider myself in the public eye. I don't care about being a star, a top-selling recording star, if that has to come at the expense of my life."

Tearful nights, angry dawns

After spending a few weeks of the summer up on her brother's Tree Frog farm in Vermont, Carly returned to New York and in late August commenced work on the *Carly Simon* album. With Holzman attending some of the early recordings, things got off to a good start with the new producer. Holzman looked on Kramer as the ideal person to give the songs the rich, instrument-heavy production that he felt would complement Carly's strong voice, and to that end brought together some of the best session musicians in the business to achieve it.

Keyboard player Paul Griffin had been a member of saxophonist King Curtis's backing band and later played on some of Dylan's first "electric" albums. He had also been one of the musicians present at Carly's Grossman sessions. Jeff Baxter was a much-sought-after session guitarist and soon to be a founding member of the band Steely Dan. Jimmy Johnson was another guitarist, one-time member of the famous Muscle Shoals Rhythm Section and co-founder of their Sound Studio. Bass guitarist Jerry Jemmott was a Grammy-winning musician who had played on albums by Aretha Franklin, Ray Charles and Wilson Pickett. Tony Levin, another bass player, had worked on jazz pianist Gap Mangione's debut album *Diana in the Autumn Wind*.

A second keyboard player, Mark "Moogy" Klingman, was also quite a gifted songwriter, and, being an associate of multi-instrumentalist Todd Rundgren, would shortly be helping him build the famous Secret Sound Studio in Greenwich Village. Carly and Jake were impressed with one of his compositions, 'Just a Sinner', and agreed to record it for the album.

Ed Freeman was an accomplished producer and arranger who had just finished working on folk singer Tom Rush's eponymous album, and was now brought in to work on certain string arrangements, which would otherwise be handled by session keyboardist Pat Rebillot. Freeman also helped to arrange some of the unfinished songs. Another familiar musician working on the album was keyboard player Billy Mernit, a friend of Jimi Hendrix who Carly remembered as one of her camp band at Indian Hill. He would also co-write with Carly and Kramer one of the songs chosen for the album. Cellist Harvey Shapiro, drummer John Siomos, and bass player Jim Wilkins were also employed during some of the recordings.

Carly and her manager also brought in two other guitarists to help out. One was David Bromberg, who had produced and played on her demo tape, and the other was Danny Armstrong's friend Jimmy Ryan.

The first song to be recorded was 'That's the Way I've Always Heard It Should Be', with Carly on piano being accompanied by a simple metronome to keep time. But for added impact, especially for the intro to the powerful chorus, Carly visualized a more dynamic sound, and suggested a tumbling tom-tom percussion. Kramer and almost everyone in the studio disagreed, reminding her it was essentially a gentle ballad that only needed the piano and a string arrangement which would be handled by Freeman. Carly insisted, and without a regular drummer available at the time, she had guitarist Jimmy Johnson stepping in to provide the tom-tom infills. Eventually, to everyone's satisfaction, they got the result they wanted, and even Kramer was in agreement. Carly was also dissatisfied with Kramer having doubled-tracked her voice, but to avoid more confrontation she went along with it. The remaining recordings went ahead as planned, although the relationship between Carly and her producer remained somewhat strained. But news of a tragedy would soon put completion of the album in jeopardy.

Toward the end of the sessions on September 18th, the news came that Jimi Hendrix had been found dead in a London apartment. Carly had met Jimi just several weeks before when she had attended the official opening of the studio, the same night that she had also been introduced by Kramer to Paul McCartney and his girlfriend Linda Eastman. Kramer was devastated with the loss of his premier recording artist, and his focus now suddenly shifted away from Carly to completing the final mixing and track selection for Jimi's *Cry of Love* album, which they had been working on for over a year.

With the distraught Kramer out of the studio, at least for a while, it meant that although Carly's basic tracks had been laid down, they still required mixing. Holzman enlisted the help of his brother Keith to supervise the album's completion, and the trouble-shooting A&R man Steve Harris was brought in to console Carly, who was now getting worried, not only about the album not being finished, but also the added fear of having to promote and perform her songs in public. Kramer did finally return to the studio to complete the recordings and do a final mix on 'That's the Way I've Always Heard It Should Be', but by October, with tensions still running high, he left the project, leaving her to do the final mixing of the songs with engineer David Palmer.

The loss of Kramer came about at the same time that Carly's manager, Jerry Brandt, also bailed out, perhaps worried too that the album would be pulled, or perhaps having second thoughts as to whether Carly had what it took to make it a success.

When Jac Holzman finally sat and listened to the recorded songs, it would be the first time he had heard 'That's the Way I've Always Heard It Should Be' in its completed form, and, being full of praise, told a surprised Carly that it had to be the first single. The album, and this unusual song that meant so much to her, was about to be introduced to a worldwide audience.

CARLY SIMON
Elektra K 42077 (UK – EKS 74082)
Recorded - Electric Lady Studios, New York, August-September 1970.
Released - February 9 1971.
Producer - Eddie Kramer
Production supervisors – Jac Holzman & Keith Holzman.
Mixing engineers – Ed Kramer & Dave Palmer.
Art direction & Design - Robert L Heimall.
Billboard Pop Albums #30; Canada #17; Australia #55
Carly Simon - guitar, piano; Jeff Baxter- pedal steel guitar; David Bromberg - guitar; Jimmy Johnson - guitar, drums; Jimmy Ryan - guitar; John Siomos - drums; Jerry Jemmott - bass; Tony Levin - bass; Jim Wilkins - bass; Billy Mernit- keyboards; Paul Griffin - keyboards; Mark "Moogy" Klingman - keyboards; Ed Freeman - arr. strings on "That's the Way I've Always Heard It Should Be," "Reunions," and "The Love's Still Growing;" Pat Rebillot - arr. strings on "Alone;" Harvey Shapiro - cello.

Side 1

That's the Way I've Always Heard It Should Be *(Carly Simon - Jacob Brackman)* *****
Single EKS-45724 b/w Alone
Released - April 1971
Billboard Pop Singles (Hot 100) #10; Billboard Adult Contemporary #6; Cashbox #9; Canada #15
Carly Simon - piano; Paul Griffin - piano; Tony Levin - bass; Jimmy Johnson - drums; Harvey Shapiro - cello; Ed Freeman - arr. cello
A sophisticated and candid description of young female angst and a musical insight into a subject matter that was already being well voiced in the current climate of women's liberation. Some angry feminists would see it as "a lame statement of resignation" rather than the condemnation that Carly intended. Drawing on Carly's distant relationship with her father and her parents' troubled marriage, Jake pens a sorrowful contemplation on commitment and compromise to complement what will become Carly's trademark unorthodox song structure. Carly is not looking to seduce the listeners or win their pity; she is telling it

straight - whether women should be dictated by society into marriage, or follow their own rules to avoid a relationship that so often fails. The way she interprets Jake's delicately-spun and complex lyrics with such melancholy is truly outstanding, and her inspired decision to use drums in such a dynamic way is indicative of how even at this early stage of her career she has a flare for production techniques. As the first track of her first album, and the first single to be released, there certainly couldn't have been a better introduction to her career.

Alone *(Carly Simon)* ***
A song about a woman seeking solitude to reflect on her relationship, while at the same time reassuring her lover that she is not leaving him. But there's something in her past she needs to come to terms with, and she can only do this by being on her own and using that time to deal with any pain those memories may bring. Jeff Baxter's spicy pedal-steel guitar is prominent, with strings arranged by Pat Rebillot. Chosen to be the flip-side of the single 'That's the Way I've Always Heard It Should Be.'

One More Time *(Carly Simon)* **
Carly Simon - guitar; Billy Mernit - piano; Jimmy Ryan - guitar; Jeff Baxter - steel guitar; Tony Levin - bass; Jimmy Johnson/John Siomos/Jim Wilkins - drums
Jaunty country-flavored song and an example of Carly's double-tracked voice, something she was opposed to, but nevertheless giving it more substance. Some reviewers criticized how basic the production was, but also praised the performance. *Rolling Stone* remarked how her voice assumed the "gliding plangency of a pedal-steel guitar."

The Best Thing *(Carly Simon)* ****
Carly's homage to her lost London love, Willie Donaldson, and a relationship she later recalls with fond memories and some regret. The reference to The Serpentine confirms the setting, as it is a lake in one of the city's famous parks. Carly examines what life would be like if she had married him, had three children, and then, like her own father, how her relationship would have been with the youngest child. Notable for the haunting, echoing female chorale, it's a sophisticated and elegant song, lyrically one of the best of her own compositions on the album.

Just a Sinner *(Mark Klingman)* ***
Carly's chance to let it rip in this semi-rocker written by keyboard player "Moogy" Klingman, and later to be featured on his own 1972 album *Moogy*. His gentle confessional lyrics in the verse are blown away by the heavy-metal chorus and display early evidence of Carly momentarily stepping away from the melancholy to bring her hard-rock side to the surface.

Side 2

Dan, My Fling *(Jacob Brackman - Fred Gardner)* ****
The second non-Carly-written song on the album, this was a collaboration between Jake and his friend, civil rights activist Fred Gardner, best known for his opposition to the Vietnam War, and based on his own song, 'Ruth My Truth'. Carly uses it as a lusty portrayal of her relationship with Danny Armstrong, and her regret over it ending so soon (more or less happening at the time of the recording). *Melody Maker* rated it as one of the album's best tracks. Carly will take the line "fall back on dreams" and use it again later on her own song, 'Haven't You Seen Me Lately'.

Another Door *(Carly Simon)* ****
Splendid piano-driven track showcasing Carly's vocal range and memorable for its evocative chorale ending. This part-philosophical, part-spiritual song is one of the best examples of Carly's writing style that will become more evident over the next half a dozen albums.

Reunions *(Carly Simon, with additional music & lyrics by Bill Mernit & Eddie Kramer)* ****
One of the album's highlights, with arguably Carly's best vocal performance. Even though it's not clear what the additional contribution may have been, it remains a tour-de-force of songwriting. Billy Mernit recalled that it was about Indian Hill, the summer camp where he first met Carly, and was "a sort of personal reflection of that experience." This bittersweet, wistful song, about an incomplete family gathering and wrong turns made, has a harpsichord and cello arrangement by Ed Freeman that adds just the right touch to give the track that emotional punch. Carly would cite this song as her mother's favorite, and it's easy to see why.

Rolling Down the Hills *(Carly Simon)* **
A jingling honky-tonk piano, busy harmonica, and a la-la chorus, manage to raise a few spirits after the emotions of the previous two tracks, but still fail to lift this song from being more than just average. The low point of an otherwise great debut album.

The Love's Still Growing *(Buzzy Linhart)* ****
Exceptional ending to the album, and although not one of her own compositions, Carly delivers a superlative double-tracked vocal, rising and falling in perfect symmetry. Percussionist and vibraphone-impresario William "Buzzy" Linhart's lyrics may seem "mantric and clichéd," but Carly's hauntingly beautiful, psychedelic-flavored performance transcends any criticism, and is far superior to Linhart's much-covered own version, which appears on his second album, *The Time to Live Is Now*, released the following year. Once again, Ed Freeman is on hand to supply the string arrangement to a song that even gets Jac Holzman raving. You can almost smell the herbs and spices burning.

Too much, too soon

With the recording in the can, the album's jacket design was now the focus. For an added touch of quality, Holzman gave it a soft, matte-pink finish, and for the cover picture called on top celebrity photographer Joel Brodsky, who had recently taken some iconic images of Jim Morrison. One of Brodsky's shots had Carly sitting on a couch looking directly into the camera, hands on knees, barefoot, and with a black shawl stretched across her arm and legs. As evocative as this was, just a simple, and less impressive head shot was finally chosen for the rear cover, revealing what many would see as her having more than just a passing resemblance to Mick Jagger. But for the front cover Holzman and his art designer Robert Heimall were looking for something more feminine. Carly then suggested they ask her brother Peter, now a professional photographer, to do the shots, and, with their agreement, she traveled up to his commune in Guilford with a suitcase full of various dresses. In a makeshift studio set up in the farmhouse Peter emulated Brodsky's original portrait by having his sister recline on an old love-chair. Staring directly at the camera, but now with her head gently resting in the palm of her hand, Carly was wearing a beautiful long pink dress that covered her crossed legs, with a yellow knitted shawl draped over the chair, and a backdrop of blue embroidered cloth.

Holzman loved it, and could see that with this image Carly was making a statement - here I am, now I want the world to notice me. Here was that decisive moment, and now there would be no going back.

Carly Simon was released on February 9th and entered Billboard's Pop Albums chart on April 24th, reaching a credible #30, and remaining on the charts for 25 weeks. In Canada it did even better, peaking at #17. The single of 'That's the Way I've Always Heard It Should Be', with 'Alone' chosen as the flip-side, was released in April and entered the *Billboard* Pop Singles top 40 on June 5th, peaking at #10 on July 10th, and remaining on the charts for a total of 17 weeks. It also climbed to #6 on their Adult Contemporary (easy listening) chart.

When the single 'That's the Way I've Always Heard It Should Be' was released, Carly's old friend, New York deejay Jonathan Schwartz, plugged it heavily on his radio show. Meanwhile, indicative of his marketing genius, Holzman had his team send out free copies of the single to radio stations ' female staff, those he believed would identify with the message of Carly's "signature" song. With the word then passed on to other female ears, he believed there was every chance for the women's lib movement to adopt it as one of their many anthems.

Carly Simon would go on to receive mainly positive reviews. The *Los Angeles Times* called it an "impressive album," while Britain's *Melody*

Maker described the songs as "unassuming excellence," predicting that Carly had "the potential to be up there with the best" and become a major force (the "best" being a reference to current hot properties Carole King, Laura Nyro, and Joni Mitchell). In their estimation, Carly also had the precious ability to "articulate the personal and convert it into the universal." *Rolling Stone* summed up the songs as simply "lovely," comparing her writing to the short stories of novelists John Updike and J D Salinger, and thus resonating with many middle-class homes. Perhaps the most critical review came from *Newsday*, which when revisiting the album in 1973 made the comment: "Simon's compositions still sound stiff and overperformed, typical rock-as-art jive. At the time, I closed my ears and hoped she would go away."

Carly never "exploded" onto the charts like the press claimed, but had just "trod lightly up to the mic," as she preferred to describe it. Reflecting on the album, she said: "It was a problem of trying to do too much too soon. I wasn't really prepared for it. The material was just a collection of odd songs I'd written over the years, plus the fact that I'd never been in a recording studio before and my producer had never produced a record before."

During the year Carly was filmed at her mother's Riverdale house for a weekly PBS television show called *The Great American Dream Machine* and gave a live performance of 'That's the Way I've Always Heard It Should Be' over a pre-recorded piano track.

On March 1st 1971 James Taylor appeared on the cover of *Time* magazine, and it didn't escape Carly's notice. In a 2015 interview she recalled: "I loved James the minute I saw him on the cover...And I will never love anyone again so much or in the same way."

Around this time Carly had also begun a brief relationship with the New Wave Czech film director Milos Forman, and had been given a small part in his movie *Taking Off*, starring Lynn Carlin, about an average couple living in the suburbs of New York whose daughter runs away from home. In the movie, Carly makes a brief appearance as an audition singer (as does Kathy Bates, also making her screen debut), but was also asked by Forman to compose a song for the soundtrack. She came up with 'Long-Term Physical Effects', co-written with Tim Sauders. The film was released in March and went on to win the Grand Prix at the Cannes Film Festival.

For Carly, due reward would finally come at the 14th Annual Grammy Awards, held in New York on March 14th 1972, and by then she had already released her second album, *Anticipation*. Nominated for Best New Artist, she beat Bill Withers to take the award, but in the category of Best Pop Vocal Performance Female, the song 'That's the Way I've Always Heard It Should Be' lost out to Carole King's album *Tapestry*. Carole stole the show by also coming away with Best Album, Best Record for 'It's Too Late', and Best Song (Lyrics) for 'You've Got a Friend'. That same night a certain James Taylor won Best Male Vocal Performance for his rendition of Carole's 'You've Got a Friend'.

Carly and the Cat

Although the Grammys were in the future, right now it was all about promoting the album. Steve Harris was now charged with putting gentle pressure on Carly to engage in a tour schedule. Carly, of course, was terrified with the idea, still wanting to be a recording artist and not a performer: "I never wanted to perform live. I thought that would be just a big burden and because of that it became hard-wired in my system that anytime I was in the center of the stage I was going to panic."

Steve and Jake did their best to quell her nerves, while at the same time suitable venues were sought to kick off her performing career. Steve struck lucky when he heard that British singer Cat Stevens would be playing at Los Angeles' premier rock club, the Troubadour, in just a little under three weeks 'time, and that its owner Doug Weston was still looking for an opening act. With a little persuasion, Steve secured the booking for three nights commencing April 6th. He then had to tell an unsuspecting Carly, who felt as if she was being thrown to the wolves. She had not performed on a stage since singing with Lucy; she had no band, and she had the added fear of flying. All these worries now conspired to bring about what she called "the Beast," a concoction of anxieties that had developed since childhood like an entity that could come to the surface at any time for any reason.

But Steve did a great job of calming her down, even agreeing to fly out there with her (although he too hated flying). Carly had been impressed with Cat Stevens' work for over a year now, and he already had two critically acclaimed albums under his belt. At the time, Carly admitted how Stevens' music influenced her: "I've had a lot of comparisons with Cat Stevens, largely because of the production of my album, but it's true that I like the way he sings so much that it's affected my vocal style." But her admiration for him didn't stop her making every excuse not to perform.

In a later interview Carly spoke about her stage fright: "I feel pinned by the spotlight like an animal in a cage. I really do get nervous claustrophobia-like. I'm in a closet without enough air to breathe. I think most performers feel certain anxieties, but unlike them I don't have the ambition to get over it." Looking back at her childhood for reasons, she admitted: "I was one of those kids who was especially afraid of the dark for much longer than most of my other friends. When I heard a plane flying overhead, I was sure that bombs were going to go off. I felt like a glass animal."

As the days flew by, Carly gradually came to terms with what had to be done. First, she had to get a band together. Guitarist Jimmy Ryan, who had played on her debut album, was invited to be her musical director, and he suggested to her using two of his friends - keyboardist Paul Glanz, who had been in Jimmy's band the Critters and had also played with The Crazy World of Arthur Brown, and Andy Newmark, an excellent session drummer who Jimmy had known for a while and who in a year or two would be replacing Gerry Gibson as a member of Sly and the Family Stone.

However, to help keep expenses down, it was decided to use a local drummer, and with Steve's help, Carly managed to get Russ Kunkel, who had recently been touring as part of James Taylor's band, until the singer was badly injured in a motorbike accident. With the tour now cut short, Kunkel was already in LA and available to sit in for the Troubadour gigs, although in a week or so Andy would become Carly's regular drummer for future concerts and go on to play on many of her albums.

The first of the sold-out nights at the Troubadour came on April 6th, and among the star-studded audience were Jack Nicholson, Leon Russell, Randy Newman, and a now recovering James Taylor with his current girlfriend Joni Mitchell. Jac Holzman was also backstage to offer encouragement. Carly, without Lucy there to support her, nervously walked on stage to perform the chosen songs - 'One More Time', 'In My Reply', (written by James Taylor's brother Livingston, a childhood friend of Carly's from the Vineyard), 'Dan, My Fling', 'The Love's Still Growing', and finally 'That's the Way I've Always Heard It Should Be'. Despite problems with a moving microphone while seated at the piano, it went well, and she received long, well-deserved applause. Backstage in her dressing room, while Cat Stevens took to the stage, Carly met James Taylor face to face for the first time since that day on the porch of the Vineyard store, many years before. The conversation was brief, but the attraction was instant. Carly would later refer to those three days at the Troubadour as life-changing.

Carly's impact was so great that on April 11th the promoter made Carly headliner for the show.

The reviews of her performances were glowing. The *LA Times* claimed after the first gig that a new artist "has arrived." On April 16th the *LA Free Press* wrote how she had "exuded confidence" with her "inspired set." *Cashbox* described her songs as "jewels," portraying "emotion in tones of whispered gray."

Anticipating good old days

Returning to New York, Carly had managed to obtain a new business manager in petite New York talent scout Arlyne Rothberg, perhaps better known for her actor-comedian clientele, and almost from the start she was inundated with calls for Carly to appear live. During this time, Carly continued writing new material around the things that inspired her. While waiting in her apartment one evening for Cat Stevens to arrive for a dinner date, she anxiously sat on her bed and in just fifteen minutes wrote the lyrics to a song she called 'These Are the Good Old Days', later to be re-named 'Anticipation'.

On May 21st Carly opened for grizzled Nashville singer Kris Kristofferson in what was to be the first of four concerts at the Bitter End in Greenwich Village, and introduced some new songs to the set, including 'These Are the Good Old Days'. Reviewing the opening night, the *Village Voice* praised Carly's performance, calling it "a rare magic of combining artistry, professionalism, and true intimacy." *The New York Times* stated: "She strikes several emotions at once and makes you feel glad to be struck," also observing that in her songs "people live on only in dreams, or else forget how to dream together," and how they bring a wonderful "fascination and curiosity" to the listener. In a later article Carly was described as being "an Amazon in gingham" and an "embodiment of a whole new ideal for women."

There were times when it seemed like reviewers were watching different concerts. Where one was critical of Carly's band for not been able "to get it together" on the night, another admired how Carly and her trio of musicians achieved a "sound wave which is quite full and perfect," and how the singer easily switched instruments depending on the song. In fact, she was "the best thing to come along in a long time." On the last night, Kris invited her back on stage to do a duet for his ballad, 'Help Me Make It Through the Night'. Everyone in attendance couldn't help but see the chemistry between them as they shared the stage, and their subsequent on-off relationship would continue for a number of months.

Just a week after the Bitter End shows, Carly again opened for Cat Stevens at a sold-out Boston Symphony Hall, and on June 5th Carly shared top billing with him at New York's Carnegie Hall, as well as a midnight performance the following evening. That same month Carly was one of the guests on the *Tonight Show with Johnny Carson*.

Meanwhile, Holzman, at Carly's urging, had invited English producer Paul Samwell-Smith to come over and watch Carly perform at Carnegie Hall. Holzman saw in him the necessary pedigree that he was looking for to work on Carly's next album. Samwell-Smith had great charm, like Willie

Donaldson, and music ran through his veins. He had been one of the founding members of the seminal British band the Yardbirds, and had since produced the last three Cat Stevens albums, all of which had been widely acclaimed. Carly had always said she would like to work with his producer, but when Holzman first offered him the job, he declined, as he was currently tied up working on Stevens' soundtrack to Hal Ashby's coming-of-age movie *Harold and Maude*. Carly persisted and asked Holzman to keep trying. He knew if he saw her sing it might persuade him to change his mind. And it worked.

Impressed by her dazzling performance, Samwell-Smith held a meeting backstage with Carly, Holzman, and her new manager to discuss plans to make her new album the following month. Carly recalled: "I had my choice of doing it in London or LA, but I jumped at the chance to record it in London." Although it meant another tearful flight for the singer to endure, it was also agreed she could take her own band and manager with her. Cat Stevens even promised to provide backing vocals on the songs when he returned home.

Central Park and the scarlet lady

On the second and third day of July 1971, Carly was invited to perform at the annual Schaefer Music Festival held at the Wollman Rink in New York's Central Park, and sponsored by the famous brewing company. With the Beach Boys headlining the show, both concerts were filmed and edited together for an hour-long ABC-TV special called *Good Vibrations from Central Park*, which would be aired on August 19th and shown across the world over the coming months. Among the other artists performing over the two days were Ike and Tina Turner and Boz Skaggs. Carly took to the stage following a raucous performance by Kate Taylor, James' younger sister. With her new band, and wearing a beautiful flowing scarlet dress, Carly appeared perfectly at ease with what was one of the largest audiences she would ever have to face, and performed an energetic rendition of 'Anticipation' on guitar, before walking across to her piano to sing 'That's The Way I've Always Heard It Should Be'. She introduced it as a "weird song about marriage" that she had heard being played on the beach earlier that day. It was a magical performance, watched from the wings by, among others, George Harrison and Art Garfunkel, but in a flash, it was all over, and Carly made way for Ike and Tina Turner. But for the thousands of music fans there and soon across the world, it would be their very first glimpse of this incredible singer.

Before departing for England in mid-July, Carly met up with photographer Jack Robinson for what was one of her first non-album photo shoots, this time for the magazine *Vogue*. On July 7th she appeared with Cat Stevens for one of the last times at Gaelic Park in the Bronx, part of what was called The Summer Scholarship Concert Series, and performed her set before another giant audience estimated to be around 5,500. Also appearing on the show was Jonathan Edwards, best known for his recent single 'Sunshine'.

In the weeks that followed, Carly continued to write and complete ten songs in readiness for the new album, all but one self-penned, and three of which were collaborations with Jake.

London calling

Arriving in London, Carly and her team began the recording sessions at Morgan Studios in Willesden, in the north-west part of the city. Barry Morgan, the drummer with British band Blue Mink, had set up the studio in the late 60s and it became a favorite recording venue for many British artists, including Donovan, Rod Stewart, and the Kinks. With Samwell-Smith at the helm, Cat Stevens had cut part of his seminal album *Tea for the Tillerman* there the previous year, and was soon to follow with *Teaser and the Firecat* in November.

Listening to Carly's previous album, Samwell-Smith was critical of the orchestrations and was now looking for a gentler, less dynamic sound in order to place more emphasis on the vocals and lyrics. This time it would be just Carly and her band, with a couple of session musicians where needed. His "little is more" approach to production sat well with Carly, and with his sympathetic and patient approach, she felt none of the pressure and intimidation she had found working with Kramer. It came as no surprise that their working together would soon take on a more intimate relationship. The musicians on the album included Carly's current band members Jimmy Ryan, Paul Glanz and Andy Newmark, as well as bass player John Ryan and British arranger and composer Derrick "Del" Newman. The recording was straightforward, with Carly first putting down a vocal track with either guitar or piano, and other instruments then being overdubbed by either Paul, Andy or Jimmy, or all three together.

Carly recalled those days: "It was completely fun, even doing the sausage sandwiches which I never would have eaten at any other time. It was just a great sense of people working together. It was one of the few band albums I have ever done."

Although the musicians had their work cut out trying to follow Carly's free-flowing and sometimes erratic methods of playing, the end result was another basic but highly charged and emotional album. She would later go on record that the sessions were unlike anything she had ever done in her career.

The recording of the album and the time spent in London were to leave Carly with some fond memories, not least of which was being introduced to Mick Jagger at one of his band's press parties. Carly dedicated the album to Steve Harris, Elektra's trouble shooter, who had supported her during some of her most anxious times.

ANTICIPATION
Elektra EKS 75016 (UK – K 42101)
Recorded - Morgan Studios, London, July-September 1971.
Released - November 1971
Producer - Paul Samwell-Smith.
Production supervisor - Jac Holzman.
Engineer - Michael Bobak.
Mastering - Lee Hulko, Sterling Sound, New York
Art direction & Design - Robert L Heimall.
US Billboard Pop Albums #30; Canada #36; Aus #12

Side 1

Anticipation *(Carly Simon)* *****
Single EKS-45759 b/w The Garden
Released - Nov 25 1971
Billboard Hot 100 #13; Billboard Adult Contemporary #3; Cashbox #10; Canada #9; Australia #64
Carly Simon- acoustic guitar, piano; Paul Glanz - piano; Jimmy Ryan - acoustic guitar, electric bass; John Ryan - acoustic bass; Andy Newmark – drums
Inspired by that dinner date with Cat Stevens, this was Carly's take on the tensions arising out of a possible romantic relationship in which either party has no idea what the outcome may be. But in a broader sense it is about all the uncertainties of love, life, and relationships, and therefore perfectly echoes the sentiments of 'That's the Way I've Always Heard It Should Be' on the previous album. Carly later admitted that she was clearly imitating Stevens, and confessed she was deeply in love with him at the time. The production, however, did not come without concerns. Carly and her band had honed the song to perfection after performing it a number of times in concert, and it seemed like it had already been recorded in her head. The question was whether it would be as good now in the studio version. Samwell-Smith's approach to production was the answer. He builds the song up from being an acoustic ballad to bringing in Newmark's suspended drumbeats that perfectly emphasize the theme of the song, before

Carly's wonderfully aggressive vocal on the chorus, accompanied by Glanz's piano, brings the message home with her choppy and extended phrasing of the key words "anticipation" and "waiting." Then, as a finale, we have a rousing anthemic coda, and the singer's advice not to worry about what will happen tomorrow, but just "stay right here," as these are truly "the good old days." The song is a fine showcase for Carly's unique style of singing. In an interview the following year she spoke about the song: "Hope is an opiate. It's so easy to get high on it. The song I wrote was like a moral lesson to myself. Trying not to think so much about what's around the corner, so I could concentrate on what's happening now. Otherwise, I wouldn't be able to be in tune with what's really going on."

Legend in Your Own Time *(Carly Simon)* ****
Single EK-45774 b/w Julie Through the Glass
Released - 1972
Billboard Hot 100 #50; Billboard Adult Contemporary #11; Cashbox #61; Canada #39
Carly Simon - acoustic guitar, piano; Paul Glanz - piano; Jimmy Ryan - acoustic guitar, electric bass; John Ryan - acoustic bass; Andy Newmark - congas, percussion.
A delightfully well-crafted character study, said to be inspired by Carly's infatuation with soon-to-be lover James Taylor, although Carly once related that it came about while she was waiting in a long line at a passport office prior to her trip to London, and a guy in front was reading an article about the late country singer Hank Williams, carrying the headline A Legend in His Own Time. It made her ponder what it would be like if she ever became a "legend" herself, and she thought about all the well-established singers sitting alone in their hotel rooms after an evening on stage in front of their loving fans and the continuing adoration bestowed on them at after-show parties, and how that legend is just another sad and lonely figure when they are without their audience. In Carly's mind, James was that legend, and she would be the one to rescue him from his loneliness. The wonderful author Sheila Weller saw it as Carly's "sarcastic take down of an arrogant man." The track is driven by Andy Newmark's congas underpinning Carly's double-tracked harmonies on the chorus.

Our First Day Together *(Carly Simon)* ****
Carly Simon - acoustic guitar
A dark and bewitching song, likened by some to the style of Joni Mitchell, which displays a quavering vulnerability in her voice. As another fine showcase for her vocal style, *The New York Times* reveled over its "remarkable, sophisticated melodic structure." A completely solo effort from Carly, who has often cited it as one of her favorite songs.

The Girl You Think You See *(Carly Simon - Jacob Brackman)* ****
Single EK-45796 c/w Share the End
Released -1972
Did not chart.

Carly Simon - acoustic piano; Paul Glanz - piano; Jimmy Ryan - acoustic guitar; John Ryan - acoustic bass; Andy Newmark - drums

Carly challenges female stereotypes and how men fantasize about how they want their women to be. It all sounds harmlessly playful as she lists the diverse roles she could willingly act out, whether it be a "foul-mouthed marine" or a "Mary Magdalene," to name just a few. But this is another poke at the male species and their "Me Tarzan, You Jane" perception of a woman's role in a relationship, and how women have to pander to their desires. More unexpected chord changes make this another fine example of her songwriting craft.

Summer's Coming Around Again *(Carly Simon - Jimmy Ryan - Paul Glanz)* ***

Paul Glanz - piano; Jimmy Ryan - acoustic guitar

The only track on the album for which Carly doesn't contribute music, this pretty bossa nova-style song about summer love owes an affectionate nod to Antonio Carlos Jobim's 'The Girl from Ipanema', with the wonderful interplay between Glanz's piano and Ryan's acoustic guitar, both musicians giving a new arrangement to a song written some time ago by Carly. One reviewer called the song "a fine cut that floats along mainly on the pure power of Carly's fine voice."

Side 2

Share the End *(Carly Simon - Jacob Brackman)* ****
Carly Simon - acoustic guitar, piano, Paul Glanz - piano; Jimmy Ryan - acoustic, electric & bass guitars; Andy Newmark - drums; John Ryan - acoustic guitar; Del Neman - arr. strings and horns

Seemingly out of place on an otherwise themed album, this apocalyptic song is both intelligent and immensely moving as the human race gathers together to face the impending end of the world. It is Carly's most operatic composition to date, and although some reviewers saw it as overblown, the powerful chorale ending with Del Newman's orchestral arrangement is one of the album's many highlights. Chosen as the flip-side of the unsuccessful single 'The Girl You Think You See'.

The Garden *(Carly Simon - Jacob Brackman)* ****
Carly Simon - acoustic guitar; Jimmy Ryan - acoustic guitar; Del Newman - arr. strings

A song that inspired the cover image. The gate is open and Carly has stolen the key to a Shangri-La garden of delights that offer a new awakening for those willing to join her. This dreamscape is a wonderful example of the melding of Carly's ethereal music and Jake's wistful lyrics, but its Carly's enchanting vocal that is the real enticement for us all to enter her paradise. The gentle song was selected to be the perfect contrast for the flip-side of the 'Anticipation' single.

Three Days *(Carly Simon)* ***
Carly Simon - acoustic guitar; Paul Glanz - piano; Jimmy Ryan - acoustic guitar; John Ryan - acoustic bass; Andy Newmark - drums

Carly is reminiscing about her intense but all-too-brief relationship with singer Kris Kristofferson, whom she had toured with recently, but after just several days their demanding careers led them to part, he to Los Angeles and she to London. Carly later confessed that she couldn't be herself when he was around, as she was just too much in awe of the grizzled singer. Sheila Weller looked on them as "two shining stars crisscrossing the heavens," on the way to their next chapter in their careers.

Julie Through the Glass *(Carly Simon)* *****
Carly Simon - acoustic piano; Paul Glanz - acoustic piano
Carly's warm and tender prayer in the shape of a lullaby for her niece Julie Levine, Lucy's daughter, who had been born in July 1969, recalling the moment she went to the hospital and looked at her for the first time through the window of the nursery. The song was written shortly afterward and long cherished by Carly. Now just two years old at the time of the recording, Julie would later have the chance to sing on a number of her aunt's seminal albums. The song was on the flip-side of the 'Legend in Your Own Time' single. According to Carly, Cat Stevens' voice is somewhere there in the background.

I've Got to Have You *(Kris Kristofferson)* *****
Carly Simon - acoustic guitar; Paul Glanz - piano; Jimmy Ryan - acoustic & electric guitar, electric bass; John Ryan - acoustic bass; Andy Newmark - drums
Carly's version of a classic Kristofferson song, and the one he had taught Carly to play when they were briefly together back in May. Samwell-Smith knew just where and when to add the subtle touches that give the lustful song that strong emotional pull that grips the listener. Like other tracks on the album, it begins as a straightforward ballad, then builds up to a swirling chorus, with Carly's voice double-tracked just at the right time, and then brings in Ryan's superb electric guitar solo, the only one on the album, to fan the flame of desire. With another producer at the helm, the song could have fallen victim to over-production, but not with this one, and from a production point of view, it's easily the best track on the album. *Rolling Stone* remarked that when Carly moans "I've Got to Have You," it's almost as if "we're being shown something so primal and private that it takes your breath away." Surprisingly, the song was only released as a single in Australia, where it was a top ten hit the following year. Kristofferson would finally record the song himself, along with future wife Rita Coolidge, and release it on their 1974 album *Breakaway*.

No one was more impressed with the album than Carly herself: "If this album had been anybody else's I think I would have been very jealous."

For the green-tinted album cover, Peter Simon's services were once again called upon to do the photo shoot. Taking advantage of London's beautiful summer gardens, he took his sister to Regent's Park for a series of iconic images, and the one chosen for the cover has her standing like a lioness guarding the elaborate iron gates to Queen Mary's Garden, dressed in a seductive diaphanous skirt and butterfly-winged top. Despite the shoot being wonderfully interrupted by a London lady walking through the gates, other images were taken with a change of outfit at nearby Primrose Hill.

As on the previous album, Peter's "here I am, look at me," pose of Carly demanded the viewer's attention. Carly was dubbed in the press as the "New Woman" or the "Woman of the Future," and beyond those gates she seemed to be offering a world of possibilities. *Rolling Stone* saw things differently and looked on Carly as just a maturing songwriter making great music, and urged its readers: "Forget the labels. Listen to the music." While in London, Peter also took the opportunity of capturing Carly and Cat Stevens relaxing in the garden at the rear patio of her rented house. Stevens had also kept his promise to Carly by providing some (uncredited) backing vocals on the album.

Carly returned to New York later that September for a string of autumn concerts. After performances in Albany and New Rochelle, she was given tickets to see a James Taylor concert at Carnegie Hall on November 9th. James was riding high with his third studio album *Mud Slide Slim and the Blue Horizon* having been released earlier in the year to critical acclaim. Among those on stage with him now were Russ Kunkel, the drummer Carly had employed for her very first concert, and Carole King, whose seminal album *Tapestry* was soon to sweep the Grammys, now playing piano for James on 'You've Got a Friend', her song that had helped him become a world-renowned star.

James

James Vernon Taylor was born in Boston on March 12th 1948, the second of five children to Harvard-educated physician Isaac "Ike" Taylor and his wife Gertrude (Trudy), a classically trained soprano. Three years later the family moved to Chapel Hill, North Carolina. They encouraged James and his siblings - older brother Alex, along with Kate, Livingston and Hugh - to become musical, but at the age of thirteen, to escape the bad influence of wayward Alex, James had been sent to a prestigious boarding school in Boston where he taught himself to play guitar. While vacationing on the Vineyard he had befriended Davy Gude and Danny "Kootch" Kortchmar, both accomplished guitar players who shared his love for folk music and blues. Carly had met James there on a couple of occasions but had never spoken to him. While finding it difficult sleeping alone in his room without company, he began having serious bouts of depression and acute tiredness, and he volunteered to attend the McLean psychiatric facility in Belmont, gaining a high school diploma at their academy in 1966. With Kortchmar's urging, he left there that year and joined him in New York as lead singer of his new band, the short-lived Flying Machine, performing songs he had written while at McLean, including 'Night Owl', an unsuccessful single release.

By the age of 18, he was being supported by his parents in his own New York apartment, and, being seemingly affluent, drew the inevitable crowd of parasites and hangers-on, and eventually became addicted to heroin. At this point he hit rock bottom, and his father came the rescue, driving all the way from North Carolina to bring him home and seek treatment.

In 1968 James arrived in London and found a flat in Notting Hill - hardly the place to kick his drug habit - and it was Kortchmar who again came to his rescue, suggesting he take a demo tape of his songs to Peter Asher, who Kortchmar had known when his band had supported Peter and Gordon on a US tour. Asher was now the A&R man at the Beatles' newly created Apple Records. Asher liked what he heard, and after auditioning for Paul McCartney and George Harrison, James became the label's first American signing. With Asher as his manager, a band was put together and his debut album *James Taylor* was recorded at Trident Studios. The album received positive reviews but, along with the single 'Carolina On My Mind', was not a commercial success, largely as a result of his addiction and failure to promote it by touring. It was during these sessions that one of his colleagues found out that, back home, one of James' close friends, Suzanne Schnerr, had taken her own life. It was decided to keep the news from him, for fear it might distract him from the chance to make his big break, and not until the album was finished was the news broken to him. The day after, the distraught singer sat down and wrote what would be the first verse of 'Fire and Rain', a song that also referenced his drug addiction, the breakup of his band, and his current rise to fame.

James returned home in November and checked into another mental institution for five months. He then did a six-night solo concert at the Troubadour in Los Angeles in July 1969, followed by an appearance at the Newport Folk Festival later that month. Following a motorbike accident on the Vineyard that summer, in which he broke both his hands and feet, he began writing new songs in earnest, including 'Sweet Baby James', inspired by the birth of his brother Alex's baby son. Once he had recovered, James relocated to California.

In September 1969, with the help of Peter Asher, who had left the disorganized Apple label to work for Warner Records, he managed to secure a new record deal. James rounded up a team of musician friends, including Kortchmar, Russ Kunkel, Charlie Larkey, and Charlie's girlfriend Carole King. Carole was about to launch her own solo career with

73

an album called *Writer*, but was persuaded to help James make his album first.

The album *Sweet Baby James*, produced by Asher, was released in February 1970, with Carole's album coming out three months later. *Sweet Baby James* went on to be a triple-platinum success, selling over three million copies worldwide. In January 1971 Carole's album *Tapestry* was recorded, with James returning the favor with his guitar and backing vocals on several of the tracks. Eventually the groundbreaking album would go on to become a multi-Grammy award winning classic. Four months later James released his third album, *Mud Slide Slim and the Blue Horizon*, which not only had Carole as pianist, but also his sister Kate Taylor and his girlfriend Joni Mitchell on backing vocals. The subsequent single, 'You've Got a Friend', penned by Carole, gave James his first US #1 that August.

This was the man and his music that Carly had long admired. Having had that all-too-brief conversation with him at the Troubadour back in April, and unaware of his heroin addiction, she was now about to see him perform live on stage. It was not only a night she would never forget; it would also be one that would have a major impact on her life. During the intermission at Carnegie, a friend of Carly's managed to get her backstage to meet James, his band members, and some of his family. Reduced to tears by the music she had just heard, the instant she met him was electric. Everyone could feel the chemistry between them, and, with her invitation for dinner accepted, he turned up at her apartment after the show.

Clouds in her coffee

A week later, Carly flew out to Los Angeles for a six-night stint at the Troubadour, commencing November 16th, and supported by singer-songwriter Don McLean, whose iconic 'American Pie' would soon be racing up the charts. Accompanying her on the outbound flight was her old Indian Hill friend Billy Mernit, who had played on her debut album. While sitting together, Billy saw the reflections of clouds in the cup she was holding, and said to her, "Look Carly, clouds in your coffee." That remark would now be firmly planted in her head. Jake Brackman and Steve Harris had also flown out there to see her. After the opening night, Carly was in her dressing room when actor Warren Beatty showed up to pay his compliments.

Billboard magazine was impressed with the Troubadour gigs, describing Carly as the "Dr Germaine Greer of rock" and putting on a "powerful display of her burgeoning charisma and fine music" in shows that were simply "spellbinding."

After the concerts, Carly flew back to New York to spend more time with James, and they went to Martha's Vineyard to see the huge wooden house he and his friends were building on a 25-acre tract of woodland James had bought with the proceeds of his first record deal. Memories of that young boy she had first encountered there must have come flooding back to her. Now she had fallen head over heels in love with him. From that day on they would become almost inseparable, almost…

Earlier that November, *Anticipation* had been released and had entered the Pop Albums chart on the 27th, finally peaking at #30 on February 12th. In Canada it reached #36. The single of 'Anticipation', backed with 'The Garden', was released on the 25th, entered the Hot 100 top 40 on January 1st 1972, and stalled at #13. It also reached an impressive #3 on the Adult Contemporary chart. A second single, 'Legend in Your Own Time', released in March and coupled with 'Julie Through the Glass', peaked at #50 on the Hot 100 on May 6th and a credible #11 on Adult Contemporary.

On September 5th 1973, *Anticipation* would be certified gold for sales of over half a million in the US alone, and at the Grammy Awards held in Nashville on March 3rd that year, Carly was nominated in the category of Best Female Vocal Performance for her song 'Anticipation', but lost out to Helen Reddy's anthemic 'I Am Woman', a song that had captured the imagination of the women's lib movement when released in May 1972.

The reviews for *Anticipation* were generally good. *Rolling Stone* admired her "frank" but "strange" carefully written songs that highlighted the emotional twists and turns of love in all its complexities. Dismissing the pretentious labels now heaped on the singer, it urged the listener to see her as the fine musician she was becoming. The *Village Voice* took its usual anti-bourgeois stance and dismissed the songs as just bland pop fodder "for the ruling class." *Melody Maker* commented later that Carly had credited *Anticipation* as being her most personal album to date, "convinced that half the songs on the record couldn't make sense to anyone but herself."

On December 15th Carly performed the first of six concerts at the Bitter End in New York. On the fourth night her whole family came to see her sing, and Carly managed to get a heavily-pregnant Lucy on stage to sing their 'Winkin, Blinkin and Nod' to rapturous applause.

As the new year got underway, Carly was now living with James in a New York apartment while his Vineyard house was slowly taking shape. Both of them had new albums to work on and were busy writing songs. But for Carly, her songs would now take on a different meaning and result in one of finest and most successful albums of her career.

When Harry met Carly

In January 1972 Carly flew out to the West Coast to appear at Elektra's four-day annual sales convention held at the Riviera Hotel in Palm Springs. On the 9th, the final night, she would be sharing top billing with Harry Chapin and performing in front of some 300 of Warner's marketing staff. Holzman had gone out of his way to impress his parent company, so rather than sending out promo copies of the albums to the relevant company salesmen, he seized the opportunity of bringing them together to see his recent signings in person.

Harry Chapin was one of Holzman's latest proteges and was about to begin recording his debut album *Heads and Tales*. Like Carly, Harry was a product of Greenwich Village, and had also begun his career singing with siblings until deciding to go solo. While cutting his teeth at the Village Gate, he was discovered by one of Holzman's talent scouts. Now he was here to showcase songs that included his iconic 'Taxi'. Holzman was master of ceremonies for the evening and did the introduction: "Remember our success last year with Carly Simon, Harry Chapin is this year's Carly Simon." After a blistering performance from Harry, it was Carly's turn. Before starting, she addressed the audience: "Harry, if you're this year's Carly Simon, you must have had some very interesting boyfriends over the past twelve months." The whole room exploded with laughter and gave her a standing ovation when she finished her set with 'Anticipation'.

After the show it was decided that it would be ideal for Harry to support her later that month. During the first of these at Boston's Symphony Hall on February 12th, Harry completed his set to thunderous applause, making his easily the standout performance of the night, and leaving Carly and her manager pondering the wisdom of choosing such a hot act to follow. It even resulted in a local review calling her performance "shallow and nervous."

On February 9th, Carly appeared on the *David Frost Show*, with a pre-recorded rendition of 'That's the Way I've Always Heard It Should Be' and 'Alone'. The following two months saw concerts in Buffalo, Providence, Rochester, and Atlanta, an appearance on the *Dick Cavett Show*, and a return in May to the Troubadour for a six-night stint which would prove to be her last public performances for several years.

With *Anticipation* now behind her, there was now the added anticipation of the next album. Carly herself admitted she was becoming tired of all the self-pity and disenchantment in her music, especially the melancholy theme of her first two albums, which related to situations that never quite turned out the way they had been planned. She felt that the next album had to be different, but it also had to be as good as or even better than before.

Carly confessed that chart success was not her ultimate goal: "My feelings do get very hurt if I'm not liked. I don't care about being No. 1 in the chart, but it's nice to see the records up there somewhere. When I made the first album I didn't think it would worry me if it made the chart or not, but once it did I wanted to see it go a little higher and then even higher. I like to be liked."

During the month of May, Cat Stevens recorded his album *Catch Bull at Four*, produced by Paul Samwell-Smith. It contained a song he had written with Carly in mind called 'Sweet Scarlet', with the memorable line, "All those dreams are gone, but the song carried on."

Around this time Carly, through one of her friends, had the chance to meet Mick Jagger in Los Angeles and interview him for the Sunday edition of the *LA Times*. Although finding him rather unresponsive to her questioning, the only positive thing that came from it was his agreement to sing on her next album. The following month, she was back in the city with James to discuss their future albums. Whilst he would be meeting up with Peter Asher in preparation for his work on *One Man Dog*, Carly would be meeting her new producer Richard Perry.

Enter Richard Perry

20-year-old Brooklyn-born Richard Perry already had several smash hit albums to his credit, including Harry Nilsson's *Nilsson Schmilsson* and Barbra Streisand's *Stoney End*. Many in the business saw him as a producer with the Midas touch, and although Carly was not too impressed by his recent work, she realized that she needed someone to foster a new approach to her creativity.

But Perry had not been her first choice. A few weeks earlier, she had had a meeting with Holzman to discuss having someone new to work with on the next album. Holzman was under the impression that singer-songwriters would soon become unfashionable, as many of them were now preferring to join bands. He believed that this album had to really stand out to make money. To that end, Carly had in mind young Paul Buckmaster, a British arranger she admired for his wonderful orchestral work on Bowie's 'Space Oddity', several of Elton John's early albums, and the Rolling Stones' *Sticky Fingers* the previous year, particularly on the track 'Moonlight Mile', one of Carly's favorite arrangements.

Despite his reservations, Holzman agreed to fund a demo that she and Buckmaster could work on. With music backing by James and Danny Kortchmar, two songs were recorded in New York with Buckmaster's arrangements. 'Angel from Montgomery' was a John Prine song about a middle-aged woman feeling older than she was and had featured on his debut album the previous year, while 'I'm All It Takes to Make You Happy' was one of Carly's earlier songs that had been demoed before. When Holzman heard the resulting tape and what Buckmaster had done with the songs, he was unimpressed and now made it clear to Carly that Perry would produce the album.

At the first meeting with Perry at Elektra studios in June, Carly sat at the piano and played some of the new songs she had been working on. One was a still-unnamed song which had the now-familiar "you're so vain" chorus, and on first hearing it made Perry sit up. Even in its unfinished state, he was hearing a hit single. With the other songs also being well received, the tension seemed to lift, and the two of them were reassured that it would all work out well. Carly now continued writing with renewed confidence.

Perry had placed his cards on the table. He had criticized the sound of some of the songs on her last album, particularly 'Anticipation', and left her convinced that, unlike her last producer, he would be calling the shots. It was also decided that the new album would be recorded in London, with the same excellent musicians that had played on *Nilsson Schmilsson*. For Carly, it seemed like all the tension and pressure she had had with Kramer might now be repeated, but she was determined to remain positive. After all, this was London, and it would bring back so many happy memories.

But what sort of album did Carly have in mind? She gave a little hint in an interview: "What I'm hoping for here is an album that doesn't lose that variety which I feel is always very helpful to an artist, because it doesn't confine them."

Returning to London

Before she prepared for the trip abroad, Carly and James made their first television appearance together on July 26th when guesting on CBS's short-lived *David Steinberg Show*, hosted by the Canadian comedian. As the weeks drew nearer to departing for England, Carly began to feel more and more anxious: "The most pressure I felt was in leaving James. I just wanted to get it done and get back to him."

In early September Carly and her manager Arlyne flew into London, along with band members Jimmy Ryan and Andy Newmark, to begin recording the new album at Trident Studios in Soho. Trident had been established in 1967 by brothers Norman and Barry Sheffield at 17, St Anne's Court in Soho, and was the first studio to use Dolby noise reduction and have an eight-track reel-to-reel recording deck, resulting in many artists keen to use their facilities. Even the Beatles had chosen Trident over EMI's

Abbey Road Studios, which still used four-track equipment, to record the song 'Hey Jude' and parts of their so-called *White Album*.

Of the new songs he had heard Carly play, Perry picked out three which had single potential, including the unfinished song that now had the working title of 'Ballad of a Vain Man', and another one called 'The Right Thing to Do'. Perry was always looking at the money-making potential of songs that he considered could be hits, and would therefore ensure they had every chance to become just that. With the excellent studio engineer Robin Cable on hand, he assembled a fine group of session musicians.

German-born artist and bass player Klaus Voormann, a great friend of the Beatles, had won a Grammy for designing the cover of their groundbreaking album *Revolver*, before going on to join the band Manfred Mann. British keyboard player Nicky Hopkins had performed on many of the Stones' and the Kinks' early albums. Other session men brought in for certain tracks included Paul Keough, David Hentschel, Lowell George, Bill Payne, Peter Robinson, and saxophonist Bobby Keys. Even Paul Buckmaster had been invited on board to add orchestral arrangements on certain tracks.

Right from the start, Carly realized that Perry was going to be a tough taskmaster and behave more like a director than the interpreter she had been hoping for, and this resulted in conflicting ideas of how the music and vocals should sound. But despite the ruffling of her feathered hair, she finally began to realize that Perry knew what he was doing, and it was beginning to come together to everyone's satisfaction. Carly wrote later that Perry was getting a hundred per cent out of her, intensifying her energy, and "pushing me off a diving board." Although there would be easier producers to work for in her career, and undoubtedly more difficult ones, Perry was undeniably one of the best.

Carly's mood had certainly improved by the third week when James flew in for a long weekend after taking part in fund-raising events for Carole King's campaign to get George McGovern elected president. During his time with Carly, he not only contributed some acoustic guitar parts to a few of her songs (although not credited), but also indicated to her that they should get married, having already asked her mother for permission. With that in mind, Carly was now given something more than her music to focus on.

During the recording, Carly made one of her first ever solo television interviews when she appeared on the BBC's music program *The Old Grey Whistle Test* (so-named after the old Tin Pan Alley phrase, when first pressings of records were heard by the old grey doormen, and if they were found whistling the tune the next, day, it had passed the "whistle test" and was a sign of it being a success). The presenter "Whispering" Bob Harris asked her about the pressures of live performances: "The more well-known I become I find it more and more difficult doing live concerts. Even though it's a great experience in one way, I think anything that is that exciting is also partly terrifying. At least it is to me."

When it came to recording the vocals for 'Vain Man', Perry and everyone else in the studio knew instinctively that this was going to be a smash hit, the money-maker that Holzman had been banking on. Carly was still critical of Perry's direction, especially his overuse of orchestration in some of the songs. With the music tracks laid down at Trident, most of the vocal sessions took place at AIR Studios in Oxford Street, which had been co-founded by Beatles' producer George Martin, and now, through his courtesy, was being made available for Perry.

Three different drummers ended up playing on the 'Vain Man' track. Perry was not satisfied with the way Andy Newmark played, so he had American session drummers Jim Keltner and Jim Gordon flown in to assist. Keltner had already worked on albums by Leon Russell and Joe Cocker, while Gordon had been part of the legendary band Derek and the Dominoes and had co-written with Eric Clapton the classic 'Layla'. It was Gordon who arrived in London first and ended up playing all the fills on the track.

It was also during the sessions for 'Vain Man' that Carly first heard Voormann's stunning bass riff which would kick off the track, and, while it was being recorded, she whispered under her breath, "son of a gun," a remark that can be heard on the final recording. After almost a hundred takes on the music track and over thirty just for the lead vocal, the song was now almost complete. All that was left to do was lay down the backing vocals on the chorus.

Amongst the artists dropping in from other studios were Paul and Linda McCartney, who at the time were working on the single 'My Love', for the new Wings album *Red Rose Speedway*. Another was Harry Nilsson, who Perry had recently worked with. Harry was best known for his hit singles 'Everybody's Talkin'' and his cover of Badfinger's 'Without You', a chart topper on both sides of the Atlantic. Like Carly, he was famously reluctant to tour and perform live.

Carly loved Harry's remarkable tenor and asked Perry if he could convince him to do backing vocals with her on the chorus to 'Vain Man'. Harry was more than happy to do so, but at the vocal session at AIR in October the initial results were unsatisfactory. During the session Carly took a call from Mick Jagger, who, through his friend Klaus Voormann, had found out she was in town. Carly took him up on his earlier offer and asked him if he wanted to come over and help with laying down the vocals. He was there in a matter of minutes and a surprised Perry invited him to join Carly and Harry at the microphone. Harry could see that there was instant electricity between Carly and Mick, and before long made his excuses to bow out.

Once they had completed the vocals, Mick requested that his name was not credited on the album. Perry, still getting over the shock that Carly had managed to get Jagger to sing, was thrilled with the result, and, after more discussions, the name of the song was given its more personal title of 'You're So Vain'.

Jagger had not only given Carly his support, but had also given her inspiration. He had seen that somewhere inside of her was a natural rock-chick waiting to surface, something that Carly was not aware of at the time, but in some of the albums that followed the world would see exactly what he meant, and for later albums would carry a little bit of that Stones 'vibe into the studio.

Another person who was taken by surprise was Jimmy Ryan, who had already recorded his wonderful guitar solo for 'You're So Vain', and when he first heard the finished vocals on the chorus, he turned to Carly and said: "Carly, why are you trying to sound like Mick Jagger?" With a little grin she replied, "Well, listen to it. Does it really sound that much like him?" Jimmy said, "Yeh." With that, Carly, now laughing, finally confessed, "It's him." Jimmy was gobsmacked.

Richard Perry was notoriously late for sessions, sometimes by four or five hours. Jimmy Ryan recalls: "We would tell Richard the session would be ten o'clock and we'd all show up at eleven or a little bit after, and inevitably we'd still be in there, but we wouldn't have wasted an hour in the studio. I'm never sure we ever let him in on the joke." But it was more of a frustration for Carly, and rather than wait around for one particular session she went downstairs and began to write a new song called 'His Friends Are More Than Fond of Robin', thinking to herself, "if we're gonna be late, I'm gonna do what I want to do." As it turned out, Perry loved the song.

Another song chosen was a cover of James Taylor's 'Night Owl', which had been a single for his band the Flying Machine in 1967 and then re-recorded in London the following year for his debut album. While recording the vocals at AIR, Carly asked Jimmy Ryan to join her and he soon arrived, along with the great session singers Doris Troy and Bonnie Bramlett (of Delaney & Bonnie fame). The three of them joined Carly at the microphone, but the initial result wasn't to Perry's satisfaction. Jimmy, however, suddenly noticed that Paul McCartney had just joined him in the control booth, having walked over from the next studio. Paul asked if he could help out with the vocals, and the result worked to perfection. As Bonnie and Doris took their leave, Paul then told the others that he had just written a song for a movie and asked if they would like to hear it so as to gauge their opinion. Walking across to the piano, he sat and gave what must have been one of his first ever performances of 'Live and Let Die'. Not only that, he invited them all to his studio the next day to hear it being recorded by George Martin with a full orchestra. It was a couple of days that the starstruck team would never forget.

On the final day of the *No Secrets* sessions Carly recorded 'Waited So Long', a new song she had written just the night before in her hotel room, and only managed to beat the deadline by just a few hours. Within a matter of days, the album would be pressed.

Once again, stand-out artwork was required for the album. During the recording, photographer Ed Caraeff was invited to do the photo shoot. Famous for his iconic *Rolling Stone* cover image of Hendrix setting fire to his guitar at the Monterey Festival, he was intent on coming up with something far removed from her two previous album covers, in which Carly was pictured in flowing dresses and skirts against decorative backdrops. Not this time. After a number of settings around London's parks, and various changes of outfits, it was getting late in the day, and there was a recording session to attend. As they arrived back at the Portobello Hotel on Stanley Gardens in Notting Hill, Carly recalled: "We had to get to the studio, so I said to him, let me just run inside and put on my clothes. I put on my red jeans and my blue top, and my red hat that matched the jeans, and my boots, and I went outside and was about to get into the cab door...." Snap! Caraeff had the shot he needed.

Carly was more than happy with the image: "It seemed just exactly like my summer was like in London." There was no secret about it, here was a woman showing that feminism could be both sexy and stylish. Caraeff recalled: "My photo captures a casual, dynamic posture of an artist caught in their natural setting...as natural and unpretentious as can be." It was only when seeing the artwork that Carly decided to give the album its title. Before that, various names had been suggested, including 'Ballad of a Vain Man'.

"I just got married today folks"

Carly returned to New York, and within a couple of days went with James to Los Angeles for final work on the mixing of the album, before having a late-September, pre-wedding honeymoon in Hawaii, accompanied by Peter Simon, who was invited along to take photographs. On November 3rd 1972, a week before the album was released, Carly and James were married by a judge in a low-key civil ceremony held in her New York apartment with just Andrea and James' parents in attendance. That night James performed

82

a concert at New York's Radio City Music Hall, and after singing an impromptu snippet of the song 'Making Whoopie', announced to the 6,000-strong audience: "I just got married today folks. I married Miss Carly Simon. That was a song to her."

James' album *One Man Dog* was released on November 1st, four weeks before *No Secrets*. Carly had provided backing vocals for the opening track, 'One Man Parade', on a portable recording console at their Vineyard home. The album reached #4 on the Pop Albums chart and was later certified gold.

NO SECRETS
Elektra EKS 75049 (UK – K-42127)
Recorded - Trident Studios & AIR Studios, London, September-October 1972
Released - November 28 1972
Producer - Richard Perry
Engineers - Robin Cable & Bill Schnee
Mixing - AIR Studios, London & Sound Labs, Los Angeles
Art direction & Design - Robert L Heimall
US Billboard Pop Albums #1; UK Album Chart #3

Side 1

The Right Thing to Do *(Carly Simon)* *****
Single EK-45843 b/w We Have No Secrets
Released - March 1973
Billboard Hot 100 #17; Billboard Adult Contemporary #4; Cashbox #10; UK Single Chart #17; Canada #20
Carly - piano; backing vocals; Jimmy Ryan - bass; Ray Cooper - congas; Andy Newmark - drums; Kirby Johnson - arr. Strings & horns;
Liz Strike - backing vocals; Vicki Brown - backing vocals
Carly's affirmation of her love for James was apparently written three months into their relationship during a flight from Cape Cod to New York: "James was asleep and I just looked at him, and looked at his face where the sun was hitting it. I thought "God, there's nothing you could do to turn me away." Before they landed, she had written the lyrics. Often dubbed as Carly's first true love song (and surely one of her best), it is performed with total conviction, and by disregarding the problems he has, is rubber stamping her selfless and undying commitment, no matter what he or anyone else does to make her turn away. On listening to the song for the first time, James showed his displeasure with the third verse, so Carly re-wrote it and gained his approval. In contrast to her feelings in 'That's the Way...' on the debut album, this Valentine card of a song is proof that Carly is now ready to take that mystery ride of marriage and to define it for herself. The title of the song had been taken from a line used in the movie *The Last Picture Show*, and the use of flowing rivers and water as an emotional metaphor for female sexuality will be increasingly evident in some of Carly's future songs. Although originally intended to be sung at a slower pace, Richard

Perry asked Carly to speed up the tempo a little bit, and most of her vocal was recorded live while playing the piano. The end result was to everyone's satisfaction.

The Carter Family *(Carly Simon - Jacob Brackman)* ****
Carly - piano; Jimmy Ryan- guitar; Klaus Voormann - bass; Andy Newmark - drums; Kirby Johnson - arr. strings & woodwinds
A boring childhood friend, a critical but caring grandmother, and a rough-hewn ex-lover are the three subjects of this gentle song, and it relates how original misguided perceptions of old friends can later lead to regret. Only the childhood friend is given a name, Gwen Carter, but we are left to wonder which grandma and lover she is referring to. In any case, the theme is that sometimes you don't realize how precious people are until they're gone from your life.

You're So Vain *(Carly Simon)* *****
Single EK-45824 b/w His Friends Are More Than Fond of Robin
Released - November 8 1972
Billboard Pop Singles #1; Billboard Adult Contemporary #1; Cashbox #1; UK Single Chart #3; Canada #1; Australia #1
Carly - piano, arr. strings; Jimmy Ryan - guitar; Klaus Voormann - bass; Jim Gordon - drums; Paul Buckmaster - strings; Richard Perry - percussion; Mick Jagger - backing vocals (uncredited)
Carly's most famous song was originally written in her New York apartment on a piano that once belonged to her aunt. According to the singer, 'Bless You, Ben', as it was originally called, was about an imaginary friend who had come into her life "when nobody else left off," and lifted her spirits when she was "mournful up in my loft," watering her plants. Not surprisingly, she was dissatisfied with the morose lyrics, but kept the interesting melody in her head. Turn the clock forward, and Carly was with a friend at a party one night when a guy walked in with his date, and her friend turned to her with the comment, "Don't they look like they've just walked onto a yacht?" The following day Carly took that off-the-cuff remark and built up a character study of a man who might be so vain as to think the song could be about him, and then mercilessly puts him down. Over the coming weeks it was given the working title of 'Ballad of a Vain Man'. Carly later stated that it was the first song with an element of vengeance that she had ever written, and was based on three or four people she knew. Carly was a hopeless romantic and by the time she had written the song she had had a succession of celebrity lovers and had been emotionally hurt by some of them. But there was no real hatred toward them. Although admitting later she tries to suppress any meanness, she confessed, "I hate myself for it, but I can still be quite a bitch." Over the years Carly has been constantly asked to reveal the name of the subject, and along the way has given several clues, even narrowing it down to three men, indicating that Warren Beatty is the subject of the second verse. Contrary to the album's title, I'm sure the secret will remain with Carly as long as the media are interested in it. Although *Creem* magazine criticized some of the odd attempts at rhyming, *Rolling Stone* called the marriage of Carly's and Jagger's voices on the chorus as "inspired alchemy," while *Disc* magazine

celebrated how the song "lodges itself in the cerebral cortex." Perhaps the drawn-out publicity over the subject matter has deflected the due praise for what is essentially a compelling combination of superior songwriting and top-notch production, and who can ever forget that superb guitar solo by Jimmy Ryan. But the fact remains that just one song has brought more attention to the singer than perhaps any other female artist can claim to have had. And that can only be good.

His Friends Are More than Fond of Robin *(Carly Simon)* *****
Carly - piano; arr. ARP synthesizer; Jimmy Ryan - acoustic guitar; David Hentschel - APR Synthesizer
Like 'The Carter Family', this is Carly in reflective mood and using a fictitious name for her homage to her great friend and collaborator Jake Brackman. By giving the title a fictitious name, Carly not only spares Jake's blushes, but also gets the media vultures searching for a past lover called Robin (Carly recently confirmed it was certainly not about the album's engineer Robin Cable, although at the time she had let him think that it was, and he loved the thought.) A reviewer wrote later: "Although a personal song, a teenager's emotions are here so perfectly described that it hardly matters whether Carly actually did know a boy named Robin or not." By any standard, this is a masterful piece of songwriting, with Carly's angelic voice on the verses underpinned by guitar and her own gentle piano playing. Jimmy Ryan recalls: "The backing track was Carly and me. I shadowed her piano part almost note for note on my acoustic guitar to give it a slightly other worldly sound of not quite a guitar and not quite a piano." But it's the chorus that really clinches it, with her double-tracked delivery preceding a short but exquisite melody supplied by Hentschel's subtle synthesizer. Arranged by Carly, it is one of the sweetest little pieces of music she has ever composed. There may be a touch of unrequited love here, but Carly has made it quite clear that she and Jake never let romance get in the way of a perfect professional relationship, and that's why their friendship has survived for so long. When asked to respond to the song, Jake simply replied: "What can I say…it's sweet." The song was rightly chosen to be the flip-side to the single 'You're So Vain'.

We Have No Secrets *(Carly Simon)* *****
Carly - acoustic guitar; Paul Keough - acoustic guitar; Jimmy Ryan - lead guitar; Klaus Voormann - bass; Jim Gordon - drums; Kirby Johnson - electric piano, strings, horns, arr. strings & horns.
In keeping with the album's theme, Carly makes no secret of the fact that this too is about James. Written just before she was leaving LA to go to London, she recalled: "There were some harrowing things that happened just before I left and he felt as if he had to tell me; he needed to come clean." Apparently, a photo of an old boyfriend had slipped from her wallet and James had asked her who it was. The conversation then turned to telling each other all about their past relationships. Carly once revealed: "The lady in the song wants to know everything about her man, as long as it doesn't include anything she doesn't want to know…The song made me realize in a concrete way how much I really would prefer to leave many things in James 'mind." No more secrets might indeed be

the message here, but sometimes too much knowledge can be painful, as it also echoes Carly's childhood and how all her family's dark secrets that plagued her as a young girl would have a lasting effect on her. Carly will strive to remain honest with herself and other people for the rest of her life, but, as *Rolling Stone* made clear, that "emotion and rationalization are often irreconcilable." Being married will now change the way Carly writes. There will be no more songs about unrequited love. Although not considered as a single, it still remains a perfect song, with thumping vocals and a wonderful string and horn arrangement by Kirby Johnson.

Side 2

Embrace Me, You Child *(Carly Simon)* *****
Carly - acoustic guitar; Jimmy Ryan - electric guitar; Klaus Voormann - bass; Andy Newmark - drums; Peter Robinson - piano; Paul Buckmaster- arr. orchestra, ARP Synthesizer & choir
Carly's childhood fantasy of her father Richard Simon, who had died in 1960 when she was just 15 years old, is one of the most extraordinary and personal songs she has written. Originally called 'Nighttime Songs', she began to write it in bed with no idea of where it was going and just let her mind flow to see where it took her. The first line she wrote down was about hearing God whispering lullabies, and in her mind, she was confusing her father with the devil. None of it made much sense, but subconsciously it began to come together. Carly had prayed every night that her father wouldn't die, but her prayers went unanswered, and he eventually passed away. For the young Carly, it felt as if both God and her father had abandoned her, but in all her confusion, she refused to blame anyone else, and kept all the emotions she had bottled up inside for many years to come. Now they appeared to be manifesting into heavy lyrics and being dictated subconsciously to her as she wrote them down. Magical it may seem, but this is a magical song. Carly later revealed to her brother Peter: "The thing which is the clearest to me is how little I knew [my father] and how clouded my vision is about our relationship....It's a little reward of insight, like a particularly interesting fragment of a dream which you remember in the middle of the afternoon."

Waited So Long *(Carly Simon)* **
Carly - acoustic guitar, backing vocals; Jimmy Ryan - electric guitar; Klaus Voormann - bass; Jim Keltner - drums; Bill Payne - organ; Nicky Hopkins - piano; Lowell George - slide guitar; James Taylor - backing vocals.
A kind of country-rocker in which Carly recalls the time when, after waiting so long, she finally loses her virginity to a green-eyed boy, and not only asks her father to celebrate the event but also begs his forgiveness. The song was actually written and recorded in the studio the day after the jam session for 'Night Owl', just in time for the deadline, and just hours before getting the afternoon flight back to New York.

86

It Was So Easy *(Carly Simon - Jacob Brackman)* *****
Carly - acoustic guitar; Paul Keough - acoustic guitar; Jimmy Ryan - electric guitar solo; Klaus Voormann - bass; Andy Newmark - drums
This nostalgic look back at youthful innocence began as just a simple la-la-la folk melody Carly gave to Jake on a cassette tape, and in no time at all he provided just the right words she was looking for for it to become one of the most endearing songs of her career. Jake recalls: "What we experience as we grew up is more like free-flowing anxiety." Jimmy Ryan's pedal steel guitar solo was done as a live take, not an overdub, and therefore ended up on the record. Just recalling those long-ago days when kids had no plan other than having fun is enough to send waves of emotion running through your body. Even today, accepting a dare with the threat of being abducted by bears is just too scary to comprehend.

Night Owl *(James Taylor)* ***
Jimmy Ryan - electric guitar, backing vocals; Klaus Voormann - bass; Ray Cooper - congas; Jim Keltner - drums; Nicky Hopkins - piano; Bobby Keys - tenor sax; Bonnie Bramlett - backing vocals, Doris Troy - backing vocals; Paul McCartney - backing vocals; Linda McCartney - backing vocals
The vocal session for James Taylor's bluesy rocker was one of the most exciting times of Carly's recording career. The song had previously been released as a single back in 1967 when James was with the Flying Machine. Taking Jagger's advice, Carly now attempts to rough it up a little and bring to the surface the rocker he had assured her was lurking inside. With the basic tracks already recorded at Trident, all that remained was to lay down the vocals and some extra instruments. At one time or another there were Mick Jagger, Nicky Hopkins, Bobby Keys, Jim Keltner, and Klaus Voormann all joining Carly and Richard in the studio for an impromptu jam session.

When You Close Your Eyes *(Carly Simon - Bill Mernit)* ****
Carly - piano; Jimmy Ryan - acoustic guitar, bass; Andy Newmark - drums; Paul Buckmaster - arr. Strings, woodwinds & synthesizer.
A fine collaboration between Carly and her old Indian Hill Camp buddy Bill Mernit. With this gentle lullaby for insomniacs only half completed when Mernit visited Carly in her New York apartment, they both sat at the piano and finished the song together, with Mernit providing the "Big surprise" bridge and then working together on the rest. The perfect ending to a wonderful album.

Pretty-near perfect

On November 8th the single 'You're So Vain' was released, backed with 'His Friends Are More Than Fond of Robin'. Entering the Hot 100 on December 2nd, it steadily rose up the chart and became Carly's first US chart topper on January 6th, replacing Billy Paul's 'Me and Mrs Jones', and remained there for three weeks until replaced by Stevie Wonder's

'Superstition' on January 27th, although it held on to the #2 spot for another month. Not only that, the single also reached #1 on the *Cashbox* 100, remaining there from January 6th to the 20th, and also spent two weeks at #1 on Adult Contemporary, becoming the first ever single to top both *Billboard* charts. Around the world, it was a chart topper in a number of countries, including Canada, Australia and New Zealand, although stalling at #3 in the UK. On January 8th it was certified gold in the US for sales of over a million.

In 1994 the song would be ranked at #72 on *Billboard's* Greatest Songs of All-Time, and twenty years later the UK's Official Chart Company listed it as the "ultimate song of the 70s." At the Grammy Awards in March 1974 Carly would receive three nominations for 'You're So Vain' - Record of the Year, Song of the Year, and Best Pop Vocal Performance (female), but lost out in each category to Roberta Flack's 'Killing Me Softly'. Thirty years later Carly would be inducted into the Grammy Hall of Fame for writing the song.

The *No Secrets* album was released on November 28th and became Carly's commercial breakthrough, entering the *Billboard* Pop Albums chart on December 9th and reaching #1 on January 13th, remaining there for five weeks, having already been certified gold on December 8th. The album also entered the UK charts on January 20th and peaked at #3. On December 12th 1997, 25 years after its release, *No Secrets* would finally be certified platinum.

A second single, 'The Right Thing to Do', coupled with 'We Have No Secrets' (which itself should have been an A-side), was released in March 1973. It entered the Hot 100 top 40 on April 21st, reaching #17 on May 26th and #4 on Adult Contemporary. It also reached at #10 on the *Cashbox* Top 100, and #17 in the UK.

The majority of critics welcomed the new album and saw a new buoyancy that previous albums had lacked. *Rolling Stone* celebrated Carly's "ingenious" phrasing and "faultless" enunciation, and a freshness in her voice that exuded "patrician generosity." *Beat Magazine* stated that Carly had never sounded better, while *Hit Parader* not only acknowledged her capacity to select the right songs to suit her vocal style, but also recognized that here was an artist who would readily accept outside influence if it made her a better musician, but at the same time equally would "bow to no one's influence if it hurt her music." *Beat Instrumental* rated the album "pretty-near perfect" but also pointed out its high production values would make it difficult for the artist to replicate the songs live, making her feel "naked" without all the musicians backing her.

With *No Secrets* becoming one of the bestselling albums of 1973 on both sides of the Atlantic, the question was now how to repeat that success.

Carly was determined to keep her feet well and truly grounded: "I refuse to be propelled in the typical way that singers are in this business, like if you've got a hit you've got to follow it up quick with a follow-up single....I've got to keep my health, my mental health, and my home life, and the things that are most important to me."

All said and done, Carly had just made one of the most celebrated albums of her career, a chart topper with a chart-topping single that elevated her onto a global stage and made her an overnight darling of the media circus, with a marvelous public relations feat for a song that to this day has never been equalled. Also, by marrying James Taylor, she had become rock royalty and one half of the newly-coined "golden couple of pop."

Carly Simon had well and truly arrived. Just two years before she had been a relatively unknown rising star beginning to make waves in the music business. Now she was riding a tidal wave of success.

Hot Cakes and Possums

"Standing under those blinding lights with everybody expecting something from you....I mean, it isn't for me, that's all. My heart races so fast I'm afraid it'll explode."

The Golden Couple

In less than two years, Carly had gone from having no money, no record label, no great desire to perform, and a personal life fraught with anxieties and a string of failed relationships, to become one of the most famous and recognizable female pop singers in the world.

The new year brought changes to Carly's record label. Elektra had now merged with Warner's Asylum label to become Elektra/Asylum Records, with Asylum founder David Geffen becoming head of the new combined label, and Holzman now appointed senior vice-president and chief technologist for Warner. This would prove to be a distraction for Carly, as she felt she had now lost Holzman, her mentor who had shown his faith in her and had steered her path to success.

On January 4th 1973, an engrossing three-part interview with the newly-married couple by Stuart Werbin appeared in *Rolling Stone*, with Peter Simon's cover picture of them taken on their pre-wedding honeymoon in Hawaii. Both of them had reservations about doing the interview, especially James, who hadn't done one since what turned out to be an embarrassment two years before. This time they spoke candidly about their marriage, their music, James 'drug addiction, and having children.

Later that month, Carly accompanied James on his three-week tour of Japan, and the long flights must have almost shattered what little nerves she had left. Based at the Tokyo Hilton, much of the media attention was focused on Carly, due to the worldwide success of 'You're So Vain'. The culmination of the tour was a sell-out concert at Tokyo's Koseinenkin Kaikan Hall on February 9th, where she joined James on stage for an encore of 'You're So Vain' and 'You Can Close Your Eyes'.

By March, with James' house still an ongoing project, the couple had moved to an apartment on New York's East 62nd Street, with Carly now expecting their first child. Although James' latest album had done reasonably well, the latest single 'One Man Parade', released in March, only managed to reach #67 in the charts, despite it being well received by critics. The lead single 'Don't Let Me Be Lonely Tonight' had been released almost simultaneously with 'You're So Vain', the first time their records had been in direct competition. It made Carly feel embarrassed with the success of her own album and chart-topping single, and her continuing desire to make him happy would continue to be compromised by their varying levels of success.

In the meantime, Carly and James contributed to Livingston Taylor's new album *Over the Rainbow*, providing backing vocals for a number of songs, including the great opening track 'Loving Be My New Horizon' and 'Pretty Woman'. But what about recording a song with James? Carly was asked the question in May and replied: "One day in the future we might write together, but I don't feel it's very likely. I've collaborated with people on songs in the past and enjoyed it, but I think James always has a total concept for a song himself - his own concept. The James Taylor way. People have told me he's much more out-going since we've been together, but in many ways he's still a very solo sort of person."

When summer came, James would return to rehab to deal with his continuing addiction. But it wasn't just drugs, as he had a drink problem too. In a diary entry in June that year, Carly confessed: "I don't seem to satisfy him much…He only seeks me out for affection when he fears its loss. I'm so sad."

Return to LA

In an interview while accompanying James on tour in Paris, Carly spoke about her next album and admitted her disappointment that musically there wouldn't be any "great departure" from *No Secrets*. She felt that she had not "grown artistically" in the last twelve months and that her personal life had taken over from her music career. On working again with Perry, she recognized the previous conflict of ideas they had, but now vowed that, whoever the producer might be, "I'll be strong and do it my way first."

With Jake Brackman once again collaborating, Carly was now focusing on new material for her next album, although she was feeling self-conscious about how she would figure in the new label's hierarchy of artists. Asylum had some of the biggest names in the business, such as Dylan, Joni Mitchell, Linda Ronstadt, the Eagles, and new signing Queen. With many of the friends she had made at Elektra now gone, she also had to deal with a rumor that new boss Geffen was not all that impressed with her music. Carly would now have to earn his respect and come up with her best work yet.

One thing that was certain was that Richard Perry wanted to produce her next album, and although she had clashed with him many times during the making of *No Secrets*, she saw no problems agreeing to it. This time, however, Geffen insisted it would not be made in England.

With production commencing that September in Los Angeles, Carly, now six months into her pregnancy, flew out there with James and rented a house in Malibu, while she got to work on the songs at the Producer's Workshop in Hollywood. After several weeks most of the new material had been completed and final production was relocated to the Hit Factory on West 54th Street in Manhattan. Perry stuck to his formula and brought in, at one time or another, a stellar group of musicians from New York's top studios and from some of the best bands in the world.

Returning from their work on *No Secrets* were Jimmy Ryan, Andy Newmark, Bobby Keys, Jim Keltner, Jim Gordon, Paul Buckmaster, and even Klaus Voormann, who was flown in specially from London. These were now joined over the coming weeks by accomplished guitarist Danny Spinozza, who had recently been working on John Lennon's album *Mind Games* as well as Paul McCartney's second solo album, *Ram*, and in just a few months would be chosen to produce James Taylor's next album, *Walking Man*. John "Buzzy" Pizzarelli was a jazz guitarist who had worked with Benny Goodman, and Kenny Ascher was a jazz pianist, former member of Woody Herman's Orchestra, and had also worked with Spinozza on *Mind Games*.

Pennsylvania-born Michael Brecker was a brilliant jazz saxophonist making his mark on the music scene in New York, while multi-instrumentalist Mac Rebennack (aka Dr John) was already a familiar figure, having just released his album, *Dr John's Gumbo*, considered by many to be a cornerstone of New Orleans music. Among the half dozen drummers were Billy Cobham, a member of the Mahavishnu Orchestra; Russ Kunkel, a favorite of Carly's making a welcome return, and 25-year-old New York drummer Richard "Rick" Marotta, a former member of the Riverboat Soul Band, who Carly would take special notice of for future reference. Another face who Carly was more than happy to see was guitarist Robbie Robertson, now flying high with the Band, and now flying in for one of the sessions. James, too, now clear-headed and focused, would prove a valuable presence in the studio.

Having the use of two recording studios and an eclectic collection of fine and expensive musicians meant recording costs would be high, something that Geffen had already pointed out, but nevertheless it went ahead as scheduled. This time there was no tension in the air, and everyone worked in harmony. There was mutual respect between producer and musicians, and a glowing Carly felt more relaxed than ever, with the low-tones of her voice now sounding more passionate.

HOTCAKES
Elektra 7E-1002 (UK – K 52005)
Recorded - Producer's Workshop, L.A (September 1973); The Hit Factory, New York (October-November 1973).
Released - January 11 1974.
Producer - Richard Perry
Engineers - Bill Schnee & Harry Maslin
Mastering - Doug Sax, Mastering Lab L.A
Art direction & Design - Vincent Ccsi
Billboard Pop Albums #3; UK Album Chart #19; Canada #7; Australia #9

Side 1

Safe and Sound *(Carly Simon - Jacob Brackman)* ***
Carly Simon - acoustic guitar; David Spinozza - electric guitar; Klaus Voormann - bass; Ken Ascher - piano; Rick Marotta - drums; Paul Buckmaster - arr. Strings and woodwinds.
Carly and Jake look at the "inside out, upside down" world around them, from "lobsters dancing on the dock" in Maine to "tornadoes turning gay" in Mexico, and come up with this humorous song about avoiding all that's weird and wacky in the world by taking a more harmonious approach and just sticking together. Maybe a declaration of how safe and sound she now feels with James by her side.

Mind on My Man *(Carly Simon)* ****
Carly Simon - acoustic piano, Fender Rhodes electric piano, whistle; Buzzy Pizzarelli - electric guitar; Richard Davis - string bass; James Taylor - acoustic guitar; Ralph McDonald - congas; George Devens - cabasa
Like 'The Right Thing to Do' on her previous album, this is another dreamy and heartfelt love letter to James, one of several on the album, and a song actually written during the recording. Carly lists all the attributes which she finds attractive in men, and James seems to tick all the boxes. It's only on the final verse that we realize it couldn't be about anyone else, with Carly describing the man on her mind as "a Northern baby and a Southern child." And, of course, she is singing it to him, her husband, sitting right here in the studio playing his acoustic guitar. Chosen as the flip-side to the single 'Haven't Got Time for the Pain'.

Think I'm Gonna Have a Baby *(Carly Simon)* ***
Carly Simon - piano, acoustic guitar; David Spinozza - electric guitar; Klaus Voormann - bass; Jim Keltner - drums; Ralph McDonald - percussion; Lucy Simon & Todd Graff - "la-la" vocals; Carl Hall, Lani Groves and Tasha Thomas - backing vocals.
Without doubt, the most important thing on Carly's mind during the making of the album. Returning to her "river" metaphor that a woman is "fluid, absorbing, and eternal" (as author Sheila Weller expertly puts it), this is a whimsical love song to her unborn child and the "immersible" nature of upcoming motherhood.

93

Lucy Simon, already a mother of a five-year-old daughter, clearly resonates with Carly's feelings and joins in with the "la-la" backing vocals.

Older Sister (Carly Simon) ***
Carly Simon - piano; David Spinozza - electric guitar; Jimmy Ryan - acoustic guitar; James Taylor - acoustic guitar; Larry Breen - bass; Jim Keltner- drums; Richard Perry - vocals (ba-yoops); Bennie Diggs and Revelation (Philip Ballou, Arthur Freeman & Arnold McCuller) - backing vocals.

In an album full of family connections, this is another trip down memory lane for Carly. Whether it be about Lucy or Joanna is irrelevant (although it's probably Joey), as it resonates with any woman who lives in the competitive, hand-me-down shadow of an older sister. Soul singer Bennie Diggs and his band Revelation add their background vocals to a joyfully ragtime track.

Just Not True (Carly Simon) ****
Carly Simon - piano, backing vocals; James Taylor - acoustic lead guitar, backing vocals; Jimmy Ryan - acoustic rhythm guitar; Klaus Voormann - bass; Jim Gordon - drums; Paul Buckmaster - arr. strings and woodwinds

Often looked on by some reviewers as a song written about another mystery man, this has the hallmarks of Carly's blossoming relationship with James. Despite his faults, Carly cannot stop loving him, even if at times she can't bring herself to say it, and if she makes him feel that her love for him is in doubt, she assures him it's not true. In the song, Carly sings backing vocals with James for the first time, and those in the studio remark just how incredible they sound.

Hotcakes (James Taylor) *
James Taylor - arr. Horns; Billy Cobham - drums; Bobby Keys - tenor sax; Barry Rogers - trombone; Steven Madaio - trumpet; Howard Johnson - tuba, baritone sax

To close side one, Carly introduces the band and gives them the chance to jazz it up a little, with James on hand to arrange the horn section.

Side 2

Misfit (Carly Simon) ***
Carly Simon - piano; Jimmy Ryan - electric guitar; James Taylor - acoustic guitar; Klaus Voormann - bass; Andy Newmark - drums; Ken Ascher - Hammond organ; Paul Buckmaster - arr. strings and woodwinds

For Carly, wife and mother to be, she sees the pitfalls of staying out late, whether it be gambling or late-night bars, when every man should be at home with their partner. Perhaps a not so subtle message to her sometimes-errant husband, but nevertheless, she is offering inviting, warm, cozy nights in front of the television or lazing under a tree, and leaving the late nights to the "young and intellectual." Who could resist? This is another song written during the making of the album, with fine arrangements by Perry and Buckmaster.

Forever My Love *(Carly Simon - James Taylor)* *****
Carly Simon - acoustic guitar; James Taylor- acoustic lead guitar; David Spinozza - electric guitar; Klaus Voormann - bass; Russ Kunkel - drums; Ken Ascher - piano, Paul Buckmaster - arr. strings and woodwinds.
Not just one of Carly's finest love songs, this ballad is up there with her finest work. Heartbreakingly beautiful in its sentiment and composition, Carly is pouring out her love for James with words that seem to have been borrowed from romantic poets of another age. Her voice shows an emotional vulnerability as if she is overcome by just having to sing the emotional lyrics, and, of course, James is right there with her on lead acoustic guitar. The atmosphere in the studio that day must have been electric. It is true that James helped a little with the writing, but when asked in an interview if she knew which parts she wrote and which were James', she simply answered, "No, not easily." Nevertheless, if James ever doubted her love for him, this song could never be more convincing.
Incidentally, the line "Time alone will tell us, lovers born in May/ may grow bitter and jealous, faded and gray" does not refer to either of them (Carly was born in June; James in March).

Mockingbird *(Inez Foxx - Charlie Foxx - James Taylor)* ****
Single EK-45880 b/w Grownup
Released - January 1974
Billboard Hot 100 #5; Billboard Adult Contemporary #10; Cashbox #3; UK Singles Chart #34; Canada #3; Australia #8
James Taylor - lead vocals; Carly Simon - backing vocals; Robbie Robertson - electric lead guitar; Jimmy Ryan - electric rhythm guitar; Klaus Voormann - bass; Jim Keltner - drums; Dr John - piano, Hammond organ; Ralph McDonald - percussion; Michael Brecker - tenor sax solo; Bobby Keys - baritone sax.
It wa James' idea s to record this old song that had been a 1963 US #7 hit for brother-and-sister act Charlie and Inez Foxx, and made popular by their alternating the lyric on a syllabic basis. James had seen them perform it live at the Apollo Theater in 1965 and had often sung it with his sister Kate while in their teens. According to Carly, it was also the one song that was guaranteed to send young Sally off to sleep at bedtime. For the new version, James would retain the alternating lyrical style but make other significant adjustments. Michael Brecker was brought in to provide a blistering tenor sax solo, along with Dr John on keyboards and Robbie Robertson on his chicken-scratch rhythm guitar, and, in the end, they produce what many consider the definitive version of the song. At the end of the decade Carly and James will also give the world the definitive live version at the No Nukes concert.

Grownup *(Carly Simon)* ****
Carly Simon - piano; Ken Ascher - piano; Paul Buckmaster - arr. strings & woodwinds.
Maybe Carly's pregnancy is reminding her of her own childhood. *Rolling Stone* once commented that Carly never apologies for writing about herself or her "well-to-do background." This is no exception, as she reflects on her passage from childhood to adulthood, with the innocence of youth, and the wonder of

what it would be like to be an adult, and how now, as an adult herself, she looks back on that time: "I started to write a song about being a little girl and standing in the doorway and listening to my parents and their friends' conversation and thinking as a child, 'How safe they are, how sure of themselves the grownups are and how when I get to be their age I'll be sure of myself too.' But really, it's the penny candy syndrome. You think I just can't wait until I have enough money to get 100 sticks of penny candy and then when you are able to afford it, it makes you fat or it puts cholesterol in your blood or you don't want it any more. It's just that whole thing about growing up and being grown up myself. Just the other night a little girl was standing in the door and looking with such awe at me for being one of the grownups. I was sitting there thinking, 'I feel so uncomfortable, so shy and unsure of myself.'" In an interview with her brother Peter, she revealed that the origin of the song was an attempt to write about their mother: "Oh Lady, you were a mother to us all, you sheltered me from the cold, and if I accuse you of being wrong, then I was too young to know." Eventually Carly rewrote it as 'Grownup'. Her mother, she readily admits, was the biggest influence on her life. The piano-driven song, shared by Carly and Ken Ascher, is as gentle as a breeze, and the key and octave range of the composition is a fine example of Carly's songwriting craft, along with her spellbinding double-tracked vocal on the chorus. Perfectly enchanting, it was chosen as the flip-side to the 'Mockingbird' single.

Haven't Got Time for the Pain *(Carly Simon - Jacob Brackman)* *****
Single EK-45887 b/w Mind on My Man
Released - April 1974
Billboard Hot 100 #14; Billboard Adult Contemporary #2; Cashbox #7; UK Singles Chart #34; Canada #5; Australia #74
Carly Simon - piano, James Taylor - acoustic lead guitar; Jimmy Ryan - acoustic rhythm guitar; Klaus Voormann - bass; Jim Keltner - drums; Ralph McDonald - percussion; Paul Buckmaster - arr. strings & woodwinds; Carl Hall - backing vocals; Lani Groves - backing vocals; Tasha Thomas - backing vocals
A spiritual celebration of love's healing properties that captures the essence of the whole album. Carly is just too madly in love with James to worry about the pain of soon having to go into labor for the very first time. Whilst in her difficult past, suffering was the one thing "that made me feel alive," this new life she now shares with her husband brings her a heart full of love and emotional calm. Jake actually wrote the "suffering" part of the lyric during the actual recording and confessed to Carly that it was inspired by his teacher of Sufi, a form of Islamic mysticism. *Rolling Stone* rated the song as Carly's best single to date. Another fine ending to a great album.

For the album cover, photographer Ed Caraeff elected for shots of the heavily-pregnant singer at a bungalow in the grounds of the Beverly Hilton Hotel, with her sitting in an all-white room, with white light pouring through the window (like the "white light pouring down from Heaven" in

'Haven't Got Time for the Pain'). It was a radical move at the time. Even on the cover of Carole King's album *Music*, released over two years before, the sign of her pregnancy had been covered by her piano, but Caraeff saw things differently. Unlike Carly's previous albums, there would be no elaborate settings, no trendy outdoors fashions, no "Here I am" statements to be made. This was just a smiling Carly, be-gowned in a simple, white-linen kaftan, and quite virginal in appearance, would it not be for the fact she was expecting a baby in a little under two months. But the image perfectly captured the mood of the album, and its warm portrayal of a woman deeply in love, enjoying life, and about to bring new life into a world which, for Carly, was right now at its very best.

On January 7th 1974 the single 'Mockingbird' was released, with 'Grownup' on the flip-side. Credited to both Carly and James, it eventually peaked at #5 on the Hot 100 on March 23rd. In the UK, it reached #34 and would be her last single to chart there for over three years. The same day as the US release, Carly gave birth to a girl, Sarah Maria Taylor (later to be known as Sally) in a New York hospital. James would later write the beautiful song 'Sarah Maria' in his daughter's honor.

Trouble with Geffen

Four days after the birth of Carly's daughter, *Hotcakes* was also released. Entering the *Billboard* Pop Albums chart on February 2nd, it climbed steadily to #3 and remained on the charts for 35 weeks. In the UK it charted at #19. *Circus* magazine applauded the album, calling Carly's songs "one joy after another" and the album not only a fitting birthday gift to their daughter, but one showing a new-found stability in Carly's personal life. Meanwhile, *Rolling Stone* saw it as "more playful" than her previous work, but still with some serious provocative undercurrents, and citing three songs in particular, 'Haven't Got Time for the Pain', 'Think I'm Gonna Have a Baby' and 'Forever My Love' as being some of her best work to date. The *Chicago Tribune* reviewed the songs as being "stamped firmly with her own personality," but still allowing listeners to apply some of the songs' sentiments to resonate with their own situations. In a more recent review, *Allmusic* looked back on it as a conceptual album that "defined domestic bliss."

Interviewed about the album in February, Carly stated: "I think that my new songs are freer and a little more whimsical in approach. My main emphasis is still on love."

In January that year Joni Mitchell, Carly's former rival for James' affections, and now her professional rival in music as one of Geffen's top recording artists, had released *Court and Spark*, destined to become her most successful and critically acclaimed album. Also, that month, Geffen had released Dylan's *Planet Waves*, another smash hit album, largely down to Geffen's heavy promotional work that seemed so lacking with Carly's record. With the likes of Joni, Linda Ronstadt, Jackson Browne, and the Eagles on board, it seemed to Carly as if Geffen was giving his major artists preferential treatment, and she took it to heart: "David Geffen came in with his whole entourage of artists that he had set up on Asylum.... I was like the ugly stepdaughter. He was sort of stuck with me, and I felt like he was putting me in the ugly closet, that I was no longer important to the label."

Hotcakes fell just short of achieving gold status in terms of sales, while Joni's album would eventually achieve double-platinum status. In frustration, Carly told Arlyne, her close friend and manager, that she had lost faith in Geffen, and, if she could, would leave the label and look elsewhere.

In April, Elektra released the single 'Haven't Got Time for the Pain', backed with 'Mind on my Man'. After a slow climb, it had finally entered the Hot 100 top 40 on June 1st, before reaching its highest position at #14 on June 22nd and remaining on the charts for 12 weeks. Meanwhile, Carly, a little unwisely, had sold the rights of the song to Heinz for $50,000 so it could be used in a humorous television ad for ketchup. She would not make that same mistake again.

Competitive rivalry

In the meantime, James had his own agenda, and that January, still off the drugs, began recording his next album *Walking Man* at the Hit Factory in New York, with producer David Spinozza, the guitarist who had just played on Carly's album. Carly would again sing backing vocals on five of the songs. Released in June, the album would reach #13 in the charts, but a couple of singles pulled from it barely received airplay. Still falling way short of Carly's success was something that James was silently having to deal with. A seven-week nationwide tour to promote James' new album followed, and Carly and their baby daughter accompanied him on the road. Most nights, Carly joined him barefoot on stage to sing and dance to a raucous version of 'Mockingbird', and it was often judged the highlight of the show.

At one point during the year the "golden couple of rock" were being considered for the lead roles in Frank Pierson's forthcoming movie remake of *A Star is Born*, but on reading the scripts sent to them, Carly realized it was "too close to our own lives, and yet not close at all." To play rock stars in a movie was just something they didn't want to get into, and the roles eventually went to Kristofferson and Streisand.

Carly and James were finding it difficult to divide their time between looking after Sarah (Sally) and writing new material for their next albums. For Carly it was a growing concern, as James was often absent and not fulfilling his parental duties. By the end of the year the family got away from the East Coast's harsh weather and rented a house in Los Angeles (one that O J Simpson would later buy), where they would spend the winter, writing and watching Sally grow, with the help of a babysitter.

During the summer Carly contributed chorus backing vocals for folk and blues singer Tom Rush's excellent song 'No Regrets', which appeared on his album *Ladies Love the Outlaws*, released in September. The Walker Brothers' version of the same song was a smash hit in the UK the following year.

Recordings of both of their new albums got underway before long, with James working on *Gorilla* at Warner's studio in Hollywood, while Carly's *Playing Possum* was done at the nearby Sound Lab Studios and Sunset Sound Recorders. What she had in mind for the next album would cause quite a stir. In an interview with *Rolling Stone* she admitted that the new songs were much more sexually daring, especially as her body was now back in shape after her pregnancy. With it, she was like a new woman, more lustful and willing to portray a highly-charged sensual persona. Just how much highly-charged would soon see a few raised eyebrows and even more raised temperatures among her record label executives and her many fans.

The stealer of ideas

Carly would write most of the new songs on the piano, as she had done with her first hit single, but many subsequent songs were done with the guitar. Having taken a few piano lessons earlier in her life, she explained in an interview: "I do believe that you never forget the fact that you've acclimated yourself to a musical instrument as a child if you've had those lessons."

Before *Possum*, Carly had commented: "The completion of one song inspires another. With me it's a confidence thing, if I have one behind me which I like, I feel good about going onto another." But what about her writing at this important stage of her career? To begin with, there was no pattern, with either music or lyric taking precedence over the other. If she happened to be sitting at the piano or with a guitar in her hands, it would usually begin with a melody with no words. She admitted that she seldom came up with an idea herself, but was more of a "stealer," good at hooking on to what other people said during a conversation and taking key words or phrases.

"I start with words that are usually emotionally brought on by having to figure out something, like having to move through an emotion and get outside myself. So, I put it on paper and look at it from the third person, and then I add the melody. I think about the rhythm. It can go in lots of different directions."

Writing on either piano or guitar would determine the song's chord progression, although she felt the piano was the more logical choice. As for subject matter, Carly always looked for interesting and uncharted sides of life, or else found a specific angle and added her own unique twist to it. This was soon to become her trademark, but as long as the listener could still identify with it. In an interview with brother Peter she said: "Most of my songs are about illusions in relationships; webs of half-spoken truths, things you can't say in time. The songs are an effort to figure it all out, or at least to free myself of the immediate dilemma."

In a later interview Carly explained how being a lyricist and composer were two very different talents: "As a lyricist, I use much more of the left side of my brain. As a composer, it's something like running water - it never stops. I can perfect it, I can edit it, I can do all kinds of things with it, but if you stop me at any point during the day or night, I will sing you the melody that's going around in my head. And it's not a familiar melody, it's a melody of mine that's being created while I'm sleeping, while I'm doing other things. The only thing that gets in its way is another melody."

With motherhood now being the focal point of Carly's world, her writing would now have an added dimension. Where before she had been compiling songs like page entries in a diary, reflecting what had been happening in her life, she now felt she had no perspective on it. Instead, she would be drawing more on hypothetical situations and becoming more a story-teller than an audio diarist: "When I'm living something, I can't write it. The writing comes from reflection, or…something else."

Carly also recognized the medicinal qualities of writing: "When I'm feeling anxious or depressed, I do find it helps to reach for a pen and paper. There is something about writing things down, that hand-eye combination, that makes me feel calmer." Whether what she writes is all true is never in question: "They are fictionalized, to a degree. I don't have to swear that everything is true."

Heat's up, tea's brewed

For the new album, Perry again brought together a top band of session musicians, including many new faces. Although Jimmy Ryan was unable to take part due to other commitments, Carly would still enjoy the company of James and her friends Billy Mernit, Andy Newmark, Klaus Voormann, and Russ Kunkel. Dr John, Jim Gordon, and Little Feat's Jeff Baxter would also be familiar from work done on previous albums.

Among the new faces were keyboard player James Newton Howard, who had been part of Elton John's recent touring band and would later become one of the great film composers of his generation; Lee Ritenour, an accomplished jazz guitarist who would soon embark on a solo career, and bassist Willie Weeks, a much-in-demand session musician. There was also young Andrew Gold, a gifted musician and songwriter recently signed by Asylum. He was the son of Marni Nixon, the famous "ghost singer" who had famously dubbed her soprano vocals in a number of Hollywood musicals, and he would later embark on a successful solo career as singer and producer. Ringo Starr and Carole King would also be turning up at some of the sessions.

PLAYING POSSUM
Elektra 7E-1033 (UK – K 52020)
Recorded - Late 1974 - March 1975, Sound Labs Studios, Sunset Sound, Crystal Sound Studios, A&M Studios, LA & Burbank Studios, CA.
Released - April 8 1975
Producer - Richard Perry
Engineers - Bill Schnee, Norm Kinney & Andrew Berliner.
Mastering - Doug Sax, Mastering Lab L.A
Art direction & Design - Glen Christensen.
US Billboard Pop Albums #10; Canada #22; Australia #25

Side 1

After the Storm *(Carly Simon)* ****
Carly Simon - acoustic piano, arr. strings & horns, backing vocals; Lee Ritenour - electric guitar; Andrew Gold - drums; Klaus Voormann - bass; Trevor Lawrence - alto sax; Alan Estes - percussion.
Kicking off the album, we have Carly writing about the added stimulus of making up and making love following a bitter argument. Inspired by a real episode shortly after heading west to make the album, Carly paints a picture of the heightened passion as the lovers put their differences aside and get under the sheets. The intensity is sharpened by Carly's solid piano playing and Trevor Lawrence's wonderful alto sax solo, also arranged by the singer. Credit also goes

to Carly's dramatic Brian Wilson-style chord changes which made a number of producers and musicians sit up and take notice. With its message of how anger can turn people on, it was a suitable choice for the flip-side to the 'Waterfall' single.

Love Out in the Street *(Carly Simon)* ****
Carly Simon - acoustic piano; Billy Mernit - acoustic piano; Willie Weeks - bass; Andy Newmark - drums; Andrew Gold - guitar, tambourine; Emil Richards - percussion; Perry Botkin Jr - orchestration; Rita Coolidge - backing vocals; Clydie King - backing vocals; Rodney Richmond - backing vocals
Carly keeps the theme of the album on course with another r&b/pop-flavored song about blissful arguing, this time taking the fight and the love outside, as if she wants to have the whole world looking as they indulge in their public spat. Top-notch orchestration by Perry Botkin, with Andrew Gold providing a short guitar solo, and Kris Kristofferson's wife Rita Coolidge joining the backing singers. Chosen as the B-side to the single 'More and More'.

Look Me in the Eyes *(Carly Simon)* ***
Carly Simon - acoustic guitar, backing vocals; James Taylor - acoustic guitar, backing vocals; James Newton Howard - electric piano, ARP synthesizer; Alan Estes - percussion; Vini Poncia - backing vocals
Carly brings the ecstasy of her love making to a tropical beach, begging her lover to make eye contact for that extra slice of intimacy. From rubbing limes all over his body and climbing on him "like a tree," this is just about as far as Carly can go without censorship stepping in, but the gentle melody, provided by James ' wonderful guitar, and a heavenly choir that includes Carly, James and Vincent "Vini" Poncia, somewhat helps to diffuse the highly-charged erotism and leaves us with a tender portrayal of love making, albeit a sexy one. Chosen as the flip-side to the single of 'It Keeps You Runnin' from the next album.

More and More *(Mac Rebennack - Alvin Robinson)* **
Single E45278 b/w Love Out in the Street
Released - 1975
Billboard Hot 100 #94; Cashbox #90
Alvin Robinson - guitar; Jeff Baxter - guitar; Malcolm Rebennack "Dr John" - acoustic piano; Klaus Voormann - bass; Ringo Starr - drums; Richard Perry - tambourine; Fred Staehle - percussion; Carolyn Willis - backing vocals; Julia Tillman Waters - backing vocals; Maxine Willard - backing vocals
Despite being a surprising choice for a commercial single, this Dr John-Alvin Robinson song is another example of Carly's occasional departure into saloon-pop with its soulful delivery. Still on the subject of sex, but now toned down as just a craving for her to give her lover that little bit extra. Nothing exceptional, although notable for Steely Dan's Jeff Baxter's guitar licks and guest drumming by Ringo Starr.

Slave *(Carly Simon - Jake Brackman)* ****
Carly Simon - acoustic piano, backing vocals; Lee Ritenour - electric guitar, mandolin; Russ Kunkel - drums; James Taylor - acoustic guitar, backing vocals; Leland Sklar - bass; Perry Botkin Jr - arr. horns & woodwinds; Rita Coolidge - backing vocals; Clydie King - backing vocals
A song that was always bound to stir up a hornet's nest of controversy among feminists taking the lyrics at face value. Carly wanted this to be a single that was a de-affirmation of everything that the women's lib movement had burned their bras for in the early 70s. But the criticism was based on its portrayal of a woman's total devotion and burning desire for a lifetime of servitude to man. Carly stated in an interview that she did indeed feel like "a victim of my own enslavement," but its real sentiment was that she was not condoning it, but really expressing her anger. At the time she was madly in love with James, almost a fixation, and deeply anxious that she might say or do something that might make him leave her. It was reminiscent of her childhood days trying to win her father's love by being what he expected her to be. Now, in trying to sustain her marriage to James, she had become his submissive "slave to love." When interviewed before the album's release, Carly commented on the song: "I myself am very old fashioned.... I feel terribly modern and very equal to my husband.... but at other times I feel just like a slave to my *own* chauvinistic emotions." Her manager was in agreement with the label that releasing the track as a single would create a backlash and be "career suicide," so 'Attitude Dancing' was released instead. *Rolling Stone* saw the song's theme as "a woman's dependence on a man" while *Advocate* claimed: "The lyrics reflect an angry ambivalence about the situation. Simon has said that it's really a crying out against that sort of dependence, a woman's version of "macho." Another reviewer wrote: "The point is that it's *all* role playing; we cannot choose *no* role, but we can choose among the number available, even the one called the path of least resistance." Others saw this as the perfect sequel to 'The Girl You Think You See'. Although far from being a suicidal addition to the album, the song, along with the album's daring cover image, would make it the most controversial of Carly's career.

Side 2

Attitude Dancing *(Carly Simon - Jake Brackman)* **
Single E-45246 b/w Are You Ticklish
Released - May 1975
Billboard Hot 100 #21; Billboard Adult Contemporary #18; Cashbox #25; Canada #21; Australia #70
Carly Simon - acoustic piano; Jim Gordon - drums; Andrew Gold - guitar; Willie Weeks - bass; Paul Riser - arr. Strings & horns; Eddie Bongo - congas; Abigail Haness - backing vocals; Carole King - backing vocals; Ken Moore - backing vocals; James Taylor - backing vocals (uncredited)
Not one of Carly's favorite songs, as she later went on record to say, especially as she was disappointed with her vocals and the fact that it was recorded in the wrong key, a "whole step too high" that had her just "croaking" the song. At the time she liked the idea of not playing it safe, and, with this song, she perhaps

went more off course than she would have preferred. Inspired by a mutual love for all the earlier dances of the 50s and 60s, which Carly once referred to as "a creative melange of self-expression," Carly and Jake's song still remains rather unmelodious, and according to a number of reviewers at the time, the least interesting track on the album. On the other hand, *Rolling Stone* called it the album's "showstopper;" Carly's voice "genuinely sassy;" and Perry's production a "tour de force." Carly had her own views on the song: "It takes me further in a direction which I only took little steps in before. I don't think I sound that good on it, but maybe I'm not the best judge." Carly did not like the mix to the song and wanted the label to release 'Slave' as a single. Two weeks before the album's release, she met with Geffen and reached a compromise, with the label waiting on feedback from radio stations. Finally, it was decided to push on with 'Attitude Dancing' and Carly and Perry had to return to the studio to do a quick and final remix, with a new vocal done live with the band.

Sons of Summer *(Billy Mernit)* ****
Billy Mernit – acoustic piano
Wonderful acoustic rendition of Billy Mernit's nostalgic look back at college days, with note-perfect harmonies from Carly, wholly reminiscent of the Simon Sisters, and another fine showcase for her vocal talents. Billy had already played the song to her and she was keen to record it, persuading him to come to LA and play piano at the session. The result is a splendid feel-good song performed by these two close friends, with Carly's triple-tracked vocal giving it incredible depth, and Billy's subtle keyboard playing as the perfect accompaniment.

Waterfall *(Carly Simon)* ***
Single E-45263 b/w After the Storm
Released - 1975
Billboard Hot 100 #78; Billboard Adult Contemporary #21; Cashbox 76
Carly Simon - acoustic piano, backing vocals; Lee Ritenour - electric guitar; Leland Sklar - bass; Russ Kunkel - drums; Lon Van Eaton - clarinet; Derrek Van Eaton - flute; Carly Simon - backing vocals; James Taylor - backing vocals
Another sensual song that takes Carly's aquatic metaphor to its utmost and describes what some commentators see as the female orgasm, the singer evidently drowning in her own desires. Carly and James again share the backing vocals to perfection. Unlike 'Attitude Dancing', this was Carly's preferred track to be the lead single.

Are You Ticklish *(Carly Simon)* **
Carly Simon - acoustic piano; Joe Mondragon - bass; Irving Cottler - drums; Perry Botkin Jr - arr. clarinets & trombones
Not so much about sex, but the flirting that leads to it, and here's Carly in waltz-like rhythm and at her playful best teasing and enticing some guy to take things to the next level. Chosen as the flip-side to the single 'Attitude Dancing'.

Playing Possum *(Carly Simon)* ****
*Carly Simon - acoustic piano; Andrew Gold - acoustic guitar, drums; Willie
Weeks - bass; Tommy Morgan - harmonica; Lon Van Eaton - sitar; Sneaky Pete
Kleinow - pedal steel guitar; James Taylor - backing vocals*
Although inspired by her brother Peter Simon, who dabbled in political rallies
before buying his farm in Vermont, this is a homage to her own generation and
the optimism of younger days. Carly was quoted as saying: "The song came out
of sadness, a concern about turning thirty, and about how things that once seemed
so important lose their magic as more practical things take over." People become
less radical with age. The wide-eyed expectations of the youth of America who
were going to live out their dreams and change the world have stagnated into a
life of lying back in bourgeois comfort. When did it all turn to this? Carly asks.
Did we all just drop out? Should we get restless again and make a change? Or, as
she says, are we all just "playing possum?"

Tasteful eroticism

The art director Glen Christensen was looking for something a little more
provocative and daring than her previous album covers. South African-born
photographer Norman Seeff specialized in soft-focus black and white
images, and when Carly arrived at his studio, quite unplanned but with the
help of a little wine, she lost herself in the moment, and revealed a skimpy
black chemise she was wearing underneath her clothes. With her high black
boots and untamed hair, Seeff began shooting away with her in a variety of
controlled but semi-erotic poses, with perhaps the least daring of them
being the one finally chosen. Even Carly's manager Arlyne, decidedly
against the song 'Slave' being included on the album, was in full agreement
with her that this image was perfect.

It was a daring decision indeed, but the label went along with the risqué
cover, maybe as it was in stark contrast to the album covers of her female
contemporaries such as Carole King and Joni Mitchell, where the former is
shown knitting alongside a seemingly bored cat, and the latter has one of
her own, nondescript, paintings featured. By comparison, Carly's was a
full-frontal advertisement for the feminist movement. In hindsight, she may
have had some regrets, and was once quoted as saying, "I was a new
mother! What could I be thinking?" although in another interview, she
quipped, "I guess it's pretty sexy. If it wasn't me, I'd probably be turned
on." One reviewer likened the images of Carly to that of a "sexy
grasshopper."

But the label's decision carried the inevitable risk, and it soon became
all too evident, when some of the larger chain record stores either refused
to stock it or at least display it. That would have an impact on eventual sales,
as would Geffen's shifting of attention to his other more bankable artists. If

105

the album wasn't going to be recognized for its music content, the cover certainly made its mark, and was nominated for a Grammy in the Best Album Package category, but at the awards the following year lost out to the Ohio Players' album *Honey*. In 1991 *Rolling Stone* ranked *Playing Possum* at #20 in its list of the 100 greatest album covers of all time (won by the Beatles' *Sgt Pepper*).

Playing Possum was released on January 11th and peaked at #10 on the Pop Albums chart, making it Carly's third consecutive album to reach the Top Ten. It also reached #22 on the Canadian chart. 'Attitude Dancing' became the first single when released in May. Backed with 'Are You Ticklish', it reached #21 on the Hot 100 on June 21st and #18 on Adult Contemporary. A second single, 'Waterfall', coupled with 'After the Storm', only managed to reach #78 on August 9th and #21 on Adult Contemporary. A final single, 'More and More', backed with 'Love Out in the Street', was a failure, scraping in to the Hot 100 at #94.

Playing Possum seduced and charmed many people. Reviews of an album that was overflowing with songs about sex, albeit elegantly, were bound to be interesting. In *People* magazine, Carly's friend and collaborator Billy Mernit was quoted as saying that listening to the music was like being invited to a party that was already under way, "a sensual sort of basking in an unrestricted way." *Advocate* claimed it was Carly's best work to date and was "progressively more sophisticated." *Rolling Stone* saw it as "a body at play," "aggressively sexy," and displaying "an aching romantic ardor." *Melody Maker* called the album "earthy and lush" and a continuation of the singer's style, while *Stereo Review* was impressed that she had "gotten her head together" at last in an album that, for the time being, summed up a number of the current social quandaries much better than might "any learned dissertation by one of the paper pundits."

Carly had her own opinion on the album, and confessed: "I see all the songs about sex, except for the one about politics. It's kind of an album about sex. Not necessarily the act of sex, but relationships between men and women. Body feelings. It's a sensual album."

Goodbye to Perry, for now

In May 1975, James Taylor's album *Gorilla* was released, featuring not only his tribute to his new-born daughter, but also the single, 'How Sweet It is (To Be Loved by You)', a cover of the Marvin Gaye hit, with Carly providing harmony vocals. This time his album, so-called after James' impression of how his wife saw him in his worst moods, had bettered Carly's by reaching #6 on the Pop Albums chart that July. With their

106

inevitable competitive, but friendly, rivalry, it placed James in a better frame of mind and keen to write new material and tour again.

During the year, Lucy Simon had also released her first eponymous album for RCA, and, although Carly did not contribute, it was a wonderful collection of songs that included Lucy's 'My Father Died', a poignant and tear-inducing memory about the day Richard Simon had passed away in his sleep.

That summer Carly and James settled back into his still work-in-progress home on Martha's Vineyard, but with James commencing a new tour to promote his album, Carly was left at home dividing her time between looking after her daughter and writing new material. She gladly provided vocals for the title track and subsequent single of her Uncle Peter's album *Four or Five Times*, released on Buddah Records.

Playing Possum had signaled the end of Carly's four-year-long relationship with Richard Perry. He had produced what were considered to be three of Carly's best albums and was largely responsible for the biggest selling single of her career. He had made Carly work harder than ever before and in doing so had helped create some of her best work. She would never forget that, and some thirty years later they would be working together on another album.

That fall Carly and James were back renting a house in the suburbs of Los Angeles in preparation for working on their new albums, and on November 7th Carly made an appearance on the *Midnight Special*, along with fellow guest Vincent Price.

Two weeks later, on November 24th, Elektra released what would be Carly's first greatest hits album, *The Best of Carly Simon*, which included eight top twenty hits from all five albums, along with two tracks from *No Secrets*. Released just in time for the Christmas market, it entered the album chart on December 12th and reached #17 on January 17th, remaining on the charts for 19 weeks. Surprisingly, it failed to make an impression on the UK charts.

On Christmas Eve Carly and James joined Linda Ronstadt and Joni Mitchell to go carol singing in Hollywood.

THE BEST OF CARLY SIMON
Elektra 6E-109 (UK – 52025)
Released - November 24th 1975
Art direction & Design - Glen Christensen
US Billboard Pop Albums #17; Canada #40; Australia #42

That's The Way I've Always Heard It Should Be/The Right Thing to Do/Mockingbird/Legend in Your Own Time/Haven't Got Time for the

Pain/You're So Vain/(We Have) No Secrets/Night Owl/Anticipation/Attitude Dancing

The glowing cover image of Carly, taken by Scottish fashion photographer Albert Watson, portrays Carly as not only a successful artist, but as a devoted wife and mother, perhaps reflecting on her life and career, and reaching out to her detractors, competitors, and maybe even her late father, and saying to them, "Look at me. I made it on my own, I *am someone*."

Despite its initial poor showing on the charts, *The Best of Carly Simon* went on to become the best-selling album of Carly's career, receiving gold status on December 18th 1976, and eventually achieving triple-platinum accreditation. Although she would not release another hits compilation for twenty years, printed on the plain black rear cover, and going almost unnoticed, was written "volume one." Indeed, the world had not seen the last of Carly Simon, and for her growing legion of fans, the best was still to come.

Bond, Boys and a Baby

"I can put myself in any musical direction and it doesn't matter whether I'm climbing an ice-capped mountain…or whether I'm in a rage at my husband. I feel emotionally available to all of the sentiments."

Templeman and the Doobies

With a new album came a new producer. Not as charismatic as Samwell-Smith or as hard-working as Perry, Ted Templeman was a 33-year-old Californian and former member of 60s sunshine band Harper's Bizarre. After getting a job in A&R at Warner, he had discovered the Doobie Brothers and had co-produced their debut album in 1971, before going on to produce their platinum-selling *Toulouse Street* the following year. Promoted to staff producer, Warner saw him as the ideal person to work with Carly on her new album *Another Passenger*.

James was now in the process of making his album *In the Pocket*, which would be his last for Warner before signing with Columbia. Meanwhile, Carly spent the first three months of 1976 working with the laid-back, less-imposing Templeman on her new songs at Sunset Sound Recorders in Hollywood, while James worked with his producers Russ Titelman and Lenny Waronker at the nearby Warner and Burbank Studios. It was inevitable that, once again, both albums would be released more or less at the same time and the two artists would be going head-to-head in the chart stakes. One theory was that there were many fans of both artists who couldn't afford to buy both albums but would be forced to choose one over the other.

Templeman liked the sound of Carly's new songs, although at the time he wasn't seeing any hit singles. But with input from the Doobie Brothers' lead singer Michael McDonald, he assured Carly that he would do his best and come up with something that would really stand out. Like before, it relied on getting some of the best musicians together. As well as James, McDonald, and many names from the previous studio sessions, Templeman had the brilliant rock and blues keyboard player Bill Payne, who had co-founded the rock band Little Feat in the late 60s; guitarist Paul Barrere and drummer Richie Haywood, both members of Little Feat; multi-instrumentalist Van Dyke Parks, a name familiar with Beach Boys fans, as he had co-written their aborted but much-celebrated album *Smile*; Milton

"Milt" Holland, a fine session percussionist and member of the famous "Wrecking Crew"; and David Campbell, an arranger who had worked with Carole King. Like before, there would also be some famous faces dropping in to sing and play.

Carly would later be critical of the production, saying it had been badly mixed, something that Templeman later agreed with. But, despite that, the album had much to be admired. With the title taken from the lyrics of 'Libby', one of the many outstanding tracks, it had none of the polish and flamboyance of Perry's productions. Carly felt completely at ease in the studio, and with the Doobies and Little Feat musicians on hand, it resulted in much looser arrangements and vocals than on previous albums. Add that to her incredible vocal range on songs that cover a number of musical genres, and the result is a remarkable piece of work.

ANOTHER PASSENGER
Elektra 32-000 (UK – K 52036)
Recorded - January-March 1976, Sunset Sound Recorders, Hollywood.
Released - June 8 1976
Producer - Ted Templeman
Engineer - Donn Landee
Art direction - Glenn Christensen
Design - Anne Gardner
US Billboard Pop Albums #29; Canada #44; Australia #44

Side 1

Half a Chance *(Carly Simon - Jacob Brackman)* ***
Single E-45341 b/w Libby
Released - 1976
Billboard Adult Contemporary #39
Carly Simon - acoustic guitar, backing vocals; Andrew Gold - electric guitar; Jeff "Skunk" Baxter - electric guitar; Patrick Simmons - electric guitar; Michael McDonald - piano; Tiran Porter - bass; John Hartman, Keith Knudsen - drums; Victor Feldman - percussion; Andrew Love - sax solo; David Campbell - arr. strings; Ellen Kearney - backing vocals; Leah Kunkel - backing vocals; Linda Ronstadt - backing vocals.
Another plea to James, maybe, urging him not to walk away when it seems an angry storm is brewing. If that's the case, this jazz-tinged song could easily be dovetailed as a perfect prequel to 'After the Storm' on the previous album. Jake's lyrics are once again in tandem with Carly's thinking about her marital life, still barely over three years old. With a fine sax solo by Andrew Love, a member of the famous Memphis Horns, and with strong backing vocals that include the great Linda Ronstadt, this is a real strong opening track.

110

It Keeps You Runnin' *(Michael McDonald)* ****
Single E-45323 b/w Look Me in the Eyes (US), Be with Me (UK)
Released - 1976
Billboard Hot 100 #46; Billboard Adult Contemporary #27; Cashbox #49;
Canada #47
Patrick Simmons - guitar; Jeff Baxter - slide guitar; Tiran Porter - bass; John Hartman - drums; Keith Knudsen - drums; Carly Simon - backing vocals; Doobie Brothers (McDonald, Hartman, Porter, Knudsen, Baxter, Simmons, Bobby LaKind & Tom Johnston) - backing vocals
Wonderful cover of a Doobie Brothers' song that had been written in 1975 after songwriter/keyboard specialist McDonald had left Steely Dan to join the Doobies as a replacement for the incapacitated Tom Johnston. Invited to perform on their next album, *Takin 'It to the Streets*, produced by Templeman, McDonald contributed a number of songs, including this one, and the album was released on March 19th 1976, peaking at #8 on the album chart. In discussions with the Doobies, Carly and her producer both agreed that 'It Keeps You Runnin' would be an ideal choice for Carly to showcase the new-found, rough-it-up vocal that Jagger had once told her she was hiding away. Carly doesn't disappoint with her energetic, almost operatic performance, but it's the incredible music that carries it along - music and backing vocals that have that indelible Doobie Brothers stamp. They, too, would release it as a single in October, charting at #37, but many critics feel that Carly's is the definitive version.

Fairweather Father *(Carly Simon)* ****
Carly Simon - keyboards, celesta, backing vocals; James Taylor - guitars, backing vocals; Klaus Voormann - bass; Victor Feldman - marimba; Milt Holland - congas; Novi Novog - viola; David Campbell - arr. strings; Jackson Browne - backing vocals
A gentle take on feminist morality. Carly had every intention to make every song she wrote about James a positive one, but then remembered that those kinds of thoughts didn't necessarily have to be about the person you're living with. So, in this evocative and light-hearted song about being an unappreciated wife and mother, Carly is singling out this "doesn't-do-diapers" husband for a mild rebuke. Ironically, she will also dedicate the album to James, "for his arrangement…and at the same time for not being one." James also contributes splendid guitar flourishes, and provides backing vocals along with Carly and singer-songwriter Jackson Browne.

Cow Town *(Carly Simon)* ****
Tom Johnston - acoustic guitar; Paul Barrere - electric guitar; Jeff Baxter - steel guitar; Bill Payne - keyboards; Richie Hayward - drums, backing vocals; David Campbell - viola; Novi Novog - viola; Carly Simon - backing vocals
Fascinating, twangy Randy Newman-style ballad, allegedly about a woman named Simone, the French daughter of one of Carly's friends, who falls in love with a Texan oil baron (and his money), and goes to live with him among the not-so-elegant surroundings of cattle, pigs and oil rigs along Buffalo Bayou. A

perfect example of Carly's bitchiness, wit, and verbal dexterity, it was at the time rated by *Rolling Stone* as the finest song she had written.

He Likes to Roll *(Carly Simon)* ***
Carly Simon - guitar; Laurindo Almeida - guitar; Klaus Voormann - electric & Earthwood acoustic bass; Jim Keltner - drums; Bud Shank - flute; Victor Feldman - marimba, percussion; Milt Holland - percussion
Catchy and seductive bossa nova-inducing song that, despite the repetitive lyric, has a gorgeous melody that hooks the listener, especially with Brazilian Laurindo Almeida's amazing guitar fills, Victor Feldman's marimba, and Bud Shank's distinctive flute. This is Carly's first venture into Brazilian-flavored music, something she will soon come to embrace.

In Times When My Head *(Carly Simon)* *****
Carly Simon - piano, backing vocals; Michael McDonald - electric piano; Steven Bruton - electric guitar; Klaus Voormann - bass; Jim Keltner - drums; Milt Holland - percussion; Kirby Johnson - arr. strings; Ellen Kearney - backing vocals; Leah Kunkel - backing vocals; Libby Titus - backing vocals; Linda Ronstadt - backing vocals
A sublime heart-wrenching song which tackles the all-too-common realities of infidelity in an otherwise seemingly sound relationship. It's all too easy to relate this to James, and in her excellent *Boys in the Trees* memoir Carly makes reference to the song in recounting one particular episode of indiscretion. But then, it could be addressing the issue on a much larger scale of how couples may sometimes lose their way but still retain their love for one another. A difficult song for Carly to write, let alone record, and one for which she seldom offers any clear interpretation. Nevertheless, despite that reluctance to offer some clarity (who was that "boy" in the backwoods?), it remains one of her greatest compositions, delivered with such intensity and depth that it eclipses much that had gone before, with superior production at the hands of Templeman. Its stunning chorus ranks among the most memorable of Carly's entire career with its sonic tapestry, and includes added vocal contributions from Linda Ronstadt, Carly's friend Libby Titus, and Russ Kunkel's wife Leah, the younger sister of the late Cass Elliot.

Side 2

One Love Stand *(Paul Barrere - Bill Payne - Kenny Gradney)* ***
Paul Barrere - electric guitar; Lowell George - slide guitar; Bill Payne - keyboards; Richie Hayward - drums; Kenny Gradney - bass; Carly Simon - backing vocals; Michael McDonald - backing vocals
Carly does justice to this cover of a Little Feat song that had first appeared on their 1975 release, *The Last Record Album*, sung by Bill Payne and Paul Barrere. With a driving beat and excellent guitar playing by Barrere and Lowell George, Carly shares backing vocals with Michael McDonald.

Riverboat Gambler *(Carly Simon - Jacob Brackman)* ****
Carly Simon - piano; Michael McDonald - electric piano; Bob Glaub - bass; Rick Jaeger - drums; David Campbell - arr. strings & woodwinds
The bluesy music and cutting lyrical detail give this Carly-Jake ballad an authentic showboat cocktail atmosphere. Another fine production with first outings for drummer Rick Jaeger and bassist Bob Glaub and solid keyboards once again by McDonald.

Darkness Til Dawn *(Carly Simon - Jacob Brackman)* ****
Van Dyke Parks - piano, marimba, arr. accordion; Robert Greenidge - steel drums; Fred Tackett - mandocellos; Carly Simon -backing vocals; Lucy Simon - backing vocals
Notable for the somewhat eccentric, but nevertheless spellbinding, piano playing by the equally eccentric Van Dyke Parks, this is undeniably another vocal masterclass from Carly, using her incredible range to great effect. Lyrically, the portrayal of a woman's feelings after a tiff with her lover is another of Jake's gems, and the sheer complexity of the music, complete with marimbas, accordion, and chimes, showcases the great working relationship that Carly is enjoying with her producer.

Dishonest Modesty *(Zach Wiesner)* ***
Carly Simon - acoustic guitar, backing vocals; Dr John - electric rhythm guitar; Paul Barrere - slide guitars; Klaus Voormann - bass; Andy Newmark - drums; Milt Holland - percussion; Alex Taylor - backing vocals
One of two songs on the album written by the one-time bass player of James Taylor's early band, the Flying Machine, and now friend and neighbor to Carly and James at their Vineyard home. The twangy ballad and its acidly accurate observations of a selfish female singer who has authenticity problems is said by some commentators to be referring to Carly's musical rival Joni Mitchell, and that she later regretted recording it. It also has James' older brother Alex on backing vocals.

Libby *(Carly Simon)* *****
Carly Simon - electric piano; Mark T Jordan - piano; Glenn Frey - guitar; Bob Glaub - bass; Rick Jaeger - drums; Bill Payne - organ; Nick DeCaro - accordion; David Campbell - arr. strings & woodwinds.
A tour-de force of songwriting and performance, and inspired by Carly's friendship with fellow singer-songwriter Elizabeth "Libby" Titus. The daughter of a Russian immigrant, Libby was born in Woodstock, New York in 1947, but her college studies had been cut short with both pregnancy and marriage at the age of nineteen to the son of Helena Rubenstein, heir to her famous cosmetic empire. Just a few years later she became the partner of musician Levon Helm, the drummer in Dylan's touring group, the Hawks, which later morphed into The Band, and who was one of the musicians present when Carly made her aborted recording with Albert Grossman. Carly and James became great friends of Levon and Libby, and Carly was so fascinated by her lively, ultra-sophisticated bohemian persona that it developed into a more intimate sisterly relationship.

113

Libby was also a talented singer-songwriter with a fragile voice and had co-written 'Love Has No Pride', a hit for Linda Ronstadt in 1973. Carly invited her to sing backing vocals on the two best tracks on her latest new album, the wonderful 'In Times When My Head' and this grandiose story of two friends, who, when their flights are grounded, find escape for a while from life's realities with a drink and a little imagination, and "take off" for an adventure in chic Paris to indulge in their fantasies. Both guilty of wasting time in search of love, Carly confesses she is just "another passenger" on their journey to a more fulfilling life. With its beautiful imagery, the song is an emotional celebration of friendship and of sharing special times together, and the production is nothing less than perfection, with lyrics, melody and vocals melding together with David Campbell's lush orchestration. Glen Frey, co-founder of the Eagles, is a guest guitarist on the track. Unfortunately, some critics just didn't get it, with *Rolling Stone* deriding its "overlong banality." Nevertheless, the song was chosen as the flip-side to the single 'Half a Chance'.

Be with Me *(Carly Simon - Zach Wiesner)* **
James Taylor - guitar; Nick DeCaro - accordion.
Another song by Vineyard neighbor Zach Wiesner, this one was co-written with Carly. Light and breezy, this has James Taylor on acoustic guitar and provides a surprisingly laid back, almost forgettable, end to an otherwise superlative and memorable album. In 1981 Carly would sing this on the compilation album *In Harmony* and later with the Muppets while guesting on an episode of *Sesame Street*. But for now, it was chosen as the flip-side to the UK release of the single 'It Keeps You Runnin'.

The cover image of the album was in marked contrast to *Playing Possum*. Taken by Carly's longtime friend, celebrated photo journalist Mary Ellen Clark, the soft-focus portrait of the singer oozes sophistication and modesty, while another image has her sitting on the desk of a 1940s-era office alongside the oft-reclusive film director Terrence Malick portraying the riverboat gambler of one of the songs.

Apart from disliking one of its finest tracks, *Rolling Stone* admired Carly's unique "monied angst of the leisured with moving conviction" and calling it "jolting stuff." *Saturday Review* rated it as a "classy job" by an artist who it saw as the most accessible among the current pantheon of female singer-songwriters, while *Stereo Review* applauded the album's maturity and how Carly's "laser-beam eye and rifle-mike ear are both softened by a civilized disinclination to judge."

In the end, sales for both Carly's and James' albums were only moderate. Released on June 8th, *Another Passenger* entered the album chart on June 26th and peaked at #29 on July 24th, remaining on the charts for 13 weeks. In the meantime, James' album *In the Pocket* did slightly better at #16 in July, although it was the lowest showing on the charts since his debut album six years before. Carly's first single, 'It Keeps You Runnin'', backed with 'Look Me in the Eyes', from *Playing Possum*, proved to be a disappointment when it topped out at #46 on the Hot 100 on July 17th and #27 on Adult Contemporary, while in the UK it was released with 'Be with Me' on the flip-side and failed to chart altogether. A second single, 'Half a Chance', coupled with 'Libby', was released, but only reached a modest #39 on Adult Contemporary. Later that summer, James' single 'Shower the People', with Carly on harmony vocals, reached #22 on the Hot 100 and #1 on Adult Contemporary.

Templeman would make no more albums with Carly, although he would soon get her together once more with Michael McDonald to write a hit single. However, the following year he would be focusing on launching the career of a band called Van Halen.

Even though touring to promote the album was still something Carly was not prepared to do, there were calls for her to do publicity appearances on television chat shows, although she always insisted that if it required her to perform it was to be pre-recorded and not done live on air. This became an issue when on May 8th, four weeks before the album's release, she was asked to appear on the hugely popular late-night satirical show, *NBC's Saturday Night*, which was hosted by a celebrity guest and featured a live musical segment. Among its regular cast were some of the country's brightest up-and-coming comics, including Chevy Chase, John Belushi and Dan Aykroyd. Chase had been one of Carly's first boyfriends back in Riverdale and he had suggested to the show's producer that they have her as a guest singer. After some haggling with Carly and Arlyne, it was finally agreed to break with tradition and allow her to pre-record the two songs for the show. Hosted by actress Madeline Kahn, Carly recorded two songs with the house band just an hour before going on air. In the first segment she performed 'Half a Chance', and in the second, with an introduction by Chase, she sat at the piano and sang a blistering version of 'You're So Vain', with Chase standing with the backing singers, wearing an apricot scarf and playing a cowbell.

In early June it was confirmed that Carly was expecting their second child. Selling their town house on East 62nd Street, they moved to a large rented apartment in the Langham Building at 135 Central Park West, just one block north of the Dakota Building. While there, Carly began a close friendship with actress Mia Farrow, who had an apartment in the same building. Meanwhile, James was once again touring with his band and thinking about switching record labels to Columbia, despite the fact that Warner were going to release his *Greatest Hits* album in time for the Christmas market, a record that would eventually go on to achieve platinum sales eleven times over.

Whilst James was on the road, Carly sang with Kate Taylor, Ellen Epstein and John Hall at the wedding of her brother Peter and his longtime girlfriend Ronni at Andrea's house on the Vineyard. During the year she also sang lead vocals on the track 'Peter', from the eponymous album by Peter Ivers, the talented musician and television presenter who would be tragically murdered in 1983.

Bond and a brand-new boy

1976 would also be the year that one of Carly's earlier dreams would finally come true. Over in London, Lewis Gilbert was in the process of directing the tenth James Bond movie called *The Spy Who Loved Me*, starring Roger Moore and Barbara Bach. When it came to recording the music score, veteran British Oscar-winning composer John Barry, who had scored all previous Bond films, was unavailable to work in the UK due to tax reasons, and American composer Marvin Hamlisch had been called in. Hamlisch had already won Oscars for his music in *The Sting* and *The Way We Were*, and he was now going to break away from the Bond tradition and give this movie a more disco-oriented sound. But for the main theme, he had in mind a "lust-drunk anthem" about Bond's sexual prowess and came up with a power ballad called 'Nobody Does It Better', the first song to be titled differently from the name of a Bond film since *Dr No*.

With lyrics supplied by his then-girlfriend Carole Bayer Sager, they now looked for a suitable female singer. Sager had co-written the lyrics for the smash hit 'A Groovy Kind of Love', and was about to launch her quirky solo single, 'You're Moving Out Today'. She recommended to Hamlisch that Carly Simon would be the ideal singer, remarking that the lyrics sounded "incredibly vain" in reference to her famous song.

Sometime in early December, Carly got the call and met up with Hamlisch at her apartment. When he sat at the piano and played the opening chords, allegedly inspired by a Mozart riff, Carly was amazed, and when she sang it from a lyric sheet, they both agreed it was a perfect match. Carly said that when it came to the recording in the new year, she wanted her old friend Richard Perry to produce it, and Hamlisch had no objections. All this, of course, was still in the future. For the time being, there was a baby to be born.

Now in the final month of her pregnancy, Carly attended the wedding of her sister Joanna to Gerald Walker, an article editor for *New York Times'* magazine. Benjamin Simon Taylor was born on January 22nd 1977, and almost right from the start there were problems with his health. Constant crying, a sleeping disorder, and bouts of high fever caused concern for parents and doctors alike, but they couldn't get to the bottom of it.

Meanwhile, despite much pleading and offer-making by Warner's executives, James had finally decided to go with Columbia to make his next album *JT*, recording of which would begin out in Los Angeles in March. Once again relocating to the West Coast, with two children and a nanny in tow, the couple were invited to stay at the home of Lou Adler, the Grammy-winning producer of Carole King's *Tapestry* and co-producer of the smash hit movie *The Rocky Horror Picture Show*.

In April James began recording his new album at the Sound Factory in Hollywood with his old friend Peter Asher, while Carly joined Richard Perry and session pianist Michael Omartian at Elektra's LA studio to record the vocal track for 'Nobody Does It Better'.

Nobody Does It Better *(Marvin Hamlisch-Carol Bayer Sager)* *****
Single Elektra E-45413-A b/w After the Storm (UK – K 12261)
Recorded - April 1977
Released - July 1977
Producer - Richard Perry
Engineer - Howard Steele
Billboard Hot 100 #2; Billboard Adult Contemporary #1; UK #7; Canada #2; Australia #8
Michael Omartian - piano; Mike Egan - acoustic guitar; Chris Rae - electric guitar; Laurence Juber - electric guitar solo; Bruce Lynch - bass; Brian Odgers - bass; Barry De Souza - drums; Richard Hewson - arr. strings & horns; Paul Buckmaster – orchestration

The Spy Who Loved Me was released in the US on July 13th 1977, and the single 'Nobody Does it Better' later that same month. Coupled with 'After the Storm' from *Playing Possum*, the single became a major worldwide hit. It entered the Hot 100 top 40 on August 27th and peaked at #2 on October 22nd, holding that spot for three consecutive weeks, and being kept off the top by Debbie Boone's 'You Light Up My Life'. It also gained the #1 spot on Adult Contemporary in late September, #2 in Canada, #7 in the UK, and #8 in Australia. Certified gold on November 9th, it became the longest-charting single of Carly's career and the most successful hit she had that was not one of her own compositions.

At the Academy Awards in February the following year, 'Nobody Does it Better' was nominated for Best Original Song, but lost out to 'You Light Up My Life', while at the Grammys that same month, it was nominated for Song of the Year, (won by 'Evergreen' from *A Star is Born*) and for Best Pop Vocal Performance (which again, was won by Streisand for

'Evergreen'.). In 2004, the American Film Institute ranked 'Nobody Does It Better' at #67 in their list of the greatest movie songs of the last 100 years.

Meanwhile in LA, Carly had teamed up with her friend Libby Titus to collaborate on her new eponymous album. Libby was well-respected at Columbia and had been given Paul Simon and Phil Ramone to produce some of the tracks. Carly was brought in to contribute and collaborate on songs. As well as her and Jake's 'Darkness Til Dawn', Carly wrote 'Wish I Could' and 'Can't Believe You're Mine' especially for her. She also co-wrote with Libby the song 'Can This Be My Love Affair?' and sang backing vocals with James on the 'Darkness Til Dawn' track. That same year Carly also contributed to Lucy's splendid second album *Stolen Time*, singing with her on the tracks 'Father to Son' and 'Partners in Crime', with their harmonizing sounding as good as ever. The album was released in August 1977.

JT and trouble with Ben

After returning to New York, Carly was finally persuaded to perform what would be her first solo concert in five years, the first of two nights at the Other End (formerly the Bitter End) in Greenwich Village on May 31st. With no prior promotion, it was done mainly for a few record executives, a sprinkling of celebrities, and the press, although members of her family were also there. Beginning around midnight, the short set included many of her hit singles, and James joined her on stage to sing 'You Can Close Your Eyes'. In the early hours of the morning, Carly announced to the audience that she would be singing the theme to the new Bond movie. On the second night, her old friend Mick Jagger was in the audience. Unfortunately, the local *Village Voice* slated the performance, calling her "too sleek and well-adjusted" and "culturally privileged."

On June 22nd James 'album *JT* was released and reached #4 in the album chart. Although James would later admit that he was still "doing drugs" during the making of the album, it is often cited as being among his best work. It produced two top twenty hit singles, 'Handy Man' and 'Your Smiling Face', as well as 'There We Are', a love letter to Carly, the philosophical ballad 'Secret O'Life', and the introspective and visionary 'Terra Nova', which was only completed with last-minute input from Carly, who provided harmony vocals. At the Grammys the following year, James won Best Male Pop Vocal Performance for 'Handy Man', while *JT* was nominated for Album of the Year, although losing out to Fleetwood Mac's *Rumours*.

During the summer, Ted Templeman had sent Carly a demo tape of a Michael McDonald song that the singer had written a melody for, but was struggling to give it a lyric. With the Doobies' latest album *Living on the Fault Line* due out soon, Templeman arranged for Carly to work remotely with McDonald on completing the song just in time for the album's release in August. Within a short time, they came up with the rocker 'You Belong to Me', although surprisingly it was not released as a single. However, Carly would soon be embracing the song herself.

On October 14th, Carly and James made their first live television appearance together on the *Dick Cavett Show*, with James performing the song 'Secret O'Life', and then joining Carly for a wonderful rendition of 'Devoted to You', at the end of which James quipped, "a sobering sentiment."

As winter approached, they both decided they would not go out to the West Coast, like they had done before, but stay home and take care of Ben, who was still having sleeping problems. Any new albums would now have to be recorded in New York.

The magic of Mardin

Over the Christmas period Carly began writing new material for her next album, *Boys in the Trees*, which would see a return to her unflinching reflective style. As the recording was to be in New York, Elektra sought out Arif Mardin, the Turkish-born producer who had joined Atlantic Records in 1955 as an A&R man. Rising through the ranks to become vice-president, Mardin was responsible with co-founder Jerry Wexler and engineer Tom Dowd for establishing the famous "Atlantic Sound." In 1967 Atlantic was sold to Warner for $17.5 million. Mardin was a sophisticated New Yorker who liked to push artists out of their comfort zones and launch them into uncharted territory. He had done it with luminaries such as Barbra Streisand, Bette Midler and Diana Ross, and he determined to do the same with Carly and bring in a wider audience than just the present rock market.

Recording commenced in December 1977 at Atlantic Studios and A&R Studios, and it was the first time Carly had recorded in the city since her debut album nearly eight years ago. With James not making another album for almost a year, he would now be able to spend much of his time with Carly in the studio, and put his stamp firmly on the recording.

New studios meant a whole new batch of session musicians, and Mardin picked some of the best the city had to offer. They would form a nucleus which would be working with Carly for years to come. The promising New York guitarist David Spinozza, keyboard player Hugh McCracken, drummer Steve Gadd, bass player Tony Levin, and saxophonist Michael Brecker were all well known to her, having played on *Hotcakes*, and had all been former members of the experiment jazz-rock outfit Mike Mainieri's White Elephant Orchestra. Another familiar face to Carly was guitarist Stuart Scharf, who she would remember from the Simon Sisters' recordings with Kapp, while percussionist Errol "Crusher" Bennett had worked on albums by Van McCoy, Bill Withers and Melba Moore.

There was also pianist Richard Tee, former student at the Manhattan School of Music; synthesizer wizard Ken Bichel, who had worked on Broadway musicals; jazz pianist Don Grolnick, who had played on the Brecker Brothers' recent albums; Jamaican jazz guitarist Eric Gale; guitarist Cornell Dupree, co-founder the jazz-funk band Stuff, along with Gadd, Tee and Gale; and Scottish guitarist Hamish Stuart from the Average White Band. The concertmaster was Gene Orloff who had worked with James on *Walking Man*, and the horn section, arranged by Mardin, consisted of former members of Mainieri's band - brothers Randy and Michael Brecker (trumpet and tenor sax respectively), Eddie Bert and Barry Rogers (trombones), Harvey Estrin and Ronnie Cuber (baritone sax), and James Buffington and Brooks Tillotson (French horns).

All the sessions were held in the afternoon so Carly could be at home to make dinner for James at their Manhattan apartment or tending to their garden on the Vineyard.

BOYS IN THE TREES
Elektra 6E-128 (UK – K 52066)
Recorded - December 1977-March 1978 Atlantic Studios, New York, with additional recordings at A&R Studios, New York.
Released - April 4 1978
Producer - Arif Mardin
Engineer - Bobby Warner
Mastering - George Piros, Atlantic Studios, New York
Art direction - Tony Lane & Johnny Lee
US Billboard Pop Albums #10; Canada #4; Australia #27

Side 1

You Belong to Me *(Carly Simon - Michael McDonald)* ****
Single E-45477 b/w In a Small Moment
Released - April 1978
Billboard Hot 100 #6; Billboard Adult Contemporary #4; Cashbox #9; Canada #5; Australia 47
Cornell Dupree - electric guitar; Eric Gale - electric guitar; Richard Tee - Fender Rhodes electric piano; Gordon Edwards - bass; Steve Gadd - drums;

Dave Sanborn - alto sax; Carly Simon - backing vocals; James Taylor - backing vocals.

When Carly received the tape of McDonald's melody, with just the line "You Belong to Me," it took her just fifteen minutes to complete the lyrics. Although they had never spoken during the writing, McDonald rewarded her by sending her a plant, so it was a kind of a bonus when she was given the chance to record it herself with her new producer. This was probably never intended to be about James, but just a frantic girl fighting to avoid losing her lover. *Rolling Stone* described it as a woman playfully giving her errant lover a warm reminder that the actual fear of ruining a relationship is the best way of not letting it happen in the first place. Or, as the great writer Jack Mauro brilliantly observed, she is "waving a contract in her lover's face" so he can observe for himself his own "rotten, faithless signature." Production-wise, it smacks of quality, with a strong rhythmic base and a great solo sax by Dave Sanborn, and once again we also have Carly and James on the backing vocals. A great positive start to the album.

Boys in the Trees *(Carly Simon)* *****
Carly Simon - acoustic guitar, backing vocals; James Taylor - acoustic guitar, backing vocals; Jeff Mironov - acoustic guitar; Richard Tee - piano; Steve Gadd - drums; David Carey - marimba; Harvey Estin & George Marge - soprano & tenor recorders

One of Carly's signature songs about adolescence and sexual awakening, this beautiful operatic title track has all the hallmarks of her songwriting craft. Whenever she looks to her past, especially her childhood, she manages to do so with a gentle intimacy that is both warming and evocative. The frustration of growing up under the doctrine that it was unbecoming and improper for young girls to play with "tree-climbing" boys, but rather to "live like a flower," was seen as a blueprint for eventual womanhood. To be unable to share in the "fruit" of the trees was to deny her own growing sexual desires, leaving her to contemplate whether she should go to them or let them come to her. Although not another outright feminist statement, it remains a candid indictment of what were the social norms of the time, and maybe to some extent even today. Musically, it is as magnificent as it is sparse, with a trio of acoustic guitars emphasizing the swirl of feelings in the song, the effective recorder playing by Harvey Estin and George Marge, and the keyboards and drums, almost going unnoticed in their subtlety. All, of course, underpinning another superlative vocal by Carly. Although the song was earmarked for a single, it was instead chosen as the flip-side to 'Devoted to You'.

Back Down to Earth *(Carly Simon)* ****
Carly Simon - acoustic guitar; James Taylor - acoustic guitar; John Hall - lead electric guitar; Jeff Mironov - electric guitar; Will Lee - bass; Steve Gadd - drums.

Another guitar-driven song with hints that it could be revealing cracks appearing in Carly's marriage to James. If it is, it stands in contradiction to other tracks on the album that are glowing tributes to her husband of over five years. If it's not, it still remains an outstanding track about relationships unable to match up to expectations, and one that will resonate with many couples. The song will appear on the flip-side to the single of 'Tranquillo (Melt My Heart)'. The track also sees the welcome return of bass guitarist Will Lee, who had played on the Simon Sisters' debut album in 1963.

Devoted to You *(Boudleaux Bryant)* ****
Single E-45506 b/w Boys in the Trees
Released - 1978
Billboard Hot 100 #36; Billboard Adult Contemporary #2; Billboard Hot Country Singles #33; Cashbox #48; Cashbox Country chart # 36; Canada #50
James Taylor - acoustic guitar; Hugh McCracken - electric guitar; Richard Tee - Fender Rhodes electric piano; Will Lee - bass; Steve Gadd - drums.
Without any doubt, to hear and even see Carly and James perform this 1958 Everly Brothers 'classic dispels any rumor that all is not well in their relationship. Singing in perfect and blissful harmony, they are expressing their undying love and devotion to one another in what will be the second and last duet of their recording career. Producer Mardin recalled what a magical session it was, and how, to best communicate their feeling of devotion, he had them singing into one microphone. In fact, Carly once stated that they seldom sang together at home.

De Bat (Fly in Me Face) *(Carly Simon)* **
James Taylor - acoustic guitar, vocal arrangement, backing vocals; Rubens Bassini - percussion; Errol "Crusher" Bennett - congas & bass drum; John Hall - backing vocals; Ken Williams - backing vocals; Luther Vandross - backing vocals; Roderick George - backing vocals.
A song with good intentions, but also seen as a little incongruent alongside the album's other songs. Inspired by Carly looking for a bat underneath the beams of the Vineyard house, she puts her playful, calypso-reggae stamp on it. With James providing both guitar accompaniment and vocal arrangement, and with Luther Vandross among the host of backing singers, it's hard to dismiss this as anything other than a bit of fun, and the song will become an audience favorite at future concerts.

Haunting *(Carly Simon)* *****
Ken Bichel - piano; Steve Gadd - drums; Phil Bodner - oboe; Gloria Agostini - harp; Margaret Ross - harp; Alyia Orme - backing vocals; Joanna Simon - backing vocals; Lucy Simon - backing vocals; Marc Embree - backing vocals; Steven Dickson - backing vocals.
Carly often cites this as her favorite track on the album, and it was the first time she had written a song as a tone poem in her head before setting it to a melody. For its inspiration, she once revealed: "At times there are situations that can become desperate, when you can't exorcise a person from your heart. But I don't mind the sensation of falling prey to my emotions." The structure of the song is truly magnificent, with the melody written freely without a background of chord progression; so freely, in fact, that every bar is "like a different time signature." The angelic and ghostly background voices include (for the first time) both

sisters, Lucy and Joanna. Carly and Mardin would later return to the song during the recording of 'Laura' on the album *Film Noir*.

Side 2

Tranquillo (Melt My Heart) *(Carly Simon - James Taylor - Arif Mardin)* ***
Single E-45544 b/w Back Down to Earth
Released 1978
Cashbox # 86
Hamish Stuart - guitar, backing vocals; Onnie McIntyre - guitar; Don Grolnick - Fender Rhodes electric piano, ARP string ensemble; Tony Levin - bass; Steve Gadd - drums; Arif Mardin - horn arrangement; James Taylor - horn arrangement, backing vocals; Carly Simon - backing vocals; Cissie Houston - backing vocals.
Latin-tinged disco-lullaby co-written with James and Mardin and inspired by Carly's 15-month-old son Ben, who was still having his sleepless nights (and still not knowing why), and who was given the nickname Tranquillo, believing it would magically induce slumber. Carly later admitted that the line "Why don't you melt my heart" had been a mistake and she had tried to re-write it, but as the background vocals had already been recorded, it was too late to change it.

You're the One *(Carly Simon)* ****
Cornell Dupree - guitar; Richard Tee - piano, Gordon Edwards - bass; Tony Levin - bass; Steve Gadd - drums; Hamish Stuart - obligatto vocal & backing vocals; Carly Simon - backing vocals; Alex Ligertwood - backing vocals
Heartfelt ballad with Carly affirming her devotion to James at a critical time in their relationship with her husband becoming more aloof as a result of his addiction. *Billboard* observed in its review: "Simon again seems to confront the issue of femininity vs. assertiveness in love relationships." Splendid piano playing by Richard Tee enhances this simple message of undying love.

In a Small Moment *(Carly Simon)* ***
Ken Bichel - electric piano, ARP synthesizer; Stuart Scarf - electric guitar; Tony Levin - bass; Steve Gadd - drums; Joe Farrell - flute; Errol "Crusher" Bennett - percussion.
In a subtle and almost tender way, Carly mentions small indiscretions of her past - taking the credit for someone else's painting at school; short changing a customer while waitressing in a restaurant; and even cheating on a lover - as being nothing more than little lies that "slip on by." But in reality, she is closely observing the larger issue of the adult preoccupations of temptation, deception, and jealousy, all things that she had witnessed from childhood to adulthood, and even now as a wife and mother. Although understated, the lyrics strike the message home without becoming judgmental. Chosen as the flip side to the single 'You Belong to Me'.

One Man Woman *(James Taylor)* ***
Cornell Dupree - guitar; Richard Tee - piano; Gordon Edwards - bass; Steve Gadd - drums; Michael Brecker - tenor sax.
A bluesy James Taylor-penned song about fidelity in which Carly self-mockingly describes what it feels like to be a "one-man woman in a two-time town." With Mardin's tight r&b influence, the bawdy, uptempo number has a rousing sax solo by Brecker, but, surprisingly, no musical input by the song's author. Like the song that follows and closes the album, it brings hope to all failing love affairs that there's still the possibility of a second chance.

For Old Times Sake *(Carly Simon - Jacob Brackman)* ***
Carly Simon - acoustic guitar, backing vocals; Stuart Scharf - acoustic guitar, auto harp; Tony Levin - bass; Arif Mardin - glass harmonica (brandy glasses)
Another song about rekindled love, with co-author Jake Brackman referring to it as being written "by a man writing a song for a girl who is singing to a man."

The cover image for the album was as daring, if not as controversial, as the one for *Playing Possum*. Deborah Turbeville, noted for her images of dancers, had Carly sitting on a chair in a Degas-inspired empty ballet studio, rolling a silk stocking up her right leg, and pictured off-center with the spaciousness of the dance floor dominating the photograph. Although portraying a more feminine than lustful image, it would never escape notice that she was also bare-breasted at the time of the shoot. Both Carly and her manager Arylene saw how this might be misconstrued as sensationalism, and with a little post-re-touching by graphic artists Jonny Lee and Tony Lane, a silky camisole top was cleverly inserted.

Carly was impressed with the production, feeling that with Arif Mardin she had at last found a producer who could put emphasis on her vocals by using a sparser production, and thereby allowing the listener to immerse themselves in the singer's emotional feelings. *Rolling Stone* also praised Mardin's custom-tailored production for what it saw as Carly's "most serene" album to date, and described the "scrubbed-down" Carly as a "mightily seductive creature" singing with "confidence and clarity," with an album of "mature intelligence." *Stereo Review* described it as a "beautifully crafted summation of what she's learned about her real self," with her lyrics having "the sensual smolder of womanliness about them at a time when most young female singers prefer to sound as androgynous as possible."

When released on April 4th 1978, *Boys in the Trees* entered the album charts on the 22nd and slowly climbed to #10 on July 1st, remaining on the charts for 29 weeks. It also became Carly's fourth album to reach the top ten and would go on to achieve gold certification on August 7th, eventually going platinum for sales in excess of one million. The single 'You Belong to Me', backed with 'In a Small Moment', was also released in April and peaked at #6 on the Hot 100 on June 24th, remaining on the charts for 18 weeks. It also reached #4 on Adult Contemporary and #9 on the *Cashbox* chart, while climbing to #5 in Canada.

Carly was also nominated for a Grammy in the category of Best Pop Female Vocalist for her performance on the single, but at the Hollywood ceremony lost out to Anne Murray's 'You Needed Me'. Art directors Johnny Lee and Tony Lane did however win the award for Best Album Package. The second single lifted off the album was 'Devoted to You', released in August with 'Boys in the Trees' on the flip-side, but only managed to reach #36 on the Hot 100 on September 30th, although topping out at #4 on Adult Contemporary.

The pressures of touring

With Elektra again putting pressure on Carly to tour, her manager Arlyne organized seven concerts, all at intimate venues, and all reasonably close to home. In the event, it turned out to be around a dozen shows. This would be her first tour with a band for nearly six years and the musicians chosen were David Spinozza and Queens-born Joe Caro on guitar; Wisconsin-born Warren Bernhardt; her old friend Billy Mernit on piano, clavinet and synthesizer; Tony Levin on bass and tuba; Mike Mainieri on keyboards, percussion and vibes, and Steve Gadd on drums.

That spring Carly and James provided backing vocals on two tracks for Kate Taylor's forthcoming eponymous second album. 'Jason and Ida' was co-written by Kate, while 'Happy Birthday Sweet Darling' was a James Taylor composition. The album was released in May. They also contributed to their friend John Hall's eponymous second album, singing backing vocals on 'The Fault', 'Good Enough', and 'Voyagers'.

On April 16th Carly performed at Villanova University in Pennsylvania, and although appearing timid at first, soon began to feel at ease. During the show she was joined on stage by James to sing 'Devoted to You' and later threw new Pampers into the audience, announcing that her children were not with them, but the Pampers were. On May 4th she did the first of three nights at the Bottom Line in New York, and any anxieties Carly may have had were dispelled by the critics 'reviews. *Rolling Stone* praised "one of the most powerful deliveries of any women in rock," while *The New York Times* simply called it "flawless," and described the image she had chosen as that of an "overtly sexual yet glossily elegant high-fashion stylist," and her intensely personal songwriting as "guarding her inner feelings as much as they reveal them."

On June 5th, while preparing to take the stage at Boston's Paradise Club, Carly became sick, and James had to take her place and perform a short impromptu set with Carly's new band. The following night, still feeling nervous and sickly, Carly gave it her very best with a set that consisted of 'Anticipation', 'We Have No Secrets', 'You Belong to Me', 'De Bat (Fly in Me Face)', 'You're So Vain', 'That's the Way I've Always Heard It Should Be', 'It Keeps You Runnin', 'Devoted To You'(with James) and finally 'Goodnight Irene', the old standard made popular by Huddie Lead Belly and given a new arrangement by James.

That summer, James once more found himself among the wrong crowd with long spells of partying and drug-taking. With him returning to his bad habits, and spending weeks away from home touring with his band, Carly was again left alone to raise her two children. When he did eventually turn up, it would often lead to vicious arguments. But Carly weathered the storm, and did her best to help her husband through these dark times, although there were times when she was in denial, forcing herself not to believe just how serious his addiction had become. She thought of her father, and even felt responsible for James' behavior.

On November 2nd Carly made a guest appearance at a gala concert held at Jones Hall in Houston, hosted by songwriter Burt Bacharach. Carly sang 'I Live in the Woods', a Bacharach composition for which she had co-written lyrics with her friend Libby Titus. Libby also performed 'Riverboat', her own collaboration with the esteemed composer. The concert, which featured the Houston Symphony Orchestra, was recorded and released on Bacharach's next album *Woman* in 1979.

Spy in the house of love

In December 1978 Carly and producer Arif Mardin got together once again to record her new album *Spy* at Atlantic Studios in New York. Not only would it be her final album with Elektra, but it would also be done with little contribution from James, who, apart from some backing vocals, would soon be jetting off to LA for three months, working on his own album *Flag* with his producer Peter Asher. During all the time he was away from home, he rarely got in touch with Carly.

In a 1972 interview Carly confessed: "Would you believe the first thing I ever wanted to be was a spy. I wanted to be involved in espionage. The raincoat and black glasses really appealed to me. I thought that would be a very glamorous career. Mind you, I was only thirteen at the time."

Carly had actually got the idea for the title of her new album from the 1954 novel *I Am a Spy in the House of Love*, written by Anais Nin, the

126

French-born American author of erotic stories who had died the previous year. On the album's inside cover, Carly would write "I am an International Spy in the House of Love." The result was her interpretation of what the effects of a failing marriage would have on a neglected wife and mother. Many would see the songs as being all too personal.

Among some of the new musicians on the recordings were members of her recent touring band, Joe Caro and Warren Bernhardt, as well as Frank Carillo, guitarist and former member of the band Doc Holliday. Mardin once again handled the strings and horns arrangements, while Gene Orloff returned as concertmaster. James would return from LA just in time to contribute backing vocals on several tracks.

SPY
Elektra 5E-506 (UK – K 52147)
Recorded - December 1978 - April 1979, Atlantic Studios, New York
Released - June 12 1979
Producer - Arif Mardin
Engineer - Lew Hahn
Mastering - George Piros, Atlantic Studios, New York
Art direction - Robert Heimall.
US Billboard Pop Albums #45; Canada #56; Australia #33

Side 1

Vengeance *(Carly Simon)* ****
Single E-46051 b/w Love You by Heart
Released - 1979
Billboard Hot 100 #48; Cashbox #52; Canada #94; Australia #90
Joe Caro - electric guitar; David Spinozza - electric guitar; Don Grolnick - piano; John Hall - electric guitar solo; Warren Bernhardt - keyboards; Ian McLagan - keyboards; Tony Levin - bass; Rick Marotta - drums; Steve Gadd - drums; Michael Brecker - tenor sax; David Sanborn - alto sax; Don Grolnick - clavinet; Richard Tee - clavinet; Randy Brecker - trumpet; Tim Curry - backing vocals.
Belting rocker about a couple betraying each other, and seen by some as a final wake-up call for James if he wants the marriage to survive. Carly has never sounded angrier, and Mardin does his very best to give the track the thunderous production it deserves, with a trio of electric guitars, a pair of top-notch drummers, including Rick Marotta, who had last played on *Hotcakes,* three excellent keyboard players, and a fine horn section. British singer and actor Tim Curry, noted for his performance in *The Rocky Horror Picture Show*, provides backing vocals. The song will later feature in a promotional video in which Carly

does her best Tina Turner impersonation with just the right amount of added panache.

Just Like You Do *(Carly Simon)* ****
David Spinozza - electric guitar; acoustic guitar; Ken Bichel - Polymoog synthesizer; Will Lee - bass; Warren Bernhardt - piano; Richard Tee - electric piano; Rick Marotta - drums; Errol "Crusher" Bennett - percussion; David Sanborn - alto sax; Carly Simon - backing vocals; James Taylor - backing vocals; Ullanda McCullough - backing vocals.
Another urging for James to return to that "brave innocence" they had once shared, and letting him know that the vulnerability brought on by his demons is akin to her own phobias and anxieties and that she feels just like him. Carly sounds uncommonly optimistic with the playful lyrics and jazz-infused melody, and, with a twist of irony, has James joining her on the backing vocals. The song had been chosen as the album's first single, but was dropped in favor of 'Vengeance'. Although it's never been made clear which track was written first, this one or 'We're So Close', the one that follows, it does seem that the optimism shown by Carly in the lyrics of this song is clearly not evident in the heartbreaking song that comes next, in which James has now become so emotionally withdrawn from her.

We're So Close *(Carly Simon)* *****
Carly Simon - piano; David Spinozza - electric guitar; Warren Bernhardt - electric piano; Ken Bichel - Polymoog synthesizer; Will Lee - bass; David Sanborn - alto sax; Errol "Crusher" Bennett - percussion.
Carly describes this song as "the most ironic song that I've ever written. It is the saddest because it implies room for so much togetherness and yet it points up to the very long, huge, lonely distances between two people who are supposedly in love." She recalled that she had written the lyrics one day while James had kept her waiting in the car for an hour while he was pulling his boat from the water, and by the time he returned she wanted to read them to him, but something had stopped her doing it. Her candid observations and mournful chords indicate what seemed to be final acceptance that her six-year marriage to James had run its course. It's almost as if she is on a therapist's couch unloading her pain and deepest emotions, with revelations of the on-going emotional conflict of her husband's errant ways and her own yearning for love, affection and even friendship. Carly has produced perhaps the most evocative song of her career, made even more poignant by it being barely a year since she and James sang 'Devoted to You', the seemingly undisputed affirmation of their love for one another. But, with James' continuing addiction, absenteeism, and apparent infidelity, coupled with his accusations that Carly was carrying a small torch for someone else, it was just fueling the fire of mistrust in both parties. As Carly admits in the song with unusual candor, it's gone so far that they can dispense with love altogether. Carly and keyboardist Warren Bernhardt provide some of the finest piano work of her career, and the evocative sax solo by David Sanborn adds just the right amount of feeling to this most sorrowful of songs.

Coming to Get You *(Carly Simon)* **

David Spinozza - electric guitar (solo); Joe Caro - acoustic guitar; Warren Bernhardt - piano; Will Lee - bass; Ken Bichel - synthesizer.

Most unusual song about a family court drama in Arkansas, in which the narrator appears to be the mother of the accused girl in a case that involves a baby. Some commentators allege it's inspired by her friend Libby Titus and her battle with her partner, singer Levon Helm, over custody of their daughter Amy, who had been born in 1970.

Never Been Gone *(Carly Simon - Jacob Brackman)* *****

Richard Tee - electric piano; Arif Mardin - arr. choir; Carly Simon - backing vocals; James Taylor - backing vocals; Lucy Simon - backing vocals.

Carly's homage to the island of Martha's Vineyard, and apparently written during a ferry crossing from the mainland. Once again, Jake was able to work his magic and get a feeling for the affection and emotional ties Carly feels for what had been her spiritual home since childhood. Carly later admits that she wrote the melody while attempting a descant to 'Greensleeves', and on listening to it it's not hard to imagine. With its wonderful hymn-like intro arranged by Mardin, and Richard Tee's sublime piano, Jake's lyrical imagery is perfect for Carly's full-throated contralto delivery, one of her very best, displaying an aching desire to return to her island home and seek solace and emotional support among her welcoming friends. James and Lucy join Carly on backing vocals to share with her their mutual love for the Vineyard.

Side 2

Pure Sin *(Carly Simon - Frank Carillo)* **

David Spinozza - guitar; Frank Carillo - guitar; Tony Levin - bass; Don Grolnick - piano; Warren Bernhardt - electric piano; Cliff Carter - synthesizer; Peter Ballin - alto sax; Lew Del Gatto - baritone sax; Michael Brecker - tenor sax; Randy Brecker -trumpet; Tom Malone - trombone; Richard Cruz - cowbell; Tim Curry - backing vocals.

Co-written by Carly and guitarist Frank Carillo, whose band Doc Holliday had made a string of albums in the early 70s, and who had more recently cut two solo albums. Although it finds Carly in rocking form once again as a woman who refuses to be contained, and has a rather raunchy Stones-style production, it falls short of having the aggressive bite of the album's lead track, 'Vengeance', and was subsequently chosen to be the flip-side for the 'Spy' single.

Love You By Heart *(Carly Simon - Jacob Brackman - Libby Titus)* ****

David Spinozza - electric & acoustic guitar; Warren Bernhardt - electric piano; Billy Mernit - acoustic piano; Tony Levin - bass; Errol "Crusher" Bennett - congas; Raphael Cruz - congas; Carly Simon - backing vocals; James Taylor - backing vocals.

Another attempt by Carly to persuade James to kick his habit and to assure him that only she can "set him straight." With lyrical help from Jake and Libby Titus, this is a beautifully produced ballad, which sees a welcome return of Billy Mernit

129

to add his keyboard skills, and with James joining her on the strikingly well-arranged backing vocals. Surprisingly, the song was selected as the flip-side for the single 'Vengeance'.

Spy *(Carly Simon - James Taylor - Arif Mardin)* ****
Single E-46514 b/w Pure Sin
Released – 1979
Billboard Adult Contemporary #34
Joe Caro - electric guitar; David Spinozza - electric guitar; acoustic guitar; Warren Bernhardt - electric piano; Will Lee - bass; Rick Marotta - drums; Hubert Laws - flute; Carly Simon - backing vocals; James Taylor - backing vocals.
The album's title track is given a disco-flavor and portrays the singer going undercover to "spy" on a man she admires from a distance until she finally wins him, but then continues as an "undercover lover" to reveal if he is living up to his reputation for letting people down. With its fine attention to detail, and with musical input from James and her producer, this is a surprisingly good stab at coming up with a potential hit single, but unfortunately it comes right at the end of the decade, and with it, the demise of disco as the chart-busting genre it had been. Carly might have had her eye on her lover, but if she now had an eye on the charts, she would be sadly disappointed.

Memorial Day *(Carly Simon)* ***
Carly Simon - piano; David Spinozza - guitar; Warren Bernhardt - electric piano; Will Lee - bass; David Sanborn - alto sax; Mike Mainieri - vibraphone.
A graphical account of a marital fight between two of her friends that Carly had witnessed first-hand. When asked to reveal their identities, Carly once replied that it was about taking her drunken drummer home after a concert one morning and then having to watch from her limo as his girlfriend accused him (wrongly) of having an affair with her.

For the album cover, photographer and Vineyard friend Pam Frank chose a film noir black and white portrait of Carly wearing a slouchy fedora pulled down across one eye, to leave her other eye firmly fixed on you.

Meanwhile that spring, James' album *Flag* had been released. It included songs from his music score to the Stud Terkel-Stephen Schwartz Broadway musical *Working*. It reached #10 on the album chart, while his cover of the Goffin-King song 'Up on the Roof' climbed to #28 on the Hot 100 in July. Carly had provided backing vocals on the track 'B.S.U.R (Be as You Are)'.

Carly's last album for Elektra was released on June 12th 1979 and entered the album chart on the 30th, finally peaking at #45 and remaining on the charts for 13 weeks. 'Vengeance', the first single taken from it, and backed with 'Love You By Heart', only reached a modest #48 on the Hot 100 on July 14th, mainly down to radio stations 'reluctance across the country to give it sufficient airplay. The follow-up single, 'Spy', coupled with 'Pure Sin', fared worse, completely missing out on the Hot 100, and only climbing to #34 on Adult Contemporary.

It was all down to the timing. The album had been released when New Wave music was just beginning to sweep over both sides of the Atlantic. The female angst portrayed in many of Carly's songs was no longer cool when compared with the music of artists like Elvis Costello, Talking Heads, Blondie, the Police, the Jam, and the Human League. Much of the new sound had a nervous, agitated feel; the music choppy, with fast tempos and a stop-start structure to the melodies, with heavy use of synthesizers and electronic productions. The singers were often high-pitched, with a distinctive visual style, even geeky and suburban, and would soon find a huge platform with the launch of the new all-music cable channel MTV and the video revolution that would follow in a couple of years.

Even before its launch, Carly had made what was to be her first music video for 'Vengeance', and as expensive as it was, it was rarely seen until two years later when MTV used clips of it in an ad for urging viewers to get stereo sound for their television sets. The single did however earn Carly a Grammy nomination for Best Rock Vocal Performance, Female, although at the following year's ceremony the award went to disco-queen Donna Summer for 'Hot Stuff'. Promotional videos were also made for 'We're So Close', and 'Never Been Gone', both showing Carly performing at the piano, but these too would rarely be shown on the music channel.

In reviewing the album, *Rolling Stone* defined Carly as still being "a confessional singer with patrician reticence," while another reviewer reveled over the album being "aurally palatial and lyrically sophisticated." *Stereo Review* simply stated how the album "thrilled." Although not critically panned, the commercial failure of the album and singles was a bitter pill for Carly to swallow; she now must have been thinking that, after having nearly a decade of relative success, with some spectacular highlights in between, her luck may have been running out.

Elektra/Asylum boss Geffen had retired in 1975 after having being wrongly diagnosed with terminal cancer, and he would not be given a clean bill of health until 1980. Taking his place as president was Joe Smith, who had been instrumental in getting the Eagles on board and would later release their greatest hits album, which would become the biggest selling album in US history. But when it came to shepherding some of his other artists, he proved most lacking, and Carly held him responsible for the failure to properly promote her last few albums.

With her recording career now in some jeopardy, Carly, in her own words, admitted she was "floundering," a young mother of two, almost raising them alone, and now with her already low self-esteem taking another battering. Worst of all, she admitted her marriage to the man she loved was unravelling, and pretending it to be anything different was never going to make it all okay.

Carly was about to enter what would be called her transitional "middle period," a time when whatever decisions she made in both her professional and personal life would be the most important she would ever have to make.

The Simon girls at the piano (left to right - Lucy, Carly and Joanna) © Richard Simon/Peter Simon Photo Archives

The Simon Sisters' debut album, April 1964 © Kapp/Geffen Records

The Simon Sisters in Concert August 1965 © Tony Gale

© Elektra Publicity Photo c1975

Relaxing in her London apartment during the recording of Anticipation,
September 1971 © Jimmy Ryan (previously unpublished)

Los Angeles, November 1971 © Jimmy Ryan (previously unpublished)

Photo shoot © RT Simon/MediaPunch

Carly and James singing "Mockingbird", No Nukes Concert, Madison Square Gardens NY, July 1979 © Everett Collection

Carly with Sally and Ben, Hard Rock Cafe, New York May 1986 © RTN Laubach/MediaPunch

HBO Concert, Martha's Vineyard June 1987 © Maggie Ryan
(previously unpublished)

Receiving the Academy Award for "Let the River Run," Hollywood Shrine
March 29 1989 © Phil Roach

Photo shoot 1997 © John Barrett

Martha's Vineyard 1999 © RT Simon/MediaPunch

Bryant Park Concert, New York May 19 2000 © MediaPunch

The Warner Years

"I am a complicated compound of paradoxes. My life is a jigsaw puzzle where the pieces have been scrambled and I've just started to piece together the outside edges. The inside pieces are still turned on the floor."

No Nukes

The summer of 1979 saw James back on the road with his band. While he was away, Carly put money into a joint project with two locals, George Brush and Herb Putnam, to build a combined restaurant and music venue called the Hot Tin Roof, to be located at the airport on Martha's Vineyard. Opening on June 7th, and affectionately known as "The Roof," it was well-advertised in both *Rolling Stone* and a number of New York and Washington newspapers, and soon attracted many celebrities, including John Travolta, Walter Cronkite (who would later be dating Joanna for a few years before his death in 2009), Jackie Onassis, John Belushi and Dan Ackroyd, and a number of singers like Leon Russell, Martha Reeves and Bonnie Raitt. For Carly, it brought back happy memories of the ambience of the island's old Mooncusser venue, where she had performed as a Simon Sister. Although sold off in 1986 and re-launched and re-named a couple of times, the music venue finally closed its doors in 2012.

On July 20th Carly made a guest appearance on the *Midnight Special*, and two weeks later played at the Robin Hood Del West, Philadelphia's premier arts center. With James now back from his long nationwide tour and supervising contractors still working on the Vineyard home, there now came an opportunity to perform together in front of their largest-ever audience as part of a huge rock charity concert in New York. Earlier in the year, Carly and James had met up with their guitarist friend John Hall, who had played on *Boys in the Trees* and *Spy*. Baltimore-born Hall brought to their attention the government's decision to license the building of nuclear power plants, many of which were to be in dangerous locations near major cities.

On March 16th the release of the movie *The China Syndrome* about safety cover-ups at a nuclear plant unsettled the nerves of many Americans, and just over a week later a partial meltdown occurred at the Three Mile Island plant on the Susquehanna River near Harrisburg, causing a serious radiation leak in what became the country's worst ever nuclear accident.

Hall told them about what had happened at Three Mile Island and about the plans to build another new plant on the Hudson close to where he lived. He announced that, along with singer Bonnie Raitt, they were about to form an artists 'activist group called Musicians United for Safe Energy (MUSE) and he invited Carly and James to attend the forthcoming press conference that had been arranged by New York publicist Danny Goldberg. Although advised by her manager not to attend any political events, Carly agreed to go ahead and she made an eloquent speech in front of a host of reporters on the dangers of radiation if more stringent safety measures were not implemented.

Over the next few months other artists joined the new activist group, including Bruce Springsteen, Jackson Browne, Graham Nash, the Doobie Brothers, David Crosby, Tom Petty, and Chaka Khan, and a series of benefit concerts were planned to raise money for the "No Nukes" anti-nuclear campaign, including five all-star shows at New York's Madison Square Garden from September 19th - 23rd which would now include Carly and James.

Around that time Carly and James also contributed vocals on the title track of John Hall's anti-nuclear album *Power*, a song that Carly would perform with Hall and others at the forthcoming concerts, which were to be directed by Danny Goldberg, Anthony Potenza and Julian Schlossberg.

At the sell-out Garden shows, which preceded a 200,000-strong anti-nuclear rally at the then-empty north end of the Battery Park City landfill, James sang a couple of his own songs with his band, before Carly joined him on stage for a rousing version of 'Mockingbird'. Wearing a green and blue jumpsuit, she gave an electric performance as the two of them sang and danced together, leading to one of the loudest standing ovations of the night. James' band consisted of Don Grolnick on keyboards, Danny Kortchmar and Waddy Wachtel on guitar, Leland "Lee" Sklar on bass, Russ Kunkel on drums, Rick Marotta on percussion, David Sanborn on sax, and Arnold McCuller and David Lasley on backing vocals. After a short anxiety attack backstage, Carly returned with James, John Hall, and Graham Nash to sing a moving version of 'The Times They Are-a Changin', before joining the ensemble with an encore of the Doobies' 'Takin' it To the Streets'.

The triple-live album *No Nukes: The MUSE Concerts for a Non-Nuclear Future*, containing selections from the Garden concerts, was released by Asylum in November 1979, peaking at #19 on the album chart, and certified gold the following year. A video of the concerts was released in 1983 on CBS Fox.

Mainieri makes the difference

Whilst writing new material for another album, Carly severed her ties with Elektra/Asylum, and with the help of manager Arlyne struck a three-album deal with Warner president Mo Ostin, on the understanding that her albums would be heavily promoted. The new label, Warner Records, was another sister company of the giant WEA. With a new label boss, Carly also found herself a new producer in Mike Mainieri, the talented musician who had not only worked with her on her last album, but had been part of her band for her recent solo concerts.

Warner were calling for a contemporary album by Carly to fit in with the changing musical landscape. Carly had no problem rising to the challenge, having already had a history of taking risks and trying out new sounds. This apparent New Wave makeover would be just another chapter in her musical education. In October work commenced on the seductively-titled album *Come Upstairs*. For the next couple of months, she worked with Mainieri on the new songs in a rented boathouse at Vineyard Haven. Fortunately for Carly, recording commenced in New York at the Power Station Studios at 441 West 53rd Street, between Ninth and Tenth Avenues, within easy walking distance from her apartment.

Returning musicians included Tony Levin, Steve Gadd, Don Grolnick, Bill Mernit, and Rick Marotta, who would now be playing drums on all but one of the tracks. The new musicians included synthesizer players Ed Walsh, Larry Fast and Ken Landrum, and guitarists Pete Hewlett and Sid McGinnis. All this indicated that the music on this album would be synthesizer-heavy with none of the lush orchestrations that some of the previous producers had preferred. Mainieri was bringing Carly's music in line with the new decade, and with his collaboration on each track, they were making something quite different from what had gone before.

As the recording of the album was nearing completion in April, Carly was asked to take part in a revival of the ABC cultural program *Omnibus*, in which three well-known artists were asked to do a portrait of her - the legendary Andy Warhol, Larry Rivers, the "godfather of Pop Art," and the French artist Marisol, "the first girl artist with glamor." A promotional video of the song 'Take Me As I Am' was made with clips taken from the program. The show, not aired until July 19th 1981, was presented by actor Hal Holbrook, and was Carly's first appearance on primetime television for five years. Carly chose Warhol's heavily-rouged, screen-print portrait to hang in her New York apartment.

146

COME UPSTAIRS
Warner BSK3443 (UK – K 56828)
Recorded - October 1979-May 1980, The Power Station Studios, New York
Released - June 16 1980
Producer - Mike Mainieri
Engineer - Scott Litt
Mastering - Bob Ludwig, Masterdisk, New York
Art direction - Peter Whorf
US Billboard Pop Albums #36; Canada #86; Australia #43

Side 1

Come Upstairs *(Carly Simon - Mike Mainieri)* ****
Single WBS 49689 b/w Them
Released - Early 1981
Did not chart
Sid McGinnis - lead guitar; Pete Hewlett - electric guitar; Billy Mernit - electric piano, Tony Levin - bass; Steve Gadd - drums; Mike Mainieri - piano, Oberheim synthesizer; Ken Landrum - Prophet 5 synthesizer; Ed Walsh - Oberheim OB-X Synthesizer programming; Carly Simon - backing vocals.
One of Carly's most seductive songs, in which she invites an acquaintance she has known for some years to disrobe and enter her bedroom where she will "give him some fire" and show him her "desire." It's easy to forget that this is a wife and mother enticing you to sin. Driven by a double dose of synthesizers to give it that 80s feel, the result is the perfect way to kick off the new decade with electronic rock, the music of which is co-written with Mainieri (as are all the tracks), and whose voice is probably heard toward the end of the song.

Stardust *(Carly Simon - Mike Mainieri)* ***
Sid McGinnis - lead guitar (soloist); Pete Hewlett - electric guitar; Tony Levin - bass, Rick Marotta - drums; Ed Walsh - Oberheim 8-voice synthesizer programming; Mike Mainieri - Prophet 5 synthesizer; Oberheim OB-X synthesizer; Carly Simon - backing vocals; James Taylor - backing vocals.
Allegedly written about Mick Jagger, someone Carly admitted that she had held a strong fascination for since first seeing him on the *Ed Sullivan Show* as a teenager. If James had issues with that, he certainly didn't think twice about sharing backing vocals with her. Chosen as the original flip-side to the hit single 'Jesse'.

Them *(Carly Simon - Mike Mainieri)* **
Sid McGinnis - lead guitar, backing vocals; Pete Howlett - electric guitar, backing vocals; Tony Levin - bass; Rick Marotta - drums; Larry Fast - synthesizer; Mike Mainieri - Yamaha cp30 synthesizer, backing vocals; Carly Simon - backing vocals; James Taylor - backing vocals; Alex Taylor - backing vocals; Hugh Taylor - backing vocals; Christine Martin - backing vocals; Laraine Newman - backing vocals; Mariah Aguiar.

Humorous look on men as being "aliens" invading the women's world and creating a battle zone with their single-minded, macho views. Another great feminist outburst, but maybe a decade too late to stir up passions. Among the backing singers are James and his brothers Alex and Hugh.

Jesse *(Carly Simon - Mike Mainieri)* *****
Single WBS 49518 b/w Stardust (later released as GWB0399 b/w Take Me As I Am)
Released - July 9 1980
Billboard Hot 100 #11; Billboard Adult Contemporary #8; Cashbox #65; Canada #12; Australia #4
Carly Simon - acoustic guitar, backing vocals; Sid McGinnis - electric slide guitar, backing vocals; Pete Hewlett - acoustic guitar, backing vocals; Don Grolnick - piano; Tony Levin - bass; Rick Marotta - drums; James Taylor - backing vocals; Alex Taylor - backing vocals; Hugh Taylor - backing vocals; Gail Boggs - backing vocals; Sally Taylor - backing vocals.
Infectious mid-tempo rocker which, according to Carly, is about how being crazy for someone can let all "good intentions go to hell," an all-important factor in the ages-old ritual of resisting or capitulating to the charms of the opposite sex. At first, she is disdainful of Jesse, a former lover, who is now back in town, but is afraid she'll let her guard down and be pulled under his spell, which is exactly what happens, to her friends 'dismay. According to Carly this was not what she had first intended the song to be about: "Jesse was originally my son, and I don't know why, I just wanted to write a song about my son at that point. And then it changed into being somebody that I didn't want to have feelings for, and then I realized that my slip was showing." Sid McGinnis's slide guitar is prominent here, with the Taylor brothers again helping with backing vocals, along with a debut for Carly's six-year-old daughter Sally. *Billboard* praised the single: "The melody is simple yet powerful, the words complex and Simon's voice had never been better."

James *(Carly Simon - Mike Mainieri)* ****
Mike Mainieri - piano; Tony Levin - electric fretless bass; Rick Marotta - drums; James Grossman - cello.
Another aching ballad in honor of her husband, and clear indication of Carly's on-going mixed feelings for him. Here she is reminiscing about happier times and maybe still hoping for things to be as they were. Short but bittersweet, the sparse instrumentation includes an evocative soft cello, but it is Carly's wistful delivery that once again steals the show. Chosen as the flip-side of the single 'Take Me As I Am'.

Side 2

In Pain *(Carly Simon - Mike Mainieri - Don Grolnick)* *****
Sid McGinnis - electric guitar (soloist); Pete Hewlett - electric guitar; Tony Levin - bass; Rick Marotta - drums.

Some commentators often refer to the next four songs as a chronicle of Carly's personal battles over the past twelve months. In one of Carly's greatest ever deliveries, she takes the listener completely by surprise, with what first appears to be a gentle ballad before turning into a wild, emotional frenzy of angry outbursts as she looks for answers from her insensitive lover. Some reviewers are critical of how her voice seems distorted, but this is Carly singing from the gut. With music co-written by Mainieri and pianist Don Grolnick, it is Sid McGinnis who provides the blistering guitar solo.

The Three of Us in The Dark *(Carly Simon - Mike Mainieri)* ****
Sid McGinnis - electric guitar; Mike Mainieri - piano; Tony Levin - bass; Rick Marotta - drums; Carly Simon - backing vocals.
"One is all the fire; one is all the spark" - the two bedfellows in this cleverly-written love triangle in which the singer ponders over which one she should choose, husband or secret lover. *Stereo Review* offered that it was perhaps about the memory of a past lover "intruding upon a current relationship, maybe about another, more critical self, doing the same." The *Boston Globe* called it "strangely compelling."

Take Me As I Am *(Carly Simon - Mike Mainieri - Sid McGinnis)* ****
Single WBS4960 b/w James
Released 1980
Billboard Hot 100 #102
Sid McGinnis - electric guitar; Pete Hewlett - acoustic guitar; Mike Mainieri - piano, synthesizer; Tony Levin - bass; Rick Marotta - drums; Ed Walsh - Oberheim synthesizer programming; Carly Simon - backing vocals.
Urgent and anthemic rocker in which Carly pleads for self-acceptance, maybe echoing her earlier image of "Here I am - Look at me now," but on the surface could be another signal to her husband about his infidelity, and how, for him, the grass may have looked greener elsewhere. Another synth-driven track with Carly at full-throttle, and a promotional video done for a television special during the recording gives a fine example of how she can perform with ease in the comfort of a closed soundstage. Chosen as the flip-side to the second single release of 'Jesse'.

The Desert *(Carly Simon - Mike Mainieri)* ***
Sid McGinnis - acoustic guitar, 12-string guitar; Billy Mernit - electric piano; Tony Levin - electric fretless bass; Rick Marotta - drums; Mike Mainieri — piano, synthesizer, marimba; Carly Simon - backing vocals.
The album closes with Carly in contemplation amid a dreamlike landscape of moonlit white sand, with no one around her disturbing her lovelorn solitude.

Carly was impressed with the recording and her work with Mainieri: "He opened my eyes to new tempos that I would've thought too fast for me. It made me see different aspects of my singing style that I would have been

149

closed to before. It feels freer than anything I've ever done before." She also admitted that the album was "more sexual than anything I've ever written; usually I cloak my sexuality in a lot of symbolism."

Come Upstairs was released on June 16th 1980, and in the liner notes Carly gave thanks to French songwriter Jacques Brel for inspiration. For the front cover, veteran British photographer Mick Rock took an image of Carly dressed in a fashionable mauve jacket with wide lapels and padded shoulders, while the rear cover portrayed her in a gold lamé jacket with black lapels, and the wildest of hair obscuring her face. Entering the Pop Album charts on July 12th, it reached #36, remaining on the charts for 32 weeks.

The single 'Jesse', backed with 'Stardust', was released the same day as the album. It eventually received sufficient airplay to get it to #11 on the Hot 100 on November 1st and #8 on Adult Contemporary, before being certified gold on December 5th, Carly's fourth single to do so. But it also proved to be one of the most expensive singles the label had ever made, due to the cost of using independent promoters, and even a figure of $300,000 was once quoted. Another single, 'Take Me As I Am', with 'James' on the flip-side, surprisingly stumbled at #102 on the Hot 100, while 'Come Upstairs', coupled with 'Them', missed out altogether on a chart place when released in early 1981.

The success of 'Jesse' did not rub off on the album, and lack of sales soon led it to being the first of her albums to fall out of print. Reviews were mixed. One recent reviewer wrote: "Simon mined her pain and refined it into nothing short of pure pop artistry." *After Dark* magazine noted Carly's "urgent, provocative edge" and how she was redirecting her musical approach to make her concerts "more accessible." Yet other reviewers felt she had stretched herself too far.

A most unhappy time

Although a summer tour had been planned to promote the album, it had to be postponed for a while when a near-tragedy hit. Around the time of the album's release, Carly's three-year-old son Ben was diagnosed with having a dysplastic kidney, the cause of all the health issues he had suffered since birth. Rushed into a hospital that June, the diseased kidney was successfully removed, but, according to Carly's manager Arlyne, James could not be contacted and only turned up after the operation, having allegedly just driven his girlfriend to the airport. Carly was uncontrollably distraught, until Andrea managed to calm her down. One person who did turn up was Carly's old friend and former neighbor John Travolta, who flew in from

California to support her during the week Ben was in hospital. Carly would remember it as "the worst day of my life," and it proved to be another nail in the coffin for her marriage to James. The next few months would see a steady path to separation.

In September 1980, James flew back to Los Angeles to work with Pete Asher on his next album, *Dad Loves His Work*, which would take until the following January to complete. For Carly, it was now time to honor her agreement with her label to do the tour. With some of her old band members and one or two who had worked on her album, she began a 14-date schedule, playing mostly at theaters. On September 25th she appeared at the Westchester Premier Theater in Tarrytown, New York, followed by performances that included the Tower Theater in Upper Darby, PA, and the Meehan Auditorium at Brown University in Providence RI. It all went to plan until October 4th when she appeared at the Stanley Theater in Pittsburgh. With Lucy coming along to give her support the show got off to a good start, but after a few numbers, Carly began to have a crippling panic attack, and although she tried to carry on with a supportive audience, she finally had to leave the stage. She then collapsed and was briefly hospitalized, with Lucy reassuring her: "There's no reason to have to put yourself through that ordeal ever again."

Years later, Carly confessed: "In retrospect, it was foolish for me to do that tour. My marriage to James was breaking up, my son Ben just had a malfunctioning kidney removed in a serious operation, and I had lost 25 pounds because of stress. I was in terrible shape, emotionally and physically." The rest of the tour was cancelled, with the promoters threatening to sue, but Carly felt humiliated and now looked on her career and personal life as becoming unglued. It all pointed to her having a complete breakdown, and it would be the last time she performed on a stage for seven years.

But making music had to continue. Before the year was out Carly managed to contribute to *In Harmony: A Sesame Street Record*, a Warner compilation of children's music produced by Lucy and her husband David Levine. Carly sang 'Be with Me', while Lucy performed 'I Have a Song'. Also featured was the Doobie Brothers 'version of 'Wynken, Blynken and Nod', which was released as a single and reached #76 on the Hot 100. There was also James' contribution of 'Jellyman Kelly', while Kate and Livingston Taylor, Linda Ronstadt, Libby Titus, Bette Midler, Al Jarreau and George Benson also performed songs. A second compilation, *Harmony 2*, was released early the following year, and featured Carly and Lucy singing 'Maryanne' and James performing 'Sunny Skies'. Both albums would go on to win Grammy Awards for Best Recording for Children.

The year came to an end with devastating news. At 10.50pm on December 8th Carly was in her apartment when she heard what sounded like four distant gunshots. Just one block south, in the entrance to the Dakota Building, John Lennon had just been murdered.

In March 1981 James 'album, *Dad Loves His Work*, was released, and a number of tracks seemed to be heartbreakingly remorseful, as if he was seeking forgiveness for his past behavior as a husband and father. It reached #11 on the Pop Albums Chart. The single 'Her Town Too', was about the aftermath of breaking up a long-term relationship, although James always claimed it was about his producer's recent divorce. Another single, 'Hard Times', was also taken as a message that his marriage was about to end, while on the track 'I Will Follow', he appears to be begging forgiveness for past wrong-doings. It would be another four long years before he would make another album.

In May, a television special *3 Sisters* aired in the US, featuring for the first time glimpses of Carly, Lucy and Joey and clips of home movies. Produced by Catherine Harrington, it was for many fans a first candid glimpse into Carly's childhood and her relationship with her older siblings.

The fine art of heartbreak

Carly's emotional upheavals began to have a marked effect on her career. Although her label and producer were keen to have her writing new material, she was in no state to do so. Instead she came up with the idea of doing an album of sentimental "torch songs," the kind where the singer laments on unrequited or lost love, either where one party is oblivious to the existence of the other, where one has moved on, or where a romantic affair has affected the relationship.

"I didn't know it was the right thing to do. I didn't know that standards were the right thing to record. But I just knew I had a very special relationship with those songs because I'd grown up listening to them, and my mother and father played them, and I was in love with Frank Sinatra.... I simply loved to sing those songs."

But they were not originally going to be torch songs: "It was going to be an album of songs that were of that particular period which is a period of songwriting occurring primarily around the Broadway plays of the 40s and 50s and the motion pictures as well, and as I got into delving into the material I found that most of the material that I liked singing were songs about lost love, the torch songs, the songs about pain and heartache."

When pitching the idea to the Warner executives, there was understandable concern. Rock stars just didn't do this kind of album,

152

although Harry Nilsson's 1973 album of standards, *A Little Touch of Schmilsson in the Night*, had done reasonably well. Carly was not going to be denied, and, in the end, she got her way, and the result was a dramatic move out of the New Wave kinetics and back to full orchestrations.

With Mainieri again at the helm, Carly was able to choose the songs that would best channel her feelings, many familiar to her from her childhood when she either heard them on the radio, or listened as her father played them on the piano: "I remember going to bed singing those songs instead of nursery rhymes. They are songs from the heart, emotions that were easily expressed."

Recording of the album commenced at the Power Station that summer and it proved to be an emotional time for Carly. Inevitably, she found it difficult singing the songs without crying, as they all resonated with what was going on in her personal life. But this was an album she just had to make in order to release some of the emotional stress she had kept suppressed over the last few months. It was to be "a study in the fine art of heartbreak." With many of the musicians on her previous album re-employed, Mainieri enlisted the help of Don Sebesky, Robert Freeman and Marti Paich for the orchestral arrangements. Paich was the father of David Paich, founding member of the band Toto.

TORCH
Warner BSK 3592 (UK – K 56935)
Recorded - Summer 1981, The Power Station Studios, New York
Released - September 29 1981
Producer - Mike Mainieri
Engineer - Scott Litt
Mastering - Bob Ludwig, Masterdisk, New York
Art direction - Bill Gerber & Simon Levy
US Billboard Pop Albums #50: Canada #50; Australia # 77

Side 1

Blue of Blue *(Nicholas Holmes; additional lyrics by Carly Simon)* ****
Hugh McCracken - guitar; Warren Bernhardt - piano; Anthony Jackson - bass; Rick Marotta - drums; David Sanborn - alto sax; Mike Mainieri - arranger; Don Sebesky - arr. orchestration
Not an old song, but nevertheless a great opener, written by Manhattan-born folk singer Nick Holmes and highlighted by David Sanborn's beautiful but urgent alto sax solo. Holmes had performed with the Serendipity Singers in the 60s before joining the prestigious jazz-rock band White Elephant in 1970, the same band that included Mainieri, McCracken, Gadd, Bernhardt, Levin and the Brecker brothers. He wrote and recorded this beautiful ballad, which appeared on his album *Sonar*.

153

He also co-wrote 'What Shall We Do with the Child'. Carly also contributes additional lyrics to set the mood for what follows.

I'll Be Around *(Alec Wilder)* ***
Hugh McCracken - guitar; Lee Ritenour - guitar; Mike Mainieri - arranger; Robert L Freeman - arr. orchestration
Written by Alec Wilder and first published in 1942 it became a well-known standard, recorded by Sinatra in 1955 for his album *In the Wee Small Hours*. A gentle take on the song by Carly, which *Rolling Stone* describes as her "matter-of-fact vow of fidelity to a straying sweetheart."

I Got It Bad and That Ain't Good *(Duke Ellington - P F Webster)* ****
Lee Ritenour - guitar; Warren Bernhardt - piano; Anthony Jackson - bass; Rick Marotta - drums; David Sanborn - alto sax; Mike Mainieri - arranger; Marti Paich - arr. orchestration.
Famous jazz standard with music by Duke Ellington and lyrics by Paul Francis Webster, first published in 1941, and introduced in the musical revue *Jump for Joy*. It was later recorded by Benny Goodman with vocals by Peggy Lee.

I Get Along Without You Very Well *(Hoagy Carmichael)* *****
Single WBS50027 b/w Body and Soul
Released -1981
Did not chart
Mike Mainieri - piano, arranger; Warren Bernhardt - synthesizer; Marti Paich - arr. orchestration.
Composed by Hoagy Carmichael in 1939, with lyrics based on a poem by Jane Brown Thompson, this song about a rejected woman trying to stifle her feelings while confronting her lover was recorded by Red Norvo and his orchestra that same year, with vocal by Terry Allen. Carly often cites this as her favorite among all the standards.

Body and Soul *(Edward Hayman -Robert Sour -Frank Eyton - Johnny Green)* ****
Warren Bernhardt - piano; Eddie Gomez - acoustic bass; Grady Tate - drums; Phil Woods - alto sax; Mike Mainieri - vibraphone, arranger; Marti Paich - arr. orchestration.
Written in 1930 with music by Johnny Green and lyrics by Edward Heyman, Richard Sour and Frank Eyton, and composed especially for British actress Gertrude Lawrence who introduced it to British audiences. It was first performed in America by Libby Holman in the 1930 Broadway revue *Three's a Crowd*. Chosen as the flip-aide of the single 'I Get Along Without You Very Well'.

Side 2

Hurt *(Jimmie Crane - Al Jacobs)* ****
Single WBS49880 b/w From the Heart

Released – 1981
Billboard Hot 100 #106
Warren Bernhardt - piano, arranger; Hugh McCracken - guitar; Anthony Jackson - bass Jerry Marotta - drums; Michael Brecker - tenor sax; Tony Bongiovi - mixing
Written in 1954 and originally a chart hit for Roy Hamilton. It became the signature tune of Timi Yuro in 1961 and also a 1975 hit for the Manhattans.

From the Heart *(Carly Simon)* *****
Warren Bernhardt - piano, arranger; Hugh McCracken - acoustic guitar.
A new Carly-penned song about a failing relationship she compares to a cold war, and maybe held back from the previous album as it appears to be another last-minute plea to James, the husband she can't seem to shake from her mind. A beautiful arrangement by pianist Warren Bernhardt. For Carly maybe there's still a flicker of a flame in the torch. Chosen as the flip-side to the single 'Hurt'.

Spring is Here *(Richard Rodgers - Lorenz Hart)* ***
Warren Bernhardt - piano, David Nadien - violin solo.
A 1938 song with music by Richard Rodgers and lyrics by Lorenz Hart and written for their musical *I Married an Angel.*

Pretty Strange *(John Hendricks - Randy Weston)* ***
Warren Bernhardt - piano, arranger; Lee Ritenour - guitar; Anthony Jackson - bass; Rick Marotta - drums; Randy Brecker - trumpet solo; Don Sebesky - arr. orchestration
Written by jazz lyricist and singer Jon Hendricks and jazz pianist Randy Weston and featured on Hendrick's first album *Good Git-Together* in 1959. Fine trumpet solo by Randy Brecker.

What Shall We Do with the Child *(Nicholas Holmes - Kate Horsey; additional lyrics by Carly Simon)* *****
Jay Berliner - classical guitar, folk guitar; Mike Mainieri - Marimba, arranger
A poignant vignette written by Nick Holmes while a member of folk group, the Serendipity Singers, and released as a single on United Artists in 1968. Many women will resonate with this guilt-driven song about separation and the all-too-often forgotten casualties - the children. One of the most emotional tear-inducing vocals of Carly's career, enhanced by the evocative guitar playing by Jay Berliner.

Not a Day Goes By *(Stephen Sondheim)* *****
Warren Bernhardt - piano, arranger; Don Sebesky - arr. orchestration
Not exactly a standard at the time, this song about the anguish of living through the breakup of a relationship was written by Sondheim for the 1981 Broadway musical *Merrily We Roll Along*, based on a 1934 play of the same name. Carly had visited the composer at his New York apartment and he had played the song for her. He then came to the studio to see her interpretation, and was blown away

155

by her tortured, trembling alto, made even more special with one of Sebesky's finest arrangements.

Later, Carly said: "Stephen was in the studio when I recorded it. He was sitting in the control booth, and I was standing in the vocal booth recording, but I didn't want to see Stephen because it was too scary. So I knelt down and sang the song on my knees. When I finished, I went into the control booth. Stephen had his face in his hands, and he was crying. I thought it was because he didn't like it, but in fact he said he was crying because he was so moved. To this day, when I want to weep, I put on 'Not a Day Goes By'."

For the dramatic cover, rock photographer Lynn Goldsmith portrayed Carly in a low-cut blue blossom gown clinging in ecstasy to the arm of a shadowy figure, turned away from the camera, but played by 26-year-old actor Al Corley, better known for his role as the young Steve Carrington in *Dynasty*. For added effect, the titles also seemed to be written in blood. Carly not only dedicated the album to her parents, musical uncles, and "especially Jonno" (her old deejay friend Jonathan Schwartz), but also to "those who made me cry."

Released on September 29th, *Torch* entered the Pop Album Chart on October 17th and peaked at #50, attaining the same chart position in Canada. The track 'Hurt' was released as a single, coupled with 'From the Heart', but stalled at #106 on the Hot 100. 'I Get Along Without You Very Well' was also issued, backed with 'Body and Soul', but failed to chart. Promotional videos were made for 'Hurt', 'I Get Along Without You Very Well', and 'Body and Soul', although it's not certain how much they were featured on MTV.

But Carly had pulled it off. She was both pleased and proud of the album, and she had a right to be, and dismissed the idea that she had risked her career by doing it: "I'll never not take risks again. I've not taken risks in the past and I've been disappointed with myself." The critics loved the album, especially her "carefully syncopated phrasing" and how she performed the songs "with an art singer's awareness."

But sophistication didn't necessarily lend itself to successful sales, and Warner were instructed by boss Mo Ostin not to promote the album in order to persuade Carly to go back to writing new material. Two years later, he saw it had been a misjudgment, when his own signing Linda Ronstadt had a huge hit with *What's New*, the first of a trilogy of albums of old standards, reaching #3 and staying on the charts for an incredible 81 weeks.

Separation

But what of the future? In a rare televised interview that year, Carly jokingly gave a hint: "The next album I do is likely to be even more of a risk than this one. I could see myself doing an album of Irish drinking songs from the 15th century." Although Carly had no regrets doing *Torch*, with all that had been going on in her life, she now had reached a point where she had no big plans for her music career. But she did have plans when it came to her marriage, and when James returned from a summer tour promoting his latest album, she took it upon herself to set the ball in motion and announce that they were to separate. James had had a string of affairs and had made no secret of the fact he had a girlfriend, and now Carly, too, was being comforted by the new man in her life, actor Al Corley, who she had embraced on the cover of *Torch*. Kansas-born Corley was eleven years her junior and had been given his big break in the first season of *Dynasty* when it was aired in January.

Carly later reflected on that time: "A rock and roll star going on the road being faithful to his wife? How many people do I know who are? It shouldn't have been a surprise to me, but it was and it burst a bubble, whether it was a fantasy that I was hoping would exist in reality."

Dozens of headlines and articles now appeared in magazines and newspapers, with Carly once again appearing on the cover of *Rolling Stone* with the headline: "Carly: Life Without James." On December 10th she was interviewed at her home for the magazine and confessed, "We failed in the context of marriage, but not as people."

During the year Carly sang 'Fight for It' with Jesse Colin Young on his album *The Perfect Stranger*, written by Young and Wendy Waldman and produced by Michael James Jackson. Young was best remembered as a founder and lead singer of the band the Youngbloods in the 70s. The song was released as a single on Elektra in July. Carly also made a couple of television appearances. In November she appeared in the special *Marvin Hamlisch: They're Playing My Songs*, along with Gladys Knight, Johnny Mathis, and Liza Minelli, and sang 'Nobody Does It Better' with Marvin at the piano. That same month she guested on the late-night talk show, *Tomorrow Coast to Coast*, hosted by Tom Snyder.

1982 came and went with Carly coming to terms with the separation, and trying to get her life back together. With no new album planned, no touring or band to worry about, she now returned to her idea of writing music for movies, but doing so in the comfort of her Vineyard home, and then having them recorded at a nearby studio. But before she had the chance to actually compose music for a film, she was offered another chance to perform. On March 7th she was invited to take part in an episode of the

PBS television series *Great Performances*, called 'Ellington -The Music Lives On', and in a fitting nightclub setting performed a sultry version of one of her favorite standards, 'I've Got It Bad and That Ain't Good'.

Carly goes disco

Later that spring Carly was approached by former New York session musicians Nile Rodgers and Bernard Edwards, who had formed a band called Chic, and had recently helmed and written the songs for Sister Sledge's smash album, *We Are Family*. They were currently working on the soundtrack to the Marvin Worth-produced sexy rom-com *Soup for One*, starring Saul Rubinek and Marcia Strassman. With Chic, Teddy Pendergrass, Debbie Harry, and Sister Sledge already on board, Carly was commissioned to sing a Rodgers - Edwards song called 'Why', an infectious, bittersweet reggae-tinged ballad that was unlike anything Carly had sung before.

Having been given vocal coaching by the producers on how they felt it should be sung, and with Carly keeping an open mind to what they suggested, it resulted in one of her most passionate vocals to date. Both movie and the soundtrack album were released at the end of April, and in the summer 'Why' was released as a single on Mirage Records, a subsidiary of Warner, with Chic's instrumental version on the flip-side. Although the movie flopped, the single had mixed success, only reaching #74 on the Hot 100 on October 2nd, and #73 on *Cashbox*, but doing better in Europe, where it climbed to #10 on the UK chart, and, as a 12-inch extended mix released in May 1989, became a Mediterranean dance-floor classic, peaking at #56 in the UK. A promotional video was also made showing Carly walking the sidewalks of the city and flirting with passers-by and café goers.

Why *(Bernard Edwards - Nile Rodgers)* ****
US 7-inch Single Mirage WTG 4051 b/w Chic -Why (live version)
UK 7-inch Single WEA K79300 b/w Chic - Why (live version)
UK 12-inch Single WEA/Mirage U-7501T/257 500-0 (extended version) b/w
Chic - Why (inst) & Carly Simon - Why (edit)
Recorded - Spring 1982 New York
Released - August 1982 (UK 12-inch May 1989)
Producers - Nile Rodgers & Bernard Edwards
Billboard Hot 100 #74; Cashbox #73; UK #10
Nile Rodgers - guitar, arranger, conductor; Bernard Edwards - bass, arranger, conductor; Tony Thompson - drums; Sammy Figueroa - percussion; Raymond Jones - keyboards; Robert Sabino - keyboards

One reviewer of 'Why' praised "the perfectly balanced backing beat with enough funk in the groove to keep it moving, while still maintaining that sentimental mood to Carly's lovely longing vocals...This is pure perfection." For the single's picture sleeve, photographer friend Lynn Goldsmith had a wonderfully-tanned Carly posing like an Amazonian jungle-woman with her signature wild, feathery hair.

Around this time, she also contributed backing vocals for the song 'Lonesome Ranger' on Nils Lofgren's album *Wonderland*, released that year on Backstreet Records.

Toward the end of the summer Carly had the chance to write and perform a song for the Larry Peerce-directed movie *Love Child*, a biopic of Terry Jean Moore, a young prisoner who falls in love with a guard and becomes pregnant, starring Golden Globe-winner Amy Madigan with Beau Bridges. The sympathetic ballad 'Something More' was co-written with Charles Fox, who had to his credit the music for Roberta Flack's hit, 'Killing Me Softly with His Song'. The song was released as a promotional single by the Ladd Company in 1983.

Last album for Warner

With new-found confidence following the movie song and the success of 'Why' in Europe, Carly was now better prepared for *Hello Big Man*, which would be her last album for Warner, and she now got to work on completing new material in the comforting surroundings of her Vineyard home. In the meantime, Warner thought Mainieri was no longer the right person to give Carly a successful commercial album, and, although Carly disagreed, it meant she now had to find a new producer. At first, she offered the job to British engineer and producer Glyn Johns, who had worked on the Eagles' first two albums, and more recently on Eric Clapton's *Slowhand* album and his hit single 'Wonderful Tonight'. She flew off to Compass Point Studios in Bermuda to work with him on the songs, but it proved to be an unhappy relationship, and, with the album now delayed for some time, it was eventually decided to bring Mainieri back to do the job.

Recording began at the Power Station in New York toward the end of the year, with strings laid down in Los Angeles, and then final mixing at Right Track in New York. Some of the songs would actually be written in the studio. This time the label wanted a more contemporary sound, and, once again, Mainieri brought together the best available musicians. Among the newcomers were Peter Wood, the English keyboardist who had co-written Al Stewart's 'Year of the Cat', guitarist Dean Parks, who had co-founded the jazz-fusion band Koinonia, and Jimmy Bralower, a gifted session drummer. Also dropping in for some of the sessions were two guitarists - Andy Summers of the British band the Police, and Elliott Randall, noted for his amazing solo on Steely Dan's hit, 'Reeling in the Years'.

The seemingly risqué title of the new album was actually inspired by the idealized story of how Carly's parents had first met at Simon & Schuster in the mid-30s. Although James Taylor would play no part in the recording, his siblings Kate and Hugh would again be given the chance to contribute vocals, as well as Carly's daughter Sally and five-year-old brother Ben, who would be making his recording debut.

HELLO BIG MAN
Warner 1-23886
Recorded - December 1982 - May 1983, The Power Station, New York (additional recordings at Village Recorders and Ocean Way Studios, LA).
Released - September 20 1983
Producer - Mike Mainieri
Engineers - Neil Dorfsman & Scott Litt
Art direction - Paula Greif
US Billboard Pop Albums #69; Billboard Hot 200 #140

Side 1

You Know What to Do *(Carly Simon - Jacob Brackman - Peter Wood - Mike Mainieri)* ****
Single 7-29484 b/w Orpheus
Released - 1983
Billboard Hot 100 #83; Billboard Adult Contemporary #36
Don Grolnick - piano; Andy Summers - electric guitar; Elliott Randall - electric guitar solo; Hugh McCracken - acoustic guitar; Tony Levin - bass; Rick Marotta - drums; Jimmy Bralower - electronic drums; Mike Mainieri - synthesizer; Peter Wood - synthesizer; Larry Williams - synthesizer, flute; Carly Simon - backing vocals; Tawatha Agee - backing vocals; Marcus Miller - backing vocals; Fonzi Thornton - backing vocals.
According to Carly, this sexually frank song was the most difficult one to record. With a music track composed by Mainieri and synth-player Peter Wood, it was originally imagined as a swing song, but then it was decided to give it a Police-style beat, thanks to Grolnick's piano and Summers' trademark pop-reggae style electric guitar playing. With that, the song developed into something quite different, with lyric changes by Carly and Jake and a new arrangement that included a memorable bass line, synthesizer riff, and echoing backing vocals. With Carly's electrically-charged vocals added, it resulted in it becoming the album's lead single and clear indication to what the label was looking for. Despite

160

having some positive reviews, *Rolling Stone* took a dim view of the song, calling it a "terribly calculated stab at trendy synth-pop."

Menemsha *(Carly Simon - Peter Wood)* ***
Peter Wood - piano; Hugh McCracken - electric guitar; Tony Levin - bass; Rick Marotta - drums; Don Grolnick - drums; Mike Mainieri -chimes, marimba; Rob Mounsey - programming, adult backing vocals; Carly Simon - adult backing vocals; Hugh Taylor - adult backing vocals; Kate Taylor - adult backing vocals; Lynn Goldsmith - adult backing vocals; Julie Levine - kids backing vocals; Sully Taylor - kids backing vocals; Ben Taylor - kids backing vocals; Elizabeth Witham - kids backing vocals; Rachel Zabar- kids backing vocals.
Carly's tribute to the little Vineyard fishing village where as a teenager she shared a cottage with her boyfriend Nick Delbanco, and a chance to experiment both lyrically and musically by giving the song a sensual West Indies flavor: "The song is a little memoir about how the place used to be and about a boy I used to know, and I wanted to write a chant." Carly showed pianist Peter Wood a photograph of the village and between them they wrote the song. To make it more of a family reunion, Carly had both Sally and Ben (making his recording debut), Lucy's daughter Julie, Kate and Hugh Taylor, and Carly's friend Lynn Goldsmith, joining others on the vocal chants at the end. The identity of the Peter mentioned in the song may remain a mystery, unless, of course, it's Carly just substituting the name for Nick.

Damn You Get to Me *(Carly Simon)* ***
Carly Simon - acoustic guitar, backing vocals; Don Grolnick - piano; Hugh McCracken - electric guitar; Tony Levin - bass; Rick Marotta - drums; Marti Paich - arr. strings; Hugh Taylor - backing vocals; Kate Taylor - backing vocals.
Although it was often said that on this song Carly's guitar playing sounded like she had picked up some of the style of James, that's where any connection with him ends, as this seductive song is probably not intended to be about him, but about her new beau Al Corley. Beautiful choral vocals by Kate and Hugh at the end. Chosen as the flip-side to the single 'Hello Big Man'.

Is This Love? *(Bob Marley)* ***
Don Grolnick - Hammond organ; Eric Gale - electric guitar; Robbie Shakespeare - bass; Sly Dunbar - drums; Errol 'Crusher" Bennett - percussion; Leon Pendarvis - arr. horns; Michael Brecker - tenor sax; Ronnie Cuber - baritone sax; Lou Marini - alto sax; Jon Faddis - trumpet; Alan Rubin - trumpet; Carly Simon - backing vocals; Tawatha Agee - backing vocals; Marcus Miller - backing vocals, Fonzi Thornton - backing vocals.
Peter Simon had always wanted his sister to record a Bob Marley song and a couple of years before had given her a backing track to this 1978 hit single from the album *Kaya* for her to sing along to. Although initially unimpressed with the song, she later listened again to this and other reggae tunes, and she decided to record it. For that reason, she wanted to get drummer Sly Dunbar and bassist Robbie Shakespeare on board. The Jamaicans were well respected as a production duo and a celebrated reggae rhythm section, and Carly managed to track them

down in the Bahamas and bring them up to New York. The result is the unusual pairing of Carly's almost operatic alto voice and an exquisite taste of Jamaican funk. The recording was done in just two hours, giving time for her and Robbie to write and record a new song 'Just a Good Boy'.

Orpheus *(Carly Simon)* *****
Jimmy Ryan - acoustic guitar; Mike Mainieri - synthesizer, piano, bass; Rick Marotta - cymbals, tom-tom; Jimmy Bralower - electronic drums.
Carly once commented that instead of taking weeks or even months to write a song, it could happen in just ten minutes. This was just one example, and another of her favorite songs. According to Carly, the inspiration came from her children, with Sally now studying Greek mythology at school and Ben sharing an interest in it too. The legend of Orpheus and Eurydice is perhaps one of the most beloved of the ancient myths, and it is little wonder that the story of love, passion, and the weakness of the human spirit so fascinated Carly. For those not familiar with the tale, Orpheus was the son of the Greek God Apollo, who taught him to play the lyre to irresistible perfection. Orpheus falls in love and marries the beautiful Eurydice, but soon after she is bitten by a snake and dies. Apollo advises his grief-stricken son to descend to the underworld to find her. Protected by the Gods he presents himself to Pluto, and by charming everyone with his lyre, is allowed to take Eurydice back with him, but with the caveat that on leaving he is never to look back at her until they returned to the light, or she will descend back into Hell and be lost forever. Of course, he does glance back at the last minute, and as she murmurs a final farewell, she dies once more and is gone. Eurydice never reproaches Orpheus, but dies with the knowledge of his unconditional love for her. This ancient melodrama about Eurydice's plight struck a chord with Carly and resonated with what had been going on in her personal life: "I wanted to be her voice and to tell Orpheus how mad I was...to say, 'Orpheus, goddam you. Why did you blow it? Why did you look back? Why did you lose faith?'" Carly sees the parallels, both past and present. It resonated with her childhood and her dying father, and how she had lost and regained faith in her belief that he did really love her. But she also saw that ending her relationship with James and moving on, although leaving her deeply regretful, had given her the faith to accept that it was his behavior that had left her with no choice. When Carly pleads with him, "It was there for us," it is echoing Eurydice's heartbreak of seeing how Orpheus gave way to temptation and as a result lost her forever. Not so much a song, but a fine work of art, taking its rightful place among Carly's greatest ever compositions, with incredible lyrics and haunting music, the latter beautifully enhanced by the superb acoustic guitar playing by her longtime friend Jimmy Ryan. Sadly, the song was relegated to just being the flip-side to the album's lead single.

Side 2

It Happens Everyday *(Carly Simon)* *****
Carly Simon - acoustic guitar; Hugh McCracken - acoustic guitar; Dean Parks - electric guitar; Don Grolnick - piano; Peter Wood - Memory Moog synthesizer; Tony Levin - bass; Rick Marotta - drums; Marti Paich - arr. strings.
With its universal theme of a relationship falling apart, Carly once again reflects on the disintegration of her own marriage to James, and recalled in an interview how her friend Al Corley had put her in a room, closed the door, and told her not to come out until she had written a song. Inspired by her love for the Everly Brothers, her double-tracked voice perfectly emulates their famous sound, and Mainieri's production is excellent, although Carly failed in her attempt not to have Marti Paich's strings added, which she felt gave it an unintended country-feel. On the 2009 album *Never Been Gone* Carly recalls that the lyric was one she paraphrased "all the long-winded philosophical ideas I've ever had about breaking up."

Such a Good Boy *(Carly Simon - Robbie Shakespeare - Mike Mainieri)* ****
Eric Gale - electric guitar; Sid McGinnis - electric guitar; Robbie Shakespeare - bass, backing vocals; Sly Dunbar - drums; Errol "Crusher" Bennett - percussion; Carly Simon - backing vocals.
With lyrics written by Carly immediately after the recording of the track 'Is This Love?' Mainieri and bass player Robbie Shakespeare came up with the music to create this bouncy reggae ditty, allegedly about how James 'new girlfriend was thought to have a controlling influence on him.

Hello Big Man *(Carly Simon - Peter Wood)* *****
Single 7-29428 b/w Damn You Get to Me.
Released - 1983
Did not chart
Hugh McCracken - acoustic guitar; electric guitar; Marcus Miller - bass; Peter Wood - synthesizer, piano; Mike Mainieri - additional synthesizer; David Sanborn - alto sax; Carly Simon - backing vocals.
The oft-told story of how Carly's parents first met each other at the offices of Simon & Schuster remains just as poignant when transformed into song by Carly. Over the years she had tried writing a number of songs about her parents, but none of them worked out. Now, some twenty years since her father passed away, she felt good about what she had produced. Working again with keyboardist Peter Wood, who co-wrote the music, it still proved a little difficult to write the last verse, trying to separate what were the realities of her parents' later relationship with the more fantasized version she wanted to portray. In the end it was her undying love for them both that led to her romantic vision winning the day: "Everybody wants that to be true of their parents. So why can't I make that a fantasy? That's the way I wanted their lives to go out. I wanted them to go out in romantic splendor. To live happily ever after."

You Don't Feel the Same *(Carly Simon)* ****
Carly Simon - electric guitar, backing vocals; Tony Levin - bass; Jimmy Bralower - electronic drums.

163

Another remorseful ballad about losing James, asking him to stay one more time when in reality she knows he's already gone. Almost a one-woman show by Carly, with her incredibly strong lead vocal, her own double-tracked background vocals, and her ultra-rare electric guitar playing.

Floundering *(Carly Simon)* **

Hugh McCracken - electric guitar; Don Grolnick - Hammond organ; Tony Levin - bass; Rick Marotta - drums, Peter Wood - synthesizer; Errol "Crusher" Bennett - percussion.

A cheerful reggae tune in which Carly pokes fun at a middle-class woman and self-help addict, who seeks a cure from therapists for a non-existent condition and is thereby left "floundering" in the process. With her own history of therapy, this may appear a little self-mocking, but if it is, she's having a lot of fun doing it.

Divorce the final word

The stylish image of Carly on the album cover is attributed to former fashion model Lynn Kohlman, now a well-respected fashion photographer, and it gave the singer that certain iconic chic look whilst still retaining warmth and humility. Many saw the album as a welcome return to the folk-based songwriting that had made her popular in the early 70s. *Rolling Stone*, although critical of some tracks, summed up saying it was once more worth giving the singer some attention.

Around the time the album was completed, Carly heard that James was filing for divorce. It came as a shock, as she had heard that he had been clean for some time now, and had asked him several times to come home and start over. Carly would blame his girlfriend, who she referred to as a "fierce woman," for dispelling any doubts he may have had about getting back together with his wife. Legal proceedings got under way, and in the settlement that followed, James gave Carly the still-unfinished Vineyard house, while he moved into an apartment near to Carly's New York home to be close to the children. He also bought land at Chilmark on the Vineyard, and had a house built for him and his wife-to-be. The divorce was finalized on August 31st 1983. Carly would now be calling her Vineyard home Hidden Star Hill.

Hello Big Man was released on September 20th. Although critically praised, it proved to be another disappointment for the label, reaching #69 on the old *Billboard* Pop Album chart, and stalling at #140 on their new Hot 200 album listings on October 8th, remaining on the charts for 17 weeks. The first single, 'You Know What to Do', backed with 'Orpheus', received little airplay and stalled at #83 on the Hot 100 and #36 on Adult Contemporary. A follow-up single, 'Hello Big Man', coupled with 'Damn You Get to Me', flopped completely.

164

Three promotional videos were made. The most successful in terms of its exposure on MTV was the voyeuristic 'You Know What to Do', directed by Dominic Orlando, which had Carly being watched as she bathed in a swimming pool, and then nervously searching in the woods for the intruder who then chases and catches her in his arms. It was her first in a string of dramatic rather than performance videos produced over the next few years. The nostalgic 'Hello Big Man' acted out the meeting of her parents with clips of home movies, and featured Al Corley, but was almost ignored by the media. Finally, 'It Happens Everyday', directed by Michael Oblowitz, was set in Munson's Manhattan diner with sister Joanna appearing as a waitress, Sally playing the younger Carly, and Libby sitting at the bar. Carly wanted 20-year-old actor Matt Dillon to play her lover, but figuring he was too young, opted for twins Richard and Paul Garcia, the 34-year-old owners of the diner. This video was shown in movie theaters as "coming attractions."

In the summer of 1983 Carly was persuaded by her friend, photographer-turned-singer Lynn Goldsmith, to collaborate on a song called 'Kissing with Confidence' for her forthcoming New-Age album, *Dancing for Mental Health*, which she was producing for Island Records. Under the pseudonym of Will Powers, Lynn used a voice recorder to make her sound like a man to provide the spoken parts, with Carly doing the singing. Co-written by Lynn and an impressive list of collaborators in Jake Brackman, Nile Rodgers, Todd Rundgren, and Steve Winwood, the single was released in August and reached a respectable #17 in the UK charts. Carly's excellent vocals remained uncredited (either for legal reasons, or perhaps at her own request), although there could be no mistaking it was her. The album was released in the US but failed to chart.

Three albums, all with disappointing sales, convinced Warner not to renew Carly's contract. Around the same time, she also lost her manager, when Arlyne Rothberg decided to move out to Los Angeles to become the manager of budding actress Roseanne Barr. Although worried about an uncertain future, Carly's spirits were lifted when she parted with Al Corey and embarked on a relationship with her old friend, drummer Russ Kunkel.

New label, new manager

Later that year, Carly signed up to the management team Champion Entertainment, run by the astute Tommy Mottola, who now managed to strike a one-album deal with Epic Records, a subsidiary of CBS. The new album, her twelfth, was to be called *Spoiled Girl*, and rather than choosing just one producer, there ended up being a total of eight, including some of the best pop and dance producers in the business. One familiar face was Carly's old friend Paul Samwell-Smith, who had produced *Anticipation* and was now brought in to work on what would be the second single. The other producers enlisted were Don Fagenson (aka Don Was), who had recently formed the band Was (Not Was); Brit Arthur Baker, who had worked with Queen, supervised dance remixes for Cyndi Lauper and Bruce Springsteen, and had produced 'I.O.U.' by Freeez, one of the year's biggest dance hits; Phil Ramone, a studio wizard renowned for his use of innovative technology; George Smith, an accomplished guitarist who had recently worked with Hall & Oates; bass player Tom "T-Bone" Wolk, well known to Carly, having already played on some of her earlier albums; singer-songwriter and multi-instrumentalist Andy Goldmark; and, finally, her current drummer-partner, Russ Kunkel. All of these musicians would produce at least one of the tracks on the new album. Another familiar face was engineer Frank Filipetti who was a proponent of surround sound and had worked well on the mixing for *Hello Big Man*. He was destined to play a large in Carly's future career.

Carly was unsure whether this diverse collection of mostly unfamiliar producers would work, but Mottola believed it was just what was needed to make a more commercial album.

One day in 1984, Carly took up an invite by Simon & Schuster's chief executive Richard Snyder to visit the offices in New York where her father had helped to build the publishing empire. She took along her two children and on eventually meeting, he looked down at Sally and Ben and asked them if they would like to work for his company one day. According to Carly, he then said, "Well, if your grandfather had been smart, this could have been yours." It was a jaw-dropping moment Carly would never forget.

Let the dance begin

In April of that year, Carly was again invited to perform a song for a movie. *Swing Shift* was a wartime rom-com directed by Jonathan Demme, and was perhaps more notable for kick-starting the long-standing relationship of its stars, Kurt Russell and Goldie Hawn. The song chosen was 'Someone Waits For You', with lyrics by the gifted Will Jennings (famous for his Oscar-winning lyrics on 'Up Where We Belong', and 'My Heart Will Go On') and music by Australian composer Peter Allen, also an Oscar-recipient for his work on 'Arthur's Theme (Best That You Can Do)' for Christopher Cross. The song was especially written for Carly and produced by her old friend Richard Perry, who knew this sumptuous, cabaret-style, waltz-tinged kind of song would perfectly match her strong, emotive voice. It served as a precursor to the kind of songs that Carly would embrace later in her career. A promotional single was released in the US on Perry's own label, Planet Records, a subsidiary of RCA.

Work on Carly's new album would begin in the late summer of 1984 and recording would take place in four separate New York studios - Right Track Recording near Times Square; Electric Lady, where Carly had cut her first album; the Hit Factory, where *Hotcakes* had been completed; and finally Arthur Baker's own newly-created Shakedown Sound. Among the new musicians were keyboardist John Fiore, who had just started his career as frontman of the arena rock band Preview, drummer Mickey Curry, formerly of the Scratch Band, guitarists John McCurry and Ira Seigel, keyboard player David LeBolt, well-known for his recent work with David Bowie and Billy Joel, and bass player Neil Jason.

Meanwhile, on September 16th, Carly and James both featured in the acclaimed television documentary *In Our Hands*, along with Lucy, Pete Seeger, Joan Baez and Peter Yarrow. Directed and produced by Robert Richter and Stan Warnow, it used a host of volunteer cameramen to film the largest peace demonstration in US history, held in New York on June 12th 1982, interweaving interviews of performers, actors, activists, and individual marchers with down-to-earth scenes of the massive gathering.

SPOILED GIRL
Epic FE-39970 (UK – EPC 26376)
Recorded - 1984-1985, Right Track Recording, Electric Lady Studios,
Shakedown Sound, & The Hit Factory (mixing) New York
Released - July 2 1985
Producers - Arthur Baker, Andy Goldmark, Russ Kunkel, Phil Ramone, G E Smith, Paul Samwell-Smith, Don Was & "T-Bone" Wolk
Engineers - Frank Filipetti, David Theoner, Dave Whitman & Andy Wallace.
Mastering - Ed Stasium, Track 5
Cover design - Allen Weinberg
US Billboard Hot 200 #88; Canada #96; Australia #97

Side 1

My New Boyfriend *(Carly Simon)* ***
Single Epic 34-05596 b/w The Wives Are in Connecticut
Released - 1985
Recorded - Right Track Recording, New York.
Producer - Paul Samwell-Smith
Engineer - Frank Filipetti
Did not chart

Robby Kilgore - electric guitar, keyboards; Jimmy Bralower - drum programming; Carly Simon - backing vocals; Paul Samwell-Smith – backing vocals; Andy Goldmark - backing vocals; Lucy Simon - backing vocals; Ron Taylor - backing vocals.

Bright uplifting song to open what will be an essentially dark album, and a little affirmation of love from the re-bound girl for new drummer-boyfriend Russ Kunkel. At the helm in the studio was Carly's old friend Paul Samwell-Smith, who she hadn't worked with since *Anticipation* in 1972. Andy Goldmark also stepped in to provide additional backing vocals with Paul, Carly's sister Lucy, and actor Ron Taylor.

Come Back Home *(Carly Simon - Jacob Brackman - Aaron Lael Zigman - Jason Scheff - Guy Thomas)* ***
Recorded- Right Track Recording New York.
Producer - Don Was
Engineer - Frank Filipetti
Ira Siegel - guitar; Robby Kilgore - keyboards; Mickey Curry - drums; T-Bone Wolk - bass; Carly Simon - backing vocals; Gordon Grody - backing vocals; John Fiore - backing vocals; Ula Hedwig - backing vocals.

A mid-tempo rocker about a plea for a nameless wandering lover to return, produced by Don Was and co-written by Carly and Jake, along with input from Aaron Zigman, who had written a string of hits for the Jets; Jason Scheff, later bass player and singer in the band Chicago; and staff songwriter Guy Thomas. Although the song was a solid candidate for single release, the label passed it by.

Tonight and Forever *(Carly Simon - Eddie Schwartz)* ****
Recorded - Right Track Recording New York.
Producer - Phil Ramone
John McCurry - guitar, backing vocals; David LeBolt - keyboards; Neil Jason - bass; Russ Kunkel - drums; Carly Simon - backing vocals; Lucy Simon - backing vocals; Rory Dodd - backing vocals; Eric Troyer - backing vocals

A fine wedding song with words and music co-written with Canadian singer-songwriter Eddie Schwartz, who had contributed to the smash hit 'Hit Me with Your Best Shot' for Pat Benatar. An outstanding production from the soon-legendary Phil Ramone, with his growing reputation for using innovative studio technology. This is Carly celebrating her recent engagement to Russ Kunkel, who plays drums on the track. The intricate backing vocals include both Carly and Lucy. A missed opportunity here to capitalize on it, as it could have been better promoted with a video and been a wedding standard for decades to come.

Spoiled Girl *(Carly Simon - Russ Kunkel – Bill Payne)* ***
Recorded - Right Track Recording New York
Producer - Russ Kunkel
John McCurry - guitar; Bill Payne - keyboards, synthesizer; Russ Kunkel - drums; Kate Taylor - backing vocals. Lottie Golden - backing vocals.

Rocking track produced, co-written and played on by Carly's new beau Russ Kunkel, about a selfish rich girl who has everything but gives her guy nothing but the runaround. In a later interview Carly was quick to point out that the song was not about her.

Tired of Being Blonde *(Larry Raspberry)* ****
Single Epic 34-05419 b/w Black Honeymoon
Released -1985
Recorded - Electric Lady Studios, New York
Producers - G E Smith & Tom "T-Bone" Wolk (additional production - Frank Filipetti & Arthur Baker)
Engineer - Frank Filipetti
Billboard Hot 100 #70; Billboard Adult Contemporary #34; Cashbox #63#
Australia #95
G E Smith - electric guitar; T-Bone Wolk - bass; Robby Kilgore - synthesizer; Russ Kunkel - drums; Jimmy Bralower - drum programming; Carly Simon - backing vocals.
With two producers with different styles, it was never going to be easy going for Carly, especially when the new label insisted that the first single was to be a song that she hadn't written herself, but penned by Memphis songwriter Larry Raspberry, former lead vocalist and guitarist of the 60s band the Gentrys. With the lyrics written in the third person, it had Carly's vocal seemingly uninvolved and detached. However, the story of a woman escaping from a loveless relationship, coupled with the subsequent impressive promotional video, would do Carly no harm at all, as it was given much radio and MTV exposure.

Side 2

The Wives Are in Connecticut *(Carly Simon)* *****
Recorded - Right Track Recording, New York
Producer - Phil Ramone
Engineer - Frank Filipetti
John McCurry - guitar, backing vocals; David LeBolt - keyboards; Neil Jason - bass; Liberty DeVito - drums; Eric Troyer - backing vocals; Rory Dodd - backing vocals.
Witty and upbeat song about the carnal goings-on in the Constitution State, and a philandering husband, "sly with his eyes," who has the tables turned on him twenty-fold by his ultra-cheating wife, whose list of potential affairs reads like a trade directory, with special attention given to the man who works the carousel. There are no generalizations here, as Carly namechecks towns all across the state with carefree abandon. Producer Phil Ramone called it "the biggest piece of salt ever poured on a wound." The music is not to be ignored, with Billy Joel's longtime drummer, Liberty De Vito, setting the finger-tapping beat with his customary energy, but it's Carly's electrifying lyrics and the attention she gives to the not-so-funny subject of adultery that soon will bring her to the attention of film director Mike Nichols and author Nora Ephron, who will be inviting her to compose the soundtrack to the movie *Heartburn*. For that reason, this would-be novelty track suddenly becomes one of the most important songs of Carly's career. Chosen as the flip-side of the single 'My New Boyfriend'.

Anyone but Me *(Carly Simon - Arthur Baker - Stuart Kimball)* *****
Recorded - Shakedown Sound Studios, New York
Producer - Arthur Baker
Engineer - Andy Wallace
Carly Simon - synthesizer, backing vocals; Jimmy Ryan - electric guitar; Arthur Baker - DMX keyboards; Stuart Kimball - acoustic guitar, keyboards; Doug Wimbush - bass; Russ Kunkel - drums; William Beard - Simmonds drums; Bashiri Johnson - percussion.
With music composed by producer Arthur Baker and guitarist Stuart Kimball, this is Carly showcasing the depth of her vocal range in an outburst of sheer raw jealousy over her man's past lovers, wishing she had been the only one, and also flirtatiously trying to make him see their lust for one another is still strong. Some may look at this as being about her ex-husband, but with her reference to "one of the world's great lovers," it allows another little mystery to foster the interest of both fans and the media alike. One of Carly's steamier performances, in which she seems to be almost growling out the message to her man. A great production piece by Baker, and also the welcome return of Carly's great friend Jimmy Ryan on electric guitar.

Interview *(Carly Simon - Don Was)* **
Recorded - Shakedown Sound Studios & Right Track Recording, New York
Producer - Arthur Baker
Engineer - Andy Wallace
Ira Siegel - guitar; Fred Zarr - keyboards, bass synthesizer, Lin drum programming; Bashiri Johnson - percussion; Jeff Smith - sax; Robby Kilgore - strings; Cindy Mizelle - backing vocals; Stephanie James - backing vocals; Tina B - backing vocals.
Carly turns the table on a star-struck interviewer, giving sensual lies for answers, and flirtatiously asking him the questions. With music by her close friend Don Was, the three excellent backing singers include Tina B, wife of producer Arthur Baker.

Make Me Feel Something *(Carly Simon)* ***
Recorded - Right Track Recording, New York
Producer - Andy Goldmark
Engineer - Frank Filipetti
Robby Kilgore - synthesizer; Andy Goldmark - arranger, synthesizer, Lin drum programming; Russ Kunkel - drums
A song about a woman who is emotionally in a state of numbness brought about by living alone with no romantic notions to make her feel alive, leaving her "much too young to feel this old." A great little production number by Andy Goldmark, who plays synthesizer along with Robby Kilgore.

Can't Give It Up *(Carly Simon - Andy Goldmark)* ****
Recorded - Electric Lady Studios, New York
Producer - Andy Goldmark
Engineer - Frank Filipetti

Ira Siegel - guitar; Robby Kilgore - synthesizer; Mickey Curry - drums; Andy Goldmark - synthesizer, Lin drum programming, backing vocals; Luther Vandross - backing vocals.

Carly's inability to stand up to unwanted desire, affirming the inescapable hold love has over her. Another fine production job by Goldmark, who also contributes the music to Carly's lyrics, and notable for another guest appearance on backing vocals by Luther Vandross, now on the cusp of a great solo career. This song was the final track on the original vinyl release.

Black Honeymoon *(Jacob Brackman - Carly Simon - Andy Goldmark)* *****
Cassette & compact disc release only
Recorded at Right Track Recording. New York
Producer - Andy Goldmark
Engineer - Frank Filipetti
Jimmy Ryan - guitar; Robby Kilgore - synthesizer; Andy Goldmark - synthesizer, electric drum programming; Tony Levin - bass; Russ Kunkel - drums; Mallett - percussion

Although released as a flip-side to the 'Tired of Being Blonde' single, amazingly this superb song was not considered good enough to make the album, and only as an afterthought was included on both the cassette version and what became the first compact disc release of a Carly album that same year. An example of misjudgment perhaps, as this is one of the best Carly-Jake collaborations, written around 1975, and now with additional music for the chorus by producer Goldmark. Dark and hauntingly atmospheric, this tale of deceit and jealousy is simply Carly at her stunning best and could have graced every previous album since *Playing Possum* and been chosen as its lead single.

The cover image of Carly by acclaimed rock photographer Duane Michals was actually taken in her New York apartment before the album had been given its title or the title song had been written, but it shows an angst-ridden Carly dressed in mini-skirt and off-the-shoulder top standing in a darkened doorway. With the light falling just on her face and naked shoulder, she has one hand holding her head, and the other seemingly reaching out for you and pulling you in to share in whatever melodrama is about to unfold. It had all the hallmarks of a spoiled girl feigning a drama to gain a reaction. It couldn't have been more perfect.

Two promotional videos were released. The first was for 'Tired of Being Blonde', directed by the British actor Jeremy Irons, who was on vacation with his actress-wife Sinead Cusack when asked by Carly to direct the video, having already been fascinated with his role in the television classic *Brideshead Revisited*. Shot in September, the video comprised a variety of vignettes with Carly donning various wigs and outfits. 'My New Boyfriend', directed by Jeff Stein and Kathy Dougherty, featured Carly in three different roles - Egyptian-queen Cleopatra, complete with a barge full of bare-chested slaves; a scantily-clad jungle goddess dancing around with native cannibals as Alex Taylor is about to get boiled in a stewpot; and finally, as a futuristic beauty in love with a robot. It was filmed in Menemsha, with local friends and members of the Taylor family serving as willing extras. Often judged as a misguided attempt to get extra airtime on MTV, which in fact had limited success, the videos at least showed Carly giving them both her very best shot.

The black sheep album

Spoiled Girl was released on July 2nd 1985, just a week after Carly celebrated her 40th birthday. Entering the Hot 200 on July 20th, it stalled at a disappointing #88, and only reached #96 on the Canadian album chart. The single 'Tired of Being Blonde', with the wonderful 'Black Honeymoon' on the flip-side, reached #70 on the Hot 100 on July 20th. But the follow-up single 'My New Boyfriend', backed with 'The Wives Are in Connecticut', proved another chart failure.

Some critics saw the album as Carly's nadir, the "black sheep" of her creative output. Despite praising the feisty, uninhibited music as being "the most listenable for years," *Rolling Stone* derided the lyrics, describing Carly's characters as just "clichés," and the album being "utterly inconsequential." In a later review it went on to call the album a "debacle," in which her voice "whines," her melodies "stall," and her lyrics "reek with contempt for herself and her men." *The New York Times* was more sympathetic, calling it a "spicy, lighthearted romp of a record." A deluxe edition of the album would be released in 2012 with bonus tracks.

Carly admitted: "If you make a record that's true to yourself, and you love the work, it can't be a flop. It can only sell poorly." Looking back, she recounted: "I didn't set out consciously to make a modern record, but to take what is most attractive about the sounds coming out now and to play with the juxtaposition between sounds that are terribly human and terribly synthetic," but later confessed that, although acknowledging the strength of the individual songs, it failed to "work all together…It's so disparate."

Beginning with *Playing Possum*, Carly had been trying to shake off the mantle of just being another of those "singer-songwriters" stuck in 70s mode by experimenting with and expanding on new sounds that both she and her label hoped would dovetail nicely into what was currently cool and hip. It was taking risks, risks that could do permanent damage to a career, but Carly always rose to the challenge and gave it one hundred per cent. It also meant having complete faith in her label, her producers and her own confidence. There are some shining moments on *Spoiled Girl*, but some of

172

the producers put too much effort into giving Carly much more than what was necessary, with overblown arrangements that conflicted with the singer's primary intentions, and even tripping over one another when working on the same track with their different approaches. Carly would be making no more albums for Epic.

One consolation was the fact that she and Russ Kunkel were now engaged, and over the next few months he was becoming a comforting and encouraging presence in her life. Unfortunately, it would not last.

During the year Carly made another venture into the movie business when she wrote and performed the song 'All the Love in the World' for the closing scenes of Thomas Wright film *Torchlight*, starring Pamela Sue Martin and Steve Railsback, about a young couple's marriage becoming unhinged by the husband's addiction to drugs. Although the movie bombed, its theme must have resonated strongly with Carly.

In June 1985 the rom-com movie *Perfect* was released, starring John Travolta and Jamie Lee Curtis. In the movie Carly makes a cameo appearance as herself, and on seeing Travolta in a crowded restaurant, goes up to him, saying, "I read that shit you wrote about me!" and then throws her drink in his face. Meanwhile, one of the songs Carly had written for *Spoiled Girl* had come to the attention of two very influential people. One was a movie director and the other a writer of romantic fiction. It would prove to be another turning point in Carly's career.

Comeback Carly

"The kids to me are really the essence of my life... Being a mother for me has really provided me with more joy than anything my career ever has"

Nora's Heartburn

With the disappointment of *Spoiled Girl* now behind her, the summer of 1985 would prove to be another defining moment in Carly's career, and it came with a call from her friend and close neighbor Mike Nichols, the film director, to write the score for his new Paramount movie, *Heartburn*. Carly had known Nichols and his wife Diane Sawyer, the CBS news anchor and correspondent, for a number of years, and Nichols had already made his name in Hollywood for directing the Oscar-winning movies *Who's Afraid of Virginia Woolf* and *The Graduate*.

Starring Meryl Streep and Jack Nicholson, the screenplay was written by Nora Ephron, and was based on her novel of the same name, a semi-autobiographical account of her failed marriage to Watergate reporter Carl Bernstein, who had a well-publicized affair with Margaret Jay, daughter of former British prime minister James Callaghan. Carly was a huge fan of Ephron's work, and this story of betrayal and redemption was a chance for her to return to the kind of sentimental songwriting that was her forte. Nichols wanted a song that ended the otherwise depressing plot with a sense of hope that love could come around once more, and had been impressed with Carly's spirited narrative of 'The Wives Are in Connecticut' on her latest album.

Meanwhile, 1986 had begun with the tragic news of the Challenger space shuttle disaster on January 28th. Schoolteacher Christa McAuliffe, one of the seven astronauts that perished, had been a huge fan of Carly's music and had announced in a press conference that she was taking some of her cassettes into space. In her honor, Carly would later contribute songs, including the haunting 'You're Where I Go', to the 2006 television documentary *Christa McAuliffe; Reach for the Stars*, narrated by Susan Sarandon.

The beginning of the year also saw another of Carly's songs written and performed for a movie, when the ballad 'Two Looking at One' was included on the soundtrack to John Avildsen's sequel *The Karate Kid, Part II*, released in June. Co-written with Jake Brackman and produced by Bill

Conti, it featured a distinctive electronic keyboard emulating the sound of Eastern music, an instrument that Carly would embrace for future albums. Unfortunately, in the movie, the song was never going to eclipse the subsequent success of Peter Cetera's powerful, Grammy-nominated, and chart-topping ballad 'The Glory of Love'.

Carly and Jake also provided the lyrics for the wonderful song 'It's Hard to be Tender', the theme song of the CBS television mini-series *Sins*, with music written by French composer Francis Lai. The series starred Joan Collins and was adapted from Judith Gould's novel of the same name, about a woman who survives the horrors of the Nazi occupation of France to make her name in the fashion world. The series premiered on February 2nd and the song was released as a single in Europe on the Phillips label, with Lai's 'Face to Face with the Mirror' on the flip-side.

With the focus back on *Heartburn*, Carly worked alongside Ephron to get inside the minds of the characters she portrayed, and collaborated with Nichols to see how best to give it an emotional punch. As a result, Carly delivered to them one of her finest ever compositions. Carly's boyfriend Russ Kunkel was also instrumental in guiding her along with the music and maintaining her self-confidence in what she was doing. For inspiration, Carly once again turned to a story from Greek mythology. Sisyphus, the King of Corinth, infamous for his behavior and twice cheating death, was punished by Zeus by eternally having to roll a huge boulder up a hill in the depths of Hades, leaving us with the moral to never give in to failures, but accept them the same way we do our achievements, and never give up until our full potential is realized.

To echo that sentiment in the lyrics, Carly remembered the old nursery rhyme 'Itsy Bitsy Spider' (also known as 'Incy Wincy Spider'), and the fable of the little arachnid continually climbing up a water spout, only to be washed out each time by the rain. Carly saw these two stories as a double analogy, relating to the wife in the movie who is trying time and time again to prop up a marriage that she sees is constantly faltering and slipping away. Nichols loved the sentiment, and with a little of his input, they came up with theme for the chorus and the title of the song, 'Coming Around Again'. With four producers on board - Russ Kunkel, Bill Payne, Paul Samwell-Smith and George Massenburg - the two versions of the song were recorded at Right Track Recording and the Power Station in New York.

In the movie, released in July 1986, the music is played over the opening credits, and clips of the song repeated throughout the movie, with the spider version sung over the closing credits as Meryl's character boards a plane with her children to begin a new life. The film was a critical success, eventually grossing $25 million in the US.

175

Signing with Arista

On July 19th Carly was invited to sing at the wedding of Caroline Kennedy to Edwin Schlossberg at Hyannis on Cape Cod and she performed the Dixie Cups ''Chapel of Love' and her own 'The Right Thing to Do'. During the reception, Carly got chatting to the bride's twice-widowed mother, Jacqueline Onassis, and the two of them hit it off immediately with their shared stories of love and conquests, thus kindling a close friendship that would last for years.

That summer, Carly also recorded the song 'If It Wasn't Love' for the Garry Marshall rom-com movie *Nothing in Common*, starring Tom Hanks and Jackie Gleason. Written by Kathy Wakefield and Patrick Leonard, and produced by Leonard, it was included on the soundtrack album released on Arista in July. The song was also featured on the 12-inch release of 'Coming Around Again' in 1986 and included as a bonus track on the Hot Shot re-issue of the album *Coming Around Again* in 2017.

Meanwhile, Clive Davis, the former Columbia supremo who had once tossed one of Carly's demo tapes across his office floor, had now become president of Arista Records. One day he got to hear 'Coming Around Again', and it made him realize that he had let an incredibly gifted singer slip through his fingers. Now he saw Carly as a solid investment and went out of his way to get her on board with a lucrative deal that would hopefully take her to a new level of commercial and creative success, and secure her music career for the next decade.

Clive Davis was now well known for nurturing the careers of female singers, having recently taken a young Whitney Houston under his wing. In the new songs Carly was now bringing to him, he saw both maturity and sophistication, something that perhaps had passed him by all those years ago. He was a totally hands-on executive producer, personally hiring and firing producers, overseeing every aspect of the recording process, from laying down basic tracks to the final mixing, and he was wise enough to know not to interfere with how she wanted to interpret her songs. He knew only too well he was dealing with someone quite special, an incredible woman who had spent nearly seventeen years in the business, and who probably knew as much about the recording process as he did.

Carly was now entering a phase of her career when she was at the top of her game as a songwriter. Gone were the days when she tried to keep up with the changing music trends and remain "cool." All she had to do was be herself, writing and recording the kind of introspective songs that meant so much to her, and once again work with a label boss who now appreciated and admired what she was doing.

The single 'Coming Around Again', backed with 'Itsy Bitsy Spider', was released by Arista on October 12th 1987 and became Carly's twelfth US top 40 hit, peaking at #18 on the Hot 100 on January 24th. It also climbed to #5 on Adult Contemporary and #38 in Canada. When released in the UK the following January it reached #10 on the singles chart. The picture sleeve featured a photo taken by Lynn Goldsmith of a relaxed Carly wearing a black dress and sitting next to her guitar, the first record cover to feature her favored musical instrument. The wonderful promotional video for the song featured Carly and a guest viewing some home movies of her childhood and proved a big hit on MTV.

So romantic, so bewildering

Recording the album *Coming Around Again*, built around the theme and success of the single, would involve a number of New York studios, with one track completed in Vancouver. There would be nine producers for the eleven tracks, including the familiar Frank Filipetti, Russ Kunkel, Bill Payne, Richard Perry, and the most welcome addition of Paul Samwell-Smith, who was specially flown in from London. Rob Mounsey was a keyboard player with the band Joe Cool, which also consisted of former sessionists Will Lee and Jeff Mironov, and had played at Simon and Garfunkel's 1981 concert in Central Park. John Boylan had worked for Epic and had produced albums for Charlie Daniels and the Little River Band before forming his own company, Great Eastern Music, while George Massenburg owned a pioneering audio electronics company. Frank Filipetti had been one of the engineers who worked on *Spoiled Girl* and now was becoming an integral part of Carly's recordings. Finally, Bryan Adams, the "groover from Vancouver" had already carved himself a place as one of Canada's finest rock singers and was currently working on his latest album, *Into the Fire*.

Apart from the producers, returning musicians included Jimmy Ryan, Hugh McCracken, Michael Brecker, Tony Levin, Robby Kilgore, Neil Jason, John McCurry and T-Bone Wolk.

Among the new musicians on the album were Scottish-born keyboardist John-Peter Vettese, former member of the band Jethro Tull, and New York jazz player and composer Scott Martin. There was also Jimmie Maelen, one of the "first call" percussionists in New York who had famously played on Barry Manilow's 'Copacabana' and the Doobies ''What a Fool Believes'. Sadly, he would succumb to leukemia in just eight months 'time. Another new face was Barbara Markay, a Julliard graduate pianist, becoming perhaps the first female session musician to appear on one of Carly's albums.

COMING AROUND AGAIN
Arista ARCD 8443 (UK – 208 140)
Recorded - 1986-1987, Right Track Recording, The Power Station, & Unique Recording, New York; Cliffhanger Studios, Vancouver
Released - April 13 1987
Producer - Bryan Adams, John Boylan, Frank Filipetti, Russ Kunkel, George Massenburg, Rob Mounsey. Bill Payne, Richard Perry and Paul Samwell-Smith
Executive producer - Clive Davis
Engineers - George Massenburg, Frank Filipetti, Richard Alderson; Bryan Adams; Tim Crich. Neil Dorfsman, Chris Lord-Alge, Ed Stasium, Bill Miranda & Leon Pendarvis.
Mastering - Ted Jensen, Sterling Sound, New York
Art direction - Howard Fritzson
US Billboard Hot 200 #25; UK Album Chart #25

Side 1

Coming Around Again *(Carly Simon)* *****
Single Arista AS1-9525 b/w Itsy Bitsy Spider
Released - October 12th 1986
Recorded - Right Track Recording & The Power Station, New York
Producers - Russ Kunkel, George Massenburg & Bill Payne, with Paul Samwell-Smith
Associate producers - Carly Simon & Frank Filipetti.
Engineers - George Massenburg & Frank Filipetti.
Mixing - Frank Filipetti
Billboard Hot 100 #18; Billboard Adult Contemporary #5; UK Singles Chart #10; Canada #38; Australia 29
Carly Simon - keyboards, backing vocals; Scott Martin - keyboards, backing vocals; Bill Payne - keyboards; Russ Kunkel - drums; Terry Hornberg - backing vocals; Paul Samwell-Smith - backing vocals
The title song and spiritual anchor of this superlative album, and Carly's biggest chart hit since 'Jesse'. The simple story of a middle-class wife going through life's daily rituals while her marriage is falling apart is the product of a singer now herself in her 40s, and one that will resonate with women of a certain age considering whether their relationships can be saved. By setting the scene for the album's optimistic theme of love lost and love regained, the wonderful song stands in stark contrast to the dance-pop sounds of *Spoiled Girl*, and is like a rebirth for the artist. There's no need for experimenting here; this is Carly returning to what she does best - writing warm and captivating songs about love, aimed solely at a rejuvenated adult contemporary pop market, thanks to the huge success of bands like Fleetwood Mac, Foreigner and Dire Straits. Carly conjures

178

up incredible images in her lyrics - paying the grocer, spoiling a soufflé, mending a broken toaster, breaking a window - and you can almost hear the woman "scream a lullaby." *Rolling Stone* praised the song as being an "emotional seesaw teetering between composure and despair" and a "portrait of embattled upper-middle-class domesticity." The brilliant writer Jack Mauro, a great friend of Carly's, best sums it up: "The bare bones of a circumstance are laid out, the music is haunting and lovely, and the two elements combine to make a sum too magnificent to be expected from any two parts."

Give Me All Night *(Carly Simon - Gerard McMahon)* *****
Single Arista AS1-9587 b/w Sleight of Hand (UK - Arista RIS 8 b/w Too Hot Girls)
Released – 1987
Recorded - Right Track Recording, New York
Producer - Paul Samwell-Smith
Associate Producers - Carly Simon & Frank Filipetti
Engineer - Frank Filipetti
Mixing - Frank Filipetti
Billboard Hot 100 #61; Billboard Adult Contemporary #5; Cashbox #70; UK Singles Chart #98; Canada # 87
Peter-John Vettese - keyboards; Hugh McCracken - guitar; Tony Levin - bass; Russ Kunkel - drums; Frank Filipetti - Linn drum; Jimmy Bralower - percussion; Carly Simon - backing vocals.
Intoxicating and lustful song about a woman tenaciously craving a full and unconditional night of passion from her lover, with no half-measures. With music composed by English-born singer-songwriter Gerald McMahon, this became the first single lifted from the album ('Coming Around Again' having already been previously released), and serves as another fine example of Carly's songwriting, with so much emotional detail put into just two verses, a short bridge, and an explosive chorus that simply oozes sexual desire. Also, another great production number from her old friend Samwell-Smith.

As Time Goes By *(Herman Hupfield)* ***
Recorded - Right Track Recording, New York
Producer - Rob Mounsey
Associate Producers - Carly Simon & Frank Filipetti
Engineers - Frank Filipetti & Richard Alderson
Rob Mounsey - MIDI (musical instrument digital interface) piano, programming, drum programming, conductor & arr. strings; Jimmy Ryan - guitar; Russ Kunkel - drums; Stevie Wonder - harmonica; David Nadien - concertmaster.
Although another cover, this great timeless song fits nicely into the overall feel of the album. Written by Hupfield for the 1931 Broadway musical *Everybody's Welcome*, it was famously covered by Dooley Wilson in the 1942 movie *Casablanca*. What makes it a welcome addition is not that it's redefining the song in any particular way, but instead perfectly showcasing Carly's incredible vocal talents, and with Mounsey's production and the added bonus of having Stevie Wonder's iconic harmonica at the end, it manages to maintain the spirit of the

179

album. Nevertheless, it had its critics, with *People Weekly* seeing Carly as "in one of her scatting moods," and "wandering all over the place." The song was chosen as the flip-side to the single 'The Stuff That Dreams Are Made Of'.

Do the Walls Come Down *(Carly Simon - Paul Samwell-Smith)* ****
Recorded - Right Track Recording, New York
Producer - Paul Samwell-Smith
Associate Producers - Carly Simon & Frank Filipetti
Engineer - Frank Filipetti
Mixing - Frank Filipetti
Carly Simon - acoustic piano, backing vocals; Russ Kunkel - drums; Jimmy Bralower - percussion; Michael Brecker - EWI (electronic wind instrument); Paul Samwell-Smith - E-Mu emulator (digital sampling synthesizer), Linn drum, backing vocals; Peter-John Vettese - backing vocals; Lucy Simon - backing vocals.
Another fine production from Samwell-Smith, who also co-authored the music with Carly and perfectly melded it with her exquisite bittersweet poetic lyrics about a woman pleading for access to a former lover who could be lowering his guard and remembering his feelings for her, or could also be concealing them so as not to let them out at all. Although its heavy use of synthesizers may deter some, it still remains for many a remarkable vocal showcase.

It Should Have Been Me *(Bryan Adams - Jim Vallance)* ****
Recorded - The Power Station, New York & Cliffhanger Studios, Vancouver.
Producer - Bryan Adams
Associate Producers - Carly Simon & Frank Filipetti
Engineers - Bryan Adams, Tim Crich & Neil Dorfsman
David Pickell - keyboards; Keith Scott - guitar; Dave Taylor - bass; Mickey Curry - drums; March LaFrance - backing vocals
One of four cover versions on the album. At the insistence of Clive Davis, Carly was asked to record a song written by Canadian rocker Bryan Adams and his longtime collaborator Jim Vallance, and first recorded by Neil Diamond for his 1986 album *Headed for the Future*. Not to be confused with the song of the same title performed by both Gladys Knight and Yvonne Fair, this mid-temp rocker was produced by Adams using his own band of musicians and completed in his home town of Vancouver. Apparently, Adams proved a difficult producer for Carly to get along with, insisting she try to emulate the voice of Steve Perry from the band Journey. Of course, Carly would have none of it, but what she finally delivers is another blazing vocal done in her own inimitable style, and a sure-fire hit if anyone had had the enterprise to release it as a single.

Side 2

The Stuff That Dreams Are Made Of *(Carly Simon)* *****
Single Arista AS1-9619 b/w As Time Goes By
Released - 1987
Recorded - Right Track Recording, New York

Producers - Russ Kunkel & John Boylan
Engineer - Frank Filipetti
Mixing - Frank Filipetti
Billboard Adult Contemporary #8; UK Singles chart #99
Carly Simon - Yamaha DX7 synthesizer; Jimmy Ryan - guitar; Rob Mounsey - acoustic piano, keyboards, arr. strings & conductor; Russ Kunkel - drums, drum machine; Timothy Wright Concert Choir - backing vocals.
Where 'Coming Around Again' gives hope that love once lost will return, this gorgeous ballad is about realizing that the love sought may never have gone away. According to Carly, it was written for her restless assistant who was bored with her marriage and about to leave her husband for "the temporary relief of passion." She urges her to think again, not to be envious of others, and take another look at what they already have. The wonderful backing vocals at the end are supplied by the celebrated gospel ensemble known as Timothy Wright's Concert Choir. The grass-always-seems-greener message has never been addressed in such an inspiring and heartfelt way, with high quality production values and Carly in splendid form, especially on the bridge.

Two Hot Girls (On a Hot Summer Night) *(Carly Simon)* *****
Recorded - Right Track Recording, New York
Producer - Paul Samwell-Smith
Associate Producers - Carly Simon & Frank Filipetti
Engineer - Frank Filipetti
Mixing - Frank Filipetti
Peter-John Vettese - keyboards; Hugh McCracken - guitar; Tony Levin - bass; Frank Filipetti - Linn drum; Michael Brecker - sax; Carly Simon - backing vocals; Jimmy Ryan - backing vocals; Lucy Simon - backing vocals.
Carly relates a true story of how she and her friend Jenny got dressed up and went into Oak Bluffs on the Vineyard "to see and be seen." During the night they were joined by one of Carly's friends who began to hit on Jenny. Carly recalls: "I felt invisible. I immediately began to resent a great friend with whom there had been no previous evidence of rivalry. It's a complicated emotion and one that needed to be looked at." Another great Samwell-Smith production and the most unusual track on the album. With the narrative style she had grown accustomed to in writing sensitive ballads, Carly uses four verses and a bridge before the final chorus which has "something quite different when all the facts are on the table." Michael Brecker once again adds his sultry sax, while Lucy joins Carly on the delicate choruses. *The New York Times* called it "quintessential Carly Simon," but identified how "psychologically complex" it appeared beneath the surface, while *Rolling Stone* claimed it to be one of her "most confused and cluttered songs." Chosen as the flip-side to the single 'All I Want is You'.

You Have to Hurt *(Frank Musker- Dominic King)* ****
Recorded - Right Track Recording, New York
Producer - Paul Samwell-Smith
Associate Producers - Carly Simon & Frank Filipetti
Engineers - Frank Filipetti, Chris Lord-Age & Ed Stasium

Mixing - Frank Filipetti

Robbie Kilgore - keyboards, programming; Jimmy Ryan - guitar, backing vocals;
Neil Jason - bass; Chuck Kentis - add. keyboards, string synthesizer; Hugh
McCracken - tiple (chordophone); Frank Filipetti - drum machine programming;
Jimmy Bralower- drum machine programming; Paul Samwell-Smith - backing
vocals, Caz Lee - backing vocals; Will Lee- backing vocals.

Written by the British songwriting partnership of Frank Musker and Dominic
King (aka Dominic Bugatti), this song has all the hallmarks of a Carly original
thanks to the fine work done by the teamwork of Samwell-Smith and Frank
Filipetti, but it's Carly who adds her personal touch to Musker's rather
impersonal lyrics.

All I Want Is You *(Carly Simon - Jacob Brackman - Andy Goldmark)* ****
Single Arista AS1-9653 b/w Two Hot Girls (UK - Arista RIS 47 b/w You Have
to Hurt)
Released - 1987
Recorded - Unique Recording & Right Track Recording, New York
Producer - John Boylan
Associate Producers - Carly Simon & Frank Filipetti
Engineers - Frank Filipetti, Chris Lord-Age & Bill Miranda
Mixing - Chris Lord-Age
Billboard Hot 100 #54; Billboard Adult Contemporary #7; Cashbox #68
Robbie Kilgore - keyboards, programming, synthesizer; John McCurry - guitar;
Jimmie Maelen - percussion; Andy Goldmark - keyboards, drum machine; Rob
Mounsey - arr. strings & conductor; David Nadien - concertmaster; Robert Flack
- backing vocals.

Another deliciously lustful single, but not quite as demanding as 'Give Me All
Night'. Carly admitted how thrilled she was about the "flaming love and the
lovely screams and passion," of Marlon Brando's character in the movie *A*
Streetcar Named Desire. With Andy Goldmark writing the music, Carly and Jake
once more come up with a catchy song that is just too irresistible not to be
considered for chart success. In the liner notes to the album, Carly gives special
thanks to the great Roberta Flack "for dashing down and saving the day" to sing
backing vocals.

Hold On To What You've Got *(Carly Simon - Joe Tex)* **
Recorded - Right Track Recording, New York
Producer - Richard Perry
Associate Producers - Carly Simon & Frank Filipetti
Engineers - Frank Filipetti & Leon Pendarvis
Mixing - Frank Filipetti
T-Bone Wolk - guitar; Leon Pendarvis - synthesizer, arrangements; Barbara
Markay - synthesizer, programming; Russ Kunkel - drums; Gordon Grody -
backing vocals; Lani Groves - backing vocals; Janice Pendarvis - backing vocals
The great Richard Perry is given the job of producing what is perhaps the album's
weakest cover. Originally written by Southern gospel singer Joe Tex as 'Hold
What You've Got', it became his first chart success when released in 1965 and

was noted for its two spoken recitations between the song's refrains, telling, first the men, and then the women, to keep on supporting their loved ones and not to take them for granted. Carly remains faithful to the original, complete with the spoken parts with just a few additional lyrics, but the overall result is somewhat disappointing.

Itsy Bitsy Spider *(Carly Simon – based on the original nursery rhyme)* ****
Recorded - Right Track Recording, New York
Producers - Russ Kunkel, George Massenburg & Bill Payne
Associate Producer - Carly Simon & Frank Filipetti
Engineer - George Massenburg
Mixing - Frank Filipetti
Carly Simon - keyboards; Bill Payne - keyboards; Russ Kunkel - drums; Alexandra Taylor - backing vocals; Ben Taylor - backing vocals; Isaac Taylor - backing vocals; Sally Taylor - backing vocals
It was Carly's inspired idea to meld this nursery rhyme and 'Coming Around Again' together as a finale for the album. The contrasting child and adult themes work beautifully together, and to give the rhyme a palpable charm has both Sally and Ben singing, as well as their cousins Isaac and Alexandra Taylor, the children of James' brother Hugh, and Aquinnah & Elizabeth Witham (Kate Taylor's children). An obvious choice for the flip-side to the single 'Coming Around Again'.

For the first and only time, the album artwork simply uses Carly's first name, and photographer Lynn Goldsmith's beautiful close-up image of that iconic smiling face negates any doubts of who it is. Not since the album *Hotcakes* had Carly been pictured looking directly at the camera, and following the sometime controversial covers, this was returning to that endearingly warm, girl-next-door persona and a woman still able to look half her age.

In the liner notes, Carly dedicated the album to her dear friend Mike Nichols "for luring the spider out of the web and over to the spout."

Coming Around Again was released on April 13th 1987 and entered the Hot 200 on the 25th. It finally peaked at #25, the highest placed album since *Boys in the Trees*, nine years before. It remained on the charts for an incredible 60 weeks, only beaten by *No Secrets* (71 weeks). In the UK it entered the album charts on May 9th and reached #25, the first of her albums to chart there since *Hotcakes*. The album produced three new singles ('Coming Around Again' having charted the previous year), and on February 1st 1988 was certified platinum, the fourth of Carly's career, following on from *No Secrets*, *The Best of Carly Simon* and *Boys in the Trees*.

'Give Me All Night', which had the hallmarks of being a great success, was released in the US with 'Sleight of Hand' on the flip-side, but surprisingly only climbed to #61 on the Hot 100 on June 20th. It did much better on Adult Contemporary, reaching #5. In the UK it was released coupled with 'Two Hot Girls', but only reached #98. The next single, 'The Stuff That Dreams Are Made Of', paired with 'As Time Goes By', missed out altogether on the Hot 100 but reached #8 on Adult Contemporary and #99 in the UK. The final single release was 'All I Want Is You', which also had alternate B-sides. In the US it was coupled with 'Two Hot Girls' and reached #54 on the Hot 100 on February 20th and #7 on Adult Contemporary, while in the UK it had 'You Have to Hurt' as the flip-side but again failed to chart.

'Sleight of Hand' was a song Carly had pre-recorded that spring for John Pielmeier's Broadway play of the same name, which was previewed on April 6th and then ran for just one week in May at the Cort Theatre on West 48th Street. The story of a drunken magician being accused of murder had critics puzzled. One commented on the inclusion of Carly's song: "It blares over the theater's sound system at intermission and at the ludicrous finale. Maybe the producers thought the song, the magic and the settings would take everyone's mind off the play. But the glitz can't disguise the fact that the evening is nothing more a few sleights of hand in search of a play."

Surprisingly, considering the commercial success of its four singles, the album only produced one more promotional video, with the breezy, sun-kissed 'Give Me All Night' shot on the Vineyard and featuring just Carly and her drummer friend Rick Marotta.

At the 1987 Grammy awards, 'Itsy Bitsy Spider' was nominated in the Best Recording for Children category but lost out to Jim Henson's 'Alphabet' from *Sesame Street*. The following year Carly was nominated for *Coming Around Again* in the Best Female Pop Vocal Performance, which was eventually won by Whitney Houston for 'I Wanna Dance with Somebody'.

Carly made a number of television appearances to promote the album over the next twelve months, including an interview and performance of 'All I Want Is You' on *Late Night with David Letterman* on October 19th, broadcast from a suite at the Milford Plaza Hotel in Manhattan. She was also invited on Roger Rose's VH1 television music show, in which she played short snippets on her keyboard of 'The Stuff That Dreams Are Made of' and 'Itsy Bitsy Spider/Coming Around Again'. The album also garnered some of the best reviews of Carly's career. *Rolling Stone* reported just what a "refreshing diversion" Carly could still be, and praised her extraordinary "cool and confident" voice, quite unlike the "frayed edges" of some of her contemporaries. People described her as "still captivating," while the *New York Times* looked back on her career and remarked how her delivery "is open-throated folk crooning punched up with a strong sense of rock rhythm."

Coming Around Again was a landmark album for Carly, and one that rejuvenated what many had seen as a flagging career. Now in her early 40s, she finally had the music industry reawakened to the fact that they should take her music more seriously, and accept her as one of the finest female singer-songwriters they had. With an album bursting with so much confidence, Carly now felt she didn't need to prove herself to anyone any longer.

Live from the Vineyard

One of the contributing factors that had led to poor album sales in the past was the labels 'reluctance to give them the degree of promotion they deserved, and Carly's reluctance to tour only compounded the problem. Despite Clive Davis's persuasive powers, he still couldn't persuade her to do a promotional tour. But there was a solution.

For what was now proposed, Carly would not even have to leave her island home. The cable television company HBO invited her to perform an open-air concert for one of their special presentations. It would take place on a stone jetty in the harbor at Menemsha, a stone's throw from her house, where a 100-man production crew spent a week erecting a stage that included a little fishing shack that would serve as a dressing room. Although *Carly Simon: Live from Martha's Vineyard* would only be for invited friends and local guests, Carly was still apprehensive and went through "about 25 different emotions" before taking to the stage on June 9th.

Produced by Jodie Wright, and directed by Jen Brian and Tony Mitchell, the original 70-minute setlist consisted of thirteen songs, eight of which were from the *Coming Around Again* album, and her band consisted of many familiar faces. The weather on that first evening was cloudy and misty, and the show had to be shortened due to the cold. Some comments overheard on the day indicate that 'That's the Way I've Always Heard It Should Be' was one of the songs dropped due to the cold conditions. Much of what was shot was deemed unusable, so it was decided to re-shoot the entire set the following day, with the weather much improved. In a number of later interviews, Carly recalled that the original idea was to film both evenings and then choose the best performances of each between them. As a result, she actually preferred the first evening's shoot with the misty weather providing an evocative backdrop, but agreed that it was not possible to intercut between the two performances.

Guitarist Jimmy Ryan recalls that first day's shoot: "Cold temperatures were an issue. We raided a local general store for all the thermal underwear we could find. We were freezing, and as you can see from the video, hair was 'blowing in the wind.' The wind chill did make things challenging. We did this with real film, not video, so there was a pause every twelve minutes or so to reload the cameras. There was also a little building stage right with a space heater. We would take turns going in there to warm our hands during the breaks. If you watch the video, there's a point where you can see me rubbing Carly's hands to warm them up."

By ignoring the many cameras and focusing on the audience, Carly pulled off what is arguably her finest live performance caught on film, with no signs of stage fright, and when premiered on television on July 25th it received excellent ratings. *The New York Times* was impressed with the way she strode "gracefully around the stage and moving naturally with the music," and delivering an "Olympian quotient of fulfillment." A live album of the concert would be released the following year.

Carly was well aware of how her latest album was seen by many to have rejuvenated her career: "Another good feature is staying in this business long enough to be able to have a comeback, to be able to have the public appreciate the fact that you've been doing this for a long time and you're back again."

Lucky Jim

Completion of *Coming Around Again* had also signaled the end of Carly's relationship with Russ Kunkel, with some observers blaming the major cultural difference between them. But by now, she had met 37-year-old James Hart, an insurance salesman and friend of Jake Brackman's. He was a divorcee, a father of a disabled child, and a recovering alcoholic, now living in a small New York apartment. Jim recalled that first meeting in July 1987 when Jake introduced him to Carly while waiting on a platform for a train: "He was standing next to this gorgeous woman. He introduced me and it was Carly. Then I followed her on to the train and we had this amazing conversation going back to New York."

There was something about Jim that fascinated Carly. For one thing, he didn't know who she was, having had little interest in music. Inevitably, a romance followed. Carly had found in him a great intellectual partner, a man who was not just like a philosopher to her, but a wonderful poet, aspiring novelist, conversationalist, and one who would be able to tend to

186

her changing emotions. Six months later, on December 23rd 1987, they were married in a church at Edgartown on the Vineyard, before honeymooning on the neighboring island of Nantucket. For Carly, this new-found love and happiness was followed by the sad news on March 17th 1988 that her uncle Peter Dean had died from cancer in Florida. He was 77.

By that summer, Carly had more or less given up on her Manhattan lifestyle and was now living full-time with her husband at the Vineyard home, with Ben attending a local school and Sally now at a mainland boarding school. During this time, she only made occasional public appearances. One was for a television special *Les Paul: He Changed the Music*, an all-star tribute to the "man who gave us rock n roll." As one half of the husband-wife duo Les Paul and Mary Ford, he had scored two chart toppers in the 50s, but was better known to musicians as the man who developed the solid-body electric guitar and an innovator of studio techniques such as overdubbing, delay effects and multi-track recording. Recorded at the Brooklyn Academy of Music, the show featured the 73-year-old legend along with a host of artists, including Steve Miller, B B King and Rita Coolidge. Carly performed a rare but nevertheless superb version of 'It Happens Everyday' playing one of his iconic electric guitars, which was presented to her after the show.

That August Carly participated in the annual Martha's Vineyard Celebrity Auction, and one of the featured items was a private performance of a song by Carly in the home of the winning bidder. She sang three songs for $26,000 each for two men who had been unable to outbid each other. The same month she appeared in an episode of the television series *Wired*, along with the band 10,000 Maniacs and the Cocteau Twins, and in November performed at the Cathedral of Saint John the Divine, New York.

Meanwhile, on August 2nd, Arista had released the album *Greatest Hits Live*, a recording of the Martha's Vineyard concert. The cover image was taken by Bob Gothard, who would be doing more album covers with her in the near future. The album reached #87 on the *Billboard* Hot 100 on September 24th, and #49 on the UK charts. It was certified gold on July 26th 1990.

GREATEST HITS LIVE
Arista AL 2586 (UK – 209 196)
Recorded - June 8-9 1987, Menemsha, Martha's Vineyard, MA
Released - August 2 1988
Producers - Carly Simon & T-Bone Wolk
Engineer - Mike Scott
Remote Recording Engineer - David Hewitt
Cover design - Dave Brubaker

US Billboard Hot 200 #87; UK Album Chart #49
Hugh McCracken - guitar; Jimmy Ryan - guitar, backing vocals; Robbie Kondor - piano, synthesizers; T-Bone Wolk - bass, piano, accordion, arranger, director; Robbie Kilgore - percussion, synthesizers; Michael Brecker - EWI, sax; Rick Marotta - drums, electronic drums, percussion; backing singers - Lani Groves, Kasey Cisyk, Frank Simms, Ben Taylor, Sally Taylor, Alexandra Taylor, Isaac Taylor, Aquinnah Witham & Elizabeth Witham

Nobody Does it Better
You're So Vain
It Happens Everyday
Anticipation
The Right Thing to Do
Do the Walls Come Down
You Belong to Me
Two Hot Girls (On a Hot Summer's Night)
All I Want Is You
Coming Around Again / Itsy Bitsy Spider
Never Been Gone

1988 had also seen Carly's friendship with Jackie Onassis begin to blossom. Whilst working as an editor for Doubleday, the former First Lady had been tasked with acquiring the rights to publish autobiographies of famous celebrities, and now suggested to Carly that she write a memoir about her fascinating life, a life that had been discussed in great detail over a number of lunches. Apprehensive at first, Carly did go ahead and began writing a draft, but eventually aborted the project when it came to involving the many well-known names that had played a part in her life. Undeterred, Jackie then reminded Carly about her childhood and the stories that her mother had told her, the ones she would later pass on to her own children, and it gave her the idea of writing her own children's stories.

It would be the beginning of another lucrative career for the singer, and with a $25,000 advance from Doubleday, Carly came up with *Amy the Dancing Bear*, the first of what would become "fragments of my own life." In collaboration with her Vineyard-artist friend Margot Datz, who supplied the illustrations, the simple story of a little bear who dances the night away while her mother wishes she would go to bed was published on September 25th 1989, and its success led to her being commissioned to write further books, *The Boy of the Bells* (September 1st 1990), *The Fisherman's Song* (September 1st 1991), *The Nighttime Chauffeur* (September 1st 1993) and finally *Midnight Farm*, published by Simon & Schuster on June 8th 1997.

Come, the new Jerusalem

Later in the year, Carly was again approached by director Mike Nichols to compose music for his new movie, *Working Girl*, written by Kevin Wade. But not just one song: this time it was for most of the score. Carly rose to the challenge and would spend almost an entire year putting her energy into writing material ready for the film's release date at the end of 1989, and doing it with as little distraction as possible.

When reading the script for the movie for the first time, Carly thought it was about a girl in the tough, unforgiving, male-orientated world of Wall Street, but after further readings she had a clearer picture of the story she wanted to portray, that of New York City, and Wall Street in particular, being the beast-killing-beast jungle it was in the mid-80s. Written initially for the film's opening sequence, Carly revealed that to get a feeling for how the song should take shape she took inspiration from Walt Whitman's book of poems *Leaves of Grass*.

Right from the beginning, she had a vision: "I knew right away that I wanted it to be a hymn over a jungle beat, and that there was something about New York that's just invariably the jungle. It has the majesty of that lady in the harbor with her arm held up with the torch in it; it has the majesty of these people aspiring to be big and tall and better, and there's a lot of ambition, and so these girls who come over on the Staten Island Ferry to work in Wall Street were there to try to partake of that same luster, that same desire to be the greatest, the winners, and what I was trying to do was to elicit that feeling of being driven to power."

At first the title was going to be 'The Wall Street Hymn', and then her husband Jim suggested using the phrase "Come the New Jerusalem," based on the poem by William Blake, and the song was then renamed 'The New Jerusalem', before finally settling on 'Let the River Run'. Carly decided to keep the Jerusalem phrase in the lyric as she saw it gave the city a holy aura of being the promised land. The end result was a divine clarion call for bringing hope and achievement to all working women struggling in a male-dominated world.

Nichols was full of praise for what Carly had achieved, and decided it would be the film's signature song, despite studio executives at one point, quite inexplicably, wanting to change it to the Eagles' 'Witchy Woman'.

'Let the River Run' was recorded at the Hit Factory in New York during the fall of 1988, and co-produced by Carly and Rob Mounsey, the keyboardist who had done sterling work on *Coming Around Again*. A version of 'Let the River Run' was also recorded with Carly singing with the choir of St Thomas's Church on Fifth Avenue. Other material Carly composed for the movie included several instrumental pieces, orchestrated by Don Sebesky, who had worked with her on the *Torch* album, and the most enchanting of these was the track 'In Love', which just begged to have lyrics written for it. 'Carlotta's Heart' and 'Looking Through Katherine's House' both had wordless vocals, although the latter had a choral backing of 'Let the River Run'.

Let the River Run (Theme from Working Girl) *(Carly Simon)*
US 7-inch Single Arista AS1-9793 b/w Turn of the Tide (UK – 112-124)
UK 12-inch Single Arista 612 124 b/w Carlotta's Heart & Coming Around Again/Itsy Bitsy Spider
Recorded - Fall 1988, The Hit Factory, New York
Released – March 1989
Producers - Carly Simon & Rob Mounsey
Engineer – Tim Leitner
Billboard Hot 100 #49; Billboard Adult Contemporary #11; Cashbox #51; UK chart #79; Australia #91
Rob Mounsey - piano; Jimmy Ryan - guitar; Mickey Curry - drums; Vivian Cherry - backing vocals; Gordon Grody - backing vocals; Kasey Cisyk - backing vocals; Frank Floyd - backing vocals; Lani Groves - backing vocals; Frank Simms - backing vocals; Vanessa Thomas - backing vocals; Kurt Yahijan – backing vocals

The movie was finally released on December 21st 1988. Starring Melanie Griffith, Harrison Ford and Sigourney Weaver, it was a rom-com box-office success, grossing $103 million worldwide. The soundtrack, which also featured music from the Pointer Sisters and Chris de Burgh, peaked at #45 on the Hot 200.

'Let the River Run' was released as a single in March 1989. Coupled with 'Turn of the Tide', it faltered at a disappointing #49 on the Hot 100 on April 15th, #51 on *Cashbox*, and only #91 in Australia. However, it did reach #11 on Adult Contemporary, while in the UK it surprisingly struggled to climb just outside the Top 75. In the UK a 12-inch version was also issued and included 'Carlotta's Heart' and 'Coming Around Again/Itsy Bitsy Spider'. The video of the song featured Carly singing aboard the Staten Island Ferry with Manhattan as the backdrop, although the actual single version of the song was not featured in the movie.

Guitarist Jimmy Ryan remembers only too well the day of the shoot. For the video a ferry had been rented and Carly had asked him if he would like to take part. Driving down from Manhattan with his outfits and guitar, he found there were no dressing rooms on the ferry, and only small bathrooms reserved for the stars. Undeterred, he went down to the car deck to get changed: "I looked around, didn't see anybody, opened the door of my car and undressed by the side. I was certain I was alone as I stripped to my undershorts, and then a gentle voice from behind me says, 'excuse me, can you close your door slightly so we can get through?' I turned around, three-quarters naked, to face Melanie Griffith and Joan Cusack standing two feet away. I don't know what I said, but they were practically peeing themselves trying not to laugh as I shuffled myself halfway into the car, pants around my ankles and pulling the door in just enough for them to pass by."

Despite its poor showing on the charts, 'Let the River Run' definitely struck a chord with the critics. At the Golden Globe Awards ceremony, which took place at the Beverly Hills Hilton in Los Angeles on January 28th 1989, the song was joint winner in the category of Best Original Song, along with Phil Collins' 'Two Hearts' from the film *Buster*. The following year, at the 32nd Grammy Awards, held at the Shrine Auditorium in Los Angeles on February 21st, Carly won in the category of Best Song Written Specifically for a Motion Picture. Then, to top it all, at the Academy Awards on March 26th, also held at the Shrine, she won the Oscar for Best Original Song, beating both 'Calling You' from *Bagdad Café* and 'Two Hearts'.

This made Carly the first of only two artists ever to win the trio of awards for a self-penned song (the other being Bruce Springsteen with 'Streets of Philadelphia'.)

In September 2001 the song 'Let the River Run' would be used as an ad by the US Postal Service. Entitled "Pride" its aim was to boost public confidence and postal worker morale in the wake of 9/11 and the 2001 anthrax attacks.

A Night at the Oscars

The exciting year rounded off for Carly with an invitation to appear in the ABC special *Free to Be...A Family*, about two groups of children, one in New York and the other in Moscow, who befriend each other over a satellite connection and find common ground. For the show Carly was asked to perform one of her most anthemic songs, 'Turn of the Tide', which she had co-written with Jake as an election campaign song for Democratic candidate Walter Mondale back in 1984. It had then been recorded in New York, produced and arranged by Arif Mardin and engineered by Frank Filipetti.

The musicians were Mick Jones (lead guitar), Hugh McCracken (guitar), Robbie Kondor (keyboards), Tony Levin (bass), and Frank Vilardi (drums). Backing vocals were supplied by Barbara Ames, Cindy Mizelle, Cissy Houston, James Hart, Jo Morris, Lucy Simon, Mark Jones, Rachele Cappelli, Reggie Griffin, Samantha Jones and Sean Lennon (son of John).

The show was the creation of the actress, author and social activist Marlo Thomas, who in 1972 had written a children's book called *Free to Be...You and Me*, inspired by her young niece who she wanted to teach about life. She went on to produce multiple recordings and television specials in the 70s, all of which related to the book's title, and encouraged gender neutrality and saluted the values of individuality and tolerance. Marlo's husband was television presenter Phil Donahue, who had been hosting a series of US-Russian satellite telecasts in the mid-80s, and this gave her the idea of using that technology to bring the message home to children from both nations via a satellite link-up.

The show was aired on December 14th with a host of performers that included Jon Bon Jovi, Lily Tomlin and the Muppets, but the highlight was Carly's performance of 'Turn of the Tide', with children from both countries singing along to the chorus with the lyric sheets provided. The soundtrack to the show was credited to Marlo Thomas & Friends and released on A&M (SP-5196). It included Carly's song as well as stories and songs by other artists such as Robin Williams, Bonnie Raitt, Pat Benatar and Whoopi Goldberg. A portion of the proceeds went to the Free To Be Foundation, while the show itself went on to win an Emmy award for Outstanding Children's Program the following year.

On March 29th 1989 Carly and her husband Jim flew out to Hollywood to attend the Academy Awards at the Shrine. It was a glittering time for the singer and the highlight of her professional career. The Oscar for 'Let the River Run' was presented to her by Sammy Davis Jr and Gregory Hines, and in her acceptance speech she gave special thanks to her "guiding light", Mike Nichols, and also to Jim Hart for "writing the best lines in the song."

During the summer, Carly was invited to sing on Mick Jones' eponymous album. Jones was better known as the lead guitarist and the only British member of the band Foreigner, and Carly joined him on the tracks 'That's the Way Love Is' and 'Write Tonight'. On August 1st she had a brief cameo in an episode of the television series *Thirtysomething* called 'Success' in which Melissa's career takes off with an assignment to photograph the singer. In an article in *Playboy* later that month it was reported that Carly had also opened an art gallery in New York called Riverrun.

Carly finds romance

Although Clive Davis still wanted Carly to do an album of new material, the end of the year found her preparing to record *My Romance*, which was going to be her second collection of standards. Despite him having reservations, he could hardly veto the triple-award winning singer's request.

The songs chosen for the album were all close to Carly's heart and brought back many happy memories of her childhood - listening to her mother sing them, her father playing them on the piano, and as a teenage girl lying face down on the bed listening to them, especially those by Sinatra. Even her favorite uncles had sung them too and taught her to play them on a ukulele. Some of the composers were well known to Richard Simon, and had visited the family home on a number of occasions and been introduced to the children. Arthur Schwartz was one of her parents 'closest friends. As she grew older Carly not only listened to these recordings, she studied the melodies and the phrasing, and in time they became the solid foundation for her musical education.

Carly expressed her thoughts on the album, saying that once hearing it, it would make you want to "dim the lights, put on something more comfortable, dab a little perfume behind the ears...and make out." In the liner notes, she wrote: "This is an album I have wanted to do for years. These are my favorite standards. This is my romance."

Carly worked with pianist and composer Michael "Koz" Kosarin on piano vocal arrangements before the sessions. Kosarin had previously worked as director and arranger on the Broadway musical *Mayor*, based on the memoir of former New York Mayor Ed Koch, and would also be joining Carly on future projects. Carly then gave the tapes to Marti Paich, who had done the orchestral work on *Torch*. In January, the songs were recorded with a live orchestra and completed in just over thirteen days at the Power Station in New York. The assembled musicians included Jimmy Ryan, Steve Gadd, and Michael Brecker, along with new bassists Jay Leonhart and Wayne Pedziwiatr, and percussionist Gordon Gottlieb. Paich co-produced the album along with Carly's old friend Frank Filipetti, and also served as arranger and conductor.

Carly included one of her own collaborations which perfectly complemented the album's theme and was a clear indication of her innate ability to write the type of songs that could easily hold their place alongside the great standards.

MY ROMANCE
Arista AL 8582
Recorded - January 1990 (UK – 210 602)
Released - March 13 1990
Producers - Frank Filipetti & Marti Paich
Associate producer & arranger - Michael Kosarin
Engineer - Frank Filipetti & Matthew "Boomer" LaMonica
Mixing - Frank Filipetti
Mastering - Ted Jensen, Sterling Sound New York
US Billboard Hot 200 #46
Carly Simon - piano; Jimmy Ryan - guitar; Michael Kosarin - piano; Wayne Pedziwiatr - bass; Jay Leonhart - acoustic bass; Steve Gadd - drums; Gordon Gottlieb - percussion; Michael Brecker - sax; Marvin Stamm - trumpet; David Nadien - concertmaster, violin; Marti Paich - arr. & orchestra conductor.

Side 1

My Romance *(Richard Rodgers - Lorenz Hart)* *****
Promo CD Single ASCD-9947
Released 1990
Written for the Billy Rose musical *Jumbo* in 1935, and sung by Doris Day in the 1962 movie. A great opening track that Carly truly makes her own with her exquisite vocal range.

By Myself / See Your Face Before Me *(Howard Dietz - Arthur Schwartz)* ****
Both songs originally featured in the 1937 show *Between the Devil*. The jazz standard 'Be Myself' was performed by Jack Buchanan and was also featured in the 1953 movie *The Bandwagon*, while 'See Your Face Before Me' was originally sung by Evelyn Laye and Adele Dixon. But Carly manages to eclipse both these singers in this most tender of break-up songs. After all, "love is only a dance."

When Your Lover Has Gone *(Einar Aaron Swan)* ****
Jazz standard originally performed in the 1931 James Cagney movie *Blonde Crazy*. Michael Kosarin's outstanding piano accompaniment is matched by Michael Brecker's haunting Steinerphone solo.

In the Wee Small Hours of the Morning *(Bob Hilliard - David Mann)* ****
Originally appeared on Frank Sinatra's album of the same name in 1955, and also recorded by Johnny Mathis, Andy Williams, and Ella Fitzgerald. Michael Stamm plays the trumpet solo, and in the liner notes Carly gives a special dedication to Sinatra "who might as well have been singing directly to me, I felt it so strongly."

My Funny Valentine *(Richard Rodgers - Lorenz Hart)* *****
Promo Vinyl Single CARLY1 b/w My Romance
Released 1990

Jazz standard which originally featured in the 1937 Broadway show *Babes in Arms* and sung by Mitzi Green. Carly's voice oozes sophistication in this most passionate of love songs.

Something Wonderful *(Richard Rodgers - Oscar Hammerstein II)* *****
A wonderful song performed in the 1951 musical *The King and I* and sung by Dorothy Sarnoff, it was later featured in the 1956 movie version and performed by Terry Saunders. David Nadien steps in as concert master and supplies the evocative violin solo that perfectly complements Carly's incredible vocal. Watching her sing this in the subsequent concert shows how much she holds this song in reverence.

Side 2

Little Girl Blue *(Richard Rodgers - Lorenz Hart)* ***
Originally sung in the 1935 Broadway circus musical *Jumbo* by Gloria Grafton, and by Doris Day in the 1962 movie version. Doris was always going to be a hard act to follow, but Carly steps up to the mark and delivers a heartfelt performance.

He Was Too Good for Me *(Richard Rodgers - Lorenz Hart)* ****
Written for the 1930 Broadway musical *Simple Simon* but never used. A song of love gone bad has never sounded so good.

What Has She Got *(Carly Simon - Michael Kosarin - Jacob Brackman)* *****
The only "torch" song on the album, and what a fine song it is, a perfect example of how easily Carly can write music to replicate the wonderful feeling of songs that mean so much to her. With musical contribution and superb piano playing by Michael Kosarin, we could easily be listening to a song that was written six decades before. Jake's words, too, are the perfect complement to the music, and hold up nicely when compared with those legendary lyricists who share the album.

Bewitched *(Richard Rodgers - Lorenz Hart)* *****
Better known as 'Bewitched, Bothered and Bewildered', this classic song was originally featured in the 1940 Broadway musical *Pal Joey* and sung by Vivienne Seagal. Carly's rendition is nothing less than spectacular, with another great sax solo by Brecker. Guaranteed to make you whimper and simper like a child.

Danny Boy *(Frederic Weatherley - traditional)* *****
The famous ballad written in 1913 by the English lawyer and lyricist Frederic Weatherley, and set to the traditional Irish melody of 'Londonderry Air'. Carly dedicated the album to her old nanny Allie Brennan, who had lullabied her with this song "when all else failed to pacify me." Practically perfect in every way.

Time After Time *(Jule Stein - Sammy Cahn)* ****
A song first recorded by Sarah Vaughan in 1946 and sung by Frank Sinatra in the 1947 movie *It Happened in Brooklyn*. One of four tracks on the album which would later be chosen for the *Clouds in My Coffee* compilation in 1995.

"With love from Carly"

Often cited as one of Carly's favorite albums, *My Romance* was released on March 13th and climbed to a respectable #46 on the Hot 200 chart on May 12th. Unlike the dark, angst-inducing cover image of *Torch*, which portrayed a woman trying to cling on to a man who is leaving her, this new photograph, taken by Bob Gothard, is quite the opposite, showing a smiling and contented Carly, her blue eyes standing out in the monochrome image, and bathed in a warming white light that perfectly fits the theme of the songs.

Two non-commercial singles were issued: 'My Romance' was released on compact disc, complete with a picture sleeve taken by Gothard, showing Carly sitting elegantly on a bed and wearing a black off-the-shoulder dress, while 'My Funny Valentine', coupled with 'My Romance', was a pre-album vinyl issue brought out around Valentine's Day, with a pink, heart-shaped sleeve saying "With love from Carly." Unfortunately, the unromantic radio stations gave both little airplay.

With this second album of standards under her belt, Carly could now celebrate and promote her work with new-found confidence. Happy in her new marriage, she was keen to get back to doing more public appearances to promote an album that was so dear to her heart. Although touring was still something that would unnerve her, she agreed to do another televised concert for HBO, in which she reprised all the album's songs except 'Danny Boy' and added a few others: 'A New Kind of Love' (aka 'You've Brought a New Kind of Love To Me') was a 1930 song written by Sammy Fain, Irving Kahal and Pierre Norman, and first introduced in the movie *The Big Pond* by Maurice Chevalier, while 'I Don't Know Why (I Just Do)' was written by Fred E Ahlert and Roy Turk and made famous by the Andrew Sisters. In the concert, both of these were performed as duets with the young Harry Connick Jr, who also played upright bass on 'We Have No Secrets'.

The concert was recorded over three days at the Academy Theatre in New York, with a full orchestra and a stage transformed into a nightclub setting. Directed by Kathy Dougherty and produced by Charles A Carroll, it had Michael Kosarin acting as musical director and Jim Hart serving as associate producer. Carly's band for the concert consisted of Michael Kosarin on piano, Jimmy Ryan on guitar, Teese Gohl on keyboards, Steve Gadd on drums, Eddie Gomez on bass, and Michael Brecker on sax and

EWI. The hour-long *Carly in Concert: My Romance* was aired on April 15th 1990 and released later as a 73-minute-long home video.

Not all the reviews for the album were positive. *Entertainment Weekly* simply called it "hapless" and a clear indication she was unable to do the standards justice. But let it be said, Carly was never trying to reinvent these songs, but just using her remarkable voice and skilled phrasing to illustrate how truly great these songs are, especially from a lyrical point of view. In an interview with Diane Sawyer for *Primetime*, Carly stated: "I love doing the standards, because I think it opens up my voice. Every time I do sing a standard, I become more conscious of how a good song should sound."

For Carly, love had well and truly come around again, not just in her marriage to Jim, but in her devotion for the great American Songbook, and with that love came a new birth of confidence that would be reflected in her next studio album.

Not long after receiving her well-deserved Oscar, Carly got another call from movie director Mike Nichols. His next film was to be a comedy-drama adapted from actress Carrie Fisher's 1987 semi-autobiographical *Postcards from the Edge*. Meryl Streep played a recovering drug addict trying to pick up the pieces of her acting career, and Nichols wanted Carly to write another big song for the opening credits, which was to be sung by Streep. Carly came up with the song 'Have You Seen Me Lately?' and it was apparently recorded by Streep for the movie. However, when the final cut was made, Nichols dropped the song, and one of the reasons given was that Fisher, who had adapted the screenplay, felt the song was "too soft and emotional to fit the sensibility of the lead character." In addition to Fisher's comment, Nichols was unhappy with the opening credits and had them removed, leaving no room for Carly's song. As a result, just small fragments remained throughout the film, but enough to earn Carly a British BAFTA nomination for Best Original Music, although losing out to the Italian film *Cinema Paradiso*. Nichols 'film was eventually released in September and was a box-office success.

On March 17th Carly was one of many artists invited to perform in *That's What Friends Are For: Arista's 15th Anniversary Concert*, an AIDS benefit held at the Radio City Music Hall in New York. Many of the label's current artists gave performances, including Hall & Oates, Whitney Houston, Dionne Warwick, Barry Manilow and Patti Smith. A month later, CBS aired a two-hour version of the concert. Over $2.5 million was raised that night for the Arista Foundation, which gave proceeds to various AIDS organizations.

Leave out the white nights

The early part of 1990 also saw Carly beginning work on *Have You Seen Me Lately?*, an album of new material, the one that Clive Davis had been growing increasingly anxious for her to do. But she would do it without the involvement of Rob Mounsey, her musical collaborator on *Coming Around Again* and for the score on *Working Girl*. Apparently aggrieved that he had not been given due credit for his work on the award-winning 'Let the River Run', he now moved on to other projects. To produce the new album Carly turned to old friends Paul Samwell-Smith and Frank Filipetti, with Swiss-born composer Mathias "Teese" Gohl now stepping in to replace Mounsey on keyboards. Gohl had recently worked on the score for the horror movie *Pet Sematary*, and this would be the beginning of a long-lasting working relationship with the singer.

Among some of the new musicians coming on board were bass player Bruce Samuels and percussionist Nana Vasconcelos. Recording commenced at Right Track in New York. Carly had originally wanted to call the album *Happy Birthday* after one of the earliest tracks to have been written, but instead chose the title of her aborted movie song instead. It would also be the first time two of Carly's studio albums had been released in the same calendar year.

HAVE YOU SEEN ME LATELY?
Arista AL 8650 (UK – 211 044)
Recorded - Summer 1990
Released - September 25 1990
Producers - Paul Samwell-Smith & Frank Filipetti
Assist. Engineer - John Herman
Mixed - Frank Filipetti
Mastering - Ted Jensen, Sterling Sound, New York
US Billboard Hot 200 #60; Canada #67

Side 1

Better Not Tell Her *(Carly Simon)* *****
Single AS 2083 b/w Happy Birthday
Released - September 25 1990
Billboard Adult Contemporary #4; Cashbox #103; Canada #30
Carly Simon - guitar, keyboards, backing vocals; Jay Berliner - Spanish guitar; Will Lee - bass; Steve Gadd - drums; Jimmy Bralower - drum programming; Lani Groves - backing vocals, Paul Samwell-Smith - backing vocals
Superb opening track to what is an exceptional album, and another example of how Carly's fascination with the subject of romantic betrayal can lend itself to

some of her most compelling compositions. Although not seeming too guilt-ridden with her own infidelity, the narrator is reminding an apparently married ex-lover of their passionate time together and pleading with him not to erase her from his memory, finally confessing she is still in love with him. With a hint that their tryst had taken them to Madrid, the music is embellished by a Spanish guitar solo by Jay Berliner, who had last appeared on 'What Shall We Do with the Child' on the *Torch* album. A spellbinding song that can keep the listener hooked right to the very end and leave them begging for more.

Didn't I *(Carly Simon)* ****
Carly Simon - guitar, keyboards, backing vocals; Will Lee - bass.
Almost a solo performance by Carly, with just Will Lee's bass guitar in support. A remarkable ballad in which the narrator uses the two-word title to great effect in reminiscing about a past relationship with her ex-lover, and despite the light-hearted line in the bridge about being dropped on his head by his mother, it still stands up as a wonderful little love song.

Have You Seen Me Lately? *(Carly Simon)* *****
Carly Simon - guitar, keyboards, backing vocals; John McCurry - electric guitar; Will Lee - bass; Michael Brecker - EWI; Steve Gadd - drums, Jimmy Bralower - drum programming; Lani Groves - backing vocals; Paul Samwell-Smith - backing vocals; Teese Gohl - arr. strings
The song that should have appeared in the movie *Postcards from the Edge* is vindicated here with a fine production number by the "A Team" of Samwell-Smith and Filipetti. It is a touching story of a daydreaming singer reluctant to be interrupted from her sleep, preferring instead to dream of blissful love than face the awakened reality of being without it. Her final question "Was I crazy?" just adds to the mystery of it all.

Life is Eternal *(Carly Simon - Teese Gohl)* ****
Single AS 2164 b/w We Just Got Here
Released - January 1991
Did not chart
Carly Simon - guitar, keyboards, backing vocals; Will Lee - bass, additional lead vocals, backing vocals; Steve Gadd - drums; Jimmy Bralower - drum programming; Nana Vasconcelos - additional percussion; Julie Levine - backing vocals; Ben Taylor - backing vocals; Sally Taylor - backing vocals; Lani Groves - backing vocals; Paul Samwell-Smith - backing vocals
A song about contentment, the reality of getting old, and how life has been enjoyed so much to the fullest that even death is seen as nothing but a horizon, the "limit of our sight." At a time when the world was gripped by AIDS, Carly had been inspired to write the lyrics after conversations with her Vineyard friend, the Reverend Bill Eddy. With music co-written with Teese Gohl, the end result is an anthemic and philosophical meditation and a beacon of hope among the gay community. Bass guitarist Will Lee, who had played on the Simon Sisters' debut album nearly thirty years before, shares additional lead vocals with Carly, while

the choral harmonies are shared with Sally and Ben, Julie Levine, Lani Groves and Paul Samwell-Smith.

Waiting at the Gate *(Carly Simon - Jacob Brackman)* *****
Carly Simon - guitar, keyboards, backing vocals; Will Lee - bass; Steve Gadd - drums; Teese Grohl - arr. strings; Paul Samwell-Smith - backing vocals; Lani Groves - backing vocals
Another wonderful collaboration with Jake about a woman waiting for her man who has a drug and alcohol addiction to be released from rehab. From its suspenseful start, the story is put together with great sensitivity. Whether Carly is looking back at the past or to the present day, we should just marvel at the ability of these two great songsmiths to come up with a composition so frank and engrossing that it defies all criticism.

Side 2

Happy Birthday *(Carly Simon)* ****
Carly Simon - guitar, keyboards, backing vocals; Jimmy Ryan - acoustic guitar, acoustic bass, backing vocals; Steve Gadd - drums; Jimmy Bralower - drum programming; Lani Groves - backing vocals; Paul Samwell-Smith - backing vocals
On the album's release Carly is just three months past her 45th birthday, and in this poignant acoustic ballad describes some of the once-acceptable social activities that now seem frowned upon by the current health-obsessed society - drinking, smoking, sunbathing, casual sex, to name just a few. The song ends with Carly attempting to make wishes before she blows out the candles on the cake. She later described the song as "a reflection on this age of denial we've entered...a measure of being middle-aged and feeling a decaying process starting." Chosen as the flip-side to the single 'Better Not Tell Her'.

Holding Me Tonight *(Carly Simon)* ****
Single (Arista LP Cut)
Released - March 1991
Billboard Adult Contemporary #36
Carly Simon - guitar, keyboards, backing vocals; John McCurry - electric guitar; Will Lee - bass; Steve Gadd - drums; Jimmy Bralower - drum programming; Marvin Stamm - trumpet; Dirk Ziff - additional electric guitar; Lani Groves - backing vocals; Paul Samwell-Smith - backing vocals.
A nice r&b track about a man who doesn't think he is worthy of his partner. It would be nice to think this is about Jim Hart, her husband of just four years. Even if it's not, it is a sweet and tender glimpse into what can sometimes be the vulnerability of being in a relationship where love is in question. Although not released as a bona fide commercial single, it did however make a good impression on the easy listening charts as an "LP cut."

It's Not Like Him *(Carly Simon - Jacob Brackman)* *****

Carly Simon - guitar, keyboards, backing vocals; Will Lee - bass; Steve Gadd - drums; Jimmy Bralower - drum programming; Michael Brecker - EWI; Teese Gohl - arr. strings; Lani Groves - backing vocals, Paul Samwell-Smith - backing vocals.

With clever, observant lyrics, this is a classic tale of insecurity and the fear of a partner's infidelity heightened by all the not-so-subtle changes in both his actions and appearance. The song was based on a track originally produced by New York songwriter Davitt Sigerson and recorded by Brad Leigh, who had worked as engineer on the soundtrack to *Working Girl*. Beautifully scored with Carly once again providing much of the atmospheric music, perfectly matched by her incredible vocal range here in full flow. A fitting soap opera for the new decade.

Don't Wrap It Up *(Carly Simon)* ****
Carly Simon - guitar, keyboards, backing vocals; Will Lee - bass; Steve Gadd - drums; Jimmy Bralower - drum programming; Lani Groves - backing vocals; Paul Samwell-Smith - backing vocals.

Carly makes no apologies for asserting her emotional demands in this charming acoustic track, which once again showcases her musical abilities, with just minimal bass and drum accompaniment.

Fisherman's Song *(Carly Simon)* *****
Carly Simon - guitar, keyboards, backing vocals; Will Lee - bass; Teese Gohl - arr. strings; Judy Collins - backing vocals; Lani Groves - backing vocals; Lucy Simon - backing vocals; Paul Samwell-Smith - backing vocals.

A haunting and beautiful acoustic ballad that immediately and intentionally transports you back to the days of the Simon Sisters, especially when you realize the backing singers not only include sister Lucy, but also the legendary Judy Collins, one of their greatest musical inspirations. The sad tale of an all-too-brief summer affair, after falling under the spell of an island fisherman, could quite easily be referring to a possible teenage fling on Martha's Vineyard, but also could be just another puzzle in Carly's wonderful box of mysteries. One of her children's books would later be based on the song.

We Just Got Here *(Carly Simon)* *****
Carly Simon - guitar, keyboards, backing vocals; Bruce Samuels - bass; Steve Gadd - drums; Jimmy Bralower - rum programming; Teese Gohl - arr. strings; Lani Groves - backing vocals; Paul Samwell-Smith - backing vocals

Irresistibly melodic finale in which the singer reflects with her lover how summer comes and goes so fast on their island paradise (surely the Vineyard), but their love remains as strong as the day when they first arrived, despite the hint that Hurricane Hugo may be sweeping up the coast. If this is another homage to Carly's island home, it is as evocative as both the previous track and also the poignant 'Never Been Gone' on *Spy*. The perfect end to one of her greatest albums.

The images for the album cover were taken by photographer Bob Gothard, who had worked with her on the covers for her last two albums. This time he chose to show Carly casually dressed in jeans and black top outside what looks like his home on the Vineyard. Two promotional videos were also made. 'Better Not Tell Her' portrays Carly on a beach dressed just as she is on the album cover, before switching to her singing and dancing around a campfire, accompanied by two Spanish dancers and musicians. 'Holding Me Tonight' has black and white studio footage of the band interspersed with clips of her relaxing in bed and round a Vineyard harbor.

The remainder of 1990 was a relatively quiet and relaxing time for Carly. In June she appeared on the *Today* show, enchanting viewers with an incredible performance of 'Little Girl Blue' and 'He Was Too Good for Me' from the *My Romance* album. During the summer Carly had also written a song called 'Raining' for Sally and Ben to perform at her local Chilmark Community Center on the island. Recorded with producer Davitt Sigerson, it remained shelved until resurrected for the *Clouds in My Coffee* box set. Carly also continued her friendship with Jackie Onassis and spent time with her at her Chilmark estate, with the former First Lady still trying to convince her to write her autobiography. Also that year, Carly teamed up with Andy Goldmark to write the song 'A Man Who Isn't So Smooth' for Thelma Houston's album *Throw You Down*, produced by Richard Perry.

On September 25th *Have You Seen Me Lately* was released, peaking at a disappointing #60 on the Hot 200 on November 10th. The single 'Better Not Tell Her', coupled with 'Happy Birthday', failed to get into the Hot 100 but climbed to a credible #4 on Adult Contemporary, remaining on the chart for 21 weeks. 'Life is Eternal', with 'We Just Got Here' on the flip side, failed to chart altogether when released early the following year. 'Holding Me Tonight' entered the Adult Contemporary chart as an "Arista LP cut" on March 23rd, and remained at #36 for three weeks.

The New York Times called the album "superb," while *Entertainment Weekly* praised the first half of the album, but found the second half "unconvincing," and her voice at times "lifeless." However, in sum, it opined that "the candid feeling in the best songs here is worth a thousand times more than other singers 'empty perfection." Jack Mauro best summed it up as a "lush catalog of stunningly realized passions."

Movies, TV and an Opera

"There has never been a real conflict in my mind about what takes precedence in my life. It has always been Sally and Ben. It was never a conscious choice, but rather a deep instinctual fact of my being."

This Is My Life

The first half of 1991 developed into a relatively quiet period for Carly. With daughter Sally now off to the Tabor Academy, a preparatory school in Marion, Massachusetts, Carly could focus her attention on 14-year-old Ben. On January 31st she guested on NBC's *Late Night with David Letterman*, performing 'Holding Me Tonight'. She also appeared on *Good Morning America*, where she was interviewed by Joan Lunden before singing a wonderful version of 'Fisherman's Song'. Meanwhile, over in the UK, 'You're So Vain' was receiving extensive television exposure from a Dunlop tires commercial, and in April it was released there a second time and made it to #41 in the charts.

On August 9th Carly duetted with Billy Joel on 'You're So Vain' during the second night of a benefit concert at Indian Field Ranch in Montauk, Long Island. That same month she was also invited to contribute to an album of classic show songs by Placido Domingo, titled *The Broadway I Love*, and recorded a duet with the great tenor in New York on 'The Last Night of the World' from the musical *Miss Saigon*.

Having done little songwriting for some time, things were about to change. Carly received another call from her old friend Nora Ephron with an invite to write another score for a movie. The film was called *This Is My Life*, for which Nora had not only written the screenplay with her sister Della, but was also making what would be her directorial debut. Based on the novel by Brooklyn author Meg Wolitzer, the movie follows the conflict between the two main characters: smart, upwardly mobile Dottie Ingals (played by Julie Kavler) works on the cosmetics counter at Macy's and uses a microphone to harangue potential customers into buying skincare products. Her daughter Erica, the narrator of the movie (played by Samantha Mathis), has grave misgivings about her mother's ambition to be a successful comedienne. Gaby Hoffmann plays Dottie's other daughter Opal, while Carrie Fisher plays a talent scout and Dan Ackroyd her boss.

Nora explained to Carly that "it's our story," a story of raising children while trying to maintain a solid career without the benefit of a live-in father. Of course, it resonated with Carly, and she didn't have to look far for inspiration. As a result, she immersed herself into the work, and, although she considered the plot to be weak, spent much of the following year at home on the Vineyard writing material for the movie.

Recorded at three New York studios, Carly was once again surrounded by her musician friends, including the three co-producers Frank Filipetti, Andy Goldmark and Russ Kunkel, along with Jimmy Ryan, Teese Gohl, Paul Samwell-Smith and Will Lee. Ben Taylor also made his debut as a musical contributor to one of his mother's albums. Behind the scenes, Carly also had valuable guidance from Quincy Jones, the gifted producer who had recently "discovered" young actor Will Smith and launched the sitcom *The Fresh Prince of Bel-Air*. Some of the early sessions were actually conducted in her living room with Teese, Frank, Will, and Jimmy, with much of the inspiration for songs coming from memories of her late Uncle Peter. Carly and her team listened to all his old albums to get a musical feel for what she had in mind, and even the threat of Hurricane Bob was unable to stop them creating an intimate "living room" sound that resonated so much with Carly. As a result, these early sessions were never re-recorded, but just overdubbed with a little embellishment.

In November Carly surprised the audience when she joined the Crash Test Dummies on stage in New York for a cameo performance of their classic 'Superman's Song'.

THIS IS MY LIFE (Music from the Motion Picture)
Quest Records 9-26901-2 (UK – 7599 26901-4)
Recorded - Summer 1991, Right Track Recording, Bubble Hill Studio, and The Hit Factory, New York
Released - February 21 1992
Producers - Carly Simon, Frank Filipetti, Andy Goldmark & Russ Kunkel
Engineers - Frank Filipetti & James Nichols
Mixed - Frank Filipetti & Tom Lord-Alge
Mastering - Ted Jensen, Sterling Sound, New York
Art direction - Kevin Design Hosmann
Carly Simon - acoustic guitar, keyboards, whistling, backing vocals; Jimmy Ryan - acoustic guitar, electric guitar, ukulele, backing vocals; Ben Taylor - acoustic guitar; Andy Goldmark - synthesizer, drums; Teese Gohl - acoustic piano, synthesizer, backing vocals; Will Lee - bass, vocals, backing vocals; Paul Samwell-Smith - bass; Russ Kunkel - drums; Richie Morales - drums; Randy Brecker - trumpet; Jim Pugh - trombone; Jamey Haddad - percussion; Toots Thielemans - harmonica; Charles McCracken - cello; Ann Brown - vocals; Michael DeVries - backing vocals; David Elledge - backing vocals; Keith Evans -

backing vocals; Frank Filipetti - backing vocals; Diane Garisto - backing vocals; Johanna Glushak - backing vocals; Curtis King - backing vocals; Kimberly Mahon - backing vocals; Kathi Moss - backing vocals; Peter Samuels - backing vocals; Sally Taylor - backing vocals; Marty Thomas - backing vocals; Martin Vidnovic - backing vocals; Brenda White-King - backing vocals.

Love of My Life *(Carly Simon)* *****
Single PRO-CD-5356 (radio version)
Released 1992
Billboard Adult Contemporary #16
Producers - Frank Filipetti & Carly Simon
With Sally and Ben in mind, this was the first song Carly composed (aka 'You're the Love of My Life'), and chosen as the lead song for the movie. In the liner notes Carly reveals: "There has never been a real conflict in my mind about what takes precedence in my life. It has always been Sally and Ben. It was never a conscious choice, but rather a deep instinctual fact of my being." The emotions in the song certainly struck a chord with Nora and how she visualized Dottie's feelings toward her two daughters. The song would also feature twice more in the soundtrack, one version subtitled 'Drive to the City', and the other a sweet harmonica instrumental called 'Toots', played by the legendary Toots Thielemans. Carly would later re-record the song as a lullaby version for the album *Into White* in 2007, but changing the name of Woody Allen to Mia Farrow in the first verse and removing the third verse altogether. The song would also be re-imagined in 2015's *Never Been Gone*. Ben Taylor contributes additional acoustic guitar, while Jamey Haddad's subtle percussion and Charles McCracken's evocative cello give the song extra gravitas.

Back the Way (Dottie's Point of View) *(Carly Simon)* ***
Producers - Frank Filipetti & Carly Simon
Apart from the splendid opening track, the remaining songs all came about from Carly's conversations with Nora. This is one of two versions of the same nostalgic song, describing how things used to be for Dottie before the bright lights of Vegas and Hollywood had lured her away from what was a normal and happy family life.

Moving Day *(Carly Simon)* ***
Producers - Frank Filipetti & Carly Simon
Short but effective instrumental with ukulele flourishes from Jimmy Ryan.

Easy on the Eyes *(Carly Simon - Andy Goldmark)* ****
Producers - Frank Filipetti, Carly Simon & Andy Goldmark
Andy Goldmark - synthesizers; Russ Kunkel - drums
Like the track 'The Night Before Christmas', this was intended to be just "source" music, usually used as background to a scene as if heard on a radio or television, and not considered to be part of the score. Unlike the other track, the song was finally dropped altogether from the movie but was retained for the album. Co-written with Andy Goldmark, her sole collaborator, who plays

synthesizers on this track, it also sees a welcome return of Russ Kunkel on drums. A great but underrated seductive song that would grace any of her previous studio albums.

Walking and Kissing *(Carly Simon)* ***
Producers - Frank Filipetti & Carly Simon
Instrumental featuring Toots Thieleman's distinctive harmonica.

The Show Must Go On *(Carly Simon)* ***
Producers - Frank Filipetti & Carly Simon
A late addition to the score, this came about when Nora decided the movie needed a song that epitomized Dottie's showbiz persona - a big-Broadway-type showstopper. Carly rose to the challenge, although it took three weeks to complete, and she finally came up with just what Nora envisaged. Randy Brecker's trumpet and Jim Pugh trombone add to the razzamatazz.

Love of My Life (Toots) *(Carly Simon)* ***
Producers - Frank Filipetti & Carly Simon
Instrumental version of the lead song, once again showcasing Toots 'harmonica playing.

Back the Way (Girls 'Point of View) *(Carly Simon)* ****
Producers - Frank Filipetti & Carly Simon
The second version of the song from the daughters 'perspective.

Little Troopers *(Carly Simon)* **
Producers - Frank Filipetti & Carly Simon
Instrumental with Richie Morales on drums.

The Night Before Christmas *(Carly Simon)* ****
Promo single Quest/Reprise PRO-CD-5804 (album version)
Released - 1992
Promo single Arista ASCD-2940 (album version)
Released -1995
Producers - Frank Filipetti, Carly Simon & Russ Kunkel
Will Lee - bass; Paul Samwell-Smith - bass; Russ Kunkel - drums; Ben Taylor - add. acoustic guitar; Backing vocals - Brenda White-King, Curtis King, Diane Garisto, Marty Thomas, Melody Kay, Kimberly Mahon, Joel Chaiken, Parker Conrad, Marcus Bishop-Wright & Sally Taylor
Like 'Easy on the Eyes', this was also considered "source" music but was successfully retained for the movie, albeit for only twenty seconds and in a different arrangement to what appears on the album. Sally and Ben are among a host of backing singers who help make this into a modern-day Christmas carol. The song later appeared on the 2010 limited edition of *Christmas Is Almost Here*.

This is My Life Suite: A) Pleasure and Pain, B) Coming Home, C) Uncle Peter *(Carly Simon)* ***
Produced by Frank Filipetti & Carly Simon
Jimmy Ryan - ukulele, acoustic guitar; backing vocals on 'Uncle Peter' - Carly Simon, Jimmy Ryan, Will Lee, Frank Filipetti, Teese Gohl & Keith Evans
Three instrumental segments with vocal flourishes inspired by Carly's Uncle Peter and his ukulele playing, deftly handled here by Jimmy Ryan.

Love of My Life (Drive to the City) *(Carly Simon)* *****
Produced by Frank Filipetti & Carly Simon
The lead song reprised as the finale to the movie with slightly amended lyrics.

The movie was finally released on February 21st 1992 to disappointing reviews, while the soundtrack album was released two months later on April 14th, the first of Carly's albums not to be issued on vinyl. *The New York Times* called Carly's score "lilting, tuneful and an inspired accompaniment to this story."

The promotional CD single of 'Love of My Life' received sufficient airplay to have it gain #16 on the Adult Contemporary chart. 'The Night Before Christmas' was also issued as a promo single toward the end of the year, but failed to make any impact. On Mother's Day, Carly appeared on *Good Morning America* and sang 'Love of My Life' at the keyboard, and also guested on *Late Night with David Letterman*, performing that song and 'Back the Way' with Will Lee on bass, Sid McGinnis on guitar, Paul Shaffer on keyboards, and Anton Fig on drums.

A promotional video for 'Love of My Life' featured Carly with her son Ben on guitar, and was interspersed with clips from the movie. But despite the relative success of both the song and video, the whole project had to be put down as a disappointment for Carly, after devoting so much of her time to the project.

Misguided failure

With Clive Davis anxious to get her working on a studio album of new material, Carly became side-tracked to do a project which was to take her on an unexpected journey. Now well regarded as a successful composer of film scores, she was approached by the Metropolitan Opera Guild in conjunction with Washington's Kennedy Center for Performing Arts to write a contemporary family-friendly opera, one that would attract adults and children alike. It would be the prototype for the Met's New Opera for New Ears project. Having already approached Elvis Costello, they turned to Carly because "she would be familiar to baby-boomer parents" who would be drawn to watch it with their children.

Carly readily accepted the challenge and got down to work. But this would be quite a new ball game for her, and to help guide her along she turned to Jake Brackman to co-write the libretto and Teese Gohl to handle the orchestration and arrangements. For additional help in writing for operatic voices, she turned to Jeff Halpern, an accomplished theater producer and musical director, and Francesca Zambello, a renowned director in the opera world. Actress and choreographer Carmen De Lavallade was another expert enlisted for the project, and, last but not least, Carly's sister Joanna gladly volunteered her experience and valuable advice.

With something like 500 pages of notes and ideas, Carly and Jake came up with a libretto about divorce, with the lead character being a 12-year-old boy called Romulus Hunt. Rom hatches a plan to trick his headstrong divorced parents Eddie and Joanna into getting back together. Joanna (so-named after Carly's sister) is a business-oriented workaholic while Eddie is a Bohemian choreographer with a sly, but sympathetic, live-in artist girlfriend called Mica. Rom is aided by his imaginary Rastafarian friend called Zoogy, who uses his Jamaican singing and magic to help with his scheming.

Following almost two years of preparation and legal battles over who actually owned the rights to the production, rehearsals finally got underway in New York. The cast of non-opera singers consisted of Andrew Garrison as Rom, Luretta Bybee as Joanna, Greer Grimsley as Eddie, Wendy Hill as Mica, and Jeff Hairston as Zoogy. Carly scored the music for ten instruments, including rock percussion, drums, guitar, bass, piano, violin, viola, cello, harp and synthesizer. Carly's ten musicians, which included the return of Jay Berliner, Warren Bernhardt, Michael Brecker and Jimmy Bralower, found it difficult to interpret some of Carly's reggae rhythms that were necessary for Zoogy's musical scenes.

The hour-long opera had its premiere at New York's John Jay Theater on February 24th 1993, and ran until March 7th, before moving to the Eisenhower Theater at the John F Kennedy Center for the Performing Arts in Washington on April 7th. Most reviews were critical, mainly aimed at the "pallid" libretto, which the *New York Times* deemed "haplessly structured." The whole project was called "a peculiar, well-meaning but misguided failure," with the rebuke:" children have far more imagination than pandering permits. Relevance comes from dramatic power." Summing up, the reviewer blamed both the Met and Carly, claiming the singer was treating her venture into opera as "a novelty." However, *Stereo Review* saw things differently, rating it as the best American opera since *Porgy and*

Bess, and *CD Magazine* stated: "Here is a genuinely beloved artist, with years of popularity, with a vast public that American opera composers would kill for, bringing that public to opera with an ease few composers can match." Despite the mixed reviews, the opera was appreciated by the ones who mattered most - the audience.

The final recording for the subsequent soundtrack, produced by Frank Filipetti and Teese Gohl, was completed at Right Track and The Hit Factory and released on Angel Records on November 16th 1993. The singing on the album was done by the cast of five, with Kurt Ollman now playing Eddie, Andrew Leeds as Rom, and Bybee, Hairston and Hill reprising their theater roles. Carly's wonderful lead song 'Voulez Vous Danser' (would you like to dance?) appears four times on the album, first as an introduction by an unknown artist, the second a duet with Leeds and Bybee, the third a duet with Leeds and Ollman, and finally being the bonus track of Carly's version, the one which later appeared on 1995's box set *Clouds in My Coffee*.

In December 2015, Carly would be involved in the show's revival by the Nashville Opera Association at the Noah Liff Opera Center's Studio Theater, holding talkback sessions with the audience after each performance. With a new cast, the character Zoogy now sang rap instead of reggae.

ROMULUS HUNT: A FAMILY OPERA
Angel Records CDQ 0777 7 54915 2 4
Recorded - 1993, Right Track Recording & The Hit Factory, New York
Released - November 16 1993
Producers - Frank Filipetti and Teese Gohl.
Engineer - Frank Filipetti
Mastering - Ted Jensen, Sterling Sound, New York
Carly Simon - acoustic guitar; Jay Berliner - guitar; Jeff Pevar - guitar; Warren Bernhardt - piano; Teese Gohl - piano; Bill Mays - piano; Michael Kosarin - piano; Richard Martinez - keyboards; Jeff Bova - piano; John Beal - bass; Sergio Brandao - bass; Timothy Cobb - bass; Jimmy Bralower - drums; Michael Brecker - EWI; Lamar Alsop - viola; Leonard Davis - viola; Richard Sortomme - viola; Barry Finclair - violin; Guillermo Figueroa - violin; Elena Barere - violin, concert master; Cenobia Cummings - violin; Charles Libove - violin; John Pintavalle - violin; Matthew Raimondi - violin; Paul Peabody - violin; Israel Chorberg - violin; Semyon Fridman - cello; Charles McCracken - cello; Jesse Levy - cello; Emily Mitchell - harp; Cyro Baptista - percussion; Gordon Gottlieb - percussion.
Introduction (Voulez-Vous Danser)
Loose Arms
Valentine Aria

A Boy of Twelve
Man With Wings
My Dance is a Tango
Voulez-Vous Danser
Fond of the Blondes
It's My Downfall
Incantation
The Fight
The Jig
Am I Still Young?
It's Such a Glorious Day
Seduction Aria
Romulus Hunt (The Nightmare)
Where Am I
It Almost Happens on Its Own (We'll Never Leave)
Eddie's Soliloquy
Voulez Vous Danser
Voulez Vous Danser (bonus track)

Pressures and pain

Earlier in the year Carly had written the theme song 'The Promise and the Prize' for the ABC sitcom *Phenom*, which premiered on September 14th and starred Angela Goethals and Ashley Johnson. She had also been contacted by Nora Ephron to sing the standard 'In the Wee Small Hours of the Morning' for the soundtrack to her rom-com movie *Sleepless in Seattle*, which was released in June and starred Tom Hanks and Meg Ryan. Produced by Frank Filipetti and Marti Paich, the song was issued by Arista as a promotional single but not commercially released. Carly also contributed music for the American Repertory Theater's production of *Cakewalk* in Cambridge, Massachusetts.

Carly was also asked to contribute her song 'Private Eyes' on her friend Andreas Vollenweider's album *Eolian Minstrel*. Swiss-born Vollenweider was a New-Age musician and celebrated harpist. In 1975 he had designed his own modified electro-acoustic harp and had recorded several notable albums. Carly had fallen in love with the sound of the instrument: "I knew I had discovered something that was going to change me in a wonderful way. I became so obsessed with his music that anyone who came to my house was introduced to it within the first 10 or 15 minutes." She contacted the musician through CBS and arranged for him to make his US debut and personally introduced him to the audience at the Beacon Theater in New York in November 1984. Three years later his album *Down to the Moon* would earn him a Grammy. Now, seven years later, Carly's admiration for him would lead to an invitation for him to play on her next album.

In August Carly and her husband Jim took the opportunity of inviting newly-elected President Bill Clinton and First Lady Hillary for lunch, after they had arrived on the Vineyard for their summer vacation. The Clintons were huge fans of Carly's music and they would become regular summer visitors to the Simon household.

Toward the end of the year Carly was invited to sing on the Frank Sinatra album *Duets*, which featured legendary artists such as Barbra Streisand, Aretha Franklin and Tony Bennett. Although Carly was looking forward to meeting her childhood hero, Sinatra was in no shape to record, so the recordings were done by lifting an isolated pre-recorded vocal track from an earlier performance and then laying down a new background with Carly's vocal. The two songs recorded were the Jule Styne-Sammy Cahn song, 'Guess I'll Hang My Tears Out to Dry', along with 'In the Wee Small Hours', both arranged by the great Nelson Riddle. When the album was released, it entered the Hot 200 at #2 on November 20th and went on to achieve triple-platinum certification. Although critics slated the album as Sinatra's worst, they rated Carly's contribution as the album's best moment.

1993 had proved to be a productive year for Carly, but it was also tinged with sadness. Jim Hart had given up on the great novel he was writing, and his frustration was causing friction in their relationship. Eventually he moved back to New York and resumed his insurance job. However, the separation only lasted a few months and he had since returned to the Vineyard to give Carly much-needed emotional support after she found out that her mother Andrea had been diagnosed with incurable lung cancer. Her anxieties were compounded even more when her great friend Jackie Onassis was diagnosed with lymphoma following a fall from a horse. Not only this, Carly was still coming to terms with the loss of her friend Alex Taylor, James' older brother, who had died of alcoholic poisoning back in March. As though that wasn't enough for her to deal with, she now had her label boss Clive Davis once again pressing her to write material for her next studio album.

A Box of Letters

"I have a faucet dripping in my head all the time with melodies. They're not all good, but they're always there. I have to sit down alone to write words. I do it at night, when everybody's asleep...it's a habit I got into when the kids were still babies"

Losing Andrea and Jackie too

For her next album, Carly found inspiration from the contents of an old box (or suitcase in some versions of the story): "I kept a whole lot of letters that I shouldn't send to people in a box on top of my closet, and I wrote them in a fit of frothy horror and ended up not sending them."

One of these letters had been addressed to Andrea before she had been diagnosed with cancer. In the letter, she asked her mother to admit some of the responsibility for her failed marriage, citing Ronnie Klinzing and her Aunt Jo as the instigators, but saying how her and her sisters were the victims. But instead of mailing it, she recalled the wise advice that her mother had once given her to "sleep on it before you put a stamp on it" and never send a letter that had been written with strong emotions. With this in mind, the new album would be titled *Letters Never Sent*.

Carly stayed close to her mother as often as she could, but on February 15th 1994 Andrea finally lost her battle at the age of 85. At the funeral held at the Riverdale Presbyterian Church, the three sisters sang the beautiful 'May the Lord Bless You and Keep You'. It was a devastating time for everyone, and Carly would pay tribute to her mother by writing the profound 'Like a River' for her new album.

A few weeks later Carly had a final lunch date with Jackie Onassis. Before they parted, Carly gave her a sheet of paper with the lyrics to a song called 'Touched by the Sun' that she had both written for her, and been inspired by her. This would be the last time they would ever meet. On May 16th Jackie died in her Manhattan apartment. She was 64. Carly later described their relationship: "I think she saw in me something that she wanted to have a little bit of herself. I think she saw a free spirit who had the license to be, in a rock & roll kind of way, loose as a goose. And I could smoke a joint if I wanted to. She didn't have a license to be free. She was a naughty girl and she liked that in herself and she liked it in other people."

Carly's sadness over losing both her mother and Jackie in so short a space of time was eased a little at a ceremony held at the Sheraton Hotel and Towers in New York on June 1st, when she finally received her long-overdue induction to the Songwriters Hall of Fame, joining the Bee Gees, Lionel Richie and Otis Redding, who were also honored that star-studded evening.

During the summer Carly appeared on *The Late Show with David Letterman* to promote *Romulus Hunt* and gave a debut performance of her new song, 'Touched by the Sun'. She also contributed to the album *Greeting from the Gutter* by keyboardist Dave Stewart, one half of the British duo the Eurythmics, and joined him in a screwball conversation/argument on the humorous track 'Oh No, Not You Again'.

The next few months would see a surge of creativity as Carly produced some of her finest work, a collection of ten songs, some linked with short interludes, and one in particular which is considered one of her finest compositions.

Recorded at five different studios, including one in Germany, the twentieth album of her career and her first of new material for four years would once again involve a number of individual producers, although Frank Filipetti would oversee the majority of the recordings. With Teese Gohl handling most of the string arrangements, many familiar faces returned to play a part on what would be a highly emotive album. James Taylor's old friend Danny Kortchmar not only added his exceptional guitar skills but also co-wrote one of the songs, while Ben Taylor was now a much-valued member of the recording team. Last, but not least, was Carly's friend Andreas Vollenweider, who now brought his incredible harp skills to one of the sessions. There were also some new players - Puerto Rican guitarist Carlos Alomar, famous for his work for David Bowie in the mid-70s; New Jersey-born multi-instrumentalist Mick Rossi; Welsh bass player Pino Palladino, who had played on Gary Numan's debut album; and Canadian-born guitarist Peter Calo, who, like Teese Gohl, would now figure greatly in Carly's career.

LETTERS NEVER SENT
Arista 07822-18752-2 (UK – 07822 18752 2)
Recorded - Summer-Fall 1994, Right Track Recording, The Hit Factory, &
Sound on Sound, New York; Cadiloon Sound, Pawling, New York & Room with
a View Studio, Hamburg.
Released - November 1 1994
Producers - Carly Simon & Frank Filipetti, (with Teese Gohl, Paul Samwell-Smith and Danny Kortchmar)
Engineer - Frank Filipetti

Mastering - Ted Jensen, Sterling Sound, New York
Art direction - Carly Simon
US Billboard Hot 200 #129

Intro *(Carly Simon)*
Producers - Carly Simon & Frank Filipetti
Short string instrumental.

Letters Never Sent *(Carly Simon - Jacob Brackman)* ***
Producers - Carly Simon, Frank Filipetti & Teese Gohl
Carlos Alomar - electric guitar; Doug Wimbush - bass; Sammy Merendino - drums; Teese Gohl - arr. strings & conductor; Emile Chartap - strings contractor; Jerry Barnes - backing vocals; Katreese Barnes - backing vocals; Curtis King - backing vocals
The song that nicely introduces the background to the album and the discovery of one or more boxes full of letters that Carly never mailed. Thumping start with Carly and Jake's lyrics complemented by an excellent jam session with the guitar riffs of newcomer Carlos Alomar and Sammy Merendino's solid drumming. Also, a welcome return of Curtis King and siblings Jerry and Katreese Barnes on backing vocals.

Lost in Your Love *(Carly Simon)* ****
Producers - Carly Simon & Frank Filipetti
Carly Simon - acoustic guitar; Mick Rossi - guitar; Jimmy Ryan - electric guitar; T-Bone Wolk - bass; Andy Newmark - drums; Andy Snitzer - tenor sax solo; Arif Mardin - arranger; Joe Mardin - arranger & conductor; Gene Orloff - strings contractor; Dexter Redding - backing vocals; Otis Redding III - backing vocals
Carly's vocals are at full-throttle in this fiery, lust-soaked ballad about infatuation, with Arif Mardin stepping in to help with the arrangement, which includes a great sax solo by Andy Snitzer. The sons of the late, great Otis Redding supply backing vocals.

Like a River *(Carly Simon)* *****
Promo CD single ASCD-2763 (radio edit & album version)
Released 1994
Producers - Carly Simon & Frank Filipetti
Carly Simon - acoustic piano, electric piano, drum programming; Teese Gohl - acoustic piano, orchestral arrangement on We'll Never Leave; Pino Palladino - bass; Robin Gould - drums; Emile Chartap - string contractor; Jeff Halpern - orchestral conductor on We'll Never Leave; Luretta Bybee, Jeff Hairston & Wendy Hill - backing vocals on We'll Never Leave
Perhaps the most poignant of the letters Carly wrote but never mailed was the one for her mother Andrea before her cancer was diagnosed. In it, Carly asked her the unresolved questions about the effect her parents 'affairs had had on the young family. In the song, she is alone in her mother's house, still asking her questions, regretting fighting with her sisters over her pearls, and asking whether she has made peace with her father in the afterlife. Returning to her favorite water

analogy, she vows she will always wait for her mother, not like a daughter, but "like a river," washing away any doubts she may have had. Carly's haunting vocal in the final chorus is breathtaking, and just as you think the song has reached a climax, Carly choses to include the "We'll never leave" segment of the opera *Romulus Hunt* to give it that solemn final punch (although it will be omitted from the single version).

Time Works on All the Wild Young Men *(Carly Simon - Ben Taylor)* ***
Producers - Carly Simon & Frank Filipetti
Ben Taylor - vocals, acoustic guitar
A charming acoustic interlude delivered by Ben, who wrote the music for his mother's inspiring lyrics as a perfect introduction to the track that follows. He also sounds eerily like his father.

Touched by the Sun *(Carly Simon)* *****
Promo CD single ASCD-2814 (radio edit & full version)
Released - 1995
Producers- Carly Simon & Frank Filipetti
Carly Simon - acoustic guitar; Mick Rossi - acoustic piano; Peter Calo - acoustic guitar; Dirk Ziff - lead guitar; Pino Palladino - bass; Gregory Jones - bass; Rick Marotta - drums; Teese Gohl - arr. strings & conductor; Emile Chartap - string contractor; Marc Cohn - backing vocals
Carly's great tribute to her friendship with former First Lady Jackie Onassis, who had died that spring just three months after Carly's mother. In the song she imagines her reaching the "other" place and meeting up with all the great people of the world who are already there. Carly and Jackie were seen by many as two very individual women. Ben had often remarked that his mother wore her nervous system on the outside of her body, whereas Jackie was emotionally more durable. And it was that durability that Carly so much admired. In a truly breathtaking epic of a song, Carly gives arguably her greatest ever vocal performance, sounding at times almost crazed with passion, as if she had had to suppress her grief for so long, and was only now finally allowed to release, in a thunderous outburst, all that long pent-up emotion. With inspiration taken from the poem 'The Truly Great' by English poet Stephen Spender (1909-95), Carly has produced a magnificent song with outstanding production helmed by both Carly and Frank Filipetti. Rick Marotta sets the beat with dynamic drumming, and acclaimed folk-rock singer Marc Cohn ('Walking in Memphis') adds a wonderful vocal toward the end. The song undoubtedly had the makings of a great hit single, and although issued as a promo it never had a commercial release. However, the accompanying video would prove to be rather special and show Carly as we've never seen her before.

Davy *(Carly Simon)* ****
Producers - Carly Simon & Frank Filipetti
Carly Simon - acoustic guitar; Walter Keiser - drums; Andreas Vollenweider - electric harp

Lyrics that portray what appears to be an unrequited love for a real or maybe imaginary person. A lovely understated track with the distinctive electric harp of Andrew Vollenweider, and one that once again leads to the question - who is it about? Carly could very well be reminiscing about young Davy Gude, one of her earliest crushes while holidaying on the Vineyard.

Halfway Round the World *(Carly Simon)* ***
Producers - Carly Simon, Frank Filipetti & Paul Samwell-Smith
Peter Calo - acoustic guitar; Dave Stewart - acoustic & electric guitar; Teese Gohl - arr. string & conductor, synthesizer, sailor vocals; Paul Samwell-Smith - Grand Casa bass drum, tambourine, sailor vocals; Beth Miller - fiddle; Emile Chartap - string contractor; Taj Mahal - harmonica, backing vocals; Ben Taylor - sailor vocals, backing vocals
Nautical-flavored anthem in which her one-time lover is always absent and preoccupied with his official duties, giving the impression that for him it can't be far enough away. The song features guitar player Dave Stewart, the harmonica of Harlem-born blues singer Taj Mahal (aka Henry Fredericks), and "sailor" vocals provided by son Ben.

What About a Holiday *(Carly Simon)* *
Producers - Carly Simon & Frank Filipetti
Short fantastical interlude in which the narrator takes the "sweet" members of the Rolling Stones for a walk around the city.

The Reason *(Carly Simon - Danny Kortchmar)* ****
Producers - Carly Simon, Frank Filipetti & Danny Kortchmar
Carly Simon - keyboards, drum programming; Danny Kortchmar - acoustic, electric & slide guitar; Pino Palladino - bass; Steve Ferrone - drums; Teese Gohl - keyboards; Julia Levine - backing vocals; Sally Taylor - backing vocals
Carly is explaining to her would-be lover why things didn't develop the night before. There's always a reason for not doing something, especially when it comes to love, and Carly does her best to explain in a rather bizarre way the consequences of such rashness, ending with one of her greatest lines - "I can never be in love, I can only be in heat." A fine collaboration with James Taylor's great friend and former band member "Kooch" Kortchmar, with a solid performance from English drummer Steve Ferrone, the one-time member of the *Saturday Night Live* house band, and now with Tom Petty and the Heartbreakers.

Private *(Carly Simon)* ****
Producers - Carly Simon & Frank Filipetti
Carly Simon - acoustic guitar; Mick Rossi - acoustic piano; Peter Calo - acoustic guitar; Gregory Jones - bass; Rick Marotta - drums; Andy Snitzer - tenor sax; Teese Gohl - synthesizer
Sultry song in which Carly, in another unsent letter, pleads with her lover to keep their relationship a secret and not to go bragging to his friends about her. If he does, she will just lie to them. In a rare falsetto, Carly sings with subdued passion, epitomized by Andy Snitzer's evocative sax solo.

Catch It Like A Fever *(Carly Simon)* ***
Producers - Carly Simon & Frank Filipetti
Another short spoken interlude in which Carly expresses her feelings about how having an obsession for someone can lead to it becoming infectious. The perfect prelude to the track that follows.

Born to Break My Heart *(Carly Simon)* ****
Producers - Carly Simon & Frank Filipetti
Carly Simon - drum programming, keyboards; Carlos Alomar - guitar; Peter Calo - guitar; Doug Wimbush - bass; T-Bone Wolk - bass; Teese Gohl - strings, arr. strings & conductor; Jimmy Bralower - additional drum programming; Emile Chartap - string contractor; Rosanne Cash - backing vocals
Another outstanding track displaying Carly's great vocal range as she compares a lover to all those who have betrayed her in the past, and who is now leaving her "cursed to seek love again from yet another cold heart." The lyrics are both elegant and precise, and perhaps recall the bitterness of some of her own failed relationships. The great Rosanne Cash guests as backing vocalist.

I'd Rather It Was You *(Carly Simon)* ****
Producers - Carly Simon & Frank Filipetti
Carly Simon - acoustic guitar; Teese Gohl - keyboards; Jimmy Ryan - hammered dulcimer, Dobro; Sammy Merendino - drums
Excellent finale by Carly, and another song about her lusting for love, a passion flamed even brighter by the spiritual Eastern-flavored music, courtesy of some magical playing by Jimmy Ryan on a hammered dulcimer, a percussion-stringed instrument consisting of strings stretched over a resonant sound board.

In the liner notes, Carly dedicated the album to "the memory of my Astounding Mother, Andrea Simon and my much-loved friend, Jacqueline Onassis." She also gives thanks to her children "who are leaving the nest and following their dreams. May you all get there," and a final nod to old friend Paul Samwell-Smith for continuing to be "a most interesting musical influence."

Released on November 1st, the album stalled at #129 on the Hot 200 on the 19th. Surprisingly, two promotional singles of 'Touched by the Sun' and 'Like a River' failed to gain interest and neither were commercially released. Even the excellent, sure-fire chart potential of 'Born to Break My Heart' was overlooked by Arista.

However, two promotional videos were made. 'Touched by the Sun' is perhaps the most audacious, showing Carly as a near-crazed woman driving a Galaxy Ford in a desert setting (close-ups were apparently filmed near Montauk on Long Island). Shot in black and white, her wild, wet hair and dark, menacing eyes perfectly capture the mood of the music, surely making it the best ever visual interpretation of one of her compositions. In contrast, the beautifully-shot video for 'Like A River' shows Carly performing the song at the piano, along with candid childhood images of her with her mother. The exterior shots were filmed at Oyster Bay on Long Island. Like the videos for 'Hello Big Man' and 'Coming Around Again', Carly has a sentimental way of evoking memories of a much gentler time.

AllMusic looked on the album as Carly returning to passion, but concluded: "It's an unusually coquettish performance for a woman of 49 and practically weightless." *Entertainment Weekly* called the "funky, fascinating and sumptuous" album a daring move for Carly that had actually paid off.

During the year Carly also sang the Gershwins' 'I've Got a Crush on You' on the Larry Adler album *The Glory of Gershwin*, produced by George Martin as a tribute to Adler's 80th birthday, and on which the maestro plays harmonica on every track. The album peaked at #2 on the UK chart.

Grand Central and the summer tour

The pressure was now on to recoup lost sales, and Clive Davis urged Carly to press on with a summer tour and do more promotional work. One of the label's executives had described Carly as one of their "heritage artists," a rather stinging reference to her age, and as a result her relationship with Arista would now become strained.

Carly had mixed emotions about committing herself to a nationwide tour, and admitted later, "I came very close to not doing it, to losing my sense of confidence. But I did it. I was so proud of myself." For Carly it was like getting back on the horse after a fall; if she didn't do it now, she never would. With determination, she was not about to let herself down.

With her new manager Brian Doyle (of the company All Access Entertainment Management Group) now urging her to meet the label's requests and not to jeopardize her future career, and with tour dates planned to begin the following July, Carly made a flurry of television appearances. On November 14th she made a return visit to *The Late Show with David Letterman*, with fellow guests George Foreman and Brooke Shields, and performed 'Half Way Round the World'. That same month she featured on the ABC television special *Christmas at Home with the Stars*, which aired on December 17th and also starred Aretha Franklin, Toni Braxton, Barry Manilow and Kenny G. Two days later Carly was interviewed on Howard Stern's radio show, and, with her usual flirting, sang an impromptu version of 'You've Got a Friend' with revised lyrics, celebrating the fact that Stern had just saved someone from jumping from the Washington Bridge by keeping them talking until the police arrived.

1995 got under way with Carly appearing as a guest caller in an episode of *Frasier* entitled 'Roz in the Doghouse', aired on January 3rd. She also appeared at Clive Davis's annual pre-Grammy bash held at the House of Blues in Los Angeles on February 28th. During the show Carly was joined by Annie Lennox, Melissa Etheridge and Sarah McLachlan for a rendition of 'You're So Vain'. The following day she attended the 37th Annual Grammy Awards at the Shrine Auditorium in Hollywood, joining Tori Amos to present Bruce Springsteen the award for Best Male Rock Vocal for 'Streets of Philadelphia'. What proved to be a busy week continued the following day when she guested on NBC's *The Tonight Show with Jay Leno*, along with Will Smith and Haley Joel Osment.

Carly now put a band together for the forthcoming tour. It consisted of Teese Gohl (keyboards), Rick Marotta (drums), T-Bone Wolk (bass), Peter Calo (guitar) and Curtis King (backing vocals). On March 3rd they began what was to be an initial seven-date jaunt as a trial for the forthcoming summer tour. At the Galaxy Theatre in Santa Ana, with a sell-out audience of 550, the setlist included classic hits and material from *Letters Never Sent*. At the concert at Boston's Avalon nightclub on March 13th, she was joined on stage by daughter Sally (who was now attending Brown University in Providence) to sing a thumping solo version of 'Mustang Sally' that sent the crowd wild.

A week later Carly performed at the Park West Club in Chicago, which impressed the *Tribune*: "If her performing manner showed a bit less edge than before, a little less rhythmic aggression, she easily compensated with the interpretive depth and musical control of this performance…Simon offered radiant maturity rather than rambunctious youth, heart and soul rather than brass and flash." Blasting out one hit after another with no sign of nerves, she told the audience, "I'm getting in to it."

The short tour finished on March 25th at the Newport Music Hall in Columbus, Ohio, but it never escaped the press that this had been Carly's first string of concerts since that frightful evening in Pittsburgh in 1980 when she had a panic attack and collapsed backstage.

As a final prelude to the summer tour, a one-off surprise concert was arranged at New York's iconic Grand Central Station. It was directed by Englishman Nigel Dick, who in 1986 had co-founded Propaganda Films, a company which specialized in making commercial and music videos. For the concert, Dick had a stage built over the west stairs of the main concourse, where sunlight would bathe the performers through the massive eastern windows. Musical producer Frank Filipetti made it a twelve-piece band by bringing in other musicians: bassist Doug Wimbush replaced the unavailable T-Bone Wolk; Eric Brazilian, whose mandolin would substitute for Vollenweider's electric harp; guitarists Mick Rossi and Dirk Ziff; and Jake Brackman's wife Melinda "Mindy" Jostyn on violin. The backing singers were Marc Cohn and Jerry and Katreese Barnes.

During the late morning of April 2nd many bemused New York commuters were either late or missed their trains altogether as they watched Carly perform fourteen songs, including some of her greatest hits, but surprisingly no 'You're So Vain'. The set opened with Carly alone on stage singing 'Touched by the Sun' as the band members joined her one by one. Toward the end of the song, her passionate guitar playing managed to break one of the strings. Among the other highlights were rare live performances of 'Davy', and 'I've Got to Have You', plus a magnificent 'That's the Way I've Always Heard It Should Be' making what must have been its first televised performance since the No Nukes concert in 1979. The show was aired on the Lifetime Television cable channel and finally released on Laserdisc and VHS on December 12th 1995. Carly was also nominated for two CableACE (Award for Cable Excellence) awards, with 'Touched by the Sun' winning her Best Original Song, and the show itself receiving a nomination in the Performance in a Music Special category.

The same month Carly reunited with her sister Lucy to sing with Peter Yarrow and Richie Havens on the Grossman-Yarrow-Travers song 'The Great Mandela (The Wheels of Life)' on their new album *Lifelines*. The song had first been heard on Peter, Paul and Mary's 1967 album *1770*.

In May Carly made another appearance on *The Late Show with David Letterman*, with fellow guests Jack Johannsen and Bruno Kirby, and again did a superb performance of 'Touched by the Sun'. On June 3rd she took part in the annual KISS Genesis Fund concert at the Great Woods Center for Performing Arts in Mansfield, Massachusetts, along with fellow artists Paula Abdul, Chris Isaak, Duran Duran, the Human League, and, last but not least, Tom Jones, who joined Carly to sing 'You're So Vain'.

Three weeks later, on June 25th, Carly celebrated her 50th birthday.

The two-month-long tour finally got under way on July 19th, and consisted of sixteen dates mainly at festivals and club-size venues. The schedule was as follows:

Jul 19	Finger Lakes Performing Arts Center, Canandaigua, NY
Jul 21	Great Woods, Mansfield MA
Jul 23	Meadows Music Theater, Hartford CT
Jul 25	Saratoga Performing Arts, Saratoga NY
Jul 27	Mann Music Theater, Philadelphia PA
Jul 29	Jones Beach, Long Island NY
Aug 1	Garden State Arts Center, Holmdel NJ

Aug 2   Chastain Park, Atlanta GA
Aug 5   Merriweather Post Pavilion, Columbia MD
Aug 8   Kingswood Amphitheater, Toronto Canada
Aug 10   Pine Knob, Detroit MI
Aug 12   Riverbend Music Theater, Cincinnati OH
Aug 14   Polaris Amphitheater, Columbus OH
Aug 16   Blossom Music Festival, Cleveland OH
Aug 20   Gorge Theater, Seattle WA
Aug 22   Concord Pavilion, Concord CA

With the successful, chart-topping Philadelphia soul duo Daryl Hall & John Oates providing the opening act, the shows were sold out well in advance. Most evenings Carly joined them on stage to sing their smash hit, 'Everytime You Go Away', while, in turn, they joined her for 'Anticipation'. This time there were no signs of panic attacks and all the concerts went without a hitch and received glowing reviews. The girl had pulled it off.

On August 30th, eight days after returning to the Vineyard, a re-invigorated Carly reunited with James Taylor to perform solo sets at the unofficially-coined Livestock 95 benefit concert, held on the county fairgrounds at West Tilsbury on the Vineyard, the proceeds of which went to the island's struggling Agricultural Society. In front of a 10,000-strong audience, and with no media coverage allowed, a balding and rather disheveled-looking James was joined on stage by a radiant Carly to sing 'Shower the People' and 'Mockingbird'. During Carly's set she performed 'You're So Vain' with Aerosmith's Steve Tyler joining her on the chorus.

During the year Carly also became one of the featured subjects of *Intimate Portrait*, a series of televised documentaries about female celebrities. Shown on the Lifetime cable channel and directed by Kathleen Dougherty, it featured Carly with contributions from Jake Brackman, Frank Filipetti, Lynn Goldsmith, Rick Marotta, Nora Ephron, Jeannie Seligmann, T-Bone Wolk, Mia Farrow and former nanny Alice Brennan. Carly also guested in an episode of the series *Studio Sessions*, with fine performances of 'Anticipation' and 'Touched by the Sun' filmed at the VH1 Studios.

Carly was also invited to record 'Take Me Out to the Ball Game' for Ken Burns' PBS documentary, *Baseball*, which charted the history of the game. The song was a Tin Pan Alley standard written in 1908 by Jack Norworth and Albert Von Tilzer. The Emmy-award-winning film first aired on September 18th.

On October 2nd Carly was honored at the Boston Music Awards with Outstanding Female Vocalist and was also inducted into their prestigious

"Lifetime Achievement" Hall of Fame, joining James Taylor, who had been given the same honor four years before.

The act of creativity

By the fall of 1995 Carly began working with Arista on what was to be the most comprehensive and retrospective collection of her music to date, entitled *Clouds in My Coffee*, the title taken from the comment made by her friend Billy Mernit during a flight many years before. The tedious work involved cooperation with former labels and searching through her own demo tapes in her personal archive. This proved to be a difficult task, as many of the masters for some of her greatest hits could not be found and were subsequently declared lost.

Working with Frank Filipetti, a few of the early songs had to be digitally improved at Right Track Recording in New York. The resultant box set (her first) consisted of three compact discs and 58 re-mastered songs spanning her career from the Simon Sisters in 1963 to the present, including previously unreleased songs that included 'Raining' from 1990; the demo of 'I'm All It Takes to Make You Happy' from the Buckmaster sessions in 1972; 'Take Me Out to the Ball Game' from *Baseball*; 'Play With Me', her first demo, produced by John McClure from 1968; and her 1972 version of John Prine's 'Angel From Montgomery'. The box set also included a 48-page booklet with liner notes by Carly, Steve Morse of the *Boston Globe*, and her friend Jim Armstrong.

In the excellent introduction to the compilation, Carly writes about her songwriting: "I think that's what the act of creativity must be about. It's about making something you believe is better than you are, and for a moment, you merge with it and think it's you and you are it. Even when I am in a state of self-loathing, I can write something that I fall in love with. Deluded though I might be, it makes me feel better about myself and it usually inspires me to write another song."

CLOUDS IN MY COFFEE
Arista 07822-18798-2 (3-cd boxset)
Released - November 7th 1995
Executive Producers - Carly Simon & Frank Filipetti
Engineer - Frank Filipetti
Remastering - Ted Jensen
Design - Louise Fili & Mary Jane Callister

Disc 1 - The Hits
Let the River Run/You Belong to Me/Nobody Does It Better/Coming Around
Again/Jesse/The Stuff That Dreams Are Made of/You're So Vain/Touched by the
Sun/Haven't Got Time For the Pain/Better Not Tell Her/Legend in Your Own
Time/Mockingbird/That's the Way I've Always Heard It Should Be/All I Want Is
You/The Right Thing To Do/Like a River/Anticipation/Give Me All Night.

Disc 2 - Miscellaneous & unreleased
Angel From Montgomery/Raining/I'm All It Takes to Make You Happy/Easy on
the Eyes/Turn of the Tide/Libby/Have You Seen Me Lately/My New
Boyfriend/Voulez Vous Danser/The Night Before Christmas/Halfway Round the
World/Life is Eternal/We Have No Secrets/Why/Take Me Out to the Ball
Game/Back This Way/Itsy Bitsy Spider/Play With Me/My Luv Is Like a Red,
Red Rose

Disc 3 - Cry Yourself to Sleep
It Happens Everyday/Boys in the Trees/Julie Through the Glass/Orpheus/Never
Been Gone/Happy Birthday/Devoted to You/Davy/Do the Walls Come
Down/Danny Boy/Dink's Blues/We're So Close/Someone Waits For You/Born
to Break My Heart/Time After Time/What Shall We Do With the Child/I've Got
a Crush On You/Something Wonderful/You're the Love of My Life/I Get Along
Without You Very Well/Be Myself - I See Your Face Before Me

The fact that this impressive collection left out so many great songs only
serves to highlight what a fine body of work Carly had accomplished in
those thirty years. As expected, the sales for the expensive box set were
disappointing, but it remains the definitive record of Carly's career up to
that time. Further anthologies would follow in due course, but none would
match this for its scale.

The last week of January 1996 saw Carly performing four more shows
with Hall & Oates in support of the American Indian College Fund at the
Fox Arena in the Foxwoods Resort Casino in Ledyard, CT.

It would prove to be a good year for Carly. Not only did she sign a new
book deal with Simon & Schuster, she was also approached to do more
movie work. Director Jerry Zaks asked her to write a song for his movie
Marvin's Room, based on the play by Scott McPherson, about a father
called Marvin (played by Hugh Cronin) who had suffered a stroke, was left
bed ridden, and was now being cared for by one daughter, Bessie (Diane
Keaton) while completely ignored by another daughter, Lee (Meryl Streep).
Carly came up with a masterful piece of emotive songwriting with 'Two
Little Sisters', and recorded it for the movie with Streep on additional
vocals, Carly and Kenneth Bichel on piano, and John Miller on bass. The

film was released in December to good reviews, and earned Streep an Oscar nomination. A short documentary of the song's recording was also released.

In a lovestruck wonder

Also in 1996 Carly hosted a television special *Bill Clinton: Rock & Roll President* and performed concerts at the Fleet Center in Boston (September 28th) and the New York City Center Stage Theater (October 17th), but with pressure coming from Arista to make another album, she won another argument with Davis to make what would be her third collection of standards, entitled *Film Noir*, a homage to the alluring genre that had seduced her as a young girl. Shot in shadowy black and white, the films were often full of sinister plots, with femme fatales and anti-heroes who fought the gangsters of the world. Despite initial misgivings, Davis decided to put his full weight behind the project and joined forces with the AMC (American Movie Classics) Film Preservation, who were holding their 5th annual festival that fall.

At a press conference, AMC president Kate McEnroe announced the world premiere of a documentary film called *Songs in Shadow: The Making of Carly's Simon's Film Noir*, a celebration of the genre and featuring a behind-the-scenes look at the recording of Carly's album, which was to be "a wonderful, musical tribute to film noir." Sitting alongside Carly, with screen heroine Lauren Bacall and movie director and film noir enthusiast Martin Scorsese, Davis welcomed Carly's participation as "an exciting next chapter in her trendsetting career" and that it "was something we wanted to be a part of." He also announced that the one-hour special presentation would be aired on the AMC channel on October 5th.

To assist in the production, Carly was joined by her old colleague Arif Mardin, esteemed Grammy-award winning songwriter Jimmy Webb, and producer and arranger Van Dyke Parks, better known for his work with Brian Wilson on the aborted *Smile* album. The songs were recorded at five different studios. Like *My Romance*, the album would include one new song, and among the familiar musicians invited were Peter Calo, Teese Gohl, Michael Kosarin and Jeff Pevar. Carly's old friend John Travolta also came along to duet on one of the numbers.

FILM NOIR
Arista 07822-18984-2 (UK – 07822 18984- 2)
Recorded - 1996-1997, Right Track Recording, Clinton, & National Edison Studios, New York; Snowbound Sound, Pawling NY & Capitol Studios, LA.
Released - September 16 1997

Producers - Carly Simon, Jimmy Webb & Arif Mardin
Engineers - Frank Filipetti (with Bill Eric, Brian Faehndrich, Roy Hendrickson,
Michael O'Reilly & Al Schmitt)
Mixing – Frank Filipetti
Mastering - Ted Jensen, Sterling Sound New York
Art direction - Mark Burdett
US Billboard Hot 200 #84

You Won't Forget Me *(Kermit Goell - Fred Speilman)* ***
*Michael Kosarin - piano; Peter Calo - guitar; Teese Gohl - keyboards; Billy
Ward - drums; David Finck - acoustic bass; Van Dyke Parks - arranger &
conductor; Elena Barere - concertmaster*
From the 1953 movie *Torch Song* starring Joan Crawford and Michael Wilding,
and sung by Crawford (dubbed by India Adams). It was recorded the same year
by the Nelson Riddle Orchestra. Beautiful arrangement by Van Dyke Parks
underpins this largely forgotten song delivered by Carly in her inimitable style.

Ev'ry Time We Say Goodbye *(Cole Porter)* *****
*Jimmy Webb - piano, organ solo; Peter Calo - guitar; Teese Gohl - keyboards;
David Finck - acoustic bass; Billy Ward - drums; Van Dyke Parks - arranger &
conductor; Barry Finclair - concertmaster; Carly Simon - backing vocals; Ben
Taylor - backing vocals*
A popular jazz song first published in 1944 and performed by Nan Wynn and Jere
McMahon in Billy Rose's musical revue, *Seven Lively Arts*. It was also a chart hit
for Benny Goodman in 1945, but here given a more flirtatious treatment by Carly
with another splendid arrangement by Parks and backing vocals with Ben on the
fadeout.

Lili Marlene *(Mack David - Norbert Schultze - Hans Leip)* ****
*Jimmy Webb - piano; Peter Calo - guitar; Jeff Pevar - mandolin; Dominick
Cortese - accordion; Carly Simon - backing vocals; Mindy Jostyn - backing
vocals; Jill Del'Abate - backing vocals*
A German love song first written as a poem in 1915, and published as a song in
1937. Originally performed by Lale Andersen in 1939, it was made famous
forevermore by Marlene Dietrich during the Second World War. Carly delivers a
haunting rendition with mandolin and accordion giving it a nostalgic touch.

Last Night When We Were Young *(Edgar Yip Harburg - Harold Arlen)* ****
*Russ Kassoff - piano; Peter Calo - guitar; Teese Gohl - keyboards; David Finck -
acoustic bass; Billy Ward - drums; Torrie Zito - arranger & conductor; Elena
Barere - concertmaster; Carly Simon - backing vocals; Ben Taylor - backing
vocals*
First recorded by Lawrence Tibbett in 1935 and twice recorded by Judy Garland.
Frank Sinatra later recorded it for the 1955 album *In the Wee Small Hours*.
Superb work from Torrie Zito, noted for his work on Lennon's album *Imagine*,
whose arrangement here provides the perfect backdrop for Carly's sensual vocals.

Spring Will Be a Little Late This Year *(Frank Loesser)* ****
Jimmy Webb - piano; Jeff Pevar - Guitar
A song recorded by Jonnie Johnston with Paul Weston and his Orchestra in 1944 and featured in the movie *Christmas Holiday,* sung by Deanna Durbin. With minimal instrumentation, Carly duets with Jimmy Webb in perfect harmony.

Film Noir *(Jimmy Webb - Carly Simon)* *****
Jimmy Webb - piano, arranger & conductor; Peter Calo - acoustic guitar; Jeff Pevar -electric guitar; Teese Gohl - keyboards; Zev Katz - electric bass; Shawn Pelton - drums; Richard Locker - cello solo; Elena Barere - concertmaster; Carly Simon - backing vocals; Ben Taylor - backing vocals
In the midst of all these standards, Carly and Jimmy Webb come up with the perfect tribute to the genre that is both cinematic and highly evocative in portraying a simple Long Island train journey, a rainy night, and a woman's image of a movie script running around in her mind. How the serenity of the two verses explode into passionate choruses is simply stunning both lyrically and musically, and full credit goes to these two wonderful songwriters working together in perfect harmony.

Laura *(Johnny Mercer - David Raskin)* ****
Produced by Arif Mardin, Jimmy Webb & Carly Simon
Russ Kassoff - piano; Peter Calo - guitar; Teese Gohl - keyboards; David Finck - double bass; Billy Ward - drums; Arif Mardin - arranger & conductor; Barry Finclair - concertmaster
Another jazz standard written for the 1944 movie of the same name, starring Gene Tierney and Dana Andrews, with Carly here singing the male-voiced lead. Magnificently arranged by Mardin, who had the inspired idea of marrying parts of Carly's song 'Haunting' from *Boys in the Trees* into the music track.

I'm a Fool to Want You *(Frank Sinatra - Joel Herron - John Wolf)* *****
Jimmy Webb - piano, conductor; Teese Gohl - keyboards; Torrie Zito - arranger; Elena Barere - concertmaster
Lyrics co-written by Sinatra, and recorded by him with the Ray Charles Singers in 1951. Legend has it that it was inspired by Sinatra's infatuation for actress Ava Gardner. One of the best vocals on the album.

Fools Coda *(Torrie Zito)* **
Torrie Zito - arranger & conductor; Elena Barere - concertmaster
Short instrumental arranged and conducted by Torrie Zito.

Two Sleepy People *(Frank Loesser - Hoagy Carmichael)* *****
Michael Kosarin - piano arranger and performer; John Travolta - vocals; Kevin DeSimone - backing vocals; Kevin Osborne - backing vocals; Lenny Roberts - backing vocals; Daryll Tookes - backing vocals; Dick Bahrke - background vocal arrangements

Written for the 1938 movie *Thanks for the Memory*, and performed by the stars Bob Hope and Shirley Ross. Carly invites her old friend John Travolta to sing with her, and the result is spectacular.

Don't Smoke in Bed *(Willard Robison)* ***
Michael Kosarin - piano; Peter Calo - guitar; Teese Gohl - keyboards, David Finck - acoustic bass; Billy Ward - drums; Van Dyke Parks - arranger & conductor; Elena Barere - concertmaster
A jazz song first recorded by Peggy Lee with Dave Barbour and his Orchestra. It was alleged that Lee and Barbour had been concerned that Robison would not live long enough to complete the song and finished it themselves so that it would gift him the copyright and provide for his daughter when he died. In the event, he lived for another twenty years. Carly delivers this goodbye letter to her lover with her trademark passion.

Somewhere in the Night *(Billy May - Josef Myrow - Mack Gordon)* ****
Jimmy Webb - piano, arranger & conductor; Russ Kassoff - piano; Peter Calo - guitar; David Finck - acoustic bass; Billy Ward - drums; Elena Barere - concertmaster
Better known as the theme to *The Naked City* television series in the early 60s and composed by Billy May. With lyrics added by Myrow and Gordon, it is given a noirish flavor by Jimmy Webb that Carly once again delivers with steamy perfection.

Film Noir was released on September 16th 1997 and it included a booklet with noirish-style black and white images by photographer Bob Gothard and liner notes written by Martin Scorsese, who sums up the album: "Carly Simon pays tribute to everything that is lasting in these movies that continue to haunt our imaginations fifty years after they were made." Carly also thanks both Jimmy Webb and Frank Filipetti for "taking a dip in the long deep shadows, where the night can almost swallow you up if you're not saved by two big guys on either side of you, holding your hands and grinning."

The album entered the Hot 200 on October 4th and eventually peaked at #84, spending a total of eight weeks on the chart. At the Grammys in New York on February 25th 1998, Carly was nominated in the category of Best Traditional Pop Vocal Performance, but lost out to Tony Bennett.

The one-hour televised special was produced by Lewis Bogach and Don Fizzinoglia and, as expected, filmed in black and white, perfectly capturing the creative process behind the making of the album, and showing Carly in the studio working alongside Webb, Mardin, and Parks. A promotional video was made for 'Ev'ry Time We Say Goodbye', which in reality was more like a fashion shoot with Carly's frizzled hair and variety of outfits, so far removed from the album's theme as it was possible to be. Nevertheless, it once again showed the glamorous and flirtatious side of the singer, which would be that bit more appealing to MTV viewers. A more appropriate video was made of 'You Won't Forget Me', with Carly in superb voice, Jimmy Webb conducting the orchestra, and clips of some of the great movie legends of the period.

At the Film Preservation Society's gala held in Los Angeles in September, Carly was introduced by actor Michael Keaton before giving an emotionally charged performance of four songs from the album - 'You Won't Forget Me', 'Laura', 'Lili Marlene', and 'Ev'ry Time We Say Goodbye'.

On September 26th Carly guested on *The Tonight Show with Jay Leno*, and sang 'Ev'ry Time We Say Goodbye' with Sally and Ben on backing vocals, and on October 15th repeated the song on *The Late Show with David Letterman*, but this time with Jimmy Webb and a small orchestra. On the same show she also promoted her latest children's book, *Midnight Farm*. Two days later she appeared on NBC's *Rosie O'Donnell Show* and duetted with Jimmy Webb on 'Spring Will Be a Little Late This Year', which also featured a great guitar solo by Jeff Pevar. Another appearance that fall was on ABC's breakfast show *Good Morning America* where she was interviewed by Charles Gibson.

Facing her greatest challenge

Carly looked in full bloom while celebrating and promoting the critical success of *Film Noir*, truly a labor of love for the singer, but she was concealing a personal dilemma. Still living apart from husband Jim, and with the memories of her mother and Jackie's recent deaths still on her mind, she was diagnosed with breast cancer on October 21st. Carly faced it head on, and with the support of her husband, who now rallied by her side, and with the help of her family and close friends, she accepted what had to be done with amazing new-found courage.

On November 12th Carly had a mastectomy and underwent a grueling course of chemotherapy. Over the coming weeks she slipped into deep depression, but everyone did their best to encourage her and give her their full support. One friend who took a different approach was Warren Beatty, who she had run into at a Boston hotel. During a subsequent phone call, she told him the news, but instead of him offering support and sympathy, Carly felt "a fading of warmth in his voice," and an evident desire that he didn't want to meet up again. That must have struck at Carly's heart, and she would relate her feelings toward him in the song 'Scar', one of the most incisive and deeply frank compositions of her career.

Carly admitted: "Everyone has problems, and learning to share them is essential. Hiding pain requires an enormous amount of energy; sharing it is liberating." She also confessed: "When you are challenged with a serious disease, you have to struggle to get to the surface. If you let go, you can drift. I had to latch on to something in myself that was strong. It would be my music."

Carly recognized that music had a large part to play in her recovery: "I called upon that strong aspect of my life to fight a life-threatening disease with life." But with a positive always came a negative, and in April she heard the devastating news that her friend Linda McCartney had died from breast cancer at the age of 56. Carly described it as feeling emotionally "crushed."

In May 1998 Carly's spirits were lifted when she received a Doctorate of Songwriting Degree from Berklee College of Music in Boston, and on June 16th she appeared in AFI's television documentary series *100 Years...100 Movies: America's Greatest Movies*. During the year Carly also contributed the song 'In Two Straight Lines' for the finale of the family comedy film *Madeline*, adapted from the children's books and television series of the same name, and starring Francis McDormand and Hatty Jones. The film was released in July.

The following year would be spent continuing with her slow recovery.

During the winter months a lot of the songs for the new album had been written and committed to tape, but for Carly it was time for a change of scenery, and the decision to vacate her New York home for good. She now spent most of her time recuperating at her Vineyard home, and, realizing that her career had to resume at some point, had Clive Davis agree to let her record the new material at home. With that in mind, she began making demos of the songs she had already written and putting them onto an 8-track tape recorder she had installed in Sally's old bedroom. Carly was getting well adept at using a drum machine, and she learnt to lay down and mix the tracks bringing the knowledge she had amassed in the numerous recording studios over the years to good use. But this time, there was no producer present to offer suggestions that might ruffle her feathers.

On March 5th 1999 Carly's second "greatest hits" album, entitled *The Very Best of Carly Simon: Nobody Does It Better* was released. It was a nineteen-track compilation issued solely for the UK and European market on the Global Television/Warner.ESP label, and included hits from the Elektra and Arista years, as well as the surprising addition of 'Angel from Montgomery'. Despite Carly never having performed in Europe, the album sold reasonably well, reaching #22 on the UK chart.

THE VERY BEST OF CARLY SIMON: NOBODY DOES IT BETTER
Global/Warner RADCD103 (UK – RADCD103)
Released - March 5 1999
UK Album charts - #22

You're So Vain/Why/ Coming Around Again/The Right Thing To Do/We Have No Secrets/You Belong To Me/That's The Way I've Always Heard It Should Be/Mockingbird/Haven't Got Time For the Pain/Anticipation/Legend In Your Own Time/The Stuff That Dreams Are Made Of/All I Want Is You/Give Me All Night/Like a River/ /Better Not Tell Her/ Angel From Montgomery/Let the River Run.

Despite still being a recovering patient, Carly was able to contribute vocals for other artists, and during the year she performed the song 'Your Silver Sky', composed and arranged by her friend Andreas Vollenweider, for his album *Cosmopoly*. She also sang a beautiful version of the traditional lullaby 'Hush L'il Baby' for singer-songwriter and radio host Jim Brickman's album *Destiny*, accompanied by his wonderful piano score. Although the album was recorded in Vancouver, the vocals were done in Los Angeles.

Music was slowly but surely bringing health back to Carly.

Back on the Vineyard, Carly continued writing material for her new album, and it saw a return to her old style. The new album was initially called *When Manhattan Was a Maiden*, as a number of the songs made a reference to the city. Carly explained: "It had a theme because I was leaving New York City at that time. I was trying to bring together a lot of my memories and a lot of New York experiences and tie them up in a neat ribbon and leave them behind and then go to another place."

All was going to plan until the time when she suffered from a rare spell of writer's block and confessed: "Everything that came out of my mouth I hated." Fortunately, it would not last long. A chance hearing of 'Embraceable You' by George Gershwin brought back the passion and inspiration to write what was to be the last song for the album.

Around this time Carly bought an old Georgian house on Beacon Hill in Boston and began working on its renovation, but on-going problems with building inspectors and a rat infestation eventually forced her to abandon the project and sell up.

In between writing and recording new material for the album, Carly was invited to write a song for the coming-of-age movie *Anywhere but Here*, directed by Wayne Wang. Starring Susan Sarandon and Natalie Portman, it's the story of an eccentric Wisconsin woman who relocates to Beverly Hills with her daughter to realize her dreams. Recorded at Carly's home studio, the wonderful acoustic song 'Amity' was co-written and performed in perfect harmony with 25-year-old daughter Sally. Produced by Don Was, the musicians included Jimmy Parr, Stuart Kimball and Chris Lannon. The film was released in November and the song appeared on the soundtrack album.

For her new album Carly had found a new sense of freedom in her writing. "I could experiment. I could play. It allowed me to open my mind and rethink the way I'd been writing." The result was some of her most complex and richly detailed lyrics, the like of which no one had seen before on one of her albums. This was breathtaking songwriting taken to another level.

The Making of a Masterpiece

"Writing and recording it.... I got closer to my soul than I ever had in my life. There was nothing to hide. You know, it just depends on how much you want to indulge in screaming"

The Vineyard Sessions

By the middle of the summer, although still recuperating, Carly felt well enough to begin recording the new songs. She brought together a small group of musical friends, including Teese Gohl, Steve Gadd, and Tom "T-Bone" Wolk, as well as the experienced Vineyard bass player Tony Garnier, best known for his work with Bob Dylan. They all descended on her home where a small recording studio had been set up in the "play barn" basement, with the help of musical neighbors Jimmy Parr and Stuart Kimball, along with Bobby Eichorn, Frank Garfi, and Peter Moshay, who all became her teachers in recording techniques. Russ Titelman, another old colleague who Carly had originally wanted to produce the album until he moved away, was now on hand to give her confidence and valuable direction.

In the liner notes to the album, Carly confessed that when alone in the studio, she felt the presence of her past producers as if they were there in a control booth guiding her along, and thanked them all for being with her, even if just in spirit.

Over the next few weeks other musicians would turn up to do their parts, including old friends Peter Calo, Eric Brazilian, and Mindy Jostyn. There were also a few new faces, with Irish musician Liam O'Maonlai, lead singer of the successful band Hothouse Flowers, and guitarist Michael Lockwood, who in a few years would be marrying Lisa Marie Presley. For backing singers, she had the Rankin Sisters (Cookie, Heather and Raylene), members of the award-winning Canadian musical family, along with 25-year-old John Forte, a friend of Ben Taylor's, who had a long association as writer and producer with the hip-hop band the Fugees.

Moving out of the city and back to the Vineyard saw a slight change in the album's direction. With the overall landscape now becoming more generalized and less geographically centered, a few of the songs that had been written were now dropped, and the name of the album tentatively changed to *Slim Canyon*, almost an anagram of Carly's name, before settling on the more appropriate *The Bedroom Tapes*.

Carly was in her element, totally in control and focused on what she was born to do. Some twenty new songs were recorded, with further work carried out at Sonic Brothers Studio on the island, and finally mixed and completed with a number of producers and other session musicians at Right Track, Sound on Sound and Edison Recording Studios in New York. She not only had fun making the album, but knew it was going to be something really special: "All I was doing is what I had started out doing thirty years ago. Making sounds that I liked. Not thinking in an orthodox way about songs.... thinking in a new way about structure. Playing like a child with fingerpaints."

Carly was once asked how much of her work over the years was related to Martha's Vineyard: "My first album was written on the Vineyard, and many, many of my songs were written either on the Vineyard, or coming to the Vineyard. 'You're So Vain' was written on the Vineyard."

After beating cancer and spending some eight months working mainly by herself, Carly was ready to introduce eleven new songs to the music world, nine of which were self-penned, and on an album what many would later consider to be her masterpiece.

THE BEDROOM TAPES
Arista 07822-14627- 2 (UK – 07822 14627 2)
Recorded - 1999-2000, Hidden Star Hill & Sonic Brothers Studio, MV; Right Track Recording, Sound on Sound & Edison Studios, New York
Released - May 16 2000 (UK - June 12 2000)
Producers - Carly Simon, Frank Filipetti, Teese Gohl & David Field
Engineers - Frank Filipetti, Jimmy Parr, Carly Simon & Ed Tuton
Mastering - Mark Wilder at Sony Studios New York
US Billboard Hot 200 #90

Our Affair *(Carly Simon)* *****
Promo CD single ARPCD-3933
Released 2001
Producers - Carly Simon, David Field & Frank Filipetti.
Carly Simon - acoustic & electric guitar, keyboards, percussion, backing vocals; Stuart Kimball - acoustic & electric guitar; Steve Gadd - drums; T-Bone Wolk - bass.
Powerful and seductive opener about new relationships. According to Carly, this was not about an extra-marital affair, but that stimulating period between initial attraction and the final act of consummation - that "wonderful dance" that men and women engage in which can be over too quickly. Carly took inspiration from her mother's advice to play games in love and "keep the dance going." The song is almost a one-woman show, like many of the songs on the album, with only Stuart Kimball's guitars, Steve Gadd's drums and T-Bone Wolk's bass. But it serves as an eye-opener and whets the appetite for what is to come. A remix of

the song featured in the movie *Bounce* starring Ben Affleck and Gwyneth Paltrow when released later that year.

So Many Stars *(Carly Simon)* *****
Promo CD single ARPCD-3857 (radio mix/album version)
Released 2000
Producers - Carly Simon, David Field & Frank Filipetti.
Carly Simon - guitar, keyboards, bass, drum programming, backing vocals; Peter Calo - rhythm guitar; Steve Gadd - drums; T-Bone Wolk - bass, acoustic & electric guitar; acoustic piano, Dobro; Liam O'Maonlai - backing vocals; The Rankin Sisters - backing vocals
A Manhattan lullaby about a woman taking the A-Train and walking the streets of the city thinking about a relationship and how all the places that she visits remind her of their time together. In doing so Carly conjures up vivid images of city life, namechecking various locations and characters she meets along the way, from "boom box boys" to "jakeys" (tramps). As she walks from store to store she ponders over what the real meaning and substance of their relationship was, and as she looks up at the sky wonders if she would recognize him if he was just one of those millions of stars. A showcase for the steel guitar skills of T-Bone Wolk and the vocal harmonies of the Rankin Sisters. Once heard, the melody will live in the head like an ear-worm for a long time to come. A great track that should have been a sure-fire hit if the promotion people had been awake.

Big Dumb Guy *(Carly Simon - T-Bone Wolk - Larry Ciancia - Jesse Farrow)* ****
Promo CD single (radio edit)
Released 2000 (UK)
Producers - Carly Simon, David Field & Frank Filipetti.
Carly Simon - drum programming, percussion, congas; Larry Ciancia - drums; T-Bone Wolk - bass; John Forte - backing vocals; Ben Taylor - backing vocals
A powerhouse rocker which according to Carly reflects what it must be like to be loved and desired in a simpler way, where outside influences (such as the internet) are not a distraction. She portrays a lover as a kind of prehistoric caveman who is single-mindedly focused on his desire for a mate. Carly got the idea following her frustration with her computer repeatedly crashing, and then thinking how life would be so much better without having material stuff like that to deal with. Co-written with musicians Tom Wolk and Larry Ciancia, the song contains excerpts from the song 'The Hat', written by Jesse Farrow and recorded by Quicksilver Messenger Service for their album *Just for Love* in 1970.

Scar *(Carly Simon)* *****
Producers - Carly Simon, David Field & Frank Filipetti.
Carly Simon - acoustic guitar, keyboards, percussion, backing vocals; Michael Lockwood - electric & acoustic guitar; Liam O'Maonlai - bowron, flute, vocal solo, backing vocals.
One of Carly's most personal songs arising from her battle with breast cancer. Although making reference to the needles and sutures, she points out that it is

more about "the wisdom you gain from living and getting bashed. We all have so many scars." Completed around the time of her mastectomy, she revealed later that the scar was elegantly positioned, "pointing right at my heart." In the song the scar serves as a metaphor for the emotional scars that come with growing old; Carly also sings about learning to see a scar as a lovable and tender badge of honor. Indeed, Warren Beatty had stopped calling her after hearing about what she had gone through, and the song refers to him as a "poor little puppy, so scared of misfortune and always on guard." Carly later explained the importance of writing the song: "I needed to get some of the pain out. When you write songs about your feelings, that's one way of exorcising them....to get it out and look at it in an objective way, so that it doesn't cause me any serious pain by staying inside." Liam O'Maonlai displays his haunting vocal skills on the most compulsive song of the album.

Cross the River *(Carly Simon)* *****
Producers - Carly Simon, David Field & Frank Filipetti.
Carly Simon - drum programming, percussion, B3 organ; Teese Gohl - B3 organ, arrange & conductor; Steve Gadd - drums; T-Bone Wolk - bass; Liam O'Maonlai - backing vocals; The Rankin Sisters - backing vocals; Jill Dell'Abate - backing vocals
Inspired by Carly's younger days living at Riverdale, and wondering what it would be like to cross the East River and become successful in Manhattan. In the song she invents characters, the main one being Laura, who crosses the river with a rich stockbroker only to find she misses Danny, the love of her life she has left behind. Perhaps Carly is recalling her relationship with Danny Armstrong. In any case, the moral is that even if you get to where you aspire to be in life, you still look back and ponder whether things were better before.

I Forget *(Carly Simon)* *****
Producers - Carly Simon, David Field & Frank Filipetti.
Carly Simon - keyboards; Eric Brazilian - electric guitar; Steve Gadd - drums; Tony Garnier - bass
Carly's road to recovery was a long one, and the pain and anguish of her treatment and the depression it caused is highlighted in this most honest and vivid song. The course of chemotherapy brought Carly to the lowest point in her life, with the pain leading to abject memory loss, and a time when she couldn't tell anyone how she felt, becoming an expert at denial and avoidance, and putting on a fake smile. For Carly it remains one of the most difficult songs she ever had to write, and consequently took nine months to complete.

Actress *(Carly Simon)* ***
Producers - Carly Simon, David Field & Frank Filipetti.
Carly Simon - acoustic guitar, keyboards, drum programming, keyboard bass, backing vocals; Michael Lockwood - electric guitar; Steve Gadd - drums; The Rankin Sisters - backing vocals
One of the character studies of New Yorkers, which was to be the original theme of the album. Inspired by a conversation between a couple of young actresses

235

outside the Lincoln Center about their auditions, in which they discuss camera angles and even rehearse their acceptance speeches in the event that they won an award. It reminded Carly of when she was a young girl herself, standing in front of a bedroom mirror and imagining being a big star.

I'm Really the Kind *(Carly Simon)* ****
Producers - Carly Simon, David Field & Frank Filipetti.
Carly Simon - acoustic guitar, keyboards, percussion, drum programming, backing vocals; Teese Gohl - arranger & conductor; Steve Gadd - percussion; T-Bone Wolk - bass; Mindy Jostyn - violin; Liam O'Maonlai - bowron, backing vocals; The Rankin Sisters - backing vocals
Confessional song about low-esteem, of having confidence one minute and none the next, of feeling ugly one day and beautiful the day after: "The pendulum swings all over the place, and it's only when I get centered that I realize that I have it all, and that it's not based on what I say or how I look, but something far more essential – the soul."

We Your Dearest Friends *(Carly Simon)* *****
Producers - Carly Simon, David Field & Frank Filipetti (additional production - Stuart Kimball).
Carly Simon - acoustic guitar, keyboards, percussion, drum programming, keyboard bass; Stuart Kimball - electric guitar; Teese Gohl - acoustic piano; Steve Gadd - drums; T-Bone Wolk - bass, mandolin
A song about a group of gossips pretending to like someone they actually despise. Carly wrote this about one specific friend who talked about her behind her back and "undermined her happiness." Carly has never been nastier or more sarcastic in her writing, nor has she been so wonderfully imaginative. *Rolling Stone* called it a "bleakly funny tune with a surging rhythm sung from an utter paranoiac's point of view."

Whatever Became of Her *(Carly Simon)* ****
Producers - Carly Simon, David Field & Frank Filipetti.
Carly Simon - acoustic & electric guitar, organ; Stuart Kimball - acoustic & electric guitar; T-Bone Wolk - bass; Andrew Fellus — organ assistant; Steve Gadd - percussion; Mindy Jostyn - violin
Wistful song inspired by the poem 'I Go Back to May 1937' by American poet Sharon Olds, about looking at a picture of her parents the day they graduated from college. Carly's song transforms it into viewing a couple in a photograph, frozen in time, with no idea of what their futures will be. Mindy Jostyn once again contributes a haunting violin.

In Honor of You (George) *(Carly Simon- George Gershwin - Ira Gershwin)* *****
Producer - Teese Gohl

Carly Simon - African marimba; Teese Gohl - arranger & conductor;
programming all instruments; Steve Gadd - drums; Shawn Pelton - drums; Aaron
Heick – sax
A song in the shape of a letter written to the great composer, with sections of his
song 'Embraceable You' interspersed. This is remarkable in its makeup, having
no verses or chorus, with Carly basically ad-libbing the words she is struggling to
write. Apparently, the idea came to Carly at a tavern in Woods Hole waiting for
the Vineyard ferry when the Gershwin song came on the jukebox. She fantasized
about what it must have been like for the young composer fifty years ago (he died
in 1937 at the aged of 39 and had been her father's guest on a number of
occasions). She asked him questions such as "How do you do it? What were you
thinking?" and the refrain of the song was always the answer given. At the end of
the letter she vows to return to her piano to begin to write once again. One of
Carly's biggest thrills was getting permission from the Gershwin estate to use his
song. With the help of Teese Gohl they came up with a reverie-like variation of
Gershwin's chorus, with improvised verses that had no rhyme but simply were a
letter put to melody. But it worked. As Carly recalled: "Some emotions are better
left unrhymed."

Grandmother's House *(Carly Simon)* * (bonus track on the 2002 and 2015
editions)
Producers - Carly Simon & Eric Brazilian
Eric Brazilian - guitar, electric guitar, bass, keyboards, programming; Jimmy
Parr - guitar; The Rankin Sisters - backing vocals
Describing a Yuletide drive from the city to "grandmother's house" culminating
in her rather unsavory desire to even "screw" Santa. Sorry, but there are lines we
shouldn't cross.

Sangre Dolce *(Carly Simon)* *** (bonus track on the 2002 edition)
Carly Simon - electric piano; guitar, bass, percussion; Michael Lockwood -
guitar solo; T-Bone Wolk - bass; Steve Gadd - drums; Teese Gohl -
orchestration; arr. strings.
Tango-flavored song with a sad twist, based on a true story. One day when Carly
was in Central Park, she came across a woman with a baby and was told that it
wasn't hers, but she was taking care of it for someone else, and that her own baby
was back in Argentina. Now she was working to save up enough money to send
back to her family. Carly wrote this song imagining what her life must be like.
The song title translates to "sweet blood," a Spanish phrase reflecting how their
affection for their children is genuine. The song would be resurrected for the
album *This Kind of Love* in 2008.

When Manhattan Was a Maiden *(Carly Simon)* **** (bonus track on the 2015
edition)
Producer – Carly Simon
Wonderful ode to New York which really should have made the album. In 2002
Carly posted the original demo on her official website for streaming, and the song
was included on the 2015 expanded re-release of the album.

237

Bob Gothard's sophisticated cover image had Carly curled up and barefoot on the floor, dressed in red leggings with a gold silken shawl wrapped around her. Unfortunately, it did little to boost sales.

The album was released on May 16th 2000 and reached a disappointing #90 on the Hot 200. Although not a commercial success, it received overwhelming praise and some of the best reviews of Carly's entire career. *Billboard* celebrated it as "intelligent, richly crafted pop music" and a "feast for fans," while *People* described the "boffo" album as "unfolding like a one-woman show." *Rolling Stone* saw it as simply a "bang up album," while the *New York Daily News* rated it as one of her finest albums to date. *Us Weekly* extolled: "These disarmingly personal songs are pure catharsis. Who needs support groups? *The Bedroom Tapes* is classy work from one of pop's original confessors", and the *Miami Herald* raved about it being a "gem." *AllMusic* marveled about the fact that Carly, now in her mid-50s, could still charm the listeners with her songs. The UK *Daily Mail* simply called it "beautiful."

Apart from promotional singles for 'Our Affair', 'So Many Stars', and 'Big Dumb Guy', there were no commercial releases, the first album of her own material not to have one. Nor were there any promotional videos. Despite that, at the Boston Music Awards on April 11th 2002, Carly would win Female Vocalist of the Year for 'Our Affair', which was also nominated for Song of the Year.

Carly once again turned to television appearances, and on May 17th, the day after the album's release, she appeared with Andreas Vollenweider on *The Late Show with David Letterman* to perform 'Big Dumb Guy'. Two days later she took part in one of *Good Morning America*'s "Friday Break Away" free morning concerts held at New York's Bryant Park. Introduced and interviewed by hosts Charles Gibson and Diane Sawyer, Carly performed five songs, 'You're So Vain', 'Anticipation', 'So Many Stars', 'Big Dumb Guy', and 'Nobody Does it Better', with a band that consisted of Sally and Ben, Teese Gohl, T-Bone Wolk, Larry Ciancia, Stuart Kimball, Andreas Vollenweider, Mindy Jostyn, and Heather Rankin.

On May 23rd Carly was again joined by Heather to perform 'So Many Stars' and 'Anticipation' on the *Rosie O'Donnell Show*, and a week later was interviewed by Barbara Walters on the talk show *The View*, in which she sang 'So Many Stars' and 'We Have No Secrets', this time accompanied by Andreas Vollenweider on electric harp, Mindy Jostyn on violin, and with wonderful backing vocals by Raylene Rankin. There was also an appearance on *Live with Regis and Kathy Lee*, where Carly was interviewed by Kathy Lee and Roger Ebert and gave a short a capella snippet of 'We Your Dearest Friends'. A similar appearance on CBS

Sunday Morning had clips of her singing 'Our Affair' and 'Scar' in her Vineyard studio.

Goodbye to Arista

Carly felt she had produced her finest work with *The Bedroom Tapes*, and many critics agreed. Her songwriting had produced her most honest and intimate lyrics to date, and she now looked forward with increased confidence to continue giving Clive Davis her very best work. But it was not to be. By the end of the year Davis had been replaced as president of Arista by Antonio "LA" Reid, who had co-founded LaFace Records, an imprint of Arista and a magnet for black music. It was felt that 67-year-old Davis had overstayed his welcome, as the mandatory retirement age laid down by parent group BMG was 65. As a result, his 25-year contract was terminated. Reid was a champion of urban teen-oriented artists, and, after meeting with Carly, she was left feeling that there would be no further interest in a 50-year old singer whose albums and singles were not exactly storming up the charts.

Carly was devastated: "I got really lost in the mix because L A Reid came into Arista and he was determined for it to be a hip-hop and Latin label and he was very not interested in me, and I heard he had said about me, 'Let's just get rid of her record as soon as possible. It will be dead in the water by the time we have the international conference in Toronto'… I forced upon him a meeting in which I came into his office and he spent the whole time watching MTV and not even looking at me. He was that disinterested in my material. He couldn't get rid of me fast enough."

With the label seemingly unwilling to spend money on promoting her album, and rather than commit herself to record another one while still under contract, Carly made a deal with Reid to leave the label in exchange for retaining the rights to her treasured *Bedroom Tapes*. It was a bitter pill to swallow, and the album, her masterpiece, soon sank into near obscurity. But at least it now all belonged to her.

That summer John Forte, the young Grammy-winning black artist who had sung on Carly's last album, was imprisoned after being caught with a briefcase full of cocaine at Newark Airport. Sentenced to a mandatory fourteen years, it was believed that he was never given a fair trial. With unprecedented tenacity Carly got on his case, lobbying political and legal friends, including the Clintons, to secure his release. With the help of Utah Republican Senator Orrin Hatch, his sentence was first reduced by half and then finally commuted by President Bush and he was released in December

2008, free to pursue his music career. He had only one person to thank: "Carly is a mentor to me, a guide, absolutely my spiritual godmother."

On March 29th 2001 Carly appeared on the televised special *An All-Star Tribute to Brian Wilson*, at New York's famous Radio City Music Hall, performing his classic 'In My Room' with Jimmy Webb and David Crosby. Directed by Bruce Gowers and hosted by Chazz Palminteri, the show was aired on TNT on July 4th.

Son of a Gun

Weeks earlier, Carly was asked by singer-songwriter Janet Jackson if she could sample 'You're So Vain' for her new album *All for You*. Carly agreed, but only if she could re-record her vocals and write new lines. Jackson's producer Jimmy Jam sent Carly tapes of the song they had been working on, and she recorded her vocals in her home studio, preferring to rap the lyrics. Although not sure if the producer would like the idea, it was decided to marry the two tracks together, and the resulting track 'Son of a Gun (I Betcha Think This Song is About You)' (with Carly Simon, and featuring Missy Elliott) was included on the album. Released on April 24th, it peaked at #1 on the Hot 200 and #2 on the UK's R&B Chart. Later in the year the song was remixed with new vocals rapped by Missy Elliott, and when released on December 11th it reached #28 on the Hot 100. It became Carly's first official single release since 'Love of My Life' in 1992. Carly also appeared with Janet on the album's short-spoken interlude 'Clouds'.

That same year Carly was invited to play on Mindy Jostyn's new album, *Blue Stories*. Mindy had taken some time off to have a baby with Jake and now produced a wonderful album of songs about loss and healing. Carly played synthesizer and percussion, and supplied backing vocals on the tracks 'Don't Turn Away' and 'East of Eden', both written by Mindy and Jake, while Mindy also sang her own version of Carly and Jake's 'That's the Way I've Always Heard It Should Be'.

Piglet, Pooh and Christmas Too

"All kinds of positive things are happening. I'm thinking...how much I feel as I've been rejuvenated. My health seems to be fine. I'm thriving and enjoying life more than I ever had."

Room 139

During the last week of January 2002, Carly embarked on her next project, which was to be an album of Christmas songs. After singing background vocals for her son Ben at a pre-Winter Olympic concert party in Los Angeles, she met up with an old friend, producer Don Was, who she had worked with on *Spoiled Girl*, and asked him bluntly, "Want to make an album this week?" When told it was to be a Christmas album, he said, "Let's make it." Unable to find a studio at short notice, they came up with a simple idea: All that was needed was Don's laptop, Ben's band members (who happened to have a free week), and some of LA's finest session musicians who Don was able to get together, and, last but not least, the use of Carly's room at the Peninsula Hotel in Beverly Hills as a recording studio.

Microphones were provided by Don's friend, the legendary engineer Bob Clearmountain, who was best known for his work with Springsteen and the Stones, and the bed had to be moved to another room to create space for a drum kit and other recording gear. Carly and Don then went out and bought various Christmas albums to select some of the traditional songs they wanted to record.

The musicians included friends old and new. Mark Goldenberg was a an accomplished guitarist and songwriter who had co-written 'Automatic' for the Pointer Sisters; Rob Mathes was a successful producer and bass player; guitarist Dean Parks had played lead guitar with David Gates' band Bread; Benmont Tench was one of the founding members of Tom Petty and the Heartbreakers; vocalist and actor Arnold McCuller had toured with many artists including James Taylor; Chris Chaney was one of the best bass players in the business; Deron Johnson was a jazz keyboardist who had toured with the legendary Miles Davis; Joel Shearer was a highly regarded composer and session guitarist; Carly's old friend Jim Keltner had played drums on four of her earlier albums; and finally, harmonica player Mickey Raphael was noted for his work with country singer Willie Nelson. Carly

241

would nickname this hastily-assembled musical group "The Great Christmas Band from Room 139."

To Carly's delight, the great Willie Nelson himself also turned up to play on the song 'Pretty Paper', one of his own compositions. Billy Preston, the legendary singer and organist noted for his work with the Beatles, also lent his keyboard and vocals skills to a song called 'Twelve Gates to the City'. One other welcomed contributor was Carly's great friend Livingston Taylor, James 'younger brother, who offered his wonderful, self-penned seasonal song, 'Christmas Is Almost Here', which was also chosen to be the lead track and title for the new album.

In just five days the tracks had been recorded, and all that was left to do was the main mixing at the Record Plant in Hollywood. Don and Carly did wonderful work on eight of the tracks, while the remaining three were mixed back at Parr Audio on the Vineyard, with the help of Carly's friend and neighbor Jimmy Parr. The final mastering was completed at Bob Ludwig's Gateway Studio in Portland, Maine, with Carly spending hours with the award-winning engineer sequencing and unifying the tracks.

Meanwhile, Carly took time out to record vocals on the John Forte track 'Been There, Done That', for his album *I, John*, which was recorded while he was awaiting sentence for distribution charges. The album was released on April 23rd.

With Arylene Rothberg now back as manager, the remainder of Carly's year was taken up compiling songs from her back catalog for what would be another retrospective album called *Anthology*. Of course, for this, and her Christmas album too, Carly needed a new record label, and she had found the perfect partner in Rhino Records, an independent label that had been formed in 1978 and which specialized in artists 'compilations. Forty tracks were chosen for the two-disc album, and eighteen were digitally re-mastered by Bill Inglot and Dan Hersch. Overall production was handled by Carly, along with David McLees, the label's re-issue producer and project coordinator, and researcher Gary Peterson. The album saw the debut of a number of songs never seen before on compact disc, including the wonderful 'In Times When My Head', 'Orpheus' and 'Boys in the Trees'.

Of the two albums, the first to be released was *Christmas Is Almost Here* on October 22nd. Debuting on *Billboard's* Holiday Album chart three days after Christmas, it finally peaked at #14.

CHRISTMAS IS ALMOST HERE
Rhino R2 78166 (UK – 8122 78166)
Recorded - January 2002, Room 139, The Peninsula Hotel, Beverly Hills CA
Released - October 22 2002
Producers - Don Was & Carly Simon

Engineers - Don Was & Ed Cherney
Mastering - Bob Ludwig & Carly Simon, Gateway Mastering, Portland ME
US Billboard Holiday Album Chart #14

Christmas Is Almost Here *(Livingston Taylor)* ***
Dean Parks - acoustic guitar; Mark Goldenberg - electric guitar; Deron Johnson - Roland JX 8P synthesizer; Chris Chaney - bass; Jim Keltner - drums
Written by James Taylor's brother Livingston, who offered it to Carly shortly before she left for LA.

O Come All Ye Faithful *(Traditional; based on an arrangement by Richie Sambora)* ***
Dean Parks - acoustic guitar; Joel Shearer - electric Dobro
A gentle rendition of this popular seasonal hymn with just guitar accompaniment.

The Land of Christmas (Mary) *(Carly Simon)* ***
Carly Simon - acoustic guitar; Chris Chaney - bass; Jim Keltner - drums
According to Carly, the song was written during a spell of migraine, and with her experience of pain giving her a more spiritual outlook on life, she turned to Mary, "the most powerful person in the Bible."

Silent Night *(Joseph Mohr - Franz Gruber)* ***
Carly Simon - acoustic guitar; Joel Shearer - guitar; Chris Chaney - bass; Arnold McCuller - harmony vocals; Ben Taylor - harmony vocals
Carly and Ben in wonderful voice.

Twelve Gates to the City *(Traditional)* ***
Carly Simon - acoustic guitar; Billy Preston - Hammond B3 organ, vocals; Mark Goldenberg - electric guitar; Jim Keltner - drums
Notable for the great Billy Preston's organ playing bringing the song to life, although apparently done remotely.

I'll Be Home for Christmas *(Kim Gannon (lyrics) - Walter Kent (music) - Buck Ram - Carly Simon (add. lyrics))* ***
Dean Parks - acoustic guitar
Originally a hit for Bing Crosby in 1943, with songwriting credits later going to producer Buck Ram who claimed he had written a poem and song of the same name. Carly adds her own wistful lyrics.

God Rest Ye Merry Gentlemen *(Traditional)***
Joel Shearer - acoustic guitar; Mark Goldenberg - electric guitar; Benmont Tench - Wurlitzer electric piano; Chris Chaney - bass; Jim Keltner - drums, Ben Taylor - vocals; Arnold McCuller - harmony vocals
The traditional song given a reggae makeover.

Heaven *(Lucy Simon - Carly Simon)* ****
Carly - acoustic guitar; Bob Mathes - acoustic piano; Chris Chaney - bass

243

A sweet little song that Lucy had written back in 1987, and although not able to get over to LA to contribute her wonderful harmony vocals, she works with Carly to re-write the lyrics to give it a more seasonal feel. A fine production number by Don Was.

Pretty Paper *(Willie Nelson)* ***
Willie Nelson - vocals, guitar; Dean Parks - acoustic guitar; Judd Fuller - acoustic guitar, mandolin; Adam MacDougal - acoustic piano; Mickey Raphael - harmonica; Chris Chaney - bass; Jim Keltner - drums
A 1963 hit for Roy Orbison with Carly and Willie Nelson doing their vocal best.

Have Yourself a Merry Little Christmas *(Hugh Martin - Ralph Blane)* ****
Mark Goldenberg - Rickenbacker 12-string guitar
Written in 1943 for the movie *Meet Me in St Louis* and sung by Judy Garland. With just guitar accompaniment, Carly's pure contralto does justice to this most emotional of Yuletide songs.

Happy Xmas (War Is Over) *(John Lennon -Yoko Ono)* ****
Carly Simon - acoustic guitar; Joel Shearer - guitar; Mark Goldenberg - Rickenbacker 12-string guitar; Benmont Trench - Wurlitzer electric piano; Chris Chaney - bass; Jim Keltner - drums; Ben Taylor - harmony vocals; Arnold McCuller - harmony vocals
John Lennon's seasonal standard was also a protest over the Vietnam war when first released in 1971. Among the original musicians were familiar names to Carly - Jim Keltner, Nicky Hopkins, Hugh McCracken, and Stuart Scharf. This is a faithful rendition by Carly, supported by harmony vocals from both Ben and Arnold McCuller, the veteran vocalist who had appeared on many of James Taylor's albums.

White Christmas *(Irving Berlin)* ** (bonus track on 2003 re-issue)
Single R2 78038 b/w Forgive
Released - 2003
Producers - Burt Bacharach and Carole Bayer-Sager
Did not chart
Burt Bacharach - piano, vocals
Originally released in 1942 with an estimated 100 million sales in all its versions, with half that figure being for Bing Crosby's definitive record. It still remains the best-selling single of all time.

Forgive *(Carly Simon - Andreas Vollenweider)* *** (bonus track on 2003 re-issue)
Andreas Vollenweider - harp
Another fine collaboration with her friend Andreas. Carly would later provide vocals for the same song on one of his own albums. In hindsight perhaps, it should have been saved for the *Into White* album, released two years later.

The Night Before Christmas *(Carly Simon)* **** (bonus track on the 2010 limited edition)
Taken from the *This Is My Life* soundtrack

The cover images were taken by Peter Simon, showing his sister wearing a short white dress and knee-length red boots. The booklet also featured photos of the leading musicians and a wonderful closing sentiment from Carly: "May we be able to abandon ourselves to higher truths and like out friends with snowflakes in their faces and on a bobtail sled be 'laughing all the way'."

To kick off the promotional work, Carly, Ben, and Mindy Jostyn sang carols during NBC's coverage of the lighting ceremony at the Rockefeller Center in New York, and on December 13th Carly performed 'Christmas Is Almost Here' on the *Caroline Rhea Show*. She also appeared that month with host Diane Sawyer on *Good Morning America*, singing 'Twelve Gates to the City' and duetting with Ben on 'Silent Night'.

The album was re-issued in the fall of 2003 as *Christmas Is Almost Here Again*, with two bonus tracks - Irving Berlin's 'White Christmas', performed with Burt Bacharach, and the short, but beautiful, 'Forgive', the song penned by Carly and Andreas Vollenweider. Both songs were released as a single the same year but did not chart.

Seven years later, the bookstore Borders issued it as a limited edition, with the extra track, 'The Night Before Christmas', taken from 1992's *This Is My Life* soundtrack.

Meanwhile, *Anthology* had been released on November 5th, just in time for the Christmas market. The fine cover image of Carly was taken by Heidi Wild, a friend of Sally's, while the comprehensive liner notes were written by Carly's friend Jack Mauro, who, looking back on her 30-year career, wonderfully summed her up: "From Carly then to Carly now, her wry humor winks at you like the pal you like a little better than your best friend."

ANTHOLOGY
Rhino R2 78167 (UK – 8122 78167 2) (2-disc compilation)
Released - November 5th 2002
Producers - Carly Simon, David McLees and Gary Peterson
Mastering - Bill Inglot and Dan Hersch

Disc 1
That's the Way I've Always Heard It Should Be/One More Time/Anticipation/Legend in Your Own Time/Julie Through the Glass/You're So Vain/We Have No Secrets/The Right Thing to Do/Mockingbird/Haven't Got Time For the Pain/Older Sister/Waterfall/Attitude Dancing/In Times When My

Head/Nobody Does it Better/You Belong To Me/Devoted To You/Boys in the Trees/Vengeance/Come Upstairs/Jesse

Disc 2
Not a Day Goes By/Why/It Happens Every Day/Orpheus/Come Back Hone/Coming Around Again/Give Me All Night (single version)/The Stuff That Dreams Are Made Of/All I Want Is You/Let the River Run/My Romance/Better Not Tell Her/Love of My Life/Like a River/Two Little Sisters/r/Film Noir/Scar/Actress/Touched By the Sun (Live at Grand Central)

Piglet, Pooh, and Carly too

2003 saw Carly returning to the movies when she was invited to write songs for Disney's latest animation, *Piglet's Big Movie*, based on the stories by A A Milne, and directed by Francis Glebas. Working mostly on her own in her home studio, Carly found inspiration from drawings by the original animators hanging on the walls, and was occasionally joined by Sally and Ben when they returned from their respective tours. The final soundtrack was produced by Carly, along with Matt Walker, Rob Mathes and Michael Kosarin, and included eight of Carly's songs, with full orchestra, including a re-working of the Sherman Brothers' classic theme song, and all but one of the tracks performed by Carly herself. The album also included Carl Johnson's score and some of the original demos for the film. The movie was premiered on March 16th, and the soundtrack released two days later.

PIGLET'S BIG MOVIE (soundtrack)
Walt Disney Records 60081-7
Released - March 18 2003
Producers - Carly Simon, Matt Walker, Rob Mathes & Michael Kosarin

Carly's contributions and performers:

Winnie the Pooh *(Robert Sherman - Richard Sherman - Carly Simon)* ***
Carly and Ben
If I Wasn't So Small (The Piglet Song) *(Carly Simon)* **
Carly
Mother's Intuition *(Carly Simon)* ***
Carly
Sing Ho For the Life of a Bear (Exposition March) *(Carly Simon)* ***
Carly with Jim Cummings (Pooh), John Fieldler (Piglet), Kath Soucie (Kanga), Ken Sansom (Rabbit), Peter Cullen (Eeyore), and Nikita Hopkins (Roo)
The More It Snows (Tiddely Pom) *(Carly Simon)* **
Jim Cummings (Pooh), and John Fieldler (Piglet)

With a Few Good Friends *(Carly Simon)* ***
Carly and Sally Taylor
The More I Look Inside *(Carly Simon)* ***
Comforting to Know *(Carly Simon)* **
Carly, Ben and opera singer Renee Fleming
Winnie the Pooh (demo)
If I Wasn't So Small (demo) *(Carly Simon)*
Mother's Intuition (demo) *(Carly Simon)*
The More It Snows (demo) *(Carly Simon)*
The More I Look Inside (demo) *(Carly Simon)*

Not surprisingly, the movie was an international success, grossing nearly $63 million, although the subsequent soundtrack album failed to chart. However, the reviews for Carly's music were very positive. The *Boston Globe* described her songs as "honey for the pre-school set," while the *New York Times* noted how the strength of her songwriting had an "unguarded emotional directness and a gift for bluntly catching tunes." *Variety* praised the songs for their "improvisational quality," and the *Miami Herald* noted that Carly had been an "inspired choice" for the soundtrack. But perhaps the best review of all came from *Newsday*, which noted how her voice and lyrics had a way to make the viewer feel "wrapped up once more in that maternal embrace that lets you know that you are safe and sound."

A performance of 'With a Few Good Friends' appears at the end of the movie showing Carly singing in what may be her Vineyard garden, while a promotional video was also made for 'Winnie the Pooh', with Carly singing the song with some of the animated characters and scenes from the movie. She also performed the latter song on *Good Morning America*, singing to a group of invited children, and in the introductory interview described the Pooh stories as "the emblem of friendship." There were also two appearances on *Live with Regis and Kelly*, one with a pre-taped rendition of 'I'll Be Home for Christmas', followed on May 4th with 'With a Few Good Friends', a landmark in some respects, as it would be her very first live television performance.

2003 turned out to be a time of mixed emotions for Carly, with her marriage to Jim finally unravelling after his long periods of depression, his inability to complete his novel, and having to come to terms with his sexuality. On July 27th she appeared with Sally in *Singing in the Shadow: The Children of Rock Royalty*, a 90-minute Handel Production directed by Tom Puchniak and first aired on Canadian television. In the candid and revealing documentary, nine children of music legends bared their souls.

On Labor Day in September Sally married Dean Bragonier, but instead of the ceremony being held in the beautiful grounds of Carly's Vineyard home, she had decided it would be at her father's house in nearby Chilmark. Carly and James both walked Sally down to the waterfront where the ceremony took place. It would be one of the last times the two families were brought together and also one of the last times Carly would speak to her ex-husband.

That year also saw Carly appearing on the Ben Taylor Band's debut album *Famous Among the Barns*, released on Iris Records, an independent label that had been set up by Ben and his friend Larry Ciancia. The band consisted of Ben (guitar), Larry (drums), Chris Chaney (bass), Joel Shearer (keyboards) and Zac Rae (keyboards, vibraphone, guitar). Carly shared vocals on the excellent track 'Let it Grow'.

The year finally came to an end with a wonderful acoustic performance of 'Let the River Run' with singer-songwriter Brendan James at the Nobel Prize Concert in Oslo on December 11th.

In 2004 Carly once again turned to her back catalog with a deal struck with the giant BMG (Bertelsmann Music Group) which had taken over Arista and Warner. Their label BMG Heritage had been created two years before as the successor to Buddah Records, and specialized in re-issues of records that had been originally released on various labels acquired over the years. As it was to be just a single-disc collection, it proved a painstaking task to edit, but the end result proved satisfying to Carly. This new album, called *Reflections: Carly Simon's Greatest Hits*, was a more-affordable compilation of twenty songs, more or less in chronological order, and included the majority of her biggest chart hits, along with several less successful singles. The cover picture was cropped from one that Bob Gothard had taken of Carly by the Bethesda Fountain in Central Park a few years before. The US version released on May 4th also included the song 'Amity', the duet with Sally written for the movie *Anywhere but Here*, and produced by Don Was. For the UK and European version, issued on June 8th, the running order was more random, and the song 'Amity' was replaced by 'Why', as it had been far more successful there.

REFLECTIONS: CARLY SIMON'S GREATEST HITS
BMG Heritage/WEA 82876592291(UK – 8122 78970 2)
Released - May 4 2004 (UK/Europe - June 8 2004)
Executive producer - Joseph Dimuro
Remastering - Bill Inglot and Dan Hersch
US Billboard Hot 200 #22; UK Album Charts #25

US PLAYLIST: That's the Way I've Always Heard It Should Be/ Legend in Your Own Time/Anticipation/The Right Thing To Do/You're So Vain/Mockingbird/Haven't Got Time For the Pain/Nobody Does it Better/You

Belong To Me (single version)/Jesse/Coming Around Again/Give Me All Night (single version)/The Stuff That Dreams Are Made Of (single version)/All I Want Is You/Let the River Run/Better Not Tell Her (single version)Love of My Life/Like a River (single version)/Touched by the Sun/Amity (alternate mix).

UK/EU PLAYLIST: You've So Vain/Anticipation/Nobody Does it Better/That's The Way I've Always Heard It Should Be/Coming Around Again/The Right Thing To Do/Let the River Run/I've Got to Have You/Mockingbird/Legend in Your Own Time/ Why/We Have No Secrets/Haven't Got Time For the Pain/You Belong to Me (single version)/Jesse/Boys in the Trees/The Stuff That Dreams Are Made Of (single version)/Give Me All Night (single version) /Love of My Life/Touched By the Sun

Reflections was a wonderful overview of Carly's extensive catalog and well-received by critics and fans alike. It reached #22 on the Hot 200, making it Carly's first top forty album since *Coming Around Again*, and remained on the charts for 19 weeks. It also reached #43 on *Billboard*'s digital album chart and #25 on the UK chart on March 2nd. Three years later it was certified gold for sales of half a million in the US alone.

Carly now decided she needed a permanent base in New York and bought a two-floor brick town house at 46 Commerce Street in the West Village for around $1.2 million. To fulfill her promotional commitments, she appeared on a number of television shows, including performances of 'Anticipation' on *Late Night with Conan O'Brien*, and 'You're So Vain' on *Live with Regis and Kelly*. That same year Carly was given another chance to make a cameo appearance, this time in the comedy-drama *Little Black Book*, for which she also contributed some of her hits. Released on August 6th, it starred Brittany Murphy and Ron Livingston and was directed by Nick Hurran. Based on the story by Melissa Carter, it tells the story of a young woman who confronts her boyfriend after finding his former girlfriends are still listed in his little black book. Carly appears at the very end of the movie when the young woman faints when first meeting her idol for an interview.

Back to the Hundred-Acre Wood

During the fall, Carly was once again approached by Disney. This time it was for their new animation called *Pooh's Heffalump Movie*. Carly wrote five new songs for the film, and performed four of them. 'The Promise' is actually one of the finest instrumentals of her career. Sadly, the film would be the last by John Fieldler who died just four months after its release (he had voiced Piglet in all Pooh movies since 1968.) The film was released on February 11th 2005, with Disney deciding to have the soundtrack album include two of Carly's songs from *Piglet's Big Movie* - 'Winnie the Pooh' and 'With Just a Few Good Friends' - and calling it *The Best of Pooh and Heffalumps, Too*. The album was released on February 8th.

Carly never regretted her work with Disney: "That's the greatest gift I have: to get into the head of most living creatures. I don't think I could get into the head of a serial killer, or someone who's that scary to me, but a Heffalump? No problem." She later recalled: "Both movies were very well reviewed and I hope keep their place in the hall of Winnie the Pooh sweet young things. What could be better? No violence, just some nasty hitting and honey stealing."

Christmas 2004 saw Carly taking part in two rousing gospel-flavored shows at the Apollo Theater in Harlem on December 18th and 19th, and she was joined by Sally and Ben, Julie Levine (Lucy's daughter), Kate and Liz Taylor, Peter Calo, T-Bone Wolk, Teese Gohl, jazz bassist Christian McBride, and acclaimed gospel singer Bebe Winans.

THE BEST OF WINNIE THE POOH AND HEFFALUMPS, TOO
Disney Records 5008 61268-7
Released - February 11 2005
Producers - Carly Simon, Joel McNeely, Matt Walker, Rob Mathes & Michael Kosarin

Carly's contributions and performers:

Winnie the Pooh *(Robert Sherman - Richard Sherman - Carly Simon)* ***
Carly and Ben
The Horrible Hazardous Heffalumps! *(Carly Simon)* **
Carly with Jim Cummings (Pooh & Tigger), John Fieldler (Piglet), Ken Sansom (Rabbit), Peter Cullen (Eeyore) and Nikita Hopkins (Roo)
Little Mr Roo *(Carly Simon)* **
Kath Soucie (Kanga)
The Name Game *(Carly Simon)* **
Kyle Stanger (Lumpy) and Nikita Hopkins (Roo)
Shoulder to Shoulder *(Carly Simon)* **
Carly with the Heffalump chorus
In the Name of the Hundred Acre Wood/What Do You Do? *(Carly Simon)* ***
Carly with the Heffalump chorus
With a Few Good Friends *(Carly Simon)* ***
Carly with Sally and Ben
The Promise *(Carly Simon)* ****
Joel McNeely

Earlier in the year Carly had duetted with her friend Mindy Jostyn on the serene 'Angel of the Darkest Night', a track off her latest album, *Coming Home*, which was an inspiring collection of so-called "folk-hymns." But within a matter of weeks Mindy was dead, having succumbed to cancer on March 10th, after refusing treatment because of her Christian Science beliefs. The album was released several months after Mindy's death, but it was a heartbreaking time for both Jake and Carly.

Serenades Turn to Sorrow

"I want to be somebody who faces things and who doesn't get stepped on, because I've been stepped on too much in my life and I don't want my self-esteem to suffer. I feel that I've just about had enough...I'm not going to take it anymore"

Back to the standards

After a period of depression and apparent weight loss, Carly managed to get herself back together and was given the chance to return to her favorite genre and make a new album of old standards, which would be her fourth. The idea came from her old producer friend Richard Perry, who in 2002 had worked closely with Rod Stewart on *It Had to Be You - The Great American Songbook*, the first in a long series of best-selling albums of standards, and two more albums had also been released in the past couple of years.

In the liner notes to the album, Carly writes: "Maybe I've earned the right to do these songs, maybe I haven't. Let time be the judge. I have always sung standards from the time I was a little girl mooning, as most of us were, over Frank Sinatra's great classic renditions."

Striking a deal with Columbia Records, Perry now approached Carly with a similar project in mind and a whole list of songs that Stewart had not performed. Carly embraced the idea and the sessions took place that spring, with the music tracks recorded by Bobby Ginsburg and Carter Humphrey at Fox Four Five Studio and Reagan's Garage in Los Angeles, with strings recorded at nearby Westlake Recorders. Carly's vocals were then recorded by Dylan Margerum at the Cutting Room in New York. Amongst the musicians were guitarist Vin D'Onofrio, best known for his portrayal of the overweight clumsy marine in the movie *Full Metal Jacket*; multi-instrumentalist Chris Golden, who had recently been the drummer for the Oak Ridge Boys, and John Ferraro, one of the top session drummers in the business.

With recording costs kept to a minimum, Carly and Perry managed to produce a wonderful album. Once again it was a labor of love for Carly, a collection of timeless songs she said "you can dance to, make love to, and engage perhaps in a dry martini or a pre-dawn swim." Carly praised the work Perry had done and called it "a sexy and novel release." The album cover had a beautiful picture of Carly in a long white silk dress, once again taken by Bob Gothard.

On June 25th, whilst recording the vocals, Carly celebrated her 60th birthday.

MOONLIGHT SERENADE
Columbia CK 94890 (UK – 5205422)
US DualDisc version - Columbia CN 94881
Recorded - Spring-Summer 2005, Fox Four Five, Reagan's Garage &Westlake Recorders, LA, & The Cutting Room, New York
Released - July 19 2005 (UK - October 10 2005)
Producer - Richard Perry
Associate producer - Lauren Wild
Mixed - Bobby Ginsberg, Regan's Garage LA
Mastering - Robert Hadley, the Mastering Lab, LA
US Billboard Hot 200 #7; Billboard Top Internet Albums #7

Moonlight Serenade *(Glenn Miller-Mitchell Parish)* ***
Arranged by Richard Perry, Mike Thompson & Lauren Wild
Mike Thompson - piano, string synths, add. string arrangements; Vin D'Onofrio - guitar; Chris Golden - bass; John Ferraro - drums; Doug Webb - sax, clarinet; Lee R Thornburg - trumpet, trombone; Victor Lawrence - cello; Mike Robertson - violin; Sam Formicola - violin; Shalini Vijayan - violin; Sam Firscher - violin; Alyssa J Park - violin; Danny Seidenberg - viola
Glen Miller's famous signature tune, written in May 1939. Mitchell Parish supplied the subsequent lyrics. Carly recalls: "I think that the idea for the theme of the album was brought to me by Richard in one phone call when he said, 'Have you ever thought of cutting Moonlight Serenade', and I hadn't….I honestly hadn't thought the song was one I could tackle for various reasons – the most important of which being I didn't know it."

I've Got You Under My Skin *(Cole Porter)* ****
Arranged by Richard Perry, Lauren Wild & Andy Chukerman
Jim Cox - piano; Vin D'Onofrio - guitar; Chris Golden - bass; John Ferraro - drums; Doug Webb - sax solo; Andy Chukerman - synth strings; Mike Thompson - add. synth; Victor Lawrence - cello; Mike Robertson - violin; Sam Formicola - violin; Shalini Vijayan - violin; Sam Firscher - violin; Alyssa J Park - violin; Danny Seidenberg - viola
Written in 1936 and first introduced by Eleanor Powell in the movie *Born to Dance*, sung by Virginia Bruce. Later it became one of Sinatra's signature tunes and was also a chart hit for the Four Seasons in the mid-60s. Superb arrangement and a faultless delivery by Carly, helped along by Doug Webb's sultry sax.

I Only Have Eyes for You *(Harry Warren - Al Dubin)* ****
Arranged by Richard Perry, Mike Thompson & Lauren Wild

Mike Thompson - piano, synth strings, Uiber; Vin D'Onofrio - guitar; Chris Golden - bass; John Ferraro - drums; Tom Evans - sax solo; Alex Navarro - synth strings, add. string arrangements; Victor Lawrence - cello; Mike Robertson - violin; Sam Formicola - violin; Shalini Vijayan - violin; Sam Firscher - violin; Alyssa J Park - violin; Danny Seidenberg - viola
One of the great doo-wop classics of all time, written for the 1934 movie *Dames* and sung by Dick Powell to Ruby Keeler. Perry adapts it in the spirit of the classic Flamingos version of 1959 but makes Carly's different to all previous versions.

Moonglow *(Eddie DeLange - Irving Mills - Will Hudson)* ****
Arranged by Richard Perry, Mike Thompson & Lauren Wild
Mike Thompson - piano, synth strings, vibes, add. string arrangements; Vin D'Onofrio - guitar; Chris Golden - bass; John Ferraro - drums, Doug Webb - clarinet solo; Victor Lawrence - cello; Mike Robertson - violin; Sam Formicola - violin; Shalini Vijayan - violin; Sam Firscher - violin; Alyssa J Park - violin; Danny Seidenberg - viola
Written in 1933 and first recorded by Joe Venuti. Wonderful husky vocal supported by Mike Thompson's piano accompaniment and string arrangement and Doug Webb's sax solo.

Alone Together *(Howard Dietz - Arthur Schwartz)* ***
Arranged by Richard Perry, Mike Thompson & Lauren Wild
Vin D'Onofrio - guitar; Mike Thompson - Fender Rhodes, synth strings; Chris Golden - bass; Sammy Merendino - drum programming, percussion; Doug Webb - stritch solo, Victor Lawrence - cello; Mike Robertson - violin; Sam Formicola - violin; Shalini Vijayan - violin; Sam Firscher - violin; Alyssa J Park - violin; Danny Seidenberg - viola
First introduced in the 1932 Broadway show *Flying Colors* by Jean Sargent. In Carly's words, Arthur Schwartz was "almost like a member of the family, my parents 'closest friend." She visualized it having a bossa nova groove and Perry was in agreement, and this resulted in it becoming her favorite song on the album. Sammy Merendino, one of New York's top drummers, was called in to do some excellent drum programming. Carly admits she took to the vocal "like fish to water."

In the Still of the Night *(Cole Porter)* ***
Arranged by Richard Perry & Lauren Wild
Jim Cox - piano; Vin D'Onofrio - guitar; Chris Golden - bass; John Ferraro - drums; Alex Navarro - synth strings, add. string arrangements; Mike Thompson - add. synth; Andy Chukerman - add, synth; Doug Webb - flute; Victor Lawrence - cello; Mike Robertson - violin; Sam Formicola - violin; Shalini Vijayan - violin; Sam Firscher - violin; Alyssa J Park - violin; Danny Seidenberg - viola
Written for the movie *Rosalie* in 1937 and sung by Nelson Eddy. In an interview with Richard Perry Carly called this one of the "best songs ever written" and one of the first chosen for the album. Perry also recognized that it is one of Porter's

most difficult songs to perform and thereby praised Carly for her "effortless" rendition.

The More I See You *(Mack Gordon - Harry Warren)* ***
Arranged by Richard Perry, Mike Thompson & Lauren Wild
Mike Thompson - piano, synth; add. string arrangements; Vin D'Onofrio - guitar; Chris Golden - bass; John Ferraro - drums; Alex Navarro - add. Synth; Larry Lunetta - trumpet solo; Victor Lawrence - cello; Mike Robertson - violin; Sam Formicola - violin; Shalini Vijayan - violin; Sam Firscher - violin; Alyssa J Park - violin; Danny Seidenberg - viola
Straightforward adaptation of the song originally sung by Dick Haymes in the 1945 movie *Diamond Horseshoe*. Wonderful trumpet solo by the celebrated Larry Lunetta.

Where or When *(Lorenz Hart - Richard Rodgers)* ***
Arranged by Richard Perry, Mike Thompson & Lauren Wild
Mike Thompson - piano, synth strings, add. string arrangements; Vin D'Onofrio - guitar and solo; Chris Golden - bass; John Ferraro - drums; Victor Lawrence - cello; Mike Robertson - violin; Sam Formicola - violin; Shalini Vijayan - violin; Sam Firscher - violin; Alyssa J Park - violin; Danny Seidenberg - viola
Written for the 1937 movie *Babes in Arms*. Carly elevates this rather lesser-known standard with another magical vocal, together with a fine guitar solo by Vin D'Onofrio (substituted by a sax solo on the DVD release).

My One and Only Love *(Guy Wood - Robert Mellin)* ****
Arranged by Richard Perry, Mike Thompson & Lauren Wild
Mike Thompson - piano, synth strings; Vin D'Onofrio - guitar; Chris Golden - bass; John Ferraro - drums; Alex Navarro - synth strings; add. string arrangements; William Galison - harmonica solo; Victor Lawrence - cello; Mike Robertson - violin; Sam Formicola - violin; Shalini Vijayan - violin; Sam Firscher - violin; Alyssa J Park - violin; Danny Seidenberg - viola
Perhaps the least well-known standard on the album, first published in 1953 and recorded by Sinatra as the B-side to the single 'I've Got the World on a String'. Perry admits that this was the most difficult song on the album for Carly to have to sing, with the first line alone covering an octave and a half range. In his own words, "excellent achievement."

All the Things You Are *(Oscar Hammerstein II - Jerome Kern)* ****
Arranged by Richard Perry, Mike Thompson & Lauren Wild
Mike Thompson - piano, synth strings, add. string arrangements; Vin D'Onofrio - guitar; Chris Golden - bass; John Ferraro - drums; Lee R Thornburg - flugelhorn solo; Victor Lawrence - cello; Mike Robertson - violin; Sam Formicola - violin; Shalini Vijayan - violin; Sam Firscher - violin; Alyssa J Park - violin; Danny Seidenberg - viola
Written for the musical *Very Warm for May* in 1939 and first appearing in the movie *Broadway Rhythm* in 1944, when it was sung by George Murphy. Another

showcase for Carly's vocal range, and an incredible flugelhorn solo by Lee R Thornburg.

How Long Has This Been Going On *(George Gershwin - Ira Gershwin)* ****
Arranged by Richard Perry, Doug Webb & Lauren Wild
Jim Cox - piano; Vin D'Onofrio - guitar; Chris Golden - bass; John Ferrero - drums; Doug Webb - saxes, clarinet; Andy Chukerman - synth strings; Victor Lawrence - cello; Mike Robertson - violin; Sam Formicola - violin; Shalini Vijayan - violin; Sam Firscher - violin; Alyssa J Park - violin; Danny Seidenberg - viola
Written for the musical *Funny Face* in 1928 but not used; then resurrected for the musical *Rosalie* the same year. Perry adapted this from a Peggy Lee recording and cites Carly's version as the best he's ever heard.

Atlantic crossing

Moonlight Serenade was released in both regular and dual-disc (CD & DVD) formats, the latter including an interview with Carly and Richard Perry, behind-the-scenes studio footage, and the entire album in "enhanced stereo." The album proved to be a rather unexpected success. Released on July 19th, it entered the Hot 200 chart on August 6th at its peak position of #7 and remained on the charts for seven weeks. It also reached the same position on *Billboard*'s Internet Album chart, and became Carly's highest charting album since *Boys in the Trees*. No one was more surprised than Carly, who in a BBC interview quipped, "I'm only gonna get killed now. As soon as you do anything successful, everybody hates you as somebody who has 'legs' in their career."

The UK CD version, released on October 10th, included 'My Foolish Heart' and 'Let it Snow', while in the US Barnes & Noble issued it as a special copy that also included 'My Foolish Heart'. 'Let it Snow' had been written during a Hollywood heat wave by Jule Styne and Sammy Cahn in 1945 and first recorded that same year by Vaughan Monroe. It also brought later chart success for Woody Herman, Frank Sinatra, Dean Martin and Bing Crosby. A splendid black and white promotional video was also made for 'I Only Have Eyes for You'.

At the 48th Grammy Awards on February 8th the following year, *Moonlight Serenade* was nominated in the category of Best Traditional Pop Vocal Album, but lost out to Tony Bennett's *The Art of Romance*.

To promote the album, Carly made the customary television appearances, including *The View* on July 22nd. The following month she also agreed to take part in the Fox documentary series *Geraldo Rivera Reports* and performed 'Alone Together' with Sally and Ben on the *Martha Stewart Show*.

In September Carly made what proved to be her last televised concert to date with the PBS televised spectacular, *Carly Simon: A Moonlight Serenade on the Queen Mary 2*. With her band and daughter Sally, she performed two concerts on board the brand-new British luxury liner during its transatlantic voyage from New York to Southampton. Produced by Ned Doyle, the 90-minute special had Carly performing many of the songs from her recent album, plus a sprinkling of her best-known hits. With Richard Perry acting as musical director and conductor, Carly's band consisted of many of the musicians that had played on the album: John Beasley on piano; Vin D'Onofrio on guitar; Chris Golden on bass; Larry Ciancia on drums; Alex Navarro on synthesizer; Doug Webb on sax, flute and clarinet; Sally Taylor on guitar and backing vocals; and Margaret Bell and Maurice Lauchner on backing vocals. There was also the ship's orchestra directed by Jim Gable.

A short six-song acoustic set was also performed in Carly's cabin with just Sally, guitarist Vin D'Onofrio, and backing singers Bell and Lauchner, and it included wonderful versions of 'Love of My Life', 'Boys in the Trees' and 'It Was So Easy'. The subsequent DVD, released on November 22nd, included behind-the-scenes footage, and an interview with Carly. There was also a preview of the video for 'Let it Snow', Carly's latest promotional single, which had been digitally released on December 6th and reached #6 on the Adult Contemporary chart.

The songs performed on the *Moonlight Serenade* DVD are as follows:

Ballroom Set: Moonlight Serenade/I've Got You Under My Skin/Where or When/How Long Has This Been Going On/Let the River Run/I Only Have Eyes for You/Jesse/Coming Around Again/Moonglow/All the Things You Are/The More I See You/Alone Together/You Belong To Me/Nobody Does It Better/You're So Vain

Acoustic Set: No Secrets/Love of My Life/Devoted to You/It Was So Easy/Boys in the Trees/Anticipation

Returning home a few weeks later, Carly prepared for what would be called the Serenade Tour, her first for ten years. Rehearsals took place at the Hot Tin Roof on the Vineyard, which had since been sold by her co-owners. As well as Sally and Ben, the touring band consisted of Peter Calo, John Beasley, Viktor Krauss, Alex Navarro, Larry Ciancia, Jimmy Roberts, and Nick Lashley, along with backing singers Carmella Ramsey and Everett Bradley. The sell-out dates began at the Orpheum Theater in Boston on November 19th, with further dates that included the Chevrolet Theater in Wallingford, CT (Nov 21), Lincoln Theater in New York (Nov 22), Borgata Events Center in Atlantic City (Nov 25) and the D.A.R.

Constitution Hall in Washington (Nov 29). All the concerts were well received, with Carly performing a fine mixture of hits and standards. There were times when Carly showed signs of anxiety, but they were rare, and on the whole it all went as planned.

It had been an emotional year for Carly, with the death of some old friends, and now it was made even more bitter with the loss to cancer of Kate Taylor's husband.

Soothing songs and lullabies

The beginning of 2006 found Carly under a little pressure from Columbia to continue with her rejuvenated career and make another album. She approached them with the suggestion of doing a collection of r&b covers with the legendary soul maestro Booker T Jones, but it was turned down. Instead, she gave it some more thought and then came back with the idea of doing a more intimate album of gentle, soothing covers, and this they liked.

After spending a couple of months selecting the songs, all of which in some way resonated with her past, Carly turned to her friend and neighbor Jimmy Parr to produce the album, which would be called *Into White*, after the title track written by Cat Stevens. During the summer months, some twenty songs were recorded at Parr Audio, where some of the mixing had been done by Jimmy for the *Christmas Is Almost Here* album. Among the other musicians were Peter Calo, Teese Gohl and British guitarist David Saw, a songwriter friend of Ben's who would also be contributing two of his own compositions. Of all the songs recorded, fourteen made it onto the final album.

Carly recalled: "I loved doing the album, and it's one of the easiest records I've ever made in terms of not having to argue with too many people." Indeed, it was a stress-free time for everyone, with no more than three people in the studio at any one time and most of the vocals completed in one take.

Through June and July Carly worked with her friend Andreas Vollenweider on his Christmas album, *Midnight Clear*, and sang on four of the thirteen tracks - the beautiful 'Forgive', which had originally featured as a bonus track on the 2003 re-release of *Christmas Is Almost Here*, as well as 'Midnight Clear', 'Suspended Note' and 'Hymn to the Sacred Heart'. The album was recorded in Switzerland, with Carly's vocals done remotely, and released on the Kinkou label on October 24th.

During the year Carly also duetted with former brother-in-law Livingston Taylor on his single 'Best of Friends', which featured on his album *There You Are Again*. It would prove to be the last chart entry to feature Carly when it peaked at the Adult Contemporary chart at #39.

INTO WHITE
Columbia 82876 86138-2 (UK – 82876861382)
Recorded - Summer 2006, Hidden Star Hill & Parr Audio, Martha's Vineyard MA
Released - January 2 2007
Producers - Carly Simon & Jimmy Parr
Engineer - Jimmy Parr
Mixing - Jimmy Parr, Parr Audio MV
Mastering - Bob Ludwig, Gateway Mastering, Portland ME.
US Billboard Hot 200 #13; Billboard Top Internet Albums #1

Into White *(Cat Stevens)* ****
Teese Gohl - piano, keyboards, bass synth strings; Peter Calo - guitar; Jan Hyer - cello; Carly Simon - backing vocals; Jimmy Parr - backing vocals
From Cat Stevens' 1970 album *Tea for the Tillerman*. Carly was as surprised as anyone that a song she had first heard back in 1970 would one day be the title song of one of her albums 36 years later. But it's a glowing tribute to the man and his music she fell in love with all those years ago.

Oh! Susanna *(Stephen Foster)* **
Carly Simon - arranger, Kalimba, backing vocals; Teese Gohl - keyboards, synth strings, Kalimba, flute; Peter Calo - guitar, Dobro; Jimmy Parr - Kalimba, backing vocals
Minstrel song first published in 1848. One of the early contenders for the album. Peter Calo's muted guitar is accompanied by almost everyone playing kalimbas (little thumb pianos).

Blackbird *(John Lennon - Paul McCartney)* ***
Teese Gohl - Pizzicato strings, Hi strings, synth cellos, bodhran, piano; Peter Calo - guitar, Dobro slide; David Saw - guitar; Jan Hyer - cello; Carly Simon - backing vocals; Ben Taylor - backing vocals
Paul McCartney song written for the 1968 album *The Beatles* (White album). Carly resonates with the bird: "I am trying to take my broken wings and learn to fly. Not to mention those sunken eyes I need to see with."

You Can Close Your Eyes *(James Taylor)* ***
Promo Single 88697050672
Released - 2006
Teese Gohl - piano, arranger; Peter Calo - guitar, Sally Taylor - vocals; Ben Taylor - vocals.

Originally appearing on Taylor's 1971 album *Mud Slide Slim*, this track features Carly with Ben & Sally. Carly still refers to it as a "plaintive, all-time great song."

Quiet Evening *(David Saw)* ****
Teese Gohl - bass, percussion, piano; Ben Taylor - guitar, backing vocals; Peter Calo - guitar; David Saw - guitar; Carly Simon - backing vocals
The first of two new songs on the album, and one not written by Carly, but by guitarist David Saw, his very first composition. Carly describes how she had to "pilfer it and make it my own." Originally a guitar-based song, Carly was so impressed by Gohl's sensual bass playing that she turned it right up in the mix. Arguably the best track on the album.

Manha De Carnaval (Theme from *Black Orpheus*) *(Luiz Bonfa - Antonio Maria)* ***
Teese Gohl - keyboards, synth strings, bass; Peter Calo - guitar; David Saw - guitar; Jan Hyer - cello
A Brazilian bossa nova song translated as "Carnival Morning." It first appeared in the Portuguese movie *Orfeu Negro (Black Orpheus)* in 1959 and Carly describes how it conjures up romantic love and is "one of the most beautiful melodies ever heard in my lifetime."

Jamaica Farewell *(Irving Burgie)* ***
Teese Gohl - Lo and Hi kalimba; Peter Calo - guitar, 8-string guitar, Dobro; David Saw - guitar; Carly Simon - backing vocals; Ben Taylor - backing vocals
Written by American Irving Burgie (aka Lord Burgess), one of the great composers of Caribbean music. It appeared on Harry Belafonte's album *Calypso* in 1956 and was first heard by Carly at one of his concerts at Carnegie Hall in the 60s. She then learnt to strum it on her guitar and it became one of the three or four songs in the Simon Sisters' early repertoire.

You Are My Sunshine *(Jimmie Davis - Charles Mitchell)* **
Teese Gohl - piano; Peter Calo - guitar, 8-string guitar, Dobro; David Saw - guitar; Carly Simon - backing vocals; Ben Taylor - backing vocals
Originally recorded by the Pine Ridge Boys in 1939. Davis was twice governor of Louisiana. It was later recorded by Bing Crosby and Gene Autry. This was never originally intended for the album, but was unexpectedly sung by Carly in the control room (having remembered the words), and the other musicians joined in to record it.

I Gave My Love a Cherry (The Riddle Song) *(Traditional)* **
Carly Simon - arranger; Teese Gohl - piano, synth strings; Jan Hyer - cello
The famous "Riddle Song" that descends from a 15th century English folk song in which a maiden says she is advised to unite with her lover. Carly was resonated with the line "The story of I love you, it had no end."

260

Devoted to You/All I Have to Do is Dream *(Boudleaux Bryant - Felice Bryant)* ***
Teese Gohl - keyboards, synth strings, bass; Peter Calo - guitar; Jan Hyer - cello; Jimmy Parr - percussion, heartbeat; Ben Taylor - backing vocals
A faithful rendition of the two Everly Brothers classics from 1958, with 'Devoted to You' previously recorded by Carly and James on the *Boys in the Trees* album in 1978.

Scarborough Fair *(Trad. Arr. by Carly Simon)* ***
Arranged by Carly Simon
Teese Gohl - Lo Kalimba, LoDrum, piano, hammered piano, flute; Ben Taylor - guitar; Peter Calo - 8-string guitar; David Saw - guitar; Jimmy Parr - woodblock (a small slit drum made from a single piece of wood); Carly Simon - backing vocals
Traditional Celtic folk ballad traced back as far as 1670 with original 19th century melody by Frank Kidson. It was given its more familiar arrangement by Simon and Garfunkel for their 1966 album *Parsley, Sage, Rosemary and Thyme*. When researching the song Carly discovered there were some lesser-known verses, and now also added a few of her own for this melancholy arrangement.

Over the Rainbow *(Harold Arlen -Yip Harburg)* ***
Teese Gohl - piano, synth strings; Peter Calo - guitar; Jan Hyer - cello
One of the most famous songs of all time, written for the 1939 film *The Wizard of Oz*. Carly admitted how much she was in awe of the song: "It doesn't get much better than this and to do anything that Judy Garland ever sang tells you just how crazy and brave I am."

Love of My Life *(Carly Simon)* ***
Teese Gohl - synth strings, electric piano, cello, pad; Peter Calo - guitar; Jimmy Parr - bass; David Saw - guitar; Jan Hyer - cello; Carly Simon - backing vocals
A new recording of the song from the *This Is My Life* soundtrack, with Carly now singing half of the original but adding new lyrics, as well as replacing Woody Allen's name with that of Mia Farrow.

I'll Just Remember You *(Ben Taylor - David Saw)* ****
Carly Simon - acoustic guitar; Teese Gohl - acoustic & electric piano
When Carly came into the room and heard Ben and David playing this song, she thought it was a Rodgers & Hart song, as they had also been working on versions of 'Funny Valentine' and other standards. But this was a new song that had taken them just fifteen minutes to write, and, of course, she fell in love with their "perfect combination of talents."

Carly once again dedicated the album to her old friend Paul Samwell-Smith, and when released on January 2nd 2007 it became *Billboard*'s "Hot Shot Debut" when it entered the Hot 200 at #15 on the 27th, finally peaking two

261

places higher and remaining on the charts for ten weeks. It also managed to hit the top spot on *Billboard*'s Internet Album list. Like *Moonlight Serenade*, it was another solid success for Carly and Columbia.

The album's cover picture was taken by Sally in the gardens at Hidden Star Hill, while the other outdoor photographs were courtesy of Heidi Wild. Several promotional singles were issued, although none were released commercially, and a trio of excellent videos were produced for 'Into White', 'Quiet Evening', and 'Blackbird', their settings perfectly matching the theme of the album.

Over the next few weeks Carly made several television appearances, with performances of 'Quiet Evening', 'Blackbird', and 'Love of My Life on the QVC shopping channel; 'Oh! Susanna' on *This Morning with Mike and Juliet*; and a beautiful rendition of 'You Can Close Your Eyes' with Sally and Ben on *Oprah* on January 16th. In February she once again appeared on *Live with Kelly and Ryan*. During the early part of the year Carly was also a guest on the new teen show *B Intune TV*, hosted by presenter Zarah, and featured as part of its music legends segment.

The overall success of the album also led to a special edition of it being released by Barnes & Noble, with the bonus track 'Hush Little Baby/My Bonnie'.

Music from the Vineyard

2007 would be another emotional year for Carly. She finally divorced Jim Hart, although they remained the closest of friends. In February Carly got a call from her old friend Jimmy Webb, who asked her if she wanted to do an album of Brazilian music, as he believed she had the perfect voice for it. With Frank Filipetti coming on board to co-produce, she now got down to writing new material for an album which was to be called *This Kind of Love*. In an interview she described what she had in mind: "I'm setting the lyrical themes to carnival or Brazilian or slightly samba tempo so that life is joyous even in its sadness. Life is a dream even in its most painful moments, it's a dream that we can dance to."

Carly had always been fascinated by the rhythms and passion of Brazilian music and they were usually the most scratched records in the Simon household of her youth: "I realized that music could evoke passion and tragedy more than could painting or dancing or any other form of art. This being a subjective point of view, but very strongly inculcated into my system. I wondered how or if I could lend my gifts to it." The next thing to do was to find a record label.

It was a year in which the whole music industry was under threat from the burgeoning digital revolution. Record stores across the country were going out of business, with music now been downloaded and often shared, albeit illegally. That spring, Carly decided to follow in the footsteps of other well-known artists when she was invited to sign up with Hear Music to make her next album. Hear Music was a former catalog company, which in 1999 had been bought by Starbucks. In the ensuing years it had established a record label with big aspirations, with its chairman proclaiming: "We believe strongly that we can transform the retail record industry" by playing and selling their recordings in their coffee shops across the country. Paul McCartney saw Hear Music as being more excited about the musical innovation than his own record company was, and, as a result, ditched EMI to become their first signee. Other artists such as Ray Charles, Joni Mitchell and Alanis Morissette also signed up.

In a period that seemed devastating for the music industry, Starbucks seemed to represent the possibility that album shopping could once again be a physical experience for a potential mass market. But it wasn't just a case of merely stocking CDs in-store, as they began to roll out special retail kiosks where people could browse through thousands of songs and burn them on to discs for a fee. In their minds, they were reinventing record shops for the digital age.

Carly saw the potential, and after meeting with Hear Music executives, the company wooed her with an advance of between $750,000 and $1million, and a marketing plan that included stacking copies of her album next to the cash registers and having it played on a regular basis in all their coffee houses. However, by the time Carly's lawyer had got his hands on a copy of the final contract, the advance had been reduced to $575,000. Carly had already spent $100,000 of it on the recording sessions.

Those recording sessions had commenced in September on Martha's Vineyard, just a matter of days before Sally went into labor. With Webb and Filipetti handling production, the assembled musicians included the familiar Peter Calo, Teese Gohl, Steve Gadd, Michael Lockwood, David Saw, T-Bone Wolk, and also the welcome return of Rick Marotta. Among the new faces were Robby Ameen, regarded as one of the prominent drummers in the field of Latin jazz music; bassist Lincoln Goines, who had been a mainstay of New York's jazz/Latin studio scene since the early 80s; and Brazilian percussionist Cyro Baptista, well regarded in the music world for creating many of the instruments he played. The recordings took place in Carly's kitchen, Parr Audio, and Ma & Egberto's Garden in Lagoa, with final work completed at Legacy Recording Studios in New York. The album would finally be released the following April.

On October 4th 2007 Carly became a grandmother for the first time when Sally and her husband Dean Bragonier had a baby girl called Bodhi.

THIS KIND OF LOVE
Hear Music HMC 30662 (UK – 0888072308008)
Recorded - Fall 2007, Hidden Star Hill & Parr Audio MV, Ma & Egberto's Garden, Lagoa, & Legacy Recording Studios, New York
Released - April 29 2008 (UK - June 2 2008)
Producers - Carly Simon, Frank Filipetti & Jimmy Webb
Engineers - Frank Filipetti, Carly Simon & Ben Taylor
Mixed - Frank Filipetti
Mastering - Bob Ludwig, Gateway Mastering, Portland ME.

This Kind of Love *(Carly Simon- Jimmy Webb - Peter Calo)* ****
Promo Single Concord Records (UK)
Released - 2008
Peter Calo - guitar; David Saw - guitar; Lincoln Goines - bass; Teese Gohl - orchestration; Robbie Ameen - drums; Cyro Baptista - percussion; Rick Marotta - percussion, Aaron Heick - sax; Elena Barere - concertmaster; Frank Filipetti - backing vocals; Jill Dell'Abate - backing vocals; outro music by Jimmy Webb & Peter Calo; Choir - Aiden Cron, Amanda Scopelliti, Amy Cass, Ben Brooks, Emily Graffeo, Emily Powers, Josie Mangold, Lucas Mangold, Melanie Clarke, Ryan King & Sarah Barnaby
Vibrant opener with a Brazilian samba flavor, originally written as a rocker. Inspired by a comment her boyfriend had once made: "You're the fantasy that I will never forget." Complete with a children's choir at the end, the song is also notable for the impromptu wordless vocals of Jimmy Webb and Peter Calo performed in the session, which Carly insisted had to be included on the recording.

Hold Out Your Heart *(Carly Simon - Peter Calo)* ****
Carly Simon - electric piano; Peter Calo - guitar; David Saw - guitar; Lincoln Goines - bass; Robbie Ameen - drums; Teese Gohl - orchestration; Cyro Baptista - percussion; Elena Barere - concertmaster; Fonzi Thornton - backing vocals; Jill Dell'Abate - backing vocals; Tawatha Agee - backing vocals; Vaneese Thomas - backing vocals
Inspired by the time that Carly's son Ben had told her he was going surfing on a stormy winter's day, and although she begged him not to go, he went anyway, but changed his mind when he got there. She's also reaching out to Sally in the song: "I hold my heart out to my kids. The reserve is always open to them. I'm like a bank if they need me." Carly adds her lyrics to Peter Calo's sensitive composition.

People Say a Lot *(Carly Simon)* **

Peter Calo - guitar, backing vocals; Teese Gohl - orchestration; Cyro Baptista - percussion, Rick Marotta - percussion; Elena Barere - concertmaster; Sammy Merendino - programming; Carly Simon - backing vocals; Ben Taylor - backing vocals; David Saw - backing vocals; Jimmy Parr - backing vocals; Jimmy Webb - backing vocals

Another song written in anger by Carly about people who promise her a lot, but instead end up taking a lot from her. It was based on the 1950 movie *All About Eve*, in which an assistant tries to assume the identity of her boss.

Island *(Ben Taylor)* ***

Peter Calo – acoustic & electric guitar, backing vocals; Ben Taylor - acoustic guitar, backing vocals; Jimmy Webb - synthesizer; Lincoln Goines - bass; Robbie Ameen - drums; Cyro Baptista - percussion; Teese Gohl - orchestration; Elena Barere - concertmaster; Carly Simon - backing vocals; Jill Dell'Abate - backing vocals

Written by Ben for his sister Sally who had just broken up with a friend and had quickly shut off her feelings, becoming an "island." The song had originally appeared on the Ben Taylor Band album, *Famous Among the Barns*, in 2003.

How Can You Ever Forget *(Carly Simon - David Saw)* ****

Carly Simon - acoustic piano, synthesizer, percussion, backing vocals; David Saw - guitar, backing vocals; Peter Calo - mandolin; Lincoln Goines - bass; Jimmy Webb - orchestration; Aaron Heick - English horn; Elena Barere - concertmaster, Ben Taylor - backing vocals; Frank Filipetti - backing vocals; Jill Dell'Abate - backing vocals

One of Carly's favorite songs on the album. Written during a seven-minute drive to the studio on the Vineyard, she worked with guitarist David Saw to complete a song for which he had just written the first verse.

Hola Soleil *(Carly Simon - Ben Taylor - Jacob Brackman - Jimmy Webb - Peter Calo - David Saw)* ***

Peter Calo - guitar; David Saw – guitar; Lincoln Goines – bass; Rick Marotta – percussion; Cyro Baptista – percussion; Teese Gohl – orchestration, synthesizer; Elena Barere – concertmaster; Fonzi Thornton – backing vocals; Jill Dell'Abate – backing vocals; Tawatha Agee – backing vocals; Vaneese Thomas – backing vocals; Choir – Aiden Cron, Amanda Scopelliti, Amy Cass, Ben Brooks, Emily Graffeo, Emily Powers, Josie Mangold, Lucas Mangold, Melanie Clarke, Ryan King, Sarah Barnaby

A spur-of-the-moment decision to do a samba jam while all the band members were present in Carly's kitchen. David Saw and Ben began putting together some lyrics, while Carly called on Jake Brackman to help out. The result was feel-good ode to the morning, with a title translated in English as "Hello Sunshine," with the children's choir giving it that added touch of sun.

In My Dreams *(Carly Simon - Jimmy Webb - Peter Calo)* ****

Peter Calo - guitar; Jimmy Webb - acoustic piano; Aaron Heick - alto flute

Carly had been nursing lyrics to this song for almost a couple of years, and described it as a "song of dreams into death," of dreaming without being afraid, and letting the subconscious take over your thoughts. Once again Jimmy and Peter come up with the perfect melody.

When We're Together *(Sally Taylor)* ***
Peter Calo - guitar, Dobro; Lincoln Goines - bass; Robbie Ameen - drums; Cyro Baptista - percussion; Rick Marotta - percussion; Teese Gohl - orchestration; Elena Barere - concertmaster
Sun-kissed slice of bossa nova that originally appeared on Sally's debut album *Tomboy Bride.*

So Many People to Love *(Carly Simon -Wade Robson - Carole Bayer-Sager)* ***
Promo Single PRO-HM-246 (album version)
Released - April 29 2008
Producer - Wade Robson
Ben Mauro - guitar; David Campbell - arr. strings; Wade Robson - arr. strings, arr. vocals; Sheree Brown - backing vocals
Recorded the previous year in Los Angeles, where Carly had written a number of songs with Carole Bayer-Sager. For this one, they enlisted the help of Australian dancer and singer Wade Robson to complete the song. Robson taught Carly to sing in the sultry r&b style of Michael Jackson. The inspiration for the song came from the Wim Wenders' movie *Wings of Desire* with its portrayal of angels listening to the whispers of sad Berliners and then touching their shoulders to lift their spirits.

They Just Want You to Be There *(Carly Simon)* ***
Carly Simon - acoustic guitar, backing vocals; Peter Calo - guitar, Dobro; Jimmy Webb - synthesizer; Robbie Ameen - drums; Frank Filipetti - backing vocals; Jill Dell'Abate - backing vocals
Another track inspired by Carly's children, and one of the last songs composed for the album, with both melody and lyrics done at the same time. Carly remembered the strong maternal instincts she had with Sally and Ben when they were young and the unconditional love shown.

The Last Samba *(Jimmy Webb)* ***
Jimmy Webb - acoustic piano; Lincoln Goines - bass; Rick Marotta - Cahones; Cyro Baptista - percussion; Aaron Heick - alto flute
A song that shows Carly and Jimmy's shared love for Brazilian music, with Jimmy having recently worked with the great Antonio Carlos Jobim.

Sangre Dolce *(Carly Simon)* ***
Producer – Carly Simon
Carly Simon - electric piano; guitar, bass, percussion; Michael Lockwood - guitar solo; T-Bone Wolk - bass; Steve Gadd - drums; Teese Gohl - orchestration; arr. strings.

266

A track resurrected from the 2002 special edition of the album *The Bedroom Tapes*.

Too Soon to Say Goodbye *(Carly Simon)* ***
Carly Simon - electric piano; synthesizer, backing vocals; Jimmy Webb - acoustic piano; Peter Calo - guitar; Lincoln Goines - bass; Robbie Ameen - drums; William Galison - harmonica; Ben Taylor - backing vocals; David Saw - backing vocals; Fonzi Thornton - backing vocals; Jill Dell'Abate - backing vocals; Tawatha Agee - backing vocals; Vaneese Thomas - backing vocals
Carly's tribute to her friend, celebrated *Washington Post* columnist Art Buchwald, who was ill at the time and had asked her to write a song with the title of a book he had written consisting of a collection of eulogies. She let him listen to the song on a cassette shortly before he died in January 2007.

Carly dedicated the album to both Buchwald and Brazilian songwriter Antonio Carlos Jobim. Her great friend Lynn Goldsmith took the stunning cover picture of Carly wearing a black dress and gold belt. When released, the album peaked at #15 on the Hot 200 on May 17th and remained on the charts for nine weeks. Two promotional singles were issued for 'This Kind of Love' and 'So Many People to Love', but neither had a commercial release. A video was also released of Carly performing 'This Kind of Love', 'Island' and 'How Can I Forget' in a studio setting with Ben, Sally and Peter Calo and advertised on Amazon.

To promote the album, Carly embarked on a series of interviews and television appearances, sometimes revealing that she now had a new man in her life, surgeon Richard Koehler, who she described as her "new kind of lover." On May 1st she appeared with Ben in a televised documentary called *Talking Guitars*, which was a portrait of guitar craftsman Flip Scipio, and the day after performed 'Hold Out Your Heart' on *Regis and Kelly*, along with Ben, Sally and other band members. A week later Carly was invited to perform on the *Rachael Ray Show*, which also had her friend and former president Bill Clinton as a guest, and two days later made an appearance on *The Tonight Show with Jay Leno*. On May 17th Carly and Ben performed a different acoustic version of 'Anticipation' at Starbucks in Miami Beach, the same version that would later appear on her next project.

That same month Carly was also invited on the syndicated *Tavis Smiley Show* and was asked about the songs on the album written about her children. It became obvious that there had been some kind of feud with Sally, who, incidentally, had moved out of Carly's home with her husband after her son was born, and was now living in Boston, leaving them in what she referred to as "a vacuum of silence." Other appearances around this time included a guest spot on *Ellen* in which she performed 'You're So

Vain', and being interviewed by Kathy Lee and Hoda Kolb on NBC News' morning show *Today*. On June 19th she appeared with Ben on Howard Stern's radio show and sang 'You're So Vain', and just over a week later performed on an episode of *A&E's Private Sessions* to promote her album, and sang two songs, including the new version of 'Anticipation'. Reviews of the album were positive. *The Daily Telegraph* wrote: "Maternal love has seldom been so honestly, melodically sung about."

No Love for Starbucks

Although sales of *This Kind of Love* were initially good, shifting 23,000 copies in the first week, they soon began to decline, and by October 2009 it had sold just 123,000 units, barely a third of what *Moonlight Serenade* had achieved. Although the album was not being exclusively sold through Starbucks, it soon became apparent that copies of the album were no longer being replenished in their outlets. Without Carly's knowledge, Starbucks had pulled back from the music business on April 24th 2008 and had handed Carly's day-to-day business over to their partner, Concord Music. Alan Mintz, the A&R man and Carly's contact at Hear Music had also been fired (he would soon become Carly's manager). Carly began drafting message to Starbucks' COE s, Howard Schultz, but received no replies. By October, with still no response, she wrote: "Howard, Fraud is the creation of Faith/And then the betrayal. Carly."

Carly was in dire straits financially. She had put her New York house on the market without any success, and through negligence and fraud her financial manager Kenneth Starr had lost her a significant amount of money. Not only that, she still owed money on the work that had been carried out on her Vineyard home, the $575,000 advance had not been paid in full, and there had been no royalty payments received from radio plays. Carly's lawyer filed a lawsuit seeking $5-10 million from Starbucks, alleging "concealment of material facts," "tortious interference" with Carly's contract, and "unlawful, unfair and fraudulent business practices." Carly was never going to take this gently, but she eventually lost the battle, with the judge ruling that Hear Music had never been a legal division of Starbucks, and therefore her suit against them had no legal standing. Two later appeals also failed. Carly was devastated: "It felt like carrying a child to term and then having it die in childbirth."

Carly revealed: "I want to be somebody who faces things and who doesn't get stepped on, because I've been stepped on too much in my life and I don't want my self-esteem to suffer. I feel that I've just about had enough...I'm not going to take it anymore."

To help her get over her despair and anger with Starbucks, it would be her son Ben who came up with the perfect antidote.

Never Been Gone

"Looking back, maybe I would have been a bit more careful about who and what I was getting involved with because my enthusiasms can sometimes be my downfall. Some things are both your greatest assets and your biggest detriments."

Carly unplugged

It wasn't time for Carly to retire yet. She had to keep on working, and working meant making music. But that, too, was beset with problems, as she was still tied into a contract with Starbucks/Concord/Universal and therefore obliged not to record any new material until a specified time had elapsed. Upset but not deterred, she now took up a suggestion made by her son Ben. It was the summer of 2008, and with the Hidden Star Hill home filled with musician friends of Ben's working with him on his latest project, he turned to his mother one day and asked her to play to them some of her finest songs the way they had originally been written, and then suggested they do "unplugged" versions for a new album. Of course, some of Carly's contemporary artists were already doing the same thing, as they didn't own the masters to their original songs. This way, Carly would have ownership of the new recordings and receive income through licensing them in the future. It was an inspired idea.

The biggest question though was whether her fans would buy it. Looking back on her ever-changing career, she put it into context: "As a singer I tried on all these hats, these voices, these clothes, and eventually out came me."

Now it was Ben who would become the driving force and he persuaded his mother to channel her energies into this new project. To begin with, the recording would have to be done at home, but it would take time to produce, with Ben's tour commitments taking priority. With these new and largely acoustic arrangements for many of her career-defining songs, there would also be the inevitable clashes between mother and son over how to re-imagine songs that to Carly were like cherished children.

The album, aptly called *Never Been Gone*, was to be launched on the small independent label Iris Records, owned by Ben and his friend Larry Ciancia, and under temporary license to Warner. The label had already released Ben's 2006 EP *Lady Magic* and his 'Nothing I Can Do' single the following year, as well as songwriter David Saw's second album *Broken Down Figure* in 2008, done in collaboration with British singer Judy Tzuke. The production team for the new album consisted of Carly, Ben, Larry Ciancia, Peter Calo, David Saw and Ben Thomas, and collectively dubbed "Paphiopedilium." Between them they chose which of Carly's songs to record, and how and where to introduce some "never-heard-before surprises." Ben had now developed into a consummate producer, and, according to Carly, he never flattered her, but took a more "passive aggressive" role, based on a profound respect for his mother's music. No one was paid for their services. David Saw made it quite clear: "We all did it for free because we all loved the songs and because of all that she's done for us."

At first Carly suggested they all sang into one microphone, giving it a more informal, "campfire" feel, but it became impossible to separate the instruments, and what she visualized as a short week's worth of basic recording proved quite the opposite. With the musicians often called away for other projects, Carly gave her old friend Frank Filipetti a call and he came over and set up recording equipment throughout the house. Another welcome guest was her godson John Forte, recently released from his prison sentence, who was now invited over to produce one of the tracks. Although none of the final selection included post-1989 songs, there would be the addition of two previously unreleased songs. Carly also wanted to program the songs so that they sounded like a continuous symphony, with songs split into three different movements and the sequencing progressing the story of each preceding track.

With the recording of the new album taking months to complete, there were other back catalog releases in the pipeline. On December 8th 2008, the Shout Factory label had released on compact disc *Carly and Lucy Sing Songs for Children*, previously issued in 1969. Remastered by Bob Fisher, it was the second CD re-issue of the sisters' music, following on from 2006's *Winkin, Blinkin and Nod: The Kapp Recordings*, a compilation of their first two albums released exclusively online by the reissue label Hip-O-Select and produced by Pat Lawrence.

On March 31st 2009 a three-disc album called *Carly Simon's Collector's Edition* was released in Canada. Produced by Warner Custom Products, and marketed and distributed by the Canadian company Madacy Entertainment, it comprised songs from her first eleven Elektra/Warner studio albums from 1971 to 1983, including some surprising choices, and was presented in a special tin box complete with liner notes and photos taken by Bob Gothard during the *Letters Never Sent* photo shoot.

271

CARLY SIMON COLLECTOR'S EDITION
Madacy Entertainment OPCD-8336-1/Warner Music Group TCE2 54058
Released March 31 2009 (Canada)

Disc 1
Anticipation/The Right Thing to Do/That's the Way I've Always Heard It Should Be/Haven't Got Time for the Pain/Waterfall/Mockingbird/Legend in Your Own Time/Back Down to Earth/We Have No Secrets/Darkness till Dawn

Disc 2
Never Been Gone/Devoted to You/Not a Day Goes By/Boys in the Trees/It Happens Everyday/We're So Close/Julie Through the Glass/Older Sister/I Get Along Without You Very Well/For Old Times Sake

Disc 3
You're So Vain/Jesse/Vengeance/You Belong to Me/Come Upstairs/Playing Possum/You Know What to Do/The Girl You Think You See/Take Me as I Am/One More Time

With the on-going recording of the new album, Carly made fewer televised appearances. However, on September 11th 2009 she performed 'Let the River Run' with Sally and Ben for the television special *9/11 Memorial from Ground Zero, 8th Anniversary*, directed by David Stern. On October 26th, the day before the new album was released, she appeared on *Good Morning America* with a band that included Ben, Larry Ciancia and David Saw, and performed the new and well-received version of 'Let the River Run'.

NEVER BEEN GONE
Iris Records IRIS1014V (US vinyl) (UK - Rhino Records 5186584342 cd)
Recorded - Summer 2008-Fall 2009, Simon/Taylor Studios A, B, & C; Parr Audio; Pulse Music & Elk Ears Studio, MV
Released - October 27 2009
Producers - Paphiopedilium (Carly Simon, Ben Taylor, Larry Ciancia, David Saw & Ben Thomas)
Engineers - Larry Ciancia, Chris Davies, Frank Filipetti, John Forte, Jimmy Parr, Derik Lee, Carlos Pennisi & Ben Taylor
Mixed - Frank Filipetti, Legacy Recording Studios, New York & Studio B, Martha's Vineyard.
Mastering - Bob Ludwig, Gateway Mastering & DVD, Portland ME.
US Billboard Hot 200 #134; Billboard Folk Albums #11; Billboard Independent Albums #22; UK Album charts #45

272

The Right Thing to Do *(Carly Simon)* ****
Arranged by Carly Simon.
Carly Simon - acoustic guitar, piano; Peter Calo - acoustic guitar, acoustic bass;
Ben Thomas - drum programming; Ben Taylor - backing vocals
A fine guitar-based re-imagination of the hit single, which had originally been
written on the piano, and now sung in the key of G rather than C to accommodate
Carly's huskier voice. Ben's "Hallelujah" jamming at the end provides a rather
inspiring touch.

It Happens Everyday *(Carly Simon)* ***
Arranged by Ben Taylor (with Peter Calo, Larry Ciancia, David Saw & Carly
Simon)
Peter Calo - acoustic guitar, baritone guitar, backing vocals; Larry Ciancia -
Cajon, percussion; Ben Taylor - acoustic guitar, loops, backing vocals
Despite the unmistakable sound of footsteps at the start, this is another wonderful
r&b interpretation with Carly's voice sounding as good as it did on the original,
and the unexpected "give it to the girls" mantra at the end doing it no harm at all.

Never Been Gone *(Carly Simon - Jacob Brackman)* ****
Arranged by Ben Taylor (with Peter Calo, Larry Ciancia, Teese Gohl, David Saw
& Carly Simon.)
Carly Simon - acoustic guitar; Peter Calo - acoustic guitar; Larry Ciancia -
Cajon; Teese Gohl - acoustic piano; David Saw - acoustic guitar; Ben Taylor -
acoustic guitar, backing vocals; Giulia Casalina - backing vocals; Frank Filipetti
- backing vocals
Nothing could ever match the hymn-like grace of the original, but with Ben
transforming this from a foxtrot to an almost waltz-like rhythm, it feels like you
are listening to Carly with her family and friends singing it around a campfire on
a Vineyard beach. Simply enchanting, especially with Teese Gohl's exquisite
piano.

Boys in the Trees *(Carly Simon)* ****
Arranged, engineered & mixed by Carly Simon
Carly Simon - all instruments; Sally Taylor - backing vocals; John Forte - add.
backing vocals
The only track on the album which is a total Carly production, with the only
contributions coming from the gentle background vocals of Sally and John Forte.

Let the River Run *(Carly Simon)* ****
Arranged by David Saw & Ben Taylor
Peter Calo - baritone guitar; Larry Ciancia - Djembe; Teese Gohl - piano, string
pads; David Saw - acoustic guitar, backing vocals; Ben Taylor - acoustic guitar,
backing vocals; Margaret Bell - backing vocals; Meredith Sheldon - backing
vocals
Stunning choral treatment of this Oscar-winning anthem which loses none of its
impact, especially with the excellent backing vocals by Meredith Sheldon and
acclaimed Detroit-born gospel singer Margaret Bell.

You're So Vain *(Carly Simon)* ****
Arranged by David Saw & Ben Taylor
Peter Calo - acoustic guitar; Larry Ciancia - Cajon, percussion; Teese Gohl - acoustic piano; David Saw - acoustic guitar, backing vocals; Ben Taylor - acoustic guitar, backing vocals; Ben Thomas - bass
Inventive and energetic rendition of this most famous of Carly's songs, which apparently took four strenuous days to perfect the vocals.

You Belong to Me *(Carly Simon - Michael McDonald)* **
Arranged by John Forte, JK & Ben Taylor
John Forte - acoustic guitar, add. programming, backing vocals; Teese Gohl - acoustic piano; JK - lead guitar; Ben Thomas - bass, drum programming, organ; David Saw - backing vocals; Ben Taylor - backing vocals
The 1978 hit given a flavor of hip-hop which lacks some the energy of the original, but makes up for it with a George Benson-style guitar solo by JK and a funky bass by Ben Thomas.

No Freedom *(Carly Simon - David Shaw - Ben Taylor)* ***
Arranged by Ben Taylor
Larry Ciancia - drums, percussion; Ben Taylor - acoustic guitar, loops, drum programming, DJing, backing vocals; Christopher Thomas - bass
A song about ex-husband Jim that Carly had written lyrics for while on vacation with him in Anguilla after their divorce. Originally intended as a reggae tune, it was unearthed for this album with music added by David Saw, who turned it into more of a folk song. But Carly then had second thoughts, and with Ben's help changed it into a 2/4-time arrangement similar to Elton John's 'Bennie and the Jets'. One of the two tracks to have big drums.

That's the Way I've Always Heard It Should Be *(Carly Simon - Jacob Brackman)* *****
Arranged by Carly Simon
Carly Simon - arr. synth guitar, keyboard programming; Jimmy Parr - synth guitar; Teese Gohl - orchestration & conductor; Elena Barere - concert master, violin; Toni Glickman - violin; Yana Goichman - violin; Ann Lehmann - violin; Katherine Livolsi-Landau - violin; Nancy McAlhaney - violin Vincent Lionti - viola; Adria Benjamin - viola; Alyssa Smith - viola; Richard Locker - cello; Stephanie Cummins - cello; Eugene Moye - cello; Ben Taylor - backing vocals
To revisit and reinterpret one of the diamonds in the jewel box of Carly's songs, and to do it justice, would have been a daunting prospect for any other artist to face. But Carly's inspiring arrangement gives her classic collaboration with Jake an added dimension, with just the right amount of orchestration to give it an ethereal quality that transcends any criticism. Easily the stand-out track on an already fine album.

Coming Around Again *(Carly Simon)* ****
Arranged by Carly Simon & David Saw

Peter Calo - acoustic guitar; Larry Ciancia - Cajon, percussion; David Saw - acoustic guitar, backing vocals; Ben Taylor - acoustic guitar, backing vocals
Emotional performance from Carly with additional lyrics tagged on at the end, including the haunting, "It's gonna break you before it makes you." Carly later stated that this improvisation "teaches me where I am with that song's openly private sorrows."

Anticipation *(Carly Simon)* ***
Arranged by Carly Simon & David Saw
Peter Calo - acoustic & bass guitar; Larry Ciancia - Cajon; Teese Gohl - acoustic piano; David Saw - acoustic guitar, backing vocals; Jill Dell'Abate - backing vocals; Meredith Sheldon - backing vocals; Ben Taylor - backing vocals
Achingly slowed down treatment of one of Carly's greatest hits as if we are in anticipation of it speeding up a little. But Carly sings with the usual passion and it's hard to criticize such feeling.

Songbird *(Carly Simon)* ****
Carly Simon - piano; Peter Calo - Lap steel; Ben Thomas - arr. strings. add. piano; Teese Gohl - orchestration, conductor, arr. strings; Ben Taylor - backing vocals; Elena Barere - concert master, violin; Toni Glickman - violin; Yana Goichman - violin; Ann Lehmann - violin; Katherine Livolsi-Landau - violin; Nancy McAlhaney - violin; Vincent Lionti - viola; Adria Benjamin - viola; Alyssa Smith - viola; Richard Locker - cello; Stephanie Cummins - cello; Eugene Moye - cello
A demo of an unfinished song written almost forty years before in 1970 for possible inclusion on her debut album, and originally titled 'Hallelujah for the Year'. It was "re-discovered" on an old Walkman in 2009 and completed by Carly with the help of Frank Filipetti over the next few months. It is a remarkable insight into her writing craft at the time with the story of a lonely girl stuck in New York on the Fourth of July: "There was a songbird that used to come to my landing when I lived in New York…and I'd try to get melodies from its singing. You couldn't do better than a bird." Also notable for the fine string arrangement by Ben Thomas and Teese Gohl.

The album was released on vinyl in the US, but only as a CD in the UK and Europe, on the Rhino Label. Britain's *Daily Mail* also issued a special free edition in a cardboard sleeve with its newspapers. Stalling at #134 on the Hot 200, it managed to reach #11 on their Folk Album chart and #22 on the Independent Album chart. In the UK, the CD release peaked at #45, Carly's first studio album to reach their top 100 since *Coming Around Again*. A portion of the album's proceeds went to the Carly Simon Music Therapy Initiative, which was a collaboration with the Berklee College of Music in Boston. Carly dedicated the album to Jake: "May we never be gone."

On the day of the album's release, Carly appeared at the Bruno Walter Theater in New York and performed the latest versions of her songs, including 'You're So Vain', 'You Belong to Me', and 'Coming Around Again'. The following day she guested on the *Today* show and sang 'You Belong to Me'. Other appearances included an hour-long exclusive interview with Adam Weisler on Extra TV, a guest spot on *Late Night with Jimmy Fallon* on November 11th, and a lip-synced performance of 'Let the River Run' during a televised special for Macy's Thanksgiving Parade in New York on November 26th.

Carly also began using her new website carlysimon.com to maximize her profile to the growing legions of online fans, rewarding them with impromptu videos taken around her home and spontaneous renditions of some of her songs. It proved to be the ideal way of connecting with the very people who were buying her records and those who relished getting a glimpse of life behind the walls of Hidden Star Hill.

Bob's Burgers and a girl called Taylor

In March 2010 Carly made a rare visit to the UK to promote the album's release. Accompanied by Ben, she performed her very first British concert, *An Evening with Carly Simon*, to a small audience of about 100 fans at BBC's Maida Vale studio, and it was broadcast on BBC Radio on March 2nd. During her short visit she also appeared on BBC's *The One Show* (March 1st) and *Breakfast* show (March 5th), before a final appearance on ITV's *Good Morning Britain* (March 10th), singing an acoustic version of 'You're So Vain'.

Two months later Carly's former financial manager was arrested and jailed for 45 years, having stolen millions of dollars from a number of celebrity clients over the years, including Carly.

On June 15th Carly took part in the televised documentary *The Greatest Ears in Town: The Arif Mardin Story*, directed by Joe Mardin and Doug Biro, and paid tribute to her great friend. In the film, Carly recorded the Mardin song, 'Calls a Soft Voice', written for his aging mother, and it appeared on the tribute album *All My Friends Are Here*, released later that year, along with contributions from the Bee Gees, Bette Midler, Willie Nelson and Chaka Khan.

In September she performed with Ben and her godson John Forte in a benefit to aid the victims of Hurricane Earl, which had devastated the East Coast but fortunately had left Martha's Vineyard unscathed. On November 25th she was finally given what was surely one of the highest honors any artist could receive when her character appeared in the television special *Jessica Simpson: Happy Christmas*.

Over the next few years there would be no new music and no tours, but there would be a host of engagements and public appearances that kept Carly in the limelight. On June 11th 2011 she paid tribute to another musician friend when she appeared in the documentary *All You Need Is Klaus*, a portrait of bass guitarist Klaus Voormann, who had played on several of her earlier albums.

During the summer of 2011 Ernest Thompson, the famous writer and director who had written the original play *On Golden Pond* and the subsequent Oscar-winning movie screenplay, sent Carly lyrics to a song called 'Father and Daughter Dance', which he had written for a new stage adaptation of the play. Thompson wanted it to have a "Carly sound," but the singer was reluctant to take on the project. Finally, one day, Carly called him and sang the song to him over the phone. Taking a break from writing her memoir she went up to New Hampshire to record it at Squam Sound, along with engineer, guitar and synthesizer player Randy Roos, bass player Brendan Dowd, and keyboard player Joe Deleault, who co-wrote the music with Carly. After several emotional takes and a few tissues later, Carly had it nailed. Her wonderful legendary voice had provided "the perfect counterpoint to the play's most powerful sense of longing, of opportunities lost, and of a lingering optimism for the future."

On October 11th, Rhino Records released *Carly Simon: Original Album Series*, a box set of Carly's first five studio albums for Elektra. Issued as part of a series of similar albums, the discs were packaged in mini cardboard replicas of the album sleeves with original artwork, but the tracks were the original recordings, not remastered like those in other similar compilations. Nine days later, she appeared with Lucy and Ben in the 90-minute Canadian documentary *Greenwich Village: Music That Defined a Generation*, directed by Laura Archibald.

2012 saw Carly performing a new recording of 'Just Like a Woman' for the multi-artist charity album *Chimes of Freedom: The Songs of Bob Dylan*, which celebrated forty years of Amnesty International. The four-disc compilation, comprising 76 tracks, debuted at #11 on the Hot 200 in January, while a two-disc version issued by Starbucks entered the charts at #38. In July, the album *Spoiled Girl: Deluxe Edition* was released by Hot Shot Records, with the bonus tracks 'Black Honeymoon', the 7-inch version of 'Tired of Being Blonde', and two 12-inch mixes of 'My New Boyfriend'.

The following year Carly duetted with her great friend Jimmy Webb on his song 'That's Easy for You to Say' for his album, *Still Within the Sound of My Voice*, released on September 10th. It had originally been recorded by Linda Ronstadt.

During the summer of 2014 Carly got a call from pop sensation Taylor Swift asking her if she would like to sing 'You're So Vain' with her in a forthcoming leg of her sold-out Red Tour. As it would be close to home in Foxborough, Massachusetts, Carly readily agreed. On July 27th they duetted in front of a wildly enthusiastic audience. Taylor was full of admiration for the singing legend: "She has always been known for her songwriting and her honesty. She's known as an emotional person but a strong person. I really look up to that."

Another tribute took place on October 12th when Carly appeared in the PBS documentary *Marvin Hamlisch: What He Did for Love*, directed by Dori Berinstein. That same month she guested in an episode of the animated series *Bob's Burgers* called 'Work Hard or Die Trying', with the plot revolving around Gene's idea of putting on a musical version of *Working Girl*, and performed the outro song. It aired on October 5th.

Having now signed a new lucrative deal with the record giant BMG, Carly's fifth greatest hits album, *Playlist: The Very Best of Carly Simon*, was released on October 27th as part of their compilation album series. The album consisted of fourteen selected tracks, including six live recordings.

PLAYLIST: THE VERY BEST OF CARLY SIMON
Legacy/ Arista/Sony
Released - October 27 2014

Coming Around Again/Give Me All Night/All I Want Is You/Nobody Does it Better (live)/You Belong to Me (live)/My New Boyfriend/Let the River Run/The Stuff That Dreams Are Made Of/Better Not Tell Her/You're So Vain (live)/Touched by the Sun (live)/Anticipation (live)/Never Been Gone (live)/Our Affair

In November Carly finally sold her West Village house for around $2.3 million, and Hidden Star Hill became her permanent residence, a sanctuary where she could now devote her time to writing a long-overdue memoir, something that her friend Jackie Onassis had pressed her to do.

A memoir in words and music

Having signed a deal with Flatiron Publishers, the book, *Boys in the Trees - A Memoir*, turned out to be a deeply candid autobiography of her life and career up to the point where she divorced James, and revealed the episodes in her early life that inspired some of her most intimate songs. Released on November 24th 2015, five months after celebrating her 70th birthday, it had a companion two-disc album called *Songs from the Trees (A Musical Memoir Collection)*, which had been released on the Rhino label five days prior to the book.

The book received excellent reviews, with *Pop Matters* declaring: "Simon mixes candor and humor into a gripping and rhythmic language that seemingly dances on the page." *The Independent* was impressed by the way Carly had fearlessly chronicled her life, while the *Boston Globe* summed up the book's dear-diary theme as "one of longing." *The Guardian*, too, admired the clinical and compelling approach that displayed how "canny and clever" she was. *The New York Times*, however, judged it as "overripe," despite it becoming one of its prestigious "bestsellers."

The album consisted of newly mastered versions of songs that paralleled the timeframe of the book, as well as 'Two Hot Girls' from 1987. Two previously unreleased songs were also included: 'Showdown' was a Carly-penned song from the 1978 *Boys in the Trees* sessions, produced by Arif Mardin and now mixed by Frank Filipetti, and 'I Can't Thank You Enough' was a song Carly had started to write when her feelings had been hurt after an argument with Ben, which was then completed by the two of them. It was later recorded at the Vineyard's TreeSound Studios with Ben, Jimmy Parr and Ryan Casey, and re-recorded in Carly's living room and at Parr Audio.

SONGS IN THE TREES - A MUSICAL MEMOIR COLLECTION
Rhino/Elektra R2-552681 (UK – 081227949495)
Released - November 20 2015
Compilation producer – Carly Simon

Disc 1
Boys in the Trees/Winkin, Blinkin and Nod/Orpheus/Older Sister/It Was So Easy/Embrace Me, You Child/Hello Big Man/Two Hot Girls (on a Hot Summer Night)/It Happens Everyday/His Friends Are More Than Fond of Robin/I'm All It Takes To Make You Happy/That's the Way I've Always Heard It Should Be/I've Got to Have You/Anticipation/Legend in Your Own Time/Three Days

Disc 2
Julie Through the Glass/We Have No Secrets/You're So Vain/Mind on My Man/Mockingbird/After the Storm/Haunting/In Times When My Head/You Belong to Me/We're So Close/From the Heart/Come Upstairs/The Right Thing to Do/Showdown/I Can't Thank You Enough

To promote the book and album, Carly appeared with Ben and Sally on *The Late Show with Stephen Colbert* on November 24th, with Carly joining the host for a humorous rendition of 'Mockingbird' before singing the wonderful 'I Can't Thank You Enough'. The following day Carly was interviewed by Susannah Guthrie on the *Today* program. Two days later they again sang the song on *Live with Kelly and Michael*, before returning to the *Today* show on December 4th to perform 'I Can't Thank You Enough' along with 'You're So Vain'.

2016 was relatively quiet for Carly, with a sprinkling of television appearances toward the end of the year. On November 1st she was a special guest on AXS TV's *The Big Interview with Don Rather*, in which the host chatted with the singer at her Vineyard home about her career, her relationships and growing up in a famous family. On November 4th she appeared on *Extra*, a daily syndicated news/magazine program, and was interviewed by host Billy Bush, while the following month she became the subject of the UK Channel Four documentary series *The Great Songwriters*, directed by Lloyd Stanton and Paul Toogood, and was interviewed at her home by Toogood, where she discussed her fascinating life, work, and approach to songwriting, giving performances of four of her songs. The program was aired in the UK on December 1st.

On May 5th 2017 Carly appeared in an episode of the BBC/Eagle Rock documentary series *Classic Albums*, which showcased *No Secrets*. Directed by Guy Evans, it featured among others Jake Brackman, Richard Perry, engineer Bill Schnee, guitarist Jimmy Ryan, and Arylene Rothberg, and was aired in the US on AXS TV on August 9th. In October a two-disc 30th Anniversary deluxe edition of the album *Coming Around Again* was released by Hot Shot Records, with remastered versions of both the studio and live recordings.

The truth about Chibie

In an episode of *Finding Your Roots: Unfamiliar Kin*, shown on October 10th, Carly finally found out the closely-guarded truth about her grandmother Chibie. Through extensive research, they found that she had actually been born Ofelia (Elma) Oliete in Cuba on June 3rd 1888 to Spaniard Jose Oliete and Cuban Maria Baez, and was the youngest of 17 children. Chibie had arrived in America with her family in 1892, and her mother was listed on arrival as 50-year-old Maria Oliete, the oldest of the eight-named Oliete group. But their age difference came into question, and later DNA results from descendants of Maria indicated that Carly was more closely related to both Maria and 19-year-old Lauriana Oliete. At first

280

thought to be Chibie's older sister, it now raised the possibility that Maria may have been bringing up Lauriana's illegitimate child as her own. The 1900 census also showed Maria living in New York with 11-year-old Ofelia and another daughter, Sunsia.

Further research found that Maria had been baptized in Cuba in 1839, as the illegitimate daughter of Vincent Baez and Maria de Leiba, who were classed as "free mixed-race" people, probably descended from slaves. More DNA tests showed that Carly's ancestry was of 10% African origin, and she was amazed that after seventy years the truth about her beloved grandmother's mysterious past was beginning to be unravelled.

On October 13th Carly appeared in the second part of the documentary *Nile Rodgers: How to Make It in the Music Business*, directed by Christopher Bruce. Rodgers had collaborated with Carly on the singles 'Why' and 'Kissing with Confidence'.

The following March Carly performed 'Let the River Run' along with the Resistance Revival Chorus, at the annual Tibet House Benefit Concert at Carnegie Hall in New York, raising funds for the preservation of Tibet's ancient cultural traditions. On June 19th she also contributed to the documentary *A Painter Who Farms*, about Allen Whiting, a Vineyard farmer-artist whose family had been living off the land for twelve generations, and it was premiered at the Martha's Vineyard Film Festival.

Losing Peter

Tragedy hit the Simon family on November 19th 2018 when, after battling cancer for many months, Peter Simon died of a heart attack at the age of 71. Peter had lived most of his life on the island and had carved a name for himself as a nationally acclaimed photographer, photojournalist, author and music historian. He had inherited his love of photography from his father when at the age of eleven he had been given a Polaroid camera, and he took numerous images of his family, later shadowing Carly around to take iconic pictures of her over various stages of her career. He not only took photographs of the famous, but of ordinary folk too, and always with the same passion and ability to make the subject feel relaxed. After gaining a scholarship at Boston University through his photographic work, he embraced the back-to-the-land movement of the early 70s and bought a farm in Vermont which he named Tree Frog, and soon turned it into a commune. He later married and made the Vineyard his permanent home with his wife Ronni. They opened the popular Simon Gallery in Vineyard Haven in 1988, and became well respected members of the island community.

Carly missed her little brother immensely, and recalled how as a young boy, he was always "a mover and a shaker, and always originating the games we played, and he got everyone to play them."

On October 22nd 2019, Carly's second memoir *Touched by the Sun: My Friendship with Jackie Onassis*, was released by Macmillan. From their chance meeting at a Vineyard summer party in 1983, the two of them had become unlikely friends, but it was a friendship that endured. Two different women, one a free-spirited artist and divorcee on a quest to find new love and the meaning of life, and the other one of the most glamorous, esteemed, but elusive women in the country. But the insightful portrait Carly paints is a glowing example of how someone can quite unexpectedly enter your life and in a moment alter its very course. For both of these great women, it was about the values and celebration of true kinship, a feeling made even stronger when you realize it would be for just a short time. Carly never held back when expressing her feelings: "She arrived when I least expected to make a new friend and she stayed up until the time of her death. I've missed her deeply and am reminded of her every day…privately, out of the public eye, I loved her."

The book became a *New York Times* instant bestseller and was named one of ten best books of the year by *People* magazine. On the day of its release, Carly was interviewed at her home by Cynthia McFadden for the *Today* show. Despite its revelations, Jackie's life still remains elusive, "a mystery wrapped in an enigma."

A word about Lucy

While Carly and Joanna went on to carve for themselves successful paths in their chosen careers, it would be a little unjust not to mention too Lucy's significant contribution to the arts. Apart from two critically-acclaimed solo albums and her two Grammy Award-winning *In Harmony* albums shared with husband David Levine, Lucy found her forte in musical theater.

In February 1984 she was one of a number of songwriters for the Off-Broadway revue *A...My Name is Alice*, a production of the Women's Project, which opened at the American Place Theater and ran for two weeks before moving to the Top of the Gate (formerly the Village Gate) for 353 performances. Well received by critics, it went on to win an Outer Circle Award for Best Revue. The two songs co-written by Lucy were 'I Sure Like the Boys' and 'Pretty Young Men'.

She made her Broadway debut in 1991 composing for the musical version of Frances Hodgson Burnett's children's novel *The Secret Garden*, with script and lyrics written by Marsha Norman. The show had had its world premiere at the Wells Theater in Norfolk, Virginia in November 1989 before having its Broadway debut at the St James Theater on April 25th 1991. Directed by Susan Schulman, it closed in January 1993 after 709 performances, and won the Tony Award for Best Book of a Musical, Best Featured Actress in a Musical (11-year-old Daisy Egan) and Best Scenic Design. Lucy also had a Tony nomination for Best Original Score and a Drama Desk Award for Outstanding Music. Over the years production moved to Canada, the UK and Australia.

In 2006 Lucy composed the music for a musical version of Boris Pasternak's classic novel *Doctor Zhivago* with lyricists Michael Korie and Amy Powers. It had its world premiere at the La Jolla Playhouse in San Diego in May, while a new version had its debut in Australia in 2011 starring the great Australian baritone Anthony Warlow. A Broadway production opened in April 2015 with limited success and no award nominations, and four years later it had its UK premiere in London.

The record speaks for itself. When have there ever been three sisters who have contributed so much to the arts?

No regrets

On June 25th 2020 Carly celebrated her 75th birthday, and in February 2021 the music world will also be celebrating the 50th anniversary of the release of her debut album, and the start of an impressive solo career in which she has amassed 24 studio albums, one live album, nine compilation albums, one Christmas album, four soundtrack albums, one audio book, and 41 singles. Of these singles, 24 were Hot 100 hits, 13 of them reaching the top forty, five the top ten, and one topping the chart for three weeks and being dubbed the "ultimate song of the 70s." Her albums have been released on eleven different labels, with five of them going platinum, one multi-platinum, and three gold. All but three of the studio albums have charted on the Hot 200, with twelve reaching the top forty, and five in the top ten.

Carly has also had two Grammy Awards from fourteen nominations, a Golden Globe, two BAFTA nominations, and an Academy Award. She is a member of the prestigious Songwriters Hall of Fame and the Grammy Hall of Fame; a recipient of the Boston Music Awards Lifetime Achievement, a Berklee College of Music Honorary Doctor of Music Degree, and an ASCAP Founders Award. Carly is also a successful author of books for both children and adults alike, a collaborator with dozens of other artists around the world, and, perhaps what she considers to be her greatest achievement, the mother of two incredibly talented singers.

All of this was the product of a shy and insecure little girl; one who once saw herself as an ugly duckling in the shadows of two glamorous sisters; one who longed to impress a seemingly unloving father; one whose phobias and anxieties stifled any ambition she may have had; and one who just wanted to be noticed for who she was and what she could do.

But this was also a girl who had been born and raised in a musical environment, and it would be that music that worked its way under her skin, and her sisters' too. For all their failings as parents, Richard and Andrea Simon were as important in the development of their children's future as anyone. From the early days of listening to her mother singing lullabies; hearing her father playing classical music and reciting poetry; harmonizing with her two sisters; learning to perform and play instruments with her favorite uncle; and soaking up the rich atmosphere of luncheons and cocktail parties for famous musical guests, Carly Simon grew up with music well and truly running through her veins.

But the complicated lives her parents led also served to stifle any desire Carly had to have any musical ambition. Having to compete for affection, and trying to comprehend what was happening around her, all conspired to become what would be a lifetime of questions she would later seek answers for in her songwriting. But then there was Lucy, her guardian angel of a sister, who snapped her out of her self-deprecation and eventually got her to step onto a stage and into the spotlight.

Looking back on her career, would Carly have done things differently? In an interview for *Billboard* she confessed: "Maybe I would have been a bit more careful about who and what I was getting involved with because my enthusiasms can sometimes be my downfall. Some things are both your greatest assets and your biggest detriments."

Let's close now….

Of the many people Carly has to thank for being the person she became, the one that stands head and shoulders above anyone else is Carly herself. In an interview for the *Los Angeles Free Press* in April 1971, she stated that "I'm prepared for the consequences." And although those consequences, both professional and personal, came thick and fast in the years ahead, she faced them all with a gritted determination to carry on. She saw the best and the worst sides of the music business, as well as the heartbreak and infidelities of relationships, and came through them with renewed strength.

Carly will forever be noticed, not just for her incredible music, but for who she is and the influence she has had on so many people. Yes, she may have taken risks, and some of those risks backfired, but many of them succeeded, and she remains a cultural icon and long-overdue to be inducted into the Rock and Roll Hall of Fame. Hopefully 2021 will put that right and due recognition will be coming around again.

Although sometimes being a victim of injustice herself, Carly, like her mother before her, recognizes injustice for others and tenaciously fights in their corner. Her huge heart and her support of worthwhile causes have made her a valuable and highly-respected member of her beloved Martha's Vineyard community. She is as much a fixture of the island as its fishing boats and gingerbread houses. She continues making music in her small home studio with her children and island friends, enjoys her menagerie of animals (four dogs, miniature ponies, goats, sheep and donkeys), cooking, gardening, and taking photographs. Her biggest fan is her partner of thirteen years, 64-year-old island surgeon Richard Koehler, who once said of her: "She is the most creative person I have ever met. It's not just her music, either. It's her writing, her art…she is amazing."

There's only one Carly Simon, and of all the female artists that launched their careers around the same time, her record speaks for itself. None of them can really match her achievements in so many facets of the music business; I honestly doubt if anyone ever will. When you add it all together, nobody did it better.

But what of the future? She once gave us a hint: "I hope to live to be able to do all sorts of things that will help the world or to join forces with those that are helping them." In another interview she declared: "There's always some way of being creative. Even if it's not always alive musically, it's doing something somewhere in my soul." Does she have more secrets to reveal? After writing her memoir, she confessed: "I pray at night, a little confessional of my own, which I've done since forever. I'm pretty comfortable with secrets of the past, because by the end of the day, there will be a pile more."

There may not be much more new music to look forward to, but who knows? This is Carly Simon. Put a guitar in her hand and she becomes another person. All it takes is some small thing to happen in her life or some nonchalant remark overheard, and that little faucet inside her head could once again drip a melody and have her humming it all day long. "Hmmm, that sounds like a good line. Now where did I leave my pen?"

Sources

Album liner notes

Websites
carlysimon.com
carlysimonnmusic.com
carlysimonalbumcovers.blogspot.com
rollingstone.com
nytimes.com
ww.washingtonpost.com
allmusic.com
grammy.com
bostonmusicawards.com
latimes.com
www.geni.com
billboard.com
officialcharts.com (UK)
discogs.com
45.cat.com
Imdb.com

Books
Simon, Carly, *Boys in the Trees: A Memoir,* Flatiron Books 2015
Simon, Carly, *Touched by the Sun: My Friendship with Jackie.* Macmillan 2019

Harrison, Quentin, *Record Redux: Carly Simon*, Joy of Sounds 2017
Hart, James, *Lucky Jim*, Start Publishing 2017
Weller, Sheila, *Girls Like Us: Carole King, Joni Mitchell, Carly Simon and the Journey of a Generation*, Washington Square Press 2008
Whitburn, Joel, *The Billboard Albums* 6th edition. Record Research Inc. 2006
Whitburn, Joel, *Billboard Top Pop Singles 1955-2010* 13th edition. Record Research Inc. 2012

Articles

1960s-1970s

Alfred A Knopf Inc. *Carly Simon Complete*
Alterman, Lorraine, "The Three Artists of the New Consciousness: A Record Forum*," Record World* May 19 1973
Alterman, Lorraine, "I Don't Enjoy Performing Live," *Hi-Fidelity Magazine* Feb 1974
Arrington, Carol, "Rock's Carly Simon: Why Fans Terrify Me," *Us Magazine*, June 13 1978
Atlas, Jacoba, "Carly Playing Possum," *Melody Maker* Apr 19 1975

Barnard, Stephen, "Carly Simon: Clear Light," *The Story of Pop* 1975

Beat Instrumental Magazine, "King and Queen of the 70s?", March 1973

Beckley, Timothy, "Carly Simon is Devoted to You!" *Rock n Roll Special Magazine,* Spring 1979

Blinder, Elliot, "Carly Simon Rides Again," *Rolling Stone* Feb 4 1971

Breslaur, Mary, "Carly Simon's Hot Tin Roof," *Boston Globe* June 9 1979

Campbell, Mary, "Carly's Rug-Cutting Uncle Cuts an LP," *Associated Press* June 3 1973

Christgau, Georgia, "Carly Simon is Not a Folksinger," *The Village Voice* July 5 1976

Christgau, Robert, "Carly Simon as Mistress of Schlock," *Newsday* Jan 1973

Circus Magazine, "Carly Refuses Fear of Flying Role,", Nov 1975

Cohen, Debra Rae, Spy Review, *Rolling Stone* Oct 4 1979

Crouse, Timothy, "Carly Simon" (review of debut album), *Rolling Stone* April 1 1971

Davis, Stephen, "Anticipation" (review), *Rolling Stone* Dec 23 1971

Donaghue, Sue, "Carly Simon – Outspoken," *Rock Magazine* Mar 13 1972

Felice, Judith, "Songs and Stories: Mrs James Taylor is Distinctly Carly Simon," *Hit Parader* June 1973

Fong-Torres, Ben, "Carly: There Goes Sensuous Simon," *Rolling Stone* May 22 1975

Freedland, Nat, "Carly Simon / Don McLean, Troubadour LA" *Billboard Magazine* Dec 4 1971

Gautschy, Jan, "Carly Simon - The Agony of Success," *Words & Music Magazine* Oct 72

Goldman, Albert, "A New Girl Tips the Balance," *Life* Music Review Oct 8 1971

Graustark, Beverly, "The Saga of "You're So Vain," Carly, Mick and the Boys," *Circus Magazine* Mar 1973

Graustark, Beverly, "James Taylor's Leggy Lover Brightens One Man Dog," *Circus Magazine* 1973

Gross, Michael, "Carly Simon Serves Up Hotcakes," *Circus Magazine* May 1974

Harrison, Quentin, "Carly Simon's Come Upstairs Turns Forty / Anniversary Perspective" *albumism.com* June 14 2020

Harrison, Quentin, "Happy 45th Anniversary to Carly Simon's Fifth Studio Album Playing Possum," *albunism.com* April 2020

Heckman, Don, "Carly Simon Sings at the Bitter End: She's Flying High," *New York Times* Dec 18 1971

Hilburn, Robert, "Carly Simon Has Impressive Album," *Los Angeles Times* Mar 9 1971

Hilburn, Robert, "Cat Stevens and Carly Simon Sing," *Los Angeles Times* April 10 1971

Hit Parader, "Carly Simon Has to be Inspired; Talks About Songwriting, Hit Singles and Albums" Dec 1977

Holden, Stephen, "No Secrets," (review) *Rolling Stone* Jan 4 1973

Holden, Stephen, "Playing Possum," (review) *Rolling Stone,* June 19 1975

Holden, Stephen, Review of May 4 1978 appearance at the Bottom Line, *Rolling Stone* July 13 1978

Holden, Stephen, "This Year's Model," (Spy review) *The Village Voice* July 16 1979

Hugg, Judy, Article on Carly and Review of Anticipation, Dec 12 1971

Hunt, Dennis, "What a Wife, Pop Star, Mother to Do?" *Los Angeles Times* Sept 21 1977

Jahn, Mike, "Carly Writes Carly's Hits," *Cue Magazine* Dec 9-15 1974

Jensen, Michael, "Another Passenger," (review) *Star News*, Pasadena CA. July 28 1976

Jerome, Jim, "She Conquered Her Stage Fright but Motherhood Comes First for Mrs James Taylor," *People Magazine*, July 17 1978

Johnson, James, "Simon on Cool Baby James / Pointing a Finger at Vanity / and on Being a Bitch Herself," *New Musical Express*, May 5 1973

Johnson, James, "The Taylors in Paris," *New Musical Express*, Aug 18 1973

Landau, Jon, "Hotcakes," (review) *Rolling Stone,* June 6 1974

Landau, Jon, *Advocate Magazine*, May 21 1975 (Playing Possum review)

Los Angeles Times, "Carly Simon On Bill" Nov 18 1971

Maloney, Peter, "Carly Simon Live from the Bitter End," *Changes Magazine* July 15 1971

Mark, M, "Carly Simon" (performance review), *The Village Voice*, May 1977

Marsh, Dave, Spy Review, *Santa Fe New Mexican* Sept 14 1979

Maslin, Janet, Boys in the Trees, *Rolling Stone*, June 15 1978

McKenna, Kristine, "Carly Simon: Pretty and Unabrasive," *Los Angeles Times*, April 30 1978

Melody Maker, "Review of the debut album from the Songbook", May 15 1971

Naglin, Nancy, "One Love Stand: Laboring in the Vineyard with Carly Simon," *Crawdaddy magazine*, Sept 1976

Nasella, Patti, "Carly Simon Rules Fieldhouse," April 16 1977 (Villanova concert)

New York Times, "Concerts Today," June 18 1971

Nolan, Tom, "Carly," *Cleveland Akron Phonograph Magazine,* May 1975

Odessa American, "Poor Little Rich Girl with Soul," Aug 15 1971

Orloff, Katherine, *Rock n Roll Woman* (Carly chapter)

Pate, Stephen, "Carly Simon - Bob Dylan's Manager and Producer Were Sexual Predators," *NJN Network* Dec 22 2014

People Magazine, "Playing Possum," 1975

Pollock, Bruce, "Carly Simon: The Shy Superstar Whose Kids Come First," *Family Weekly*, Aug 26 1979

Reilly, Peter, "Thoughtful Report from the Home Front by Interrogator Carly Simon," *Stereo Review* 1975

Reilly, Peter, "The Laser-beam Eye and Rifle-mike Ear of the Engaging Carly Simon," (Another Passenger review) *Stereo Review*, 1976

Reilly, Peter, "Boys in the Trees," *Stereo Review* July 1978

Robinson, Lisa, "Carly Simon: No More Time for the Pain*," Hit Parader* Oct 1974

Rock Magazine, "Carly Simon: "A Rock Schizophrenic Existence, Really," Nov 6 1972

Rock Star Magazine, "Very Much a Part of the Family," 1974

288

Rockwell, John, "Live at the Bottom Line," *New York Times* May 6 1978

Rockwell, John, "Carly Simon: The Fans Don't Scare Her Anymore," *New York Times* June 12 1977

Rockwell, John, "Pop: Comeback," *New York Times* May 15 1977

Rosin, Mark, "Carly Simon: Letting Her Mind Flow," *Harper's Bazaar* Nov 1972

Rubin, Stephen, "Carly Simon: Gin versus Begonias," *Saturday Review* Oct 16 1976

Rubin, Stephen, "No Sad Songs for Carly," *Chicago Tribune*, Aug 5 1976

Ruhlmann, William, Spy Review, *AllMusic* 1979

Schruers, Frederick, "The Princess of Pop Bites the Bullet," *Globe and Mail* Nov 24 1979

Shapiro, Jane, "Carly Simon, Are There Any More at Home Like You?" *Ms Magazine* Feb 1977

Shapiro, Susin, "I Bet You Think This Piece Is About You," *The Village Voice*, May 23 1977

Soocher, Stan, "Carly Simon Stages Dramatic Re-Entry - Boys in the Trees is Return to Folk Simplicity and Power," *Circus Magazine*, June 8 1978

Symes, Phil, "Carly," *Disc and Music Echo Magazine* Mar 4 1972

Tann, Anne, "Live at the Bitter End, with Kristofferson,*" The Village Voice* May 27 1971

Tann, Anne, "Carly Simon: The Scenic Route to the Top," *Circus Magazine* Feb 1972

Taylor, Andrew, "Carly Simon – A Hit at Last," *Disc Magazine* Jan 1973

Tucker, Ken, "Another Passenger," *Rolling Stone* Aug 12 1976

Unknown, "Carly's a Spy in the House of Love," unknown source 1979

Valentine, Penny, "No Secrets," *Rock Magazine* May 7 1973

Van Matre, Lynn, "A "Spark" of Strengths, with "Hotcakes" of Humor," *Chicago Tribune*, Feb 17 1974

Van Matre, Lynn, "Carly's Still Anticipating," *Chicago Tribune,* April 17 1972

Ward, Ed, "The Queens of Rock: Ronstadt, Mitchell, Simon and Nicks Talk of Their Men, Music and Life on the Road," *Us Magazine* Feb 21 1978

Washington Post and Times-Herald, "Carly Simon Concert Is Off,", Nov 25 1971

Werbin, Stuart, "James Taylor & Carly Simon," *Rolling Stone* Jan 4 1973

Wickham, Vicki, "Carly Simon," *Hit Parader Magazine* Jan 1972

Wilson & Alroy, Spy Review (on-line reviewers)

Windeler, Robert, "Carly Simon," *Stereo Review Magazine* Sept 72

Young Miss Magazine, "The Carly Simon Nobody Knows,", May 1976

Young, Charles M, "First in Five Years – Carly Simon Plays Solo Concert," *King Features Syndicate*, May 31 1977

Young, Charles M, "Carly Simon: Life, Liberty and the Pursuit of Roast Beef Hash," *Rolling Stone* June 1 1978

Young, Charles M, "Carly Simon's Land of Milk & Honey," *Rolling Stone* June 1 1978

Arrington, Carl, "No Nukers Carly Simon and James Taylor Have a New Cause: Stopping Fission at Home," *People Magazine* October 6 1980

Bernstein, Fred, "Carly Simon in Take One," *People Magazine*, April 30 1984

Boston Globe, "Simonizing Paradise: Carly Simon Learns to Let Go," June 26 1980

Chronicle-Telegram, "Art for a Cause," (Opening of New York Gallery), April 20 1989

Come Upstairs Press Kit from Warner Bros.1980

Considine, J D, "Spoiled Girl" review, *Rolling Stone,* Sept 26 1985

Fears, Stephen, "For the Real Carly Simon, living a Quiet Life Is the Right Thing to Do," *Chicago Tribune* Oct 2 1983

Fissinger, Laura, "Carly Simon: Anticipating a Revived Career", *USA Today*, July 26 1985

Friedman, Roger, "Carly Simon: Has She Got Time for the Pain," *Fame Magazine,* January 1989

Hall, Jane, "After an Onstage Collapse and a Six-Year Battle with Stage Fright, Carly Simon Braves a Comeback," *People Magazine,* August 17 1987

Harrison, Quentin, Happy 40th Anniversary to Carly Simon's Ninth Studio Album Come Upstairs, 2020

Hilburn, Robert, "Carly Simon Will Raise the Roof," *Los Angeles* Times Sept 26 1980

Hoerburger, Rob, "Coming Around Again" review, *Rolling Stone*, June 18 1987

Holden, Stephen, "The Pop Life: A Spicy New Album by Carly Simon" (Spoiled Girl review), *New York Times*, Aug 7 1985

Holden, Stephen, "The Pop Life: Carly Simon, Again" *New York Times*, Feb 22 1989

Holden, Stephen, "Recordings: Carly Simon's Emotion-Laden Self Portrait (Coming Around Again review), *New York Times*, May 3 1987

Holden, Stephen, TV: Carly on HBO (Martha's Vineyard Concert), *New York Times*, July 25 1987

Holden, Stephen, "Torch" review, *Rolling Stone*, Dec 10 1981

Holden, Stephen, "Carly Simon Triumphs Over Her Own Panic," *New York Times*, June 17 1987

Holden, Stephen, "The Pop Life: Carly Simon is Planning Feature-length Videodisk," *New York Times*, Oct 12 1983

Howe, Dessan, "Working Girl:" A Bull Market," *Washington Post*, Dec 23 1988

Hunter, James, Come Upstairs review, *Village Voice,* October 1 1980

Jarvis, Jeff, "Picks and Pans Review: Carly Simon's Coming Around Again," *People Magazine*, July 27 1987

Kozak, Roman, "Simon's WB deal: $1 million for each LP." *Billboard Magazine* March 29 1980

Knickerbocker, Suzy, Hello Big Man review, *Syracuse Herald-Journal*, Oct 21 1983

Lloyd, Jack, "Wearing a New Legend in Her Own Time," *Washington Post* July 15 1980

Marchese, Joe, Spoiled Girl Expanded Edition Review, *The Second Spin*, July 9 2012

Morse, Steve, "Simon Voice Reflects New Person," *Boston Globe*

Murphy, Mary, "Just a Family Affair," (It Happens Every Day Video) *New York Magazine* April 23 1984

Nemes, Keystone, Interview, *Hello Magazine* April 15 1989

Novak, Ralph, Coming Around Again, *People Weekly*, April 27 1987

Rea, Steven, "Chez Carly," *High Fidelity Magazine*, November 1983

Reilly, Peter, "Enormous Vitality, Fierce Intelligence" (Come Upstairs review), *Stereo Review*, October 1980

Scherer, Ron, "Carly Simon's Pop Opera," *The Christian Science Monitor*, March 9 1993

Shewey, Don, "Hello Big Man" review, *Rolling Stone*, Nov 24 1983

Steele, Alison, "The Garbo of Rock Emerges," *After Dark Magazine*, November 1980

Tosches, Nick, "Free, White and Pushing 40," *Creem magazine* January 1984

Tucker, Ken, "Come Upstairs" review, *Rolling Stone,* Sept 4 1980

Van Matre, Lynn, "Bold Plans for Stage-Shy Carly Simon," *Chicago Tribune,* July 20 1980

Van Matre, Lynn, "Carly Simon Carrying a Torch for the 40s Sound," *Chicago Tribune*, March 7 1982

Wadler, Joyce, "Carly Simon: Anxiety & Essence," *Washington Post*, Oct 30 1983

White, Timothy, "Carly: Life Without James," *Rolling Stone*, Dec 1981

White, Timothy, "James Taylor," *Rolling Stone*, June 11 1981

Yorke, Jeffrey, "Carly Simon's Sudden Serenade" *Washington Post*, April 17 1987

1990s

Armstrong, Jim, "Clouds in My Coffee" album liner notes, Nov 7 1995

Brenner, Marie, "I Never Sang for My Mother, *Vanity Fair,* August 1995

Feibleman, Peter, "A Day in the Country with Carly Simon, *Lears Magazine*, Dec 1990

Helmbreck, Valerie, "Simon Has a Life Full of Romance," (My Romance review) 1990

Hiltbrand, David, "Picks and Pans Review: Carly in Concert: My Romance," *People Magazine* 1990

Holden, Stephen, "Carly Simon: "I've Stopped Running from Problems," *Redbook magazine*, July 1990

Holden, Stephen, "The Pop Life: Rap and Peace and Love," (Have You Seen Me Lately review), *New York Times*, Oct 31 1990

Holden, Stephen, "Pop Music's Romance with the Past," (My Romance review) *New York Times*, April 29 1990

Holden, Stephen, "Carly Simon: "Have You Seen Me Lately," *New York Times*, Sept 23 1990

Holden, Stephen, "The Pop Life: A New Album of Popular Standards by Carly Simon," (My Romance review), *New York Times,* March 7 1990

Holden, Stephen, "The Pop Life: Carly Simon Looks at Middle Age and Lost Pleasures," *New York Times* Oct 31 1990

Maslin, Janet, "Being Both Monstrous and Charming" (This Is My Life review), *New York Times,* Feb 21 1992

Milwood, John, "For Carly Simon, Success is Sweeter the Second Time Around" (Have You Seen Me Lately preview) *TV Guide* April 14 1990

Morse, Steve, "Singing Against the Grain," (My Romance review) *Boston.com* April 15 1990

Morse, Steve, "Clouds in My Coffee," album liner notes, Nov 7 1995

New York Times, "She's Got Her Nerves,", May 17 1992

Newman, Melinda, "Carly Pays Tribute to Film Noir," *Billboard Magazine* 1997

Philadelphia Enquirer, "A Resurgent Carly Simon Brings Her New Album to HBO," (My Romance) 1990

Raposa, Laura & Gayle Fee, "Jackie Robinson is Big with Carly," *Boston Herald,* April 20 1997

Reich, Howard, "Carly's Coming Around After a 14-year Hiatus" (Coming Around Again review), *Chicago Tribune,* March 21 1995

Roca, Octavia, "Carly Simon's Artful Hunt" (Romulus Hut review), CD Review Magazine, Feb 13 1994

Rush, George & Joanna Molloy, "Carly Simon Downplays her Battle with Cancer" *New York Daily News,* May 1998

Sandow, Greg, Have You Seen Me Lately review, *Entertainment Weekly,* Oct 5 1990

Travers, Peter, This Is My Life review, *Rolling Stone* Feb 21 1992

West, Carinthia, "Carly Simon Catches a New Wave," *Cleo Magazine* 1990

2000s

Abelson, Max, "He's So Vain: Carly Simon and the Wannabe Madoff" *The Observer* June 6 2010

Astin, Martin, "Carly Simon – The Golden Hued Contralto on Heartbreak, Candid Memoirs, and Henry Root," *Mojo Magazine,* April 2016

Bautz, Mark, The Bedroom Tapes review, *Entertainment Weekly,* May 19 2000

Blacker, Terence, "Sex Addict, Crack Fiend and Moralist," *The Independent,* June 28 2005

Blythe, Will, "Carly Simon Says..." *Mirabella Magazine,* May 2000

Boston Globe and Mail, "Letters Never Sent" article, 2000

Brown, Helen, "No Secrets," (This Kind of Love review) *Daily Telegraph* May 27 2008

Campbell, Mary, "Comeback Carly," (The Bedroom Tapes) 2000

Chagollan, Steve, Music for Screens" (review of her career), *Variety Magazine,* Spring 2012

Clegg, Douglas, "A Room of Her Own: Carly Simon Captures a New Side of Herself ..." (The Bedroom Tapes), Barnes & Noble 2000

Clifford, Stephanie, "Suing Her Label, Not Retiring: Carly Simon Won't Go Gently," *New York Times,* Oct 11 2009

Cohen, Howard, "Random Thoughts with Carly Simon," *Miami Herald*, May 10 2008

Davis, Cooper, "Classic Carly Simon: Its Never Been Gone," *Vineyard Gazette* on-line Oct 23 2009

Donovan, Charles, "A Sound Recovery" (The Bedroom Tapes) *Amazon UK* 2000

Farndale, Nigel, "Coming Around Again: The Seventies Songstress on Famous Friendships, Affairs and Therapy," *The Telegraph* March 3 2010

Fitzharris, Dustin, "Carly Simon: Still Living Like a Flower While the Boys Grow in the Trees" *HuffPost* Dec 16 2015

Flick, Larry, "Carly Simon Finds Strength on New Arista Set," (The Bedroom Tapes) *Billboard Magazine*

Galanes, Philip, "Carly Simon on Music, Fame, Sibling Rivalry, and, Yes, James Taylor." *New York Times* April 24 2015

Gardner, Elysa, "Carly Simon Has a Quiet Rhythm of Life and a New "Love" *USA Today*, May 13 2008

Heathcote, Charlotte, Interview with Carly, *Sunday Express*, May 25 2008

Holden, Stephen, "A Sex Symbol of the 1970's Does Lawrence Welk for Hip Seniors," (Moonlight Serenade) *New York Times*, July 19 2005

Holden, Stephen, "Hush, Little Baby, Mama's Crooning," (Into White review) *New York Times*, Jan 1 2007

Hunter, James, "The Bedroom Tapes," *Rolling Stone*, May 25 2000

Kors, Michael, "Carly Simon," *Interview* July 2004

Lahr, John, "Petrified: The Horrors of Stagefright," *The New Yorker*, Aug 28 2006

Lewis, Randy, "Carly's Family Album," *Los Angeles Times* June 1 2008

Maslin, Janet, "Review: In Carly Simon's Memoir, Few Secrets Left Untold" *New York Times* Nov 25 2015

Mauro, Jack, "Anthology" album liner notes, Nov 5 2002

Mitchell, Gail, "Carly Simon has "good time" revisiting old songs." (Never Been Gone review) *Billboard* Oct 24 2009

Newman, Melinda, "Carly Simon Reflects on Her Career," *Billboard Magazine* April 30 2004

Newman, Melinda, "I Love My Early Hits," *Billboard Magazine,* April 27 2008

Newman, Melinda, "Carly Simon Reflects on Her Career" (Reflections review), *Billboard Magazine*, April 30 2004

Pennington, Juliet, "Carly Simon Recalls Her Friend Jackie Kennedy In New Book…" (Touched by the Sun), *Boston Globe*, Oct 24 2019

Pennington, Juliet, "On the Vineyard with Carly," *New England Living* December 4 2017

Proudfoot, Jenny, "13 of our all-time favorite Carly Simon quotes, *Marie Claire* July 14 2016

Ragona, Mike, "Never Been Gone: A Conversation with Carly Simon," *Huffpost.com* March 18 2010

Rogers, Jude, "Boys in the Trees: A Memoir by Carly Simon review, *The Guardian* Dec 27 2015

Schwartz, Robin, Letters Never Sent review, *Entertainment Review*, 2000

Sexton, Paul, "Carly Simon: True Confessions," *The Independent,* Jan 13 2006

Shea, Jack, "Carly Simon Discusses New Book…" (Touched by the Sun), *New York Times*, January 8th 2020

Simon, Carly, "How Lyrics Work," www.doubletakemagazine.org Nov 9 2006

Simon, Lizzie, "Simon Unseen," *Gotham Magazine*, May 2004

Sturgis, Fiona, "Carly Simon, Boys in the Trees: "More Pain Than Vain," book review The Independent Dec 11 2015

This Kind of Love – Track by Track 2008

Wall Street Journal, "Carly Simon Sings at the WSJ Café, Talks About Her Suit Against Starbucks," Nov 20 2009

Weller, Sheila, "The Counterintuitive Wisdom of Carly Simon," *The Observer* Dec 10 2015

Wilkane, Christian, "Tales from the Trees: An Interview with Carly Simon," *Pop Matters.com*, Nov 20 2016

Wolfson, C K, "Catching Up with Carly Simon," *Martha's Vineyard Times*, Oct 22 2009

CPSIA information can be obtained
at www.ICGtesting.com
Printed in the USA
BVHW042056161120
593496BV00016B/404